HYPER POLICE™

ハイパーポリス

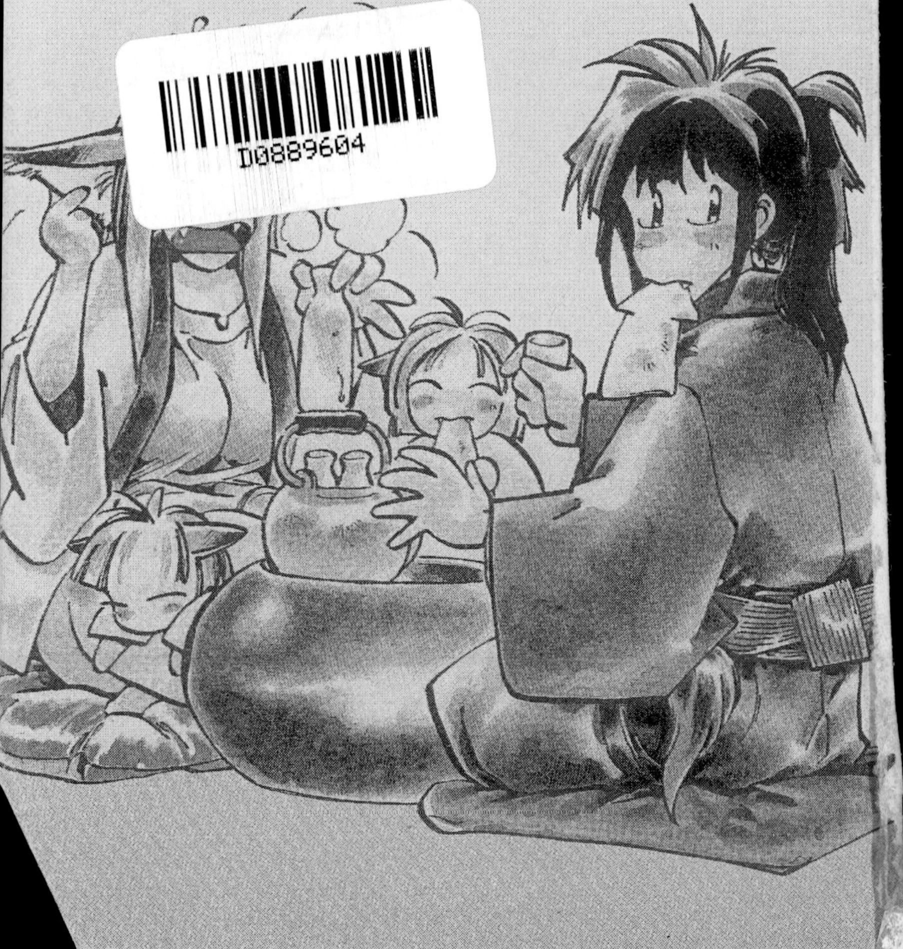

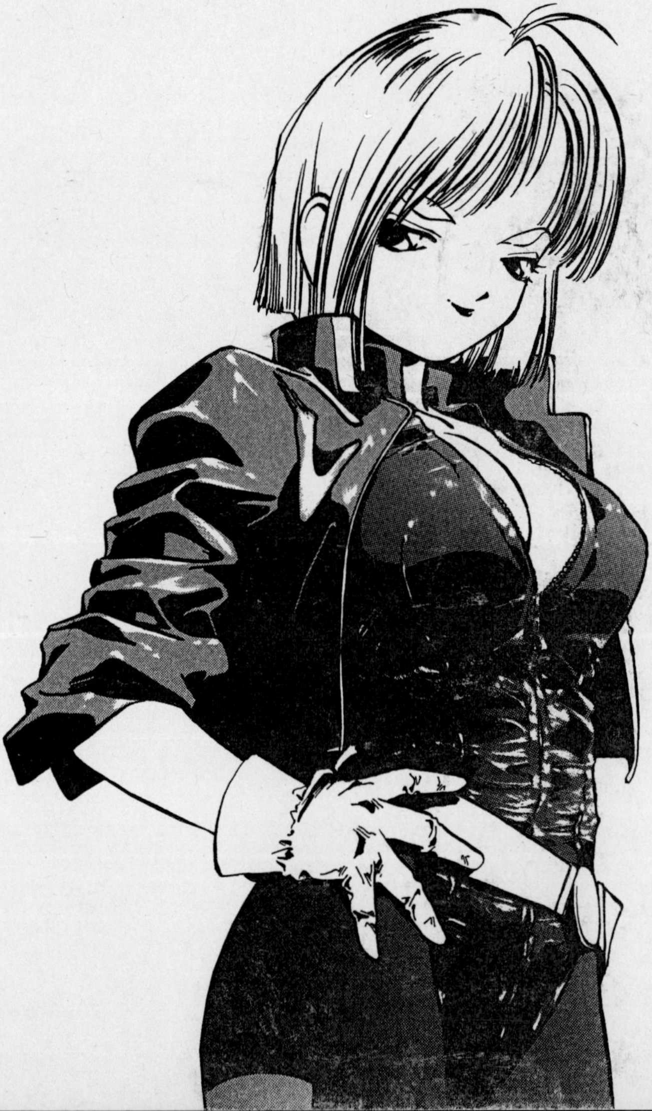

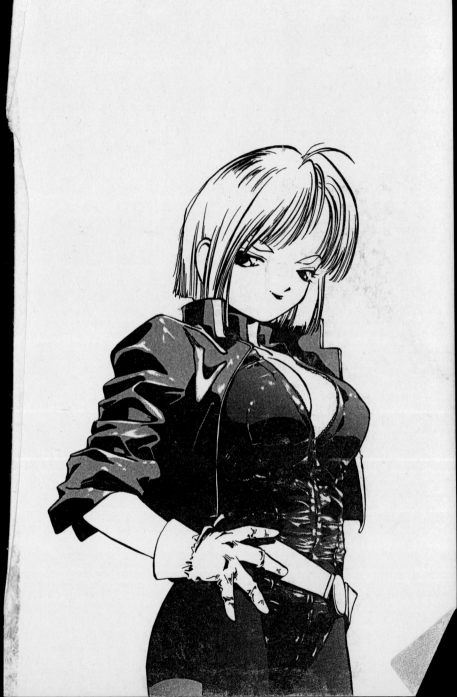

HYPER POLICE

ハイパーポリス ™

Hyper Police Vol. 3
Created by MEE

Translation - David Ury
English Adaptation - Aaron Sparrow
Retouch and Lettering - Eric Pineda
Producion Artist - James Dashiell
Cover Design - Kyle Plummer

Editor - Tim Beedle
Digital Imaging Manager - Chris Buford
Pre-Press Manager - Antonio DePietro
Production Managers - Jennifer Miller and Mutsumi Miyazaki
Art Director - Matt Alford
Managing Editor - Jill Freshney
VP of Production - Ron Klamert
Editor-in-Chief - Mike Kiley
President and C.O.O. - John Parker
Publisher and C.E.O. - Stuart Levy

A  Manga

TOKYOPOP Inc.
5900 Wilshire Blvd. Suite 2000
Los Angeles, CA 90036

E-mail: info@TOKYOPOP.com
Come visit us online at www.TOKYOPOP.com

ISBN: 1-59532-296-5
First TOKYOPOP printing: June 2005
10 9 8 7 6 5 4 3 2 1
Printed in Canada

HYPER POLICE™

by

MEE

Volume 3

TOKYOPOP®

HAMBURG // LONDON // LOS ANGELES // TOKYO

HYPER POLICE™

ハイパーポリス

The Story So Far...

It is the year 22 H.C. (Holy Century), and the human race has all but disappeared. The Japanese city of Shinjuku has become a haven for "monsters"—intelligent creatures that possess human-like anatomy with distinctly animal features. While most monsters are benevolent, all possess the ability to cause destruction, due largely to an internal struggle that is both constant and unwavering. Their evolved minds recognize the necessity for order and respect the sanctity of life, but the animal inside each of them is never too far beneath the surface...

Natsuki Sasahara is one such monster. A rookie at Police Company, a private police organization, she makes her living as a bounty hunter. She was scouted for the position by Batanen Fujioka, a werewolf who harbors a secret attraction for the young cat girl. Cool under pressure and stunningly efficient, Batanen is a seasoned veteran of the hunter trade. With his partner Tomy, Batanen always tops the list of monthly arrests. Recently, Police Company welcomed a new officer to their ranks. Sakura is part nine-tailed fox—or rather she WOULD be if her ninth tail would finish growing in. Partnered with Natsuki, Sakura has formed an uneasy friendship with the young cat girl. While Sakura has come to depend on Natsuki as a partner and roommate, she also hides a vicious desire to eat her. It is her hope that the strong magical essence Natsuki possesses will finally allow Sakura's stumpy tail to grow.

All four of our fearless hunters have learned to deal with budget cutbacks and faulty, obsolete equipment. However, none of them were prepared for the recent bankruptcy of Police Company, forcing them into the sad contract-to-contract life of a freelancer. To complicate matters further, a rift in the space/time continuum has tossed a feudal-age samurai on our intrepid heroes' doorsteps—a man out of time that Sakura mistakenly believes may have taken certain liberties with her while she was unconscious!

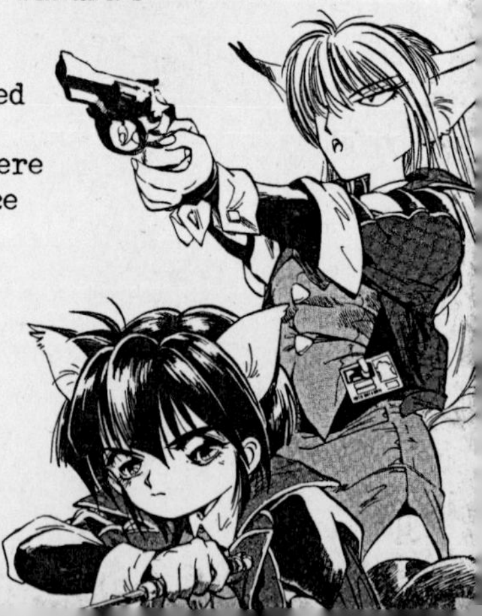

CHARACTERS

Natsuki

A rookie bounty hunter with magical powers and wicked sword skills. Her magic manifests itself as electrical energy capable of frying anything in sight, and is further amplified through the assistance of her two pet parasites: Raijin and Fujin.

Natsuki's partner and a fellow rookie, Sakura is a nine-tailed fox whose ninth tail has yet to grow in. To trigger its growth, Sakura plans to eat the highly magical Natsuki...as soon as she can figure out how.

Sakura

A clean shot and a brutal brawler, Batanen is one of the best hunters in the biz. He was Police Company's pride and joy, and has been equally successful as a freelancer, largely due to his possession of something the others lack: a license.

Batanen

Resourceful, quiet and clever, Tomy prefers to keep busy behind the scenes. He's proven to be an efficient yin to Batanen's yang, often accompanying the great hunter on some of his greatest hunts.

Tomy

CONTENTS

HYPER POLICE
MEE

Report #15
Blossoms Scattered

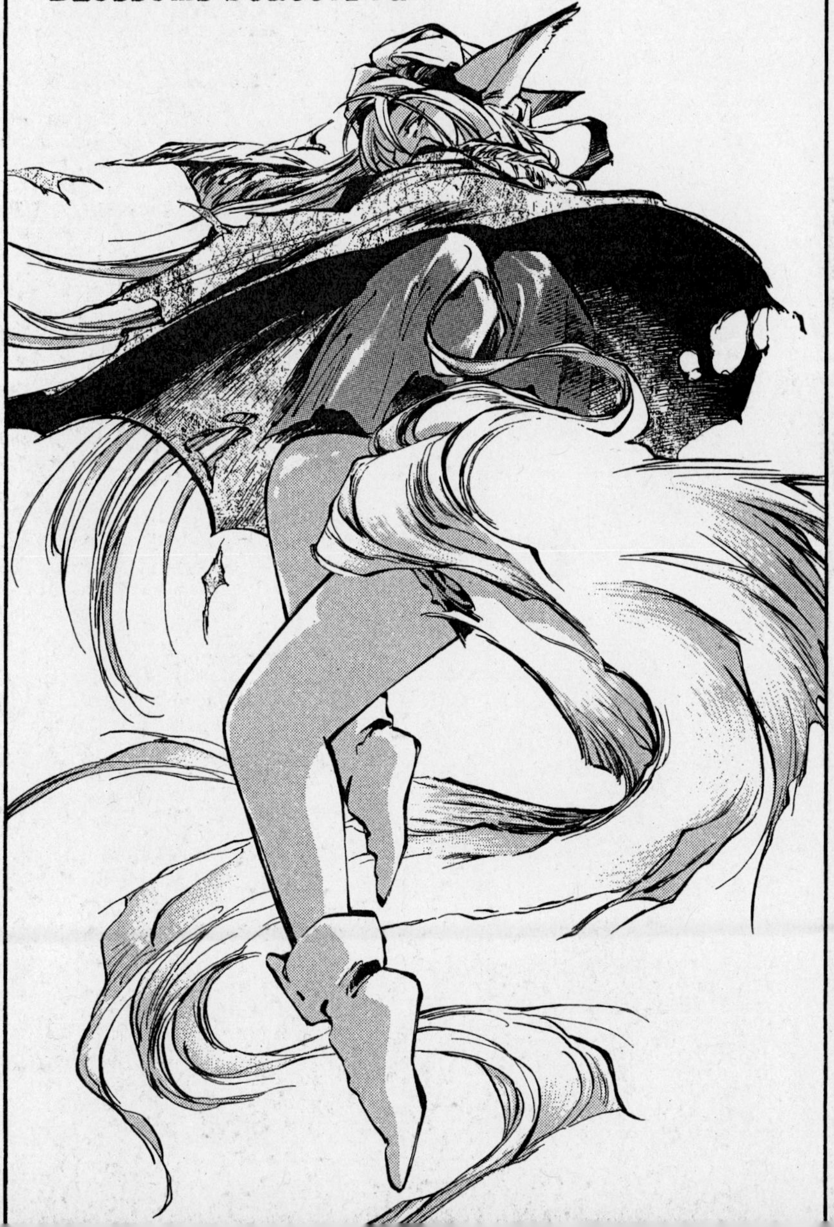

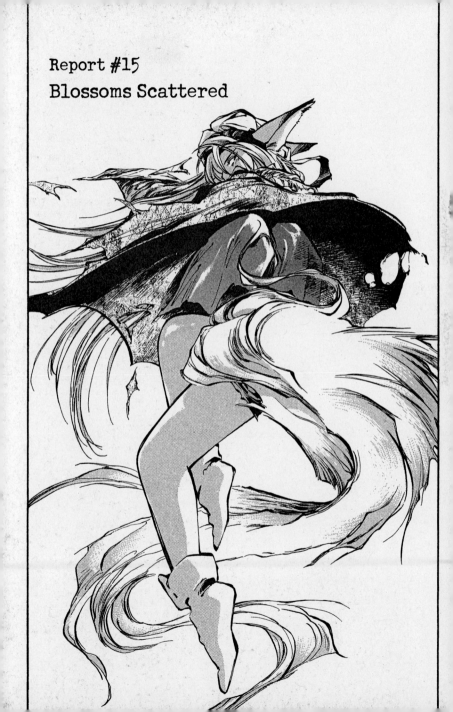

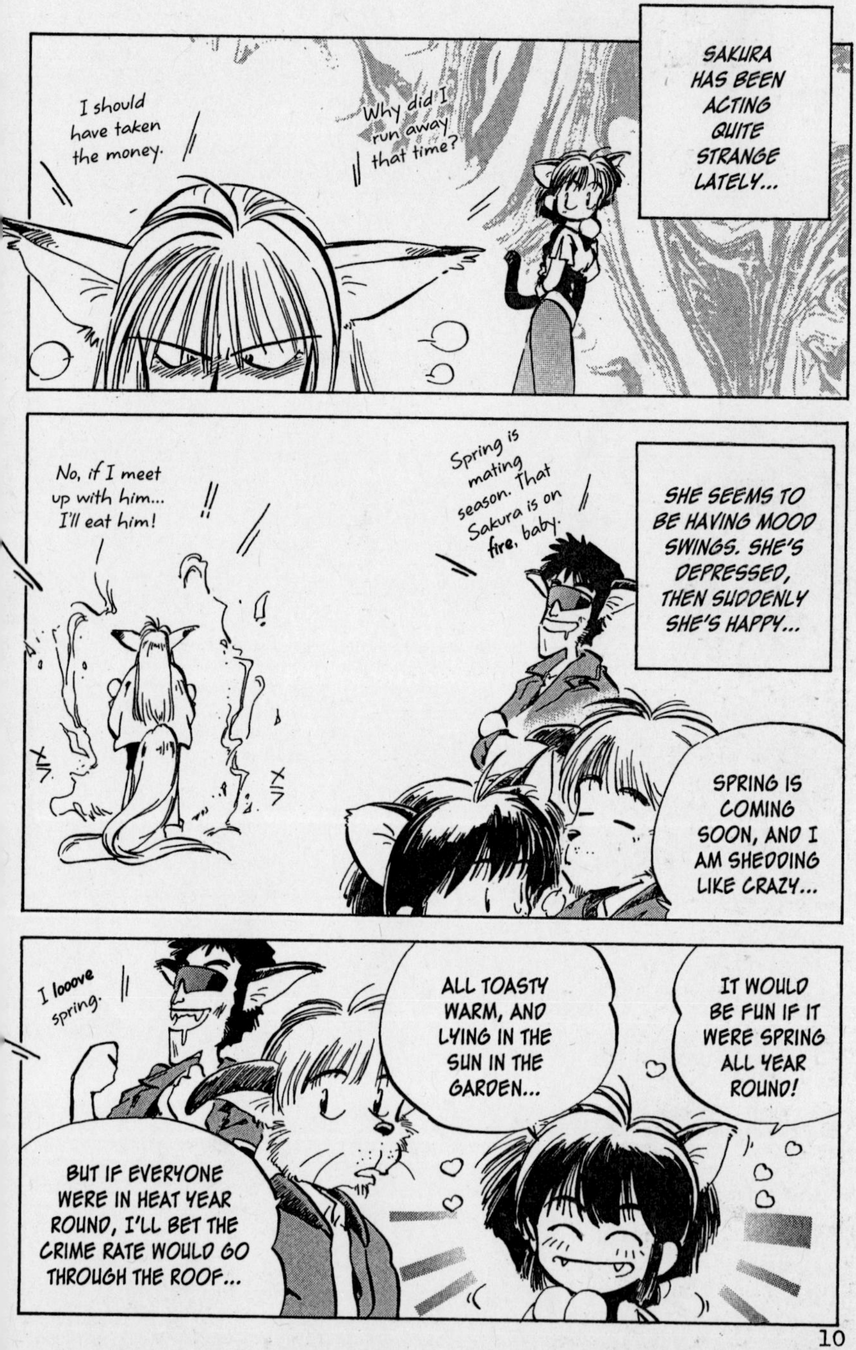
SAKURA HAS BEEN ACTING QUITE STRANGE LATELY...
Why did I run away that time?
I should have taken the money.
SHE SEEMS TO BE HAVING MOOD SWINGS. SHE'S DEPRESSED, THEN SUDDENLY SHE'S HAPPY...
SPRING IS COMING SOON, AND I AM SHEDDING LIKE CRAZY...
Spring is mating season. That Sakura is on fire, baby.
No, if I meet up with him... I'll eat him!
IT WOULD BE FUN IF IT WERE SPRING ALL YEAR ROUND!
ALL TOASTY WARM, AND LYING IN THE SUN IN THE GARDEN...
I looove spring.
BUT IF EVERYONE WERE IN HEAT YEAR ROUND, I'LL BET THE CRIME RATE WOULD GO THROUGH THE ROOF...

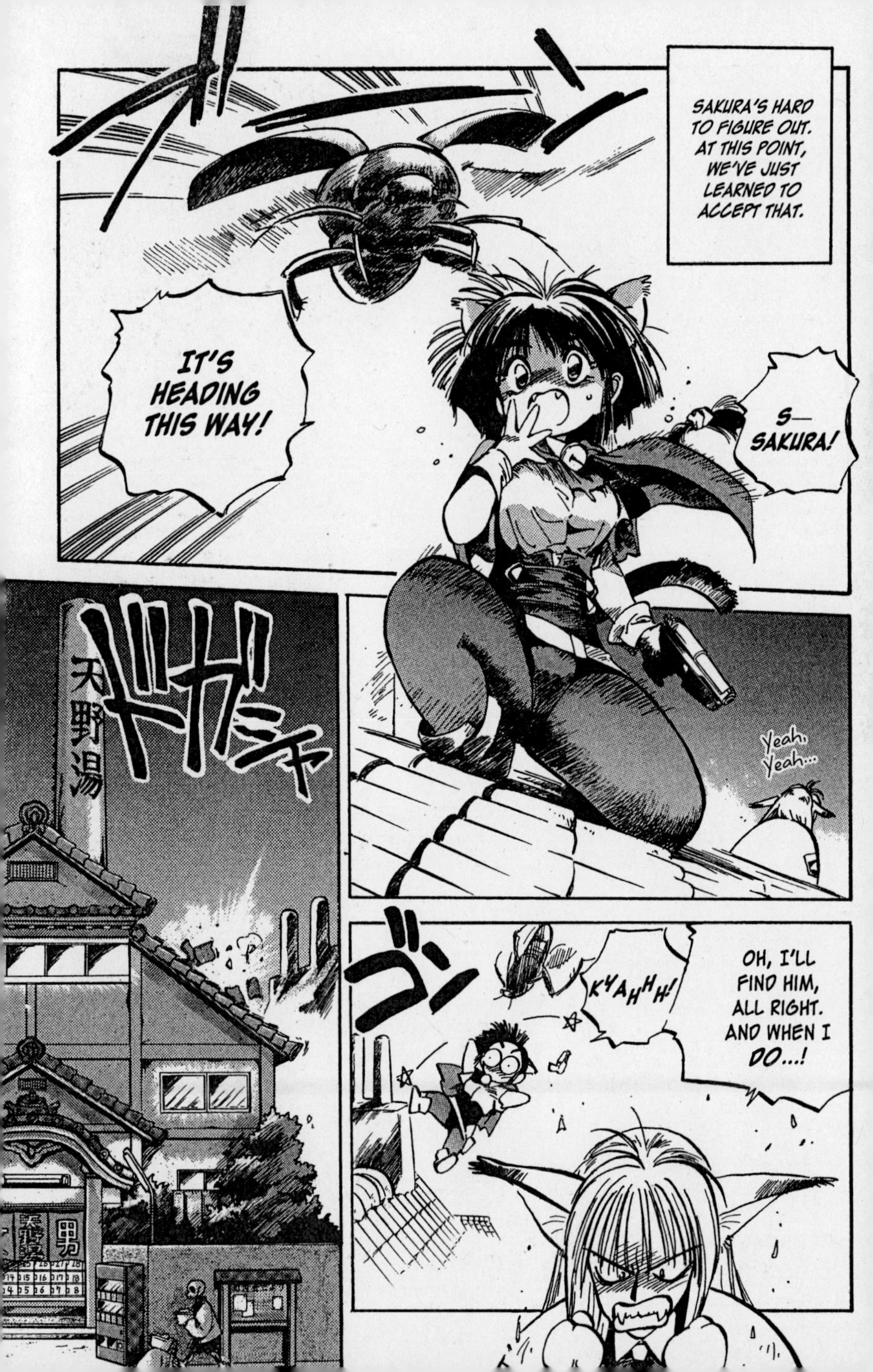
SAKURA'S HARD TO FIGURE OUT. AT THIS POINT, WE'VE JUST LEARNED TO ACCEPT THAT.
S— SAKURA!
IT'S HEADING THIS WAY!
Yeah, Yeah...
OH, I'LL FIND HIM, ALL RIGHT. AND WHEN I DO...!
KYAHHH!
ゴン
天野湯
ドガシャ

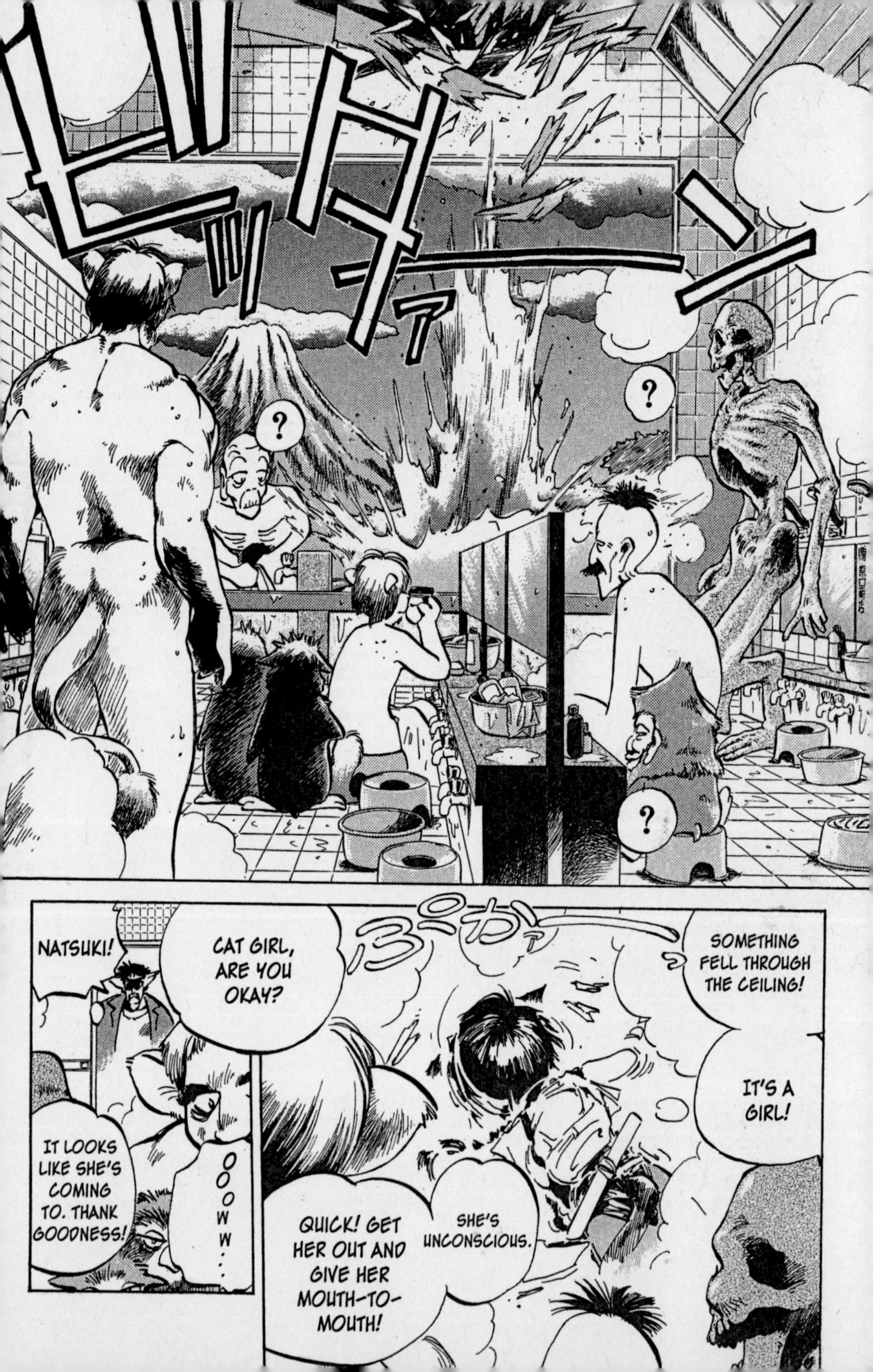
ビッダァーン
SOMETHING FELL THROUGH THE CEILING!
IT'S A GIRL!
SHE'S UNCONSCIOUS.
QUICK! GET HER OUT AND GIVE HER MOUTH-TO-MOUTH!
CAT GIRL, ARE YOU OKAY?
NATSUKI!
OOOWW...
IT LOOKS LIKE SHE'S COMING TO. THANK GOODNESS!

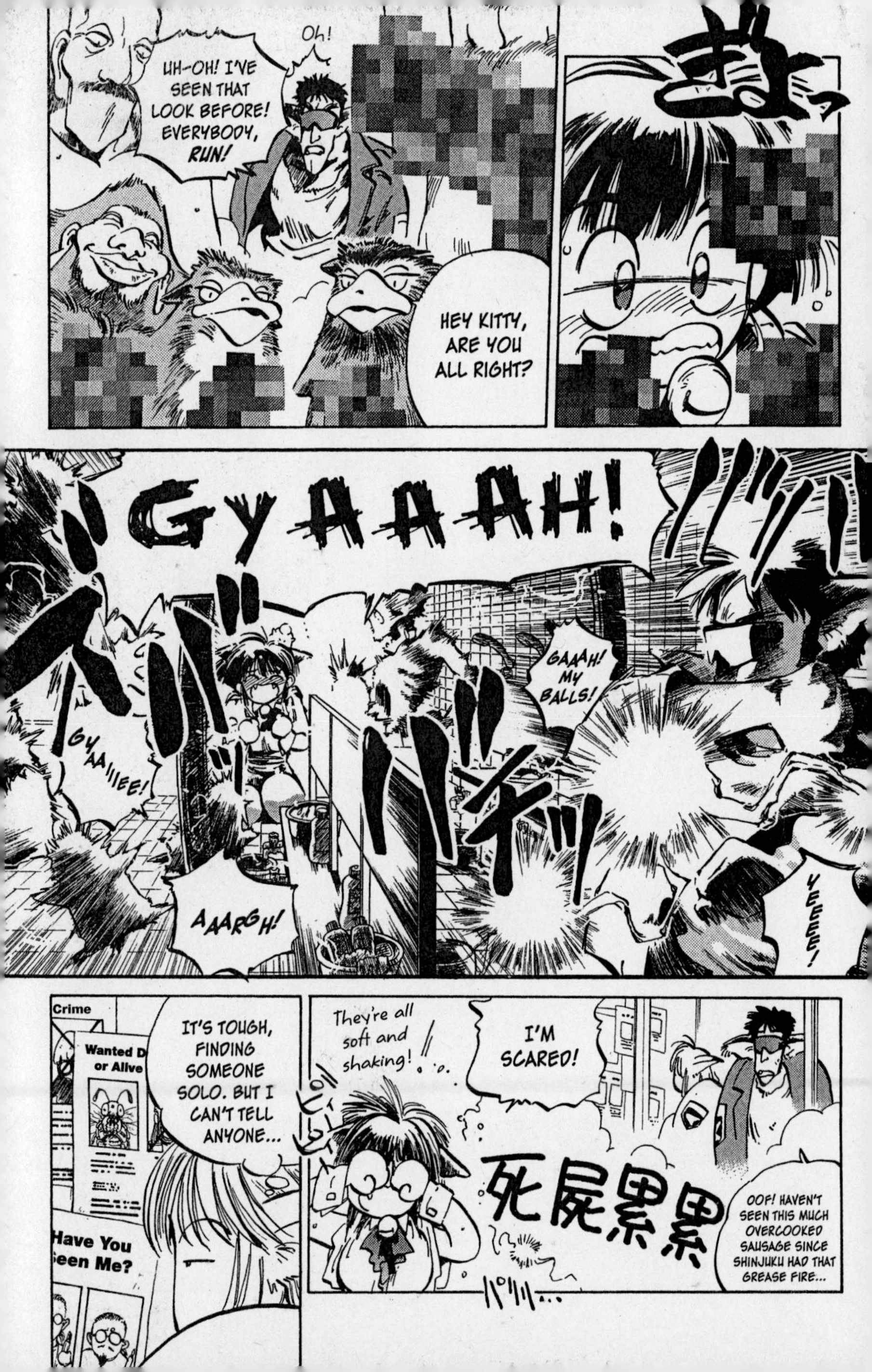
Oh!
UH-OH! I'VE SEEN THAT LOOK BEFORE! EVERYBODY, RUN!
HEY KITTY, ARE YOU ALL RIGHT?
GYAAAAH!
GAAAH! MY BALLS!
YEEEE!
GYAAIIEEE!
AAARGH!
I'M SCARED!
They're all soft and shaking!
OOF! HAVEN'T SEEN THIS MUCH OVERCOOKED SAUSAGE SINCE SHINJUKU HAD THAT GREASE FIRE...
死屍累累
Crime
Wanted D
or Alive
IT'S TOUGH, FINDING SOMEONE SOLO. BUT I CAN'T TELL ANYONE...
Have You
een Me?

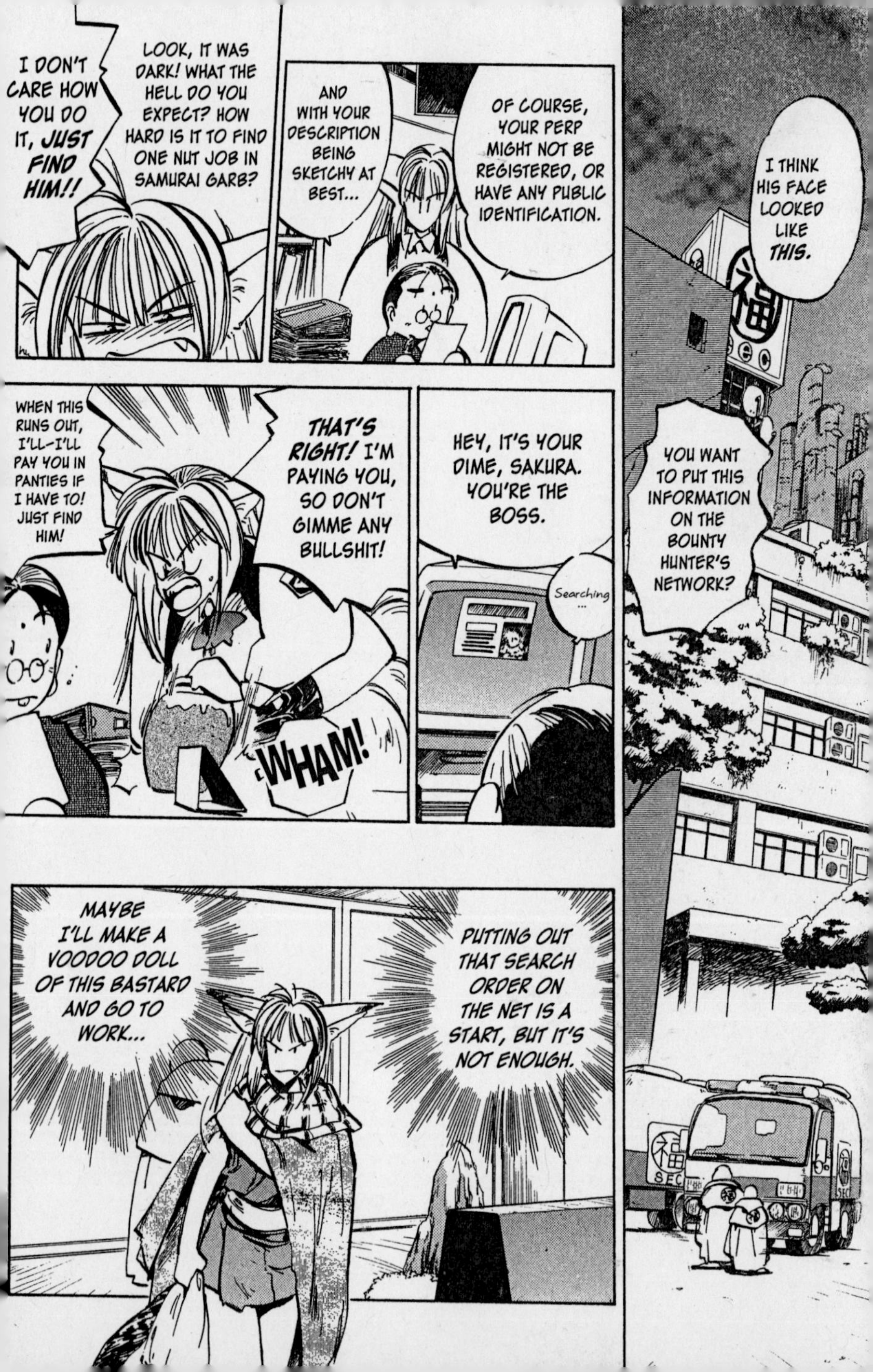

I THINK HIS FACE LOOKED LIKE THIS.
YOU WANT TO PUT THIS INFORMATION ON THE BOUNTY HUNTER'S NETWORK?
OF COURSE, YOUR PERP MIGHT NOT BE REGISTERED, OR HAVE ANY PUBLIC IDENTIFICATION.
AND WITH YOUR DESCRIPTION BEING SKETCHY AT BEST...
LOOK, IT WAS DARK! WHAT THE HELL DO YOU EXPECT? HOW HARD IS IT TO FIND ONE NUT JOB IN SAMURAI GARB?
I DON'T CARE HOW YOU DO IT, JUST FIND HIM!!
HEY, IT'S YOUR DIME, SAKURA. YOU'RE THE BOSS.
Searching ...
THAT'S RIGHT! I'M PAYING YOU, SO DON'T GIMME ANY BULLSHIT!
WHEN THIS RUNS OUT, I'LL-I'LL PAY YOU IN PANTIES IF I HAVE TO! JUST FIND HIM!
WHAM!
PUTTING OUT THAT SEARCH ORDER ON THE NET IS A START, BUT IT'S NOT ENOUGH.
MAYBE I'LL MAKE A VOODOO DOLL OF THIS BASTARD AND GO TO WORK...

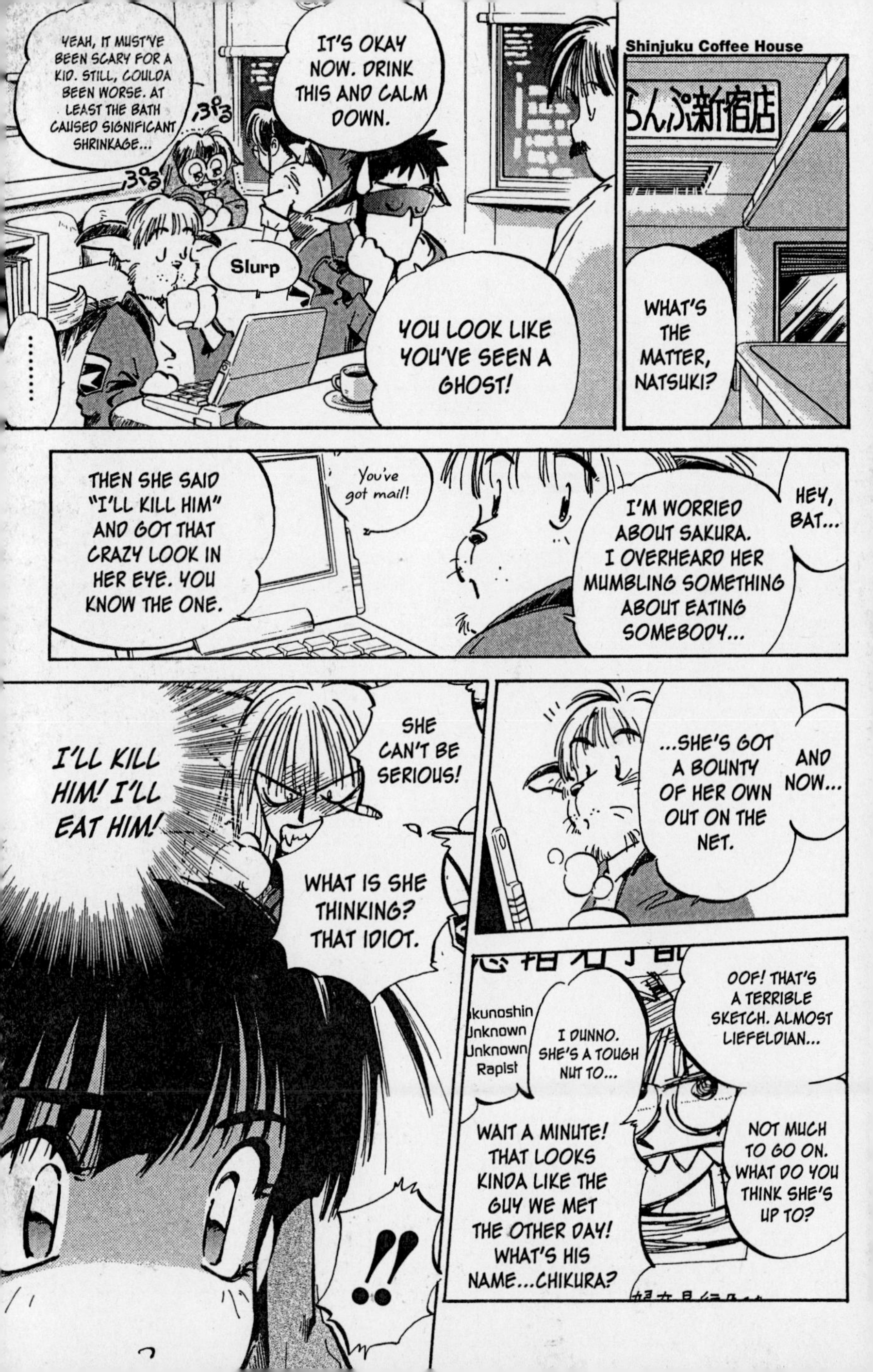

Shinjuku Coffee House
らんぷ新宿店
WHAT'S THE MATTER, NATSUKI?
YOU LOOK LIKE YOU'VE SEEN A GHOST!
IT'S OKAY NOW. DRINK THIS AND CALM DOWN.
YEAH, IT MUST'VE BEEN SCARY FOR A KID. STILL, COULDA BEEN WORSE. AT LEAST THE BATH CAUSED SIGNIFICANT SHRINKAGE...
ぷる
ぷる
Slurp
......
HEY, BAT...
I'M WORRIED ABOUT SAKURA. I OVERHEARD HER MUMBLING SOMETHING ABOUT EATING SOMEBODY...
You've got mail!
THEN SHE SAID "I'LL KILL HIM" AND GOT THAT CRAZY LOOK IN HER EYE. YOU KNOW THE ONE.
AND NOW...
...SHE'S GOT A BOUNTY OF HER OWN OUT ON THE NET.
OOF! THAT'S A TERRIBLE SKETCH. ALMOST LIEFELDIAN...
NOT MUCH TO GO ON. WHAT DO YOU THINK SHE'S UP TO?
I DUNNO. SHE'S A TOUGH NUT TO...
akunoshin
Unknown
Unknown
Rapist
WAIT A MINUTE! THAT LOOKS KINDA LIKE THE GUY WE MET THE OTHER DAY! WHAT'S HIS NAME...CHIKURA?
SHE CAN'T BE SERIOUS!
I'LL KILL HIM! I'LL EAT HIM!
WHAT IS SHE THINKING? THAT IDIOT.
!!

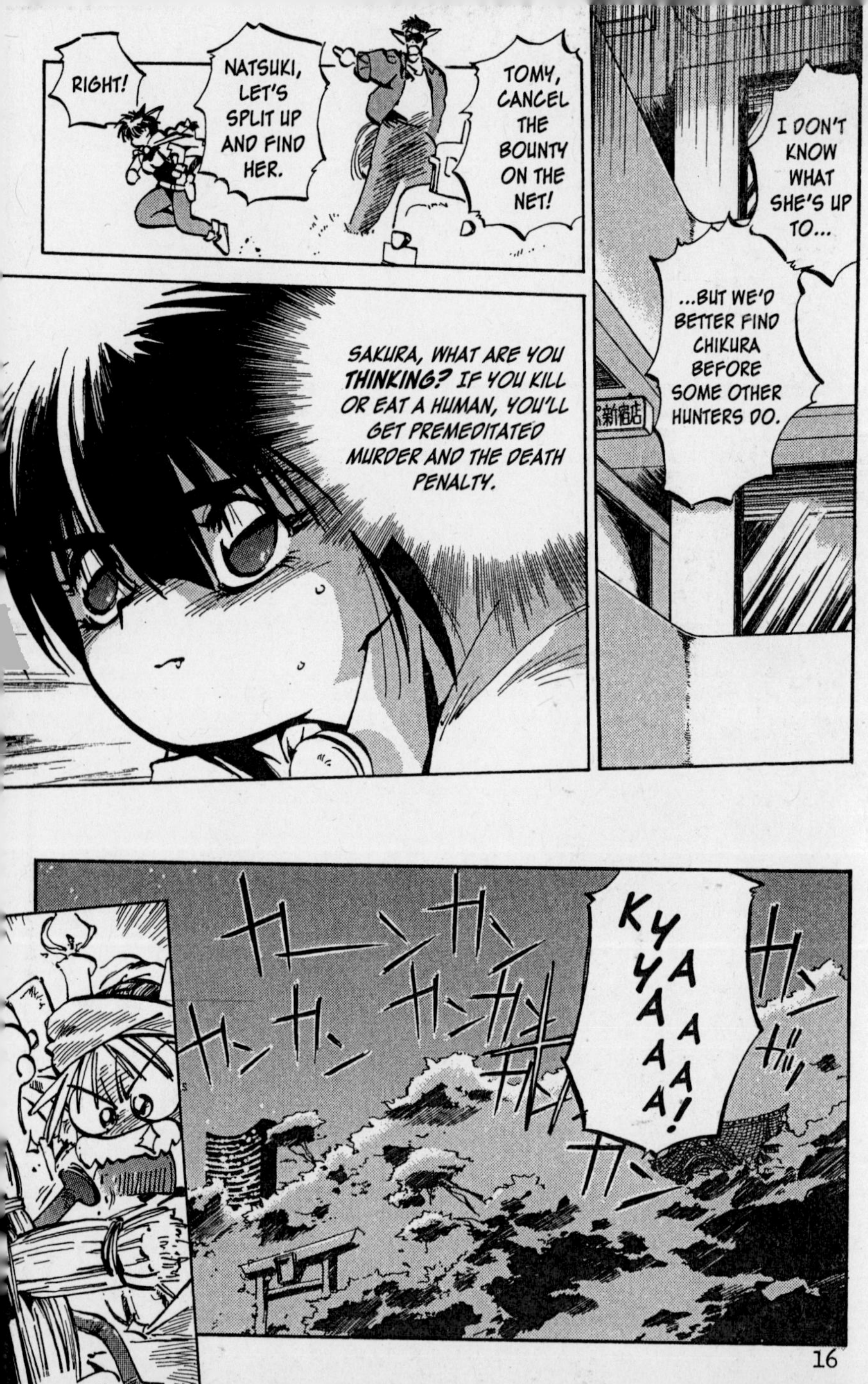
I DON'T KNOW WHAT SHE'S UP TO...
...BUT WE'D BETTER FIND CHIKURA BEFORE SOME OTHER HUNTERS DO.
TOMY, CANCEL THE BOUNTY ON THE NET!
NATSUKI, LET'S SPLIT UP AND FIND HER.
RIGHT!
SAKURA, WHAT ARE YOU **THINKING?** IF YOU KILL OR EAT A HUMAN, YOU'LL GET PREMEDITATED MURDER AND THE DEATH PENALTY.
KYYAAAAAA!

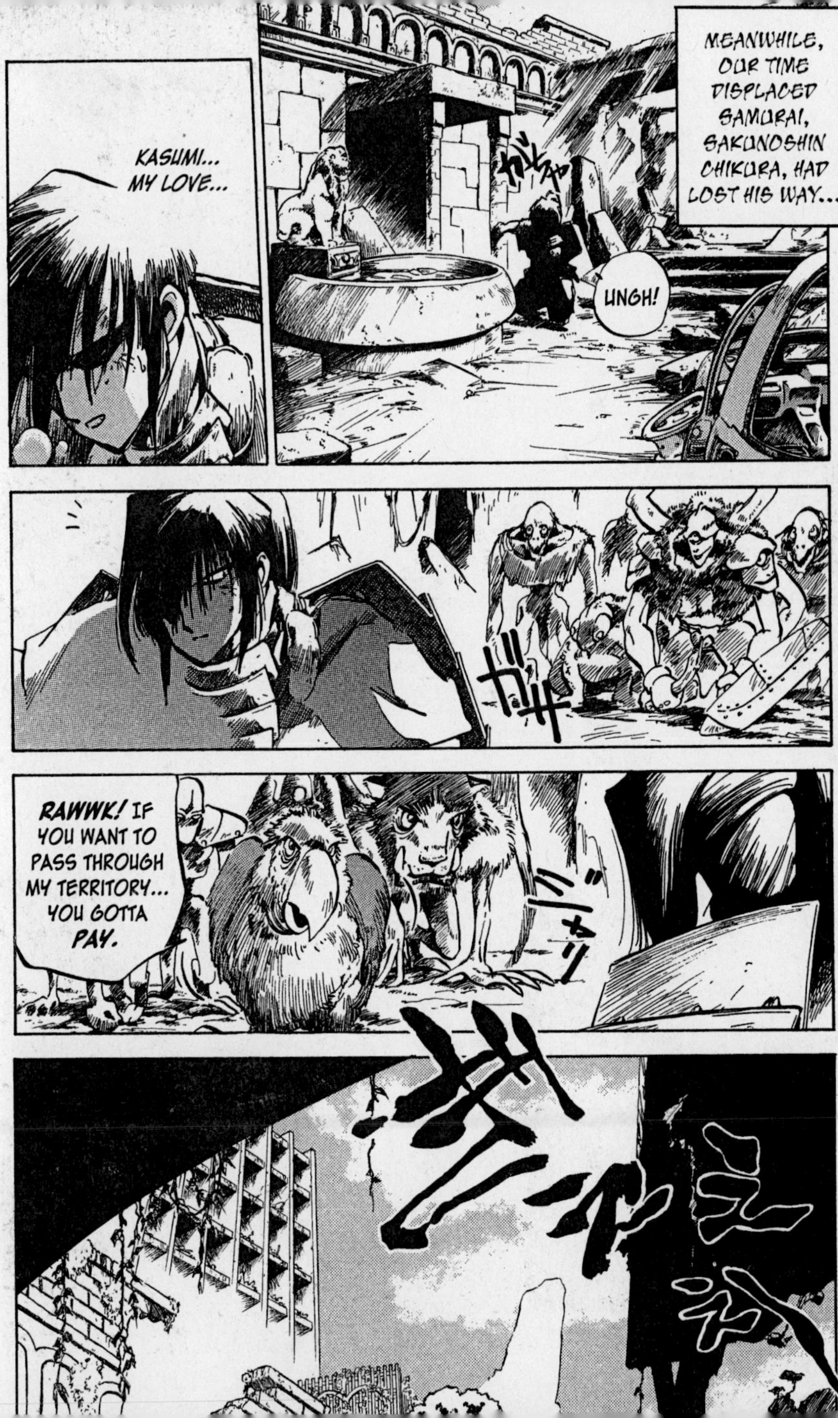
MEANWHILE, OUR TIME DISPLACED SAMURAI, SAKUNOSHIN CHIKURA, HAD LOST HIS WAY...
UNGH!
KASUMI... MY LOVE...
RAWWK! IF YOU WANT TO PASS THROUGH MY TERRITORY... YOU GOTTA PAY.

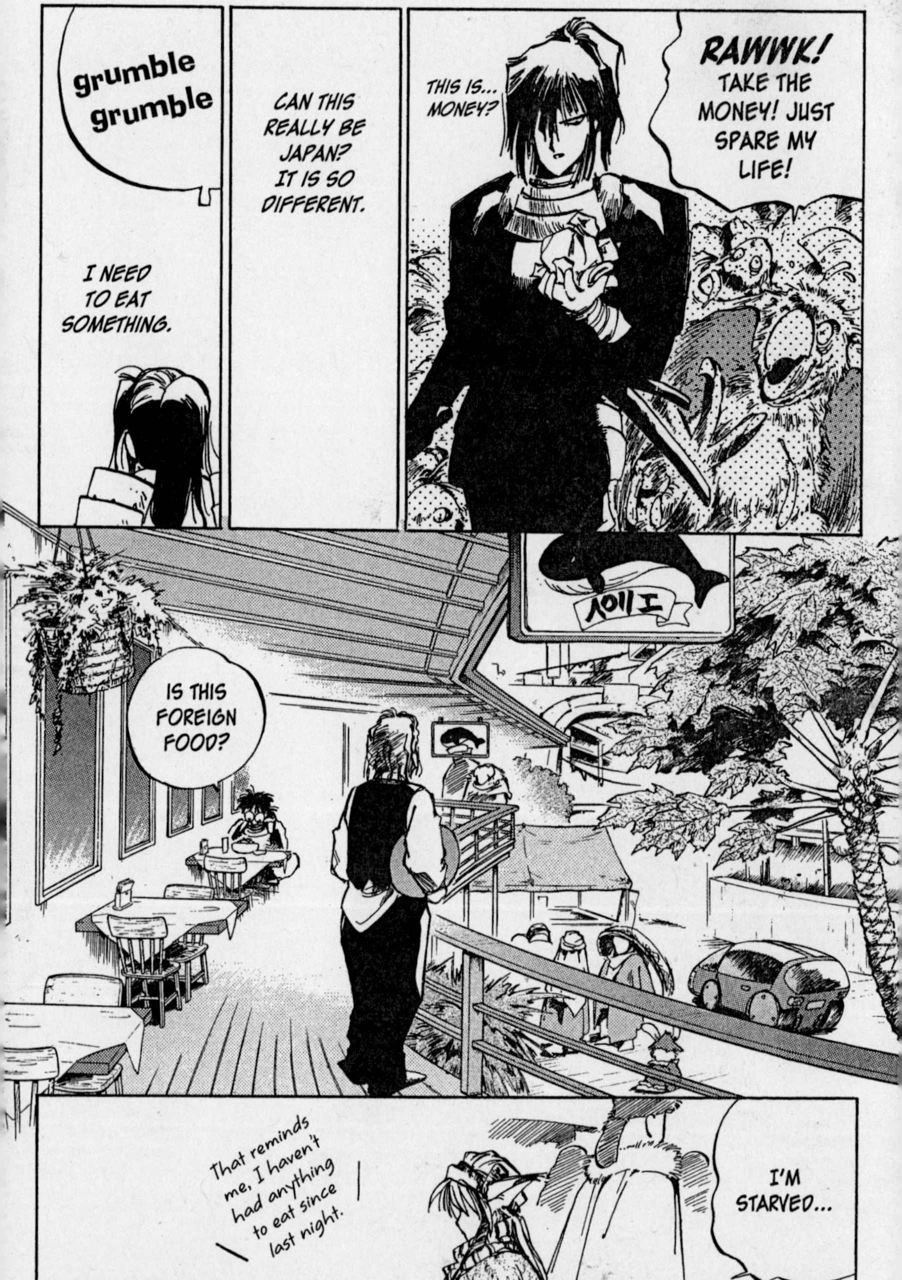
RAWWK!
TAKE THE MONEY! JUST SPARE MY LIFE!
THIS IS... MONEY?
CAN THIS REALLY BE JAPAN? IT IS SO DIFFERENT.
grumble grumble
I NEED TO EAT SOMETHING.
IS THIS FOREIGN FOOD?
I'M STARVED...
That reminds me, I haven't had anything to eat since last night.

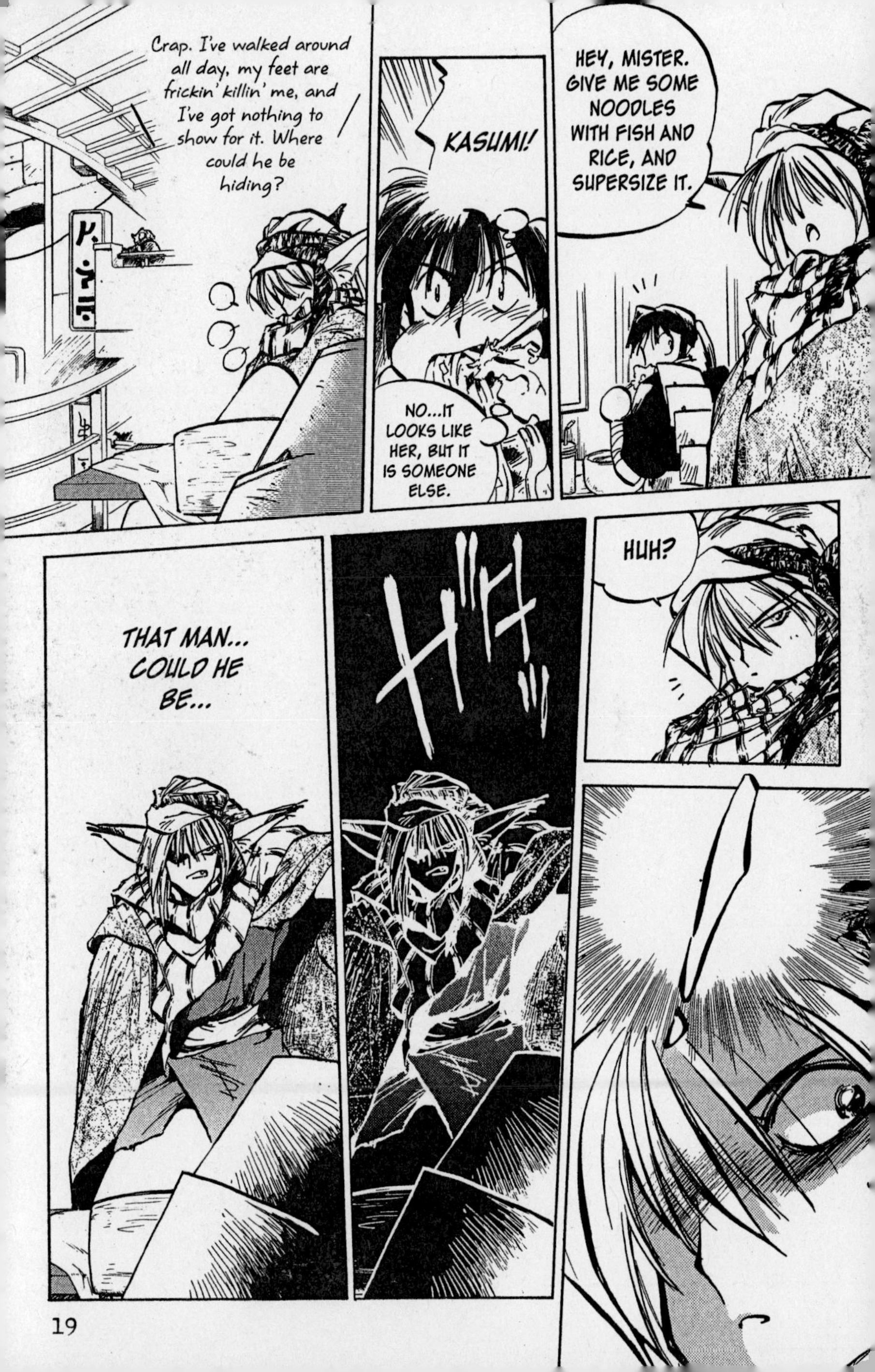
HEY, MISTER. GIVE ME SOME NOODLES WITH FISH AND RICE, AND SUPERSIZE IT.
KASUMI!
NO...IT LOOKS LIKE HER, BUT IT IS SOMEONE ELSE.
Crap. I've walked around all day, my feet are frickin' killin' me, and I've got nothing to show for it. Where could he be hiding?
HUH?
THAT MAN... COULD HE BE...

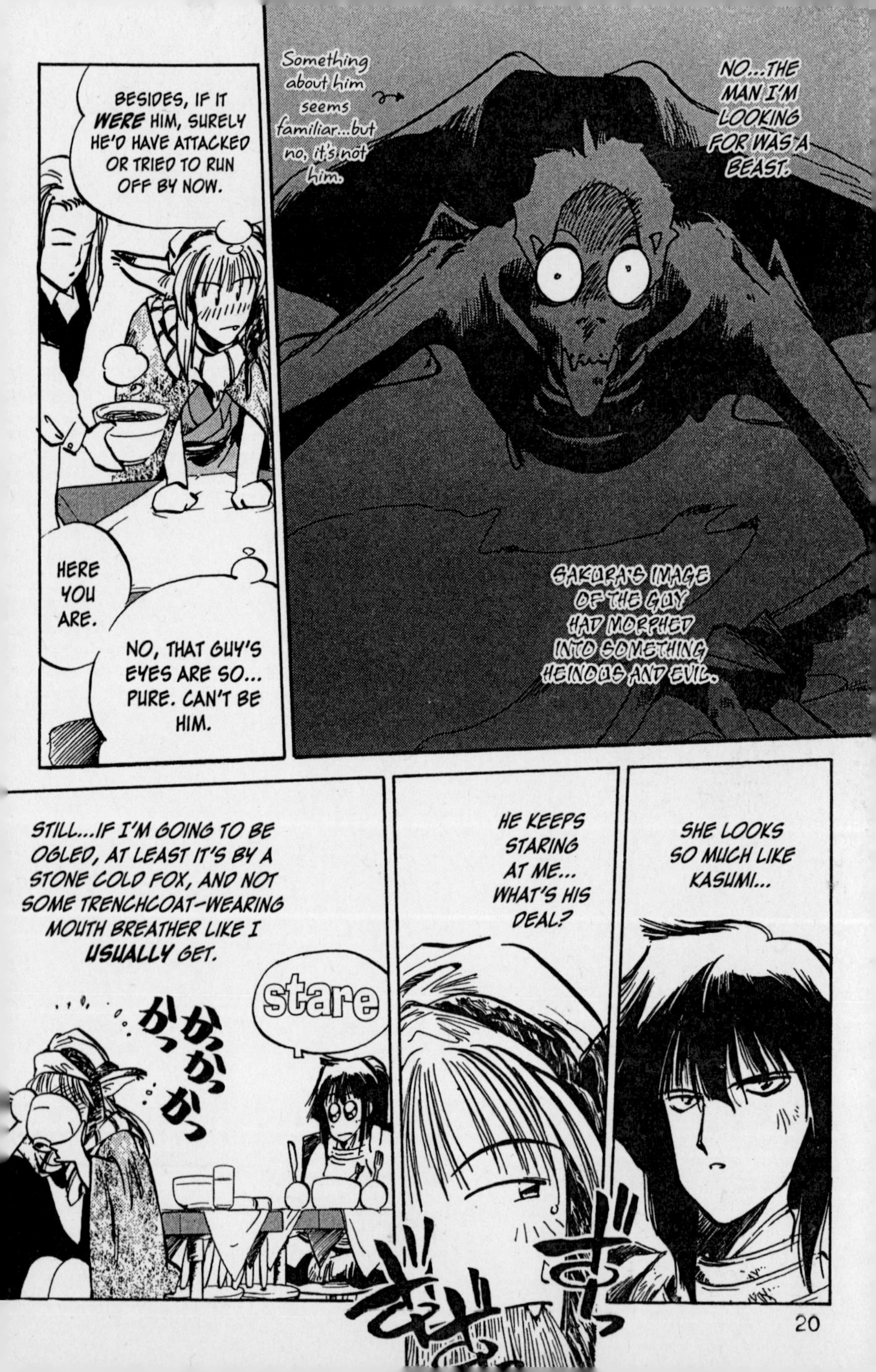
NO...THE MAN I'M LOOKING FOR WAS A BEAST.
Something about him seems familiar...but no, it's not him.
SAKURA'S IMAGE OF THE GUY HAD MORPHED INTO SOMETHING HEINOUS AND EVIL.
BESIDES, IF IT WERE HIM, SURELY HE'D HAVE ATTACKED OR TRIED TO RUN OFF BY NOW.
HERE YOU ARE.
NO, THAT GUY'S EYES ARE SO... PURE. CAN'T BE HIM.
SHE LOOKS SO MUCH LIKE KASUMI...
HE KEEPS STARING AT ME... WHAT'S HIS DEAL?
STILL...IF I'M GOING TO BE OGLED, AT LEAST IT'S BY A STONE COLD FOX, AND NOT SOME TRENCHCOAT-WEARING MOUTH BREATHER LIKE I USUALLY GET.
stare

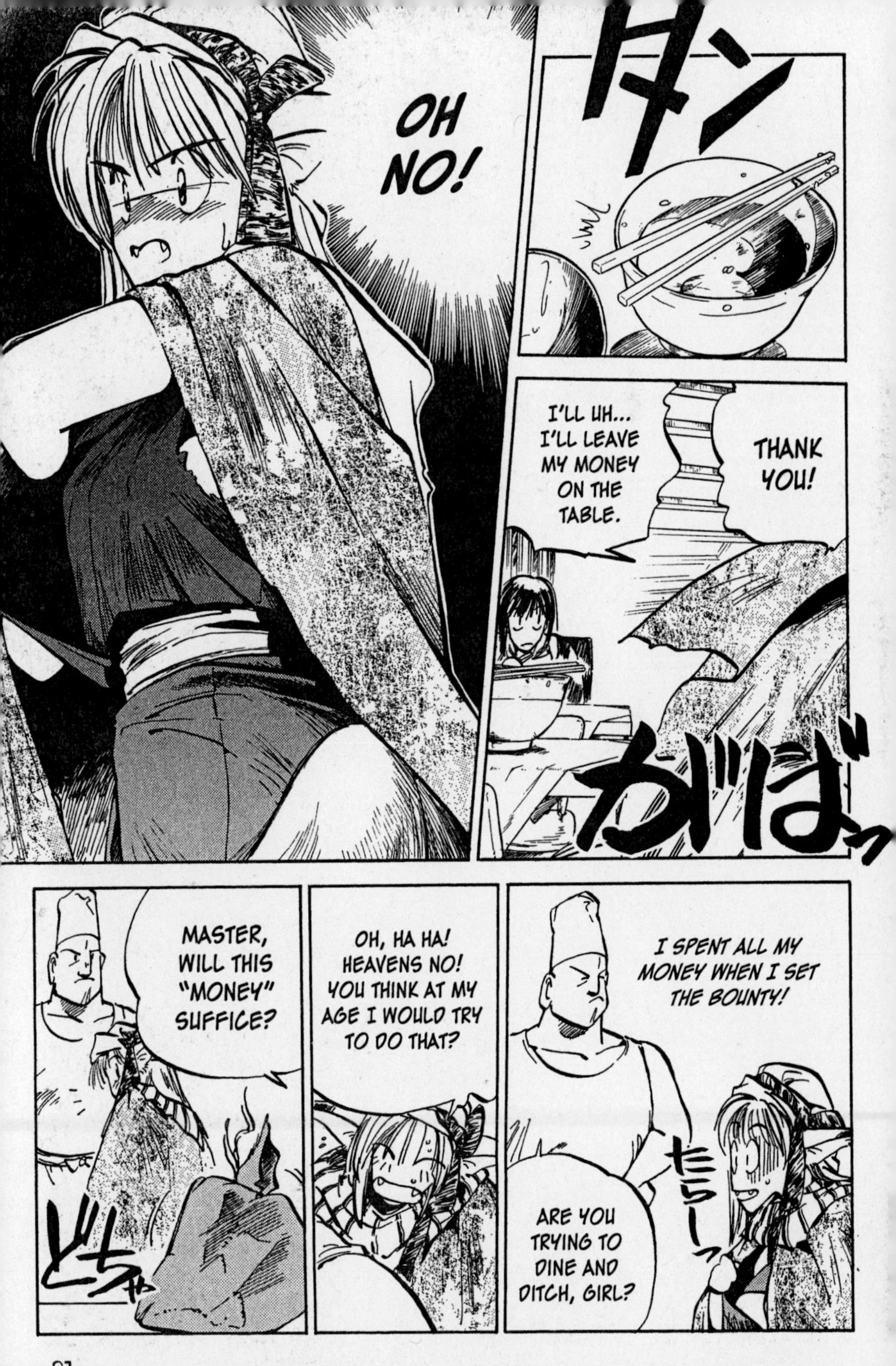
ダン
I'LL UH... I'LL LEAVE MY MONEY ON THE TABLE.
THANK YOU!
がばっ
OH NO!
I SPENT ALL MY MONEY WHEN I SET THE BOUNTY!
たらーっ
ARE YOU TRYING TO DINE AND DITCH, GIRL?
OH, HA HA! HEAVENS NO! YOU THINK AT MY AGE I WOULD TRY TO DO THAT?
MASTER, WILL THIS "MONEY" SUFFICE?
どちゃ

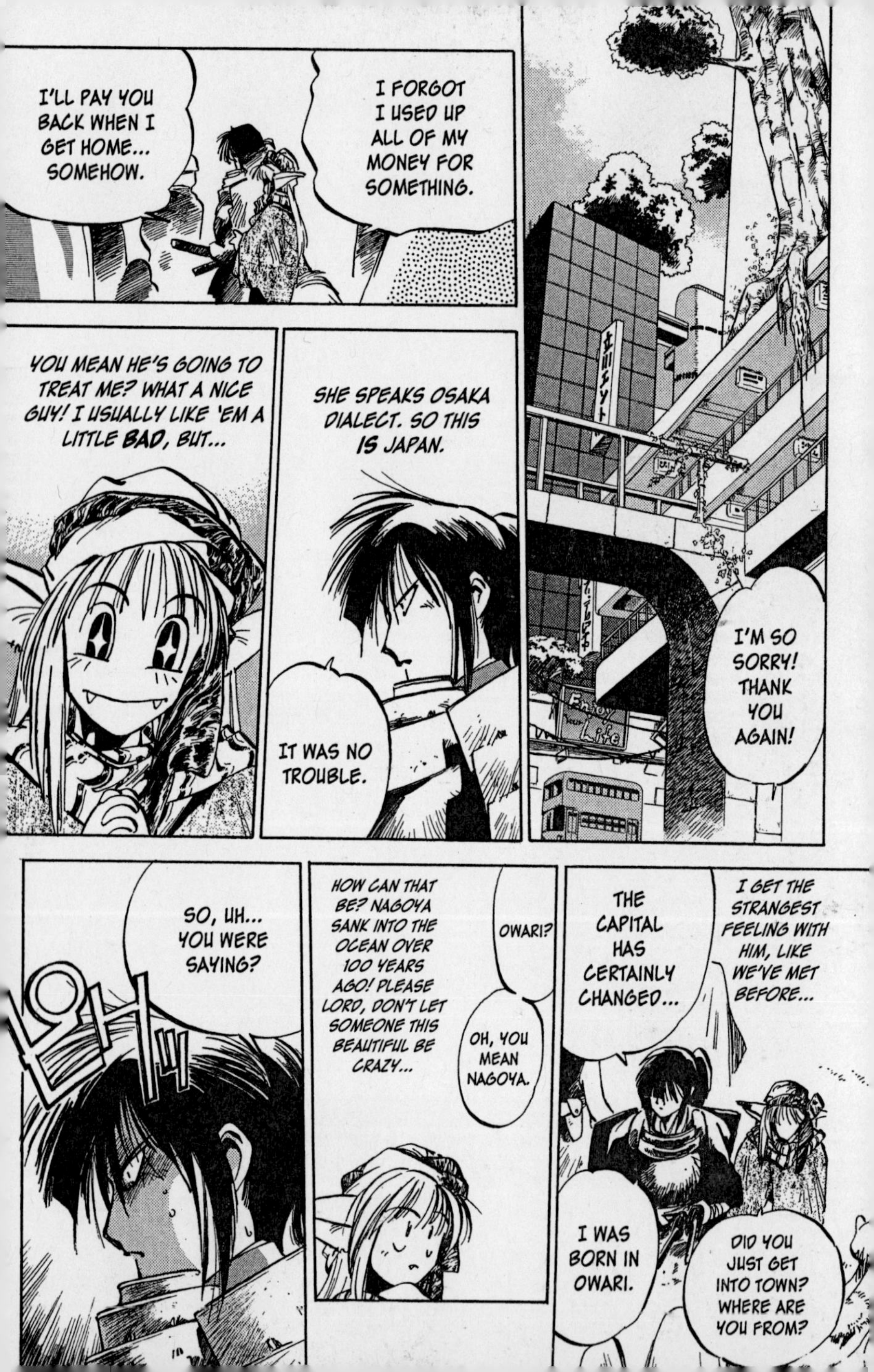

I'M SO SORRY! THANK YOU AGAIN!
I FORGOT I USED UP ALL OF MY MONEY FOR SOMETHING.
I'LL PAY YOU BACK WHEN I GET HOME... SOMEHOW.
SHE SPEAKS OSAKA DIALECT. SO THIS IS JAPAN.
IT WAS NO TROUBLE.
YOU MEAN HE'S GOING TO TREAT ME? WHAT A NICE GUY! I USUALLY LIKE 'EM A LITTLE BAD, BUT...
I GET THE STRANGEST FEELING WITH HIM, LIKE WE'VE MET BEFORE...
THE CAPITAL HAS CERTAINLY CHANGED...
DID YOU JUST GET INTO TOWN? WHERE ARE YOU FROM?
I WAS BORN IN OWARI.
OWARI?
OH, YOU MEAN NAGOYA.
HOW CAN THAT BE? NAGOYA SANK INTO THE OCEAN OVER 100 YEARS AGO! PLEASE LORD, DON'T LET SOMEONE THIS BEAUTIFUL BE CRAZY...
SO, UH... YOU WERE SAYING?

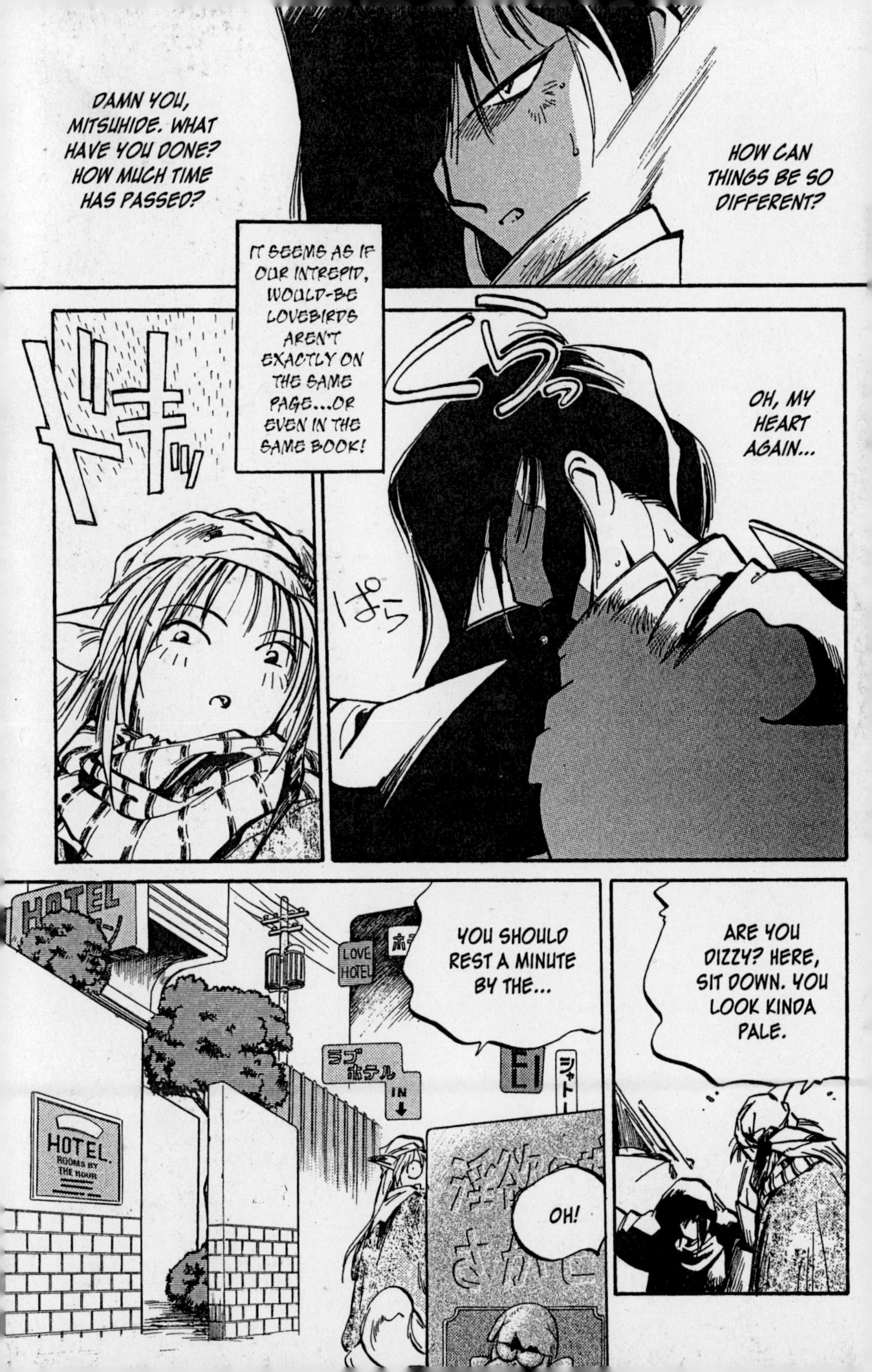
HOW CAN THINGS BE SO DIFFERENT?
DAMN YOU, MITSUHIDE. WHAT HAVE YOU DONE? HOW MUCH TIME HAS PASSED?
IT SEEMS AS IF OUR INTREPID, WOULD-BE LOVEBIRDS AREN'T EXACTLY ON THE SAME PAGE...OR EVEN IN THE SAME BOOK!
くらっ
OH, MY HEART AGAIN...
ぱら
ドキッ
ARE YOU DIZZY? HERE, SIT DOWN. YOU LOOK KINDA PALE.
HOTEL
YOU SHOULD REST A MINUTE BY THE...
LOVE HOTEL
ラブホテル
IN
シャトー
HOTEL. ROOMS BY THE HOUR
OH!

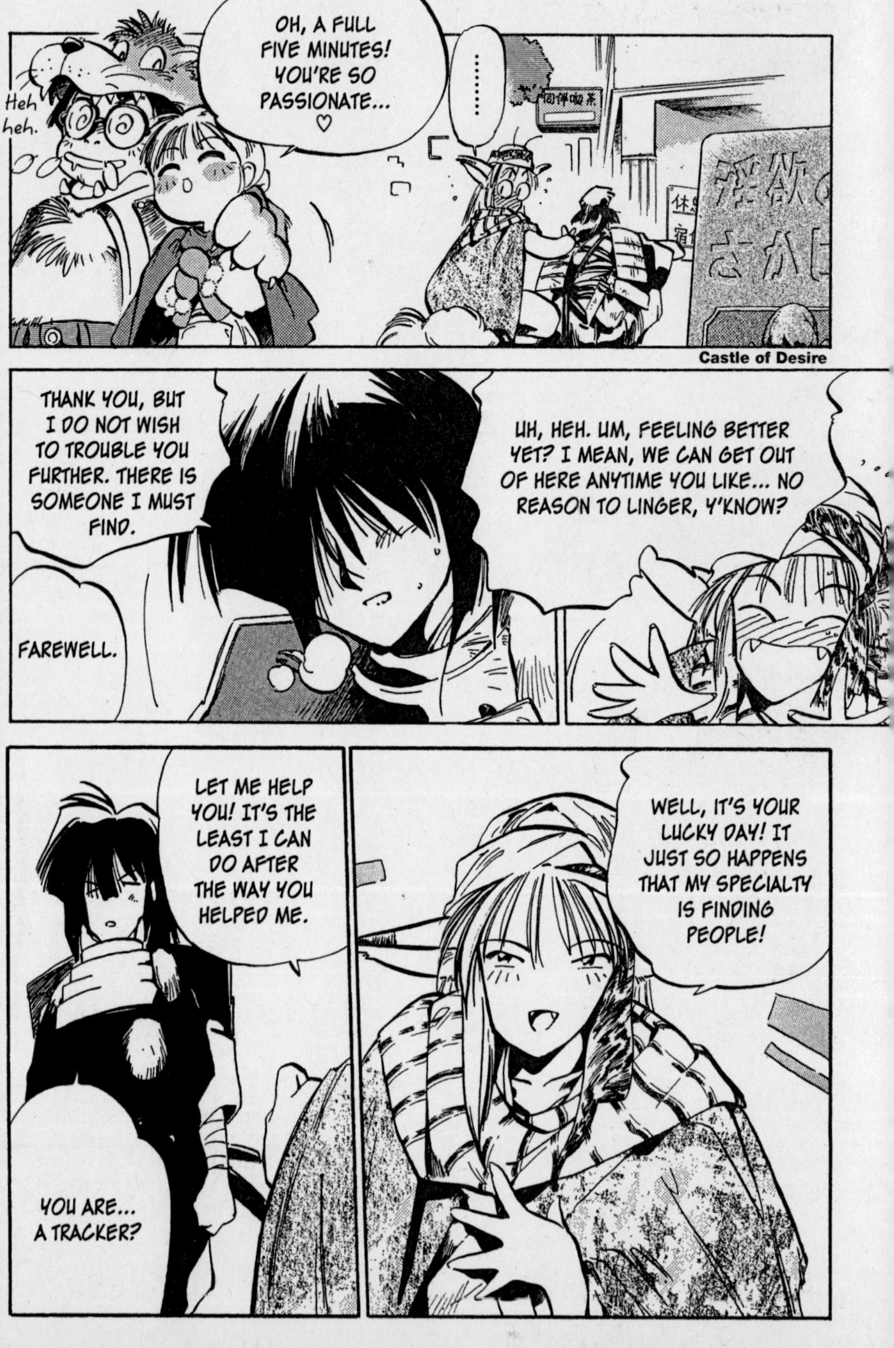
......
OH, A FULL FIVE MINUTES! YOU'RE SO PASSIONATE... ♡
Heh heh.
UH, HEH. UM, FEELING BETTER YET? I MEAN, WE CAN GET OUT OF HERE ANYTIME YOU LIKE... NO REASON TO LINGER, Y'KNOW?
THANK YOU, BUT I DO NOT WISH TO TROUBLE YOU FURTHER. THERE IS SOMEONE I MUST FIND.
FAREWELL.
WELL, IT'S YOUR LUCKY DAY! IT JUST SO HAPPENS THAT MY SPECIALTY IS FINDING PEOPLE!
LET ME HELP YOU! IT'S THE LEAST I CAN DO AFTER THE WAY YOU HELPED ME.
YOU ARE... A TRACKER?

Castle of Desire

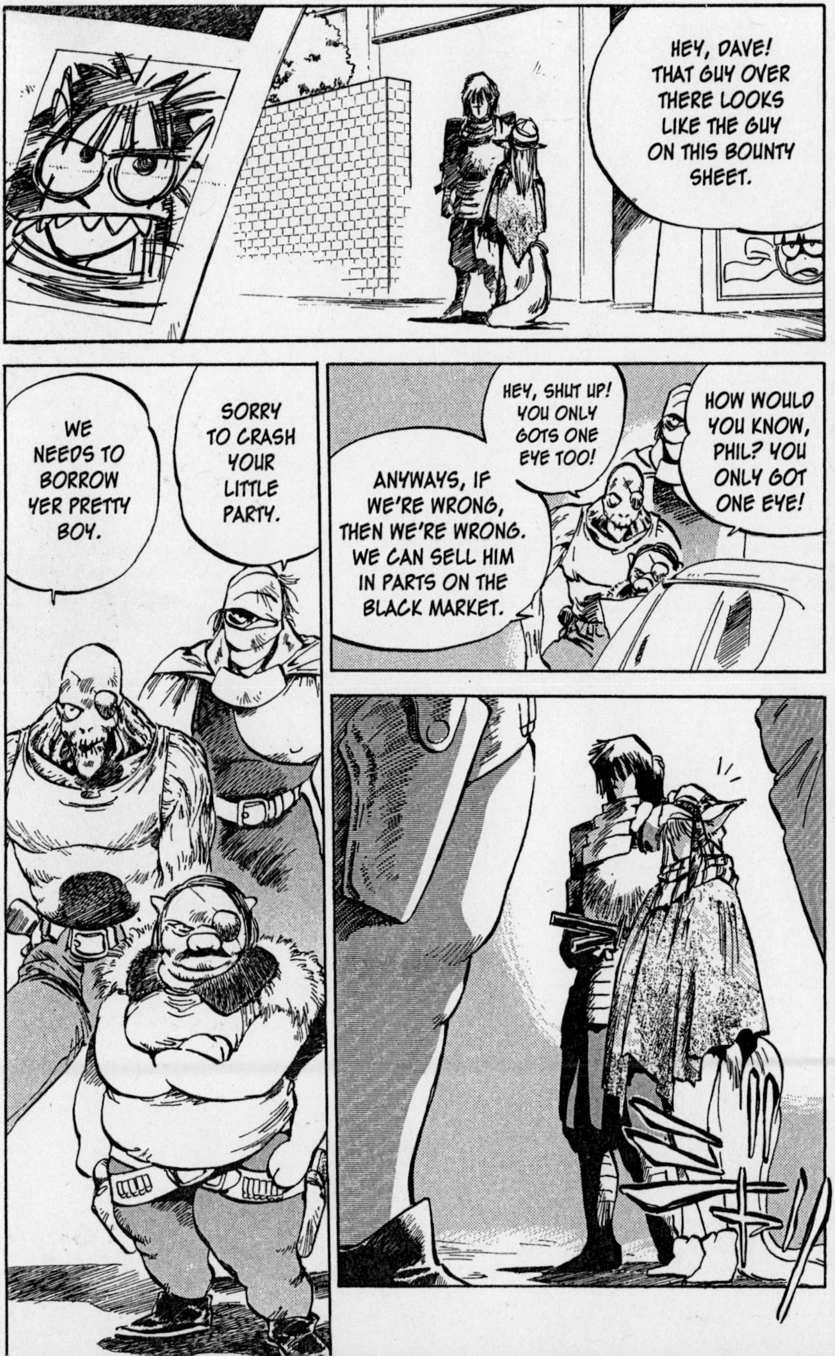
HEY, DAVE! THAT GUY OVER THERE LOOKS LIKE THE GUY ON THIS BOUNTY SHEET.
HOW WOULD YOU KNOW, PHIL? YOU ONLY GOT ONE EYE!
HEY, SHUT UP! YOU ONLY GOTS ONE EYE TOO!
ANYWAYS, IF WE'RE WRONG, THEN WE'RE WRONG. WE CAN SELL HIM IN PARTS ON THE BLACK MARKET.
SORRY TO CRASH YOUR LITTLE PARTY.
WE NEEDS TO BORROW YER PRETTY BOY.

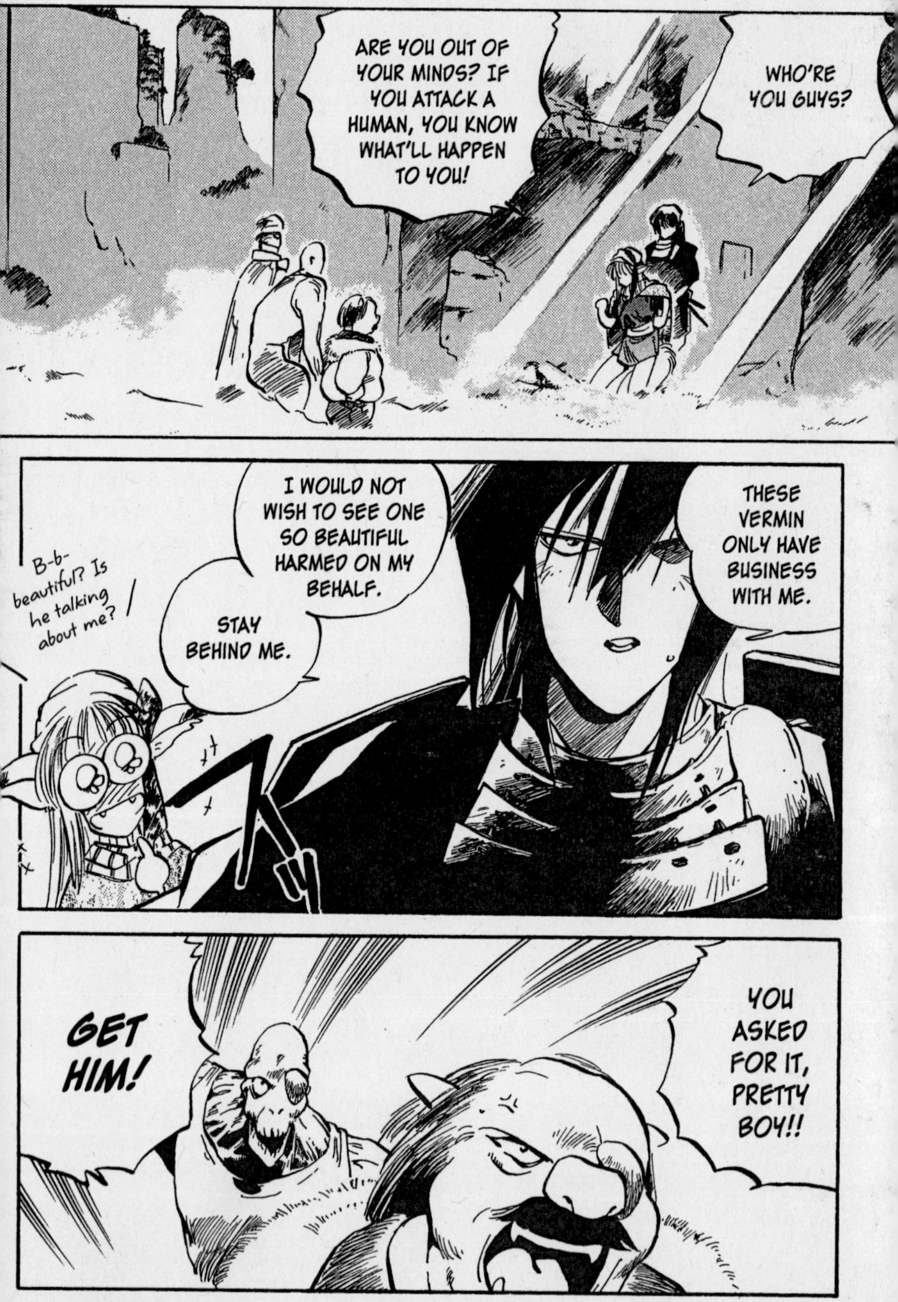
WHO'RE YOU GUYS?
ARE YOU OUT OF YOUR MINDS? IF YOU ATTACK A HUMAN, YOU KNOW WHAT'LL HAPPEN TO YOU!
THESE VERMIN ONLY HAVE BUSINESS WITH ME.
I WOULD NOT WISH TO SEE ONE SO BEAUTIFUL HARMED ON MY BEHALF.
STAY BEHIND ME.
B-b-beautiful? Is he talking about me?
YOU ASKED FOR IT, PRETTY BOY!!
GET HIM!

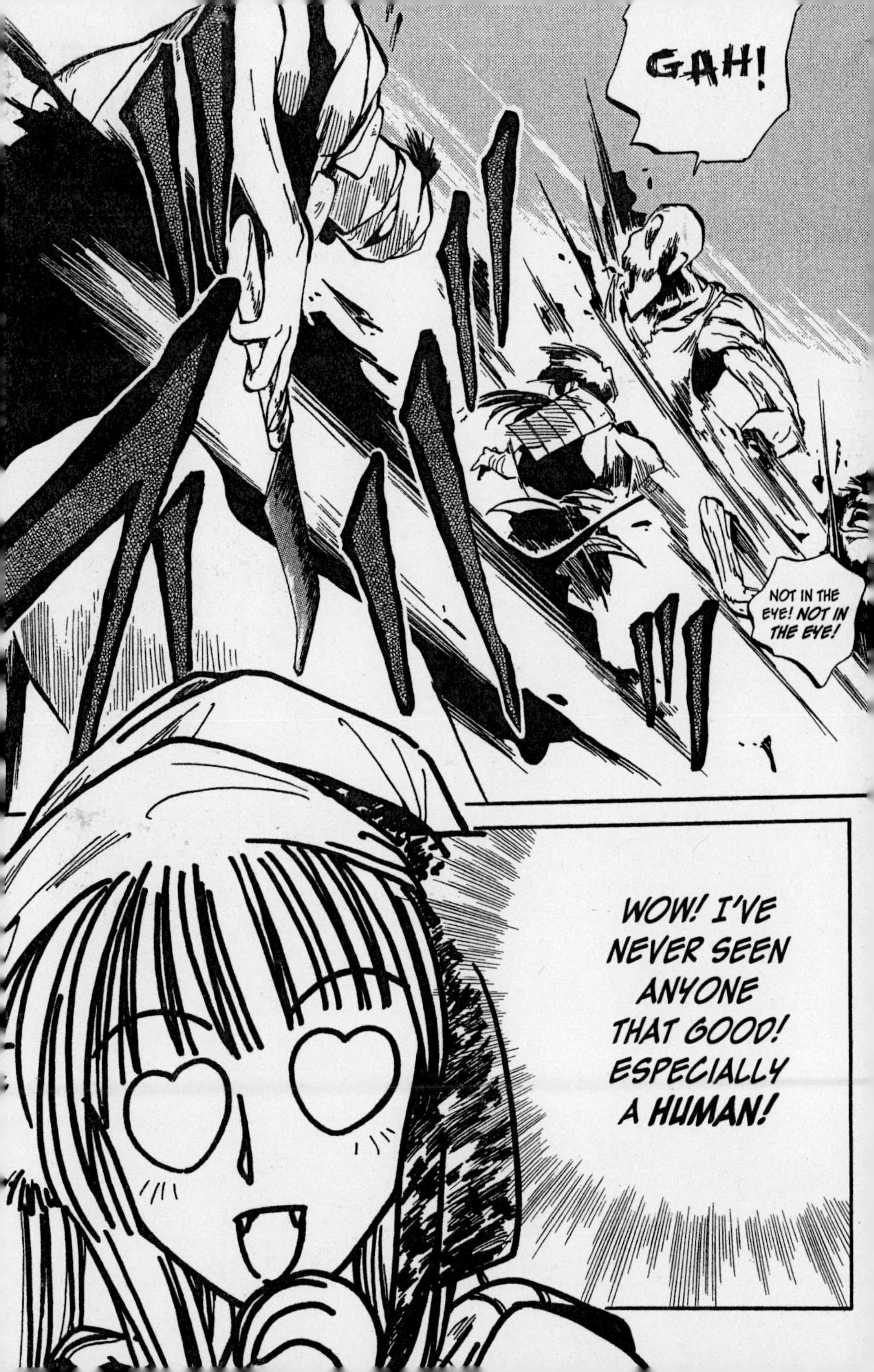
GAH!
NOT IN THE EYE! NOT IN THE EYE!
WOW! I'VE NEVER SEEN ANYONE THAT GOOD! ESPECIALLY A HUMAN!

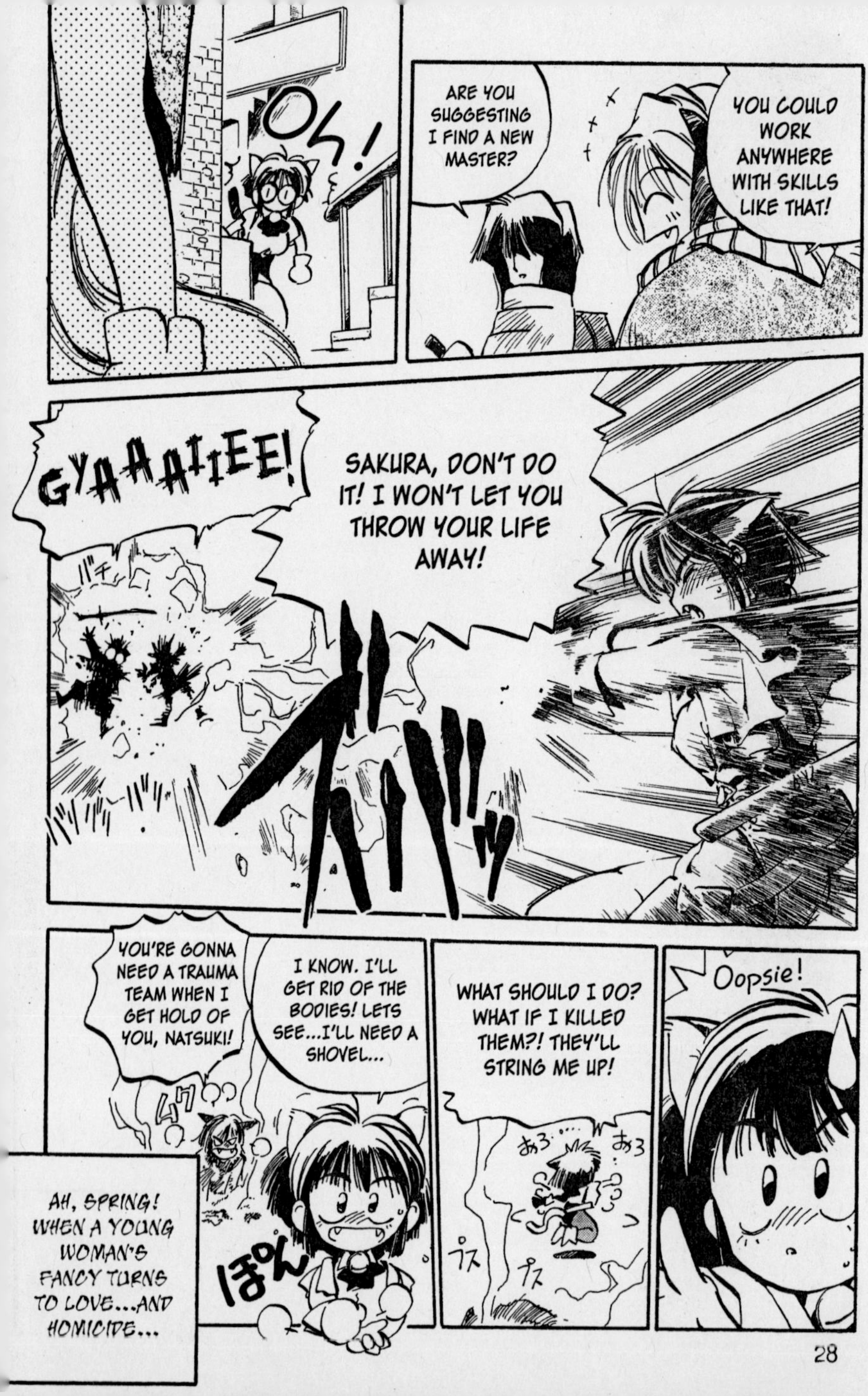
YOU COULD WORK ANYWHERE WITH SKILLS LIKE THAT!
ARE YOU SUGGESTING I FIND A NEW MASTER?
OH!
SAKURA, DON'T DO IT! I WON'T LET YOU THROW YOUR LIFE AWAY!
GYAAAIIEEE!
Oopsie!
WHAT SHOULD I DO? WHAT IF I KILLED THEM?! THEY'LL STRING ME UP!
I KNOW. I'LL GET RID OF THE BODIES! LETS SEE...I'LL NEED A SHOVEL...
YOU'RE GONNA NEED A TRAUMA TEAM WHEN I GET HOLD OF YOU, NATSUKI!
ぽん
AH, SPRING! WHEN A YOUNG WOMAN'S FANCY TURNS TO LOVE...AND HOMICIDE...

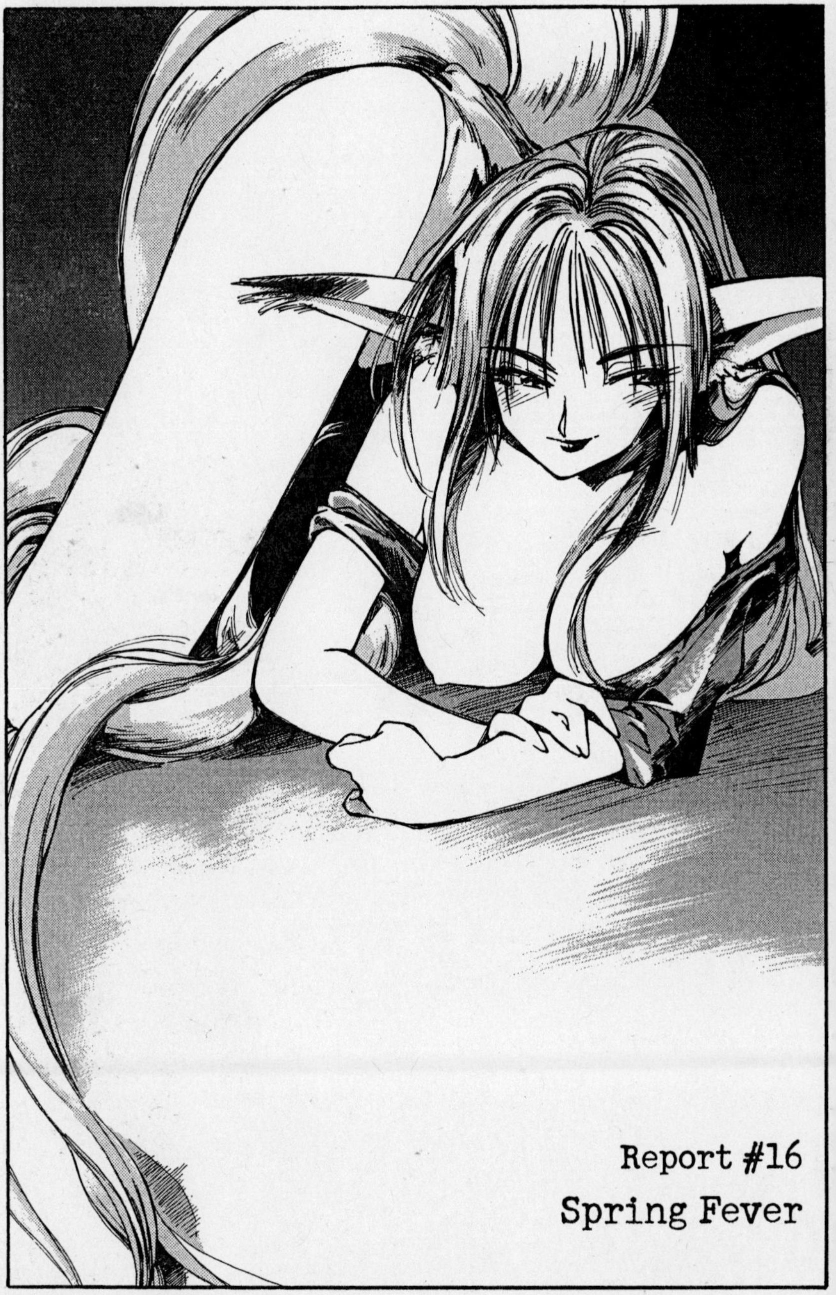
Report #16
Spring Fever

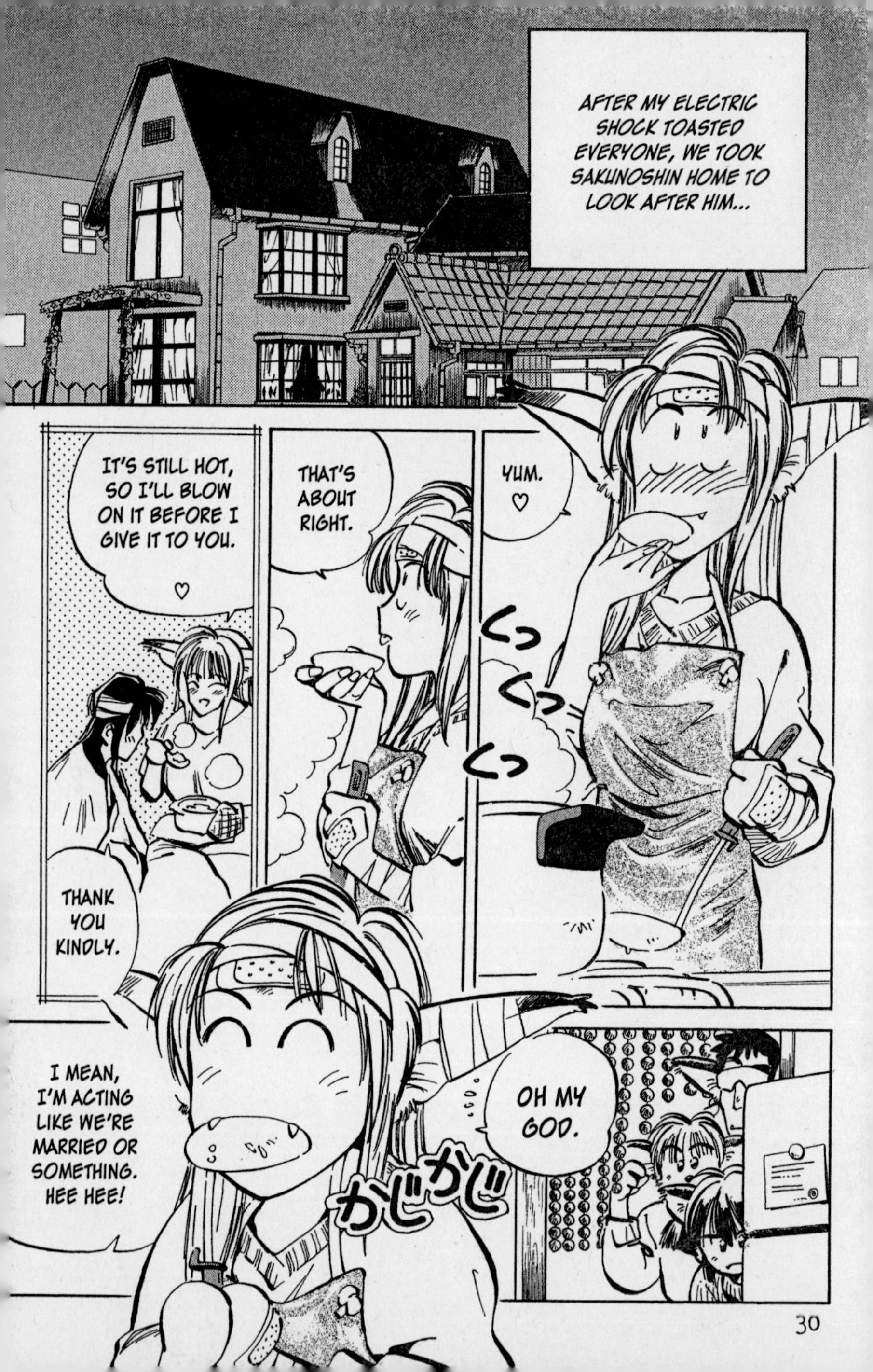
AFTER MY ELECTRIC SHOCK TOASTED EVERYONE, WE TOOK SAKUNOSHIN HOME TO LOOK AFTER HIM...
YUM. ♡
くっ
くっ
くっ
THAT'S ABOUT RIGHT.
IT'S STILL HOT, SO I'LL BLOW ON IT BEFORE I GIVE IT TO YOU. ♡
THANK YOU KINDLY.
OH MY GOD.
かじかじ
I MEAN, I'M ACTING LIKE WE'RE MARRIED OR SOMETHING. HEE HEE!

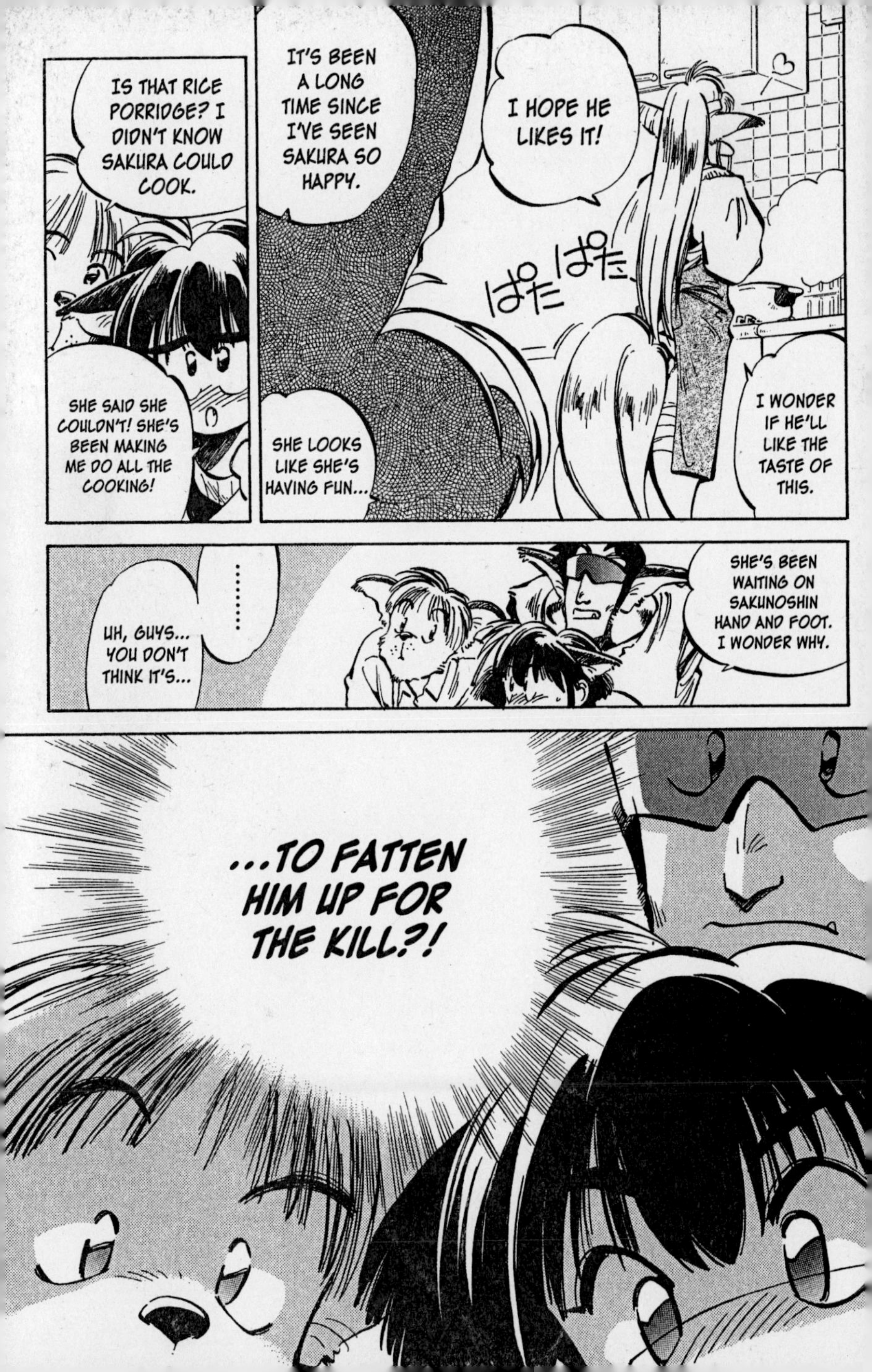
I HOPE HE LIKES IT!
ぱたぱた
I WONDER IF HE'LL LIKE THE TASTE OF THIS.
IT'S BEEN A LONG TIME SINCE I'VE SEEN SAKURA SO HAPPY.
SHE LOOKS LIKE SHE'S HAVING FUN...
IS THAT RICE PORRIDGE? I DIDN'T KNOW SAKURA COULD COOK.
SHE SAID SHE COULDN'T! SHE'S BEEN MAKING ME DO ALL THE COOKING!
SHE'S BEEN WAITING ON SAKUNOSHIN HAND AND FOOT. I WONDER WHY.
......
UH, GUYS... YOU DON'T THINK IT'S...
...TO FATTEN HIM UP FOR THE KILL?!

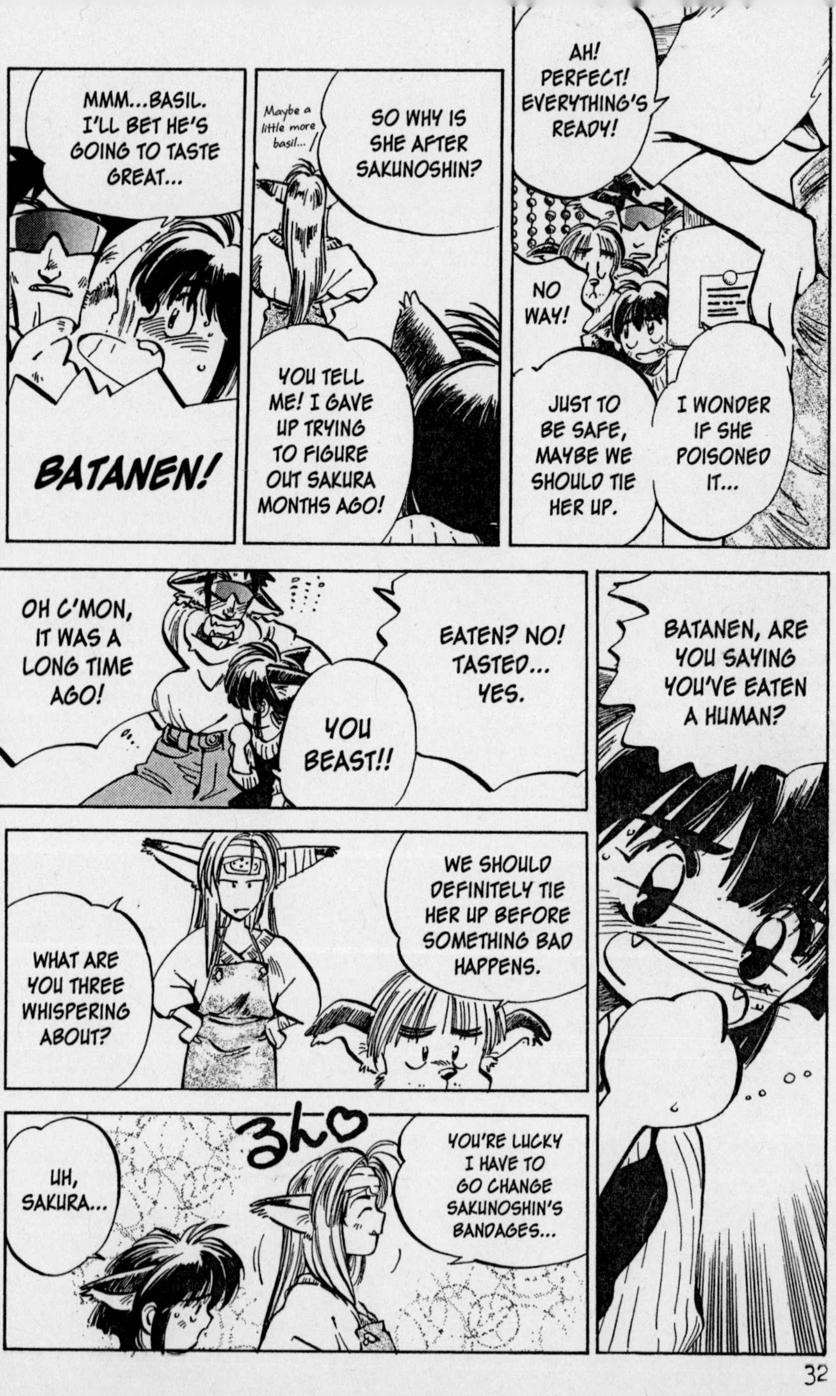
AH! PERFECT! EVERYTHING'S READY!
I WONDER IF SHE POISONED IT...
NO WAY!
JUST TO BE SAFE, MAYBE WE SHOULD TIE HER UP.
SO WHY IS SHE AFTER SAKUNOSHIN?
Maybe a little more basil...
YOU TELL ME! I GAVE UP TRYING TO FIGURE OUT SAKURA MONTHS AGO!
MMM...BASIL. I'LL BET HE'S GOING TO TASTE GREAT...
BATANEN!
BATANEN, ARE YOU SAYING YOU'VE EATEN A HUMAN?
EATEN? NO! TASTED... YES.
YOU BEAST!!
OH C'MON, IT WAS A LONG TIME AGO!
WE SHOULD DEFINITELY TIE HER UP BEFORE SOMETHING BAD HAPPENS.
WHAT ARE YOU THREE WHISPERING ABOUT?
YOU'RE LUCKY I HAVE TO GO CHANGE SAKUNOSHIN'S BANDAGES...
うん♡
UH, SAKURA...

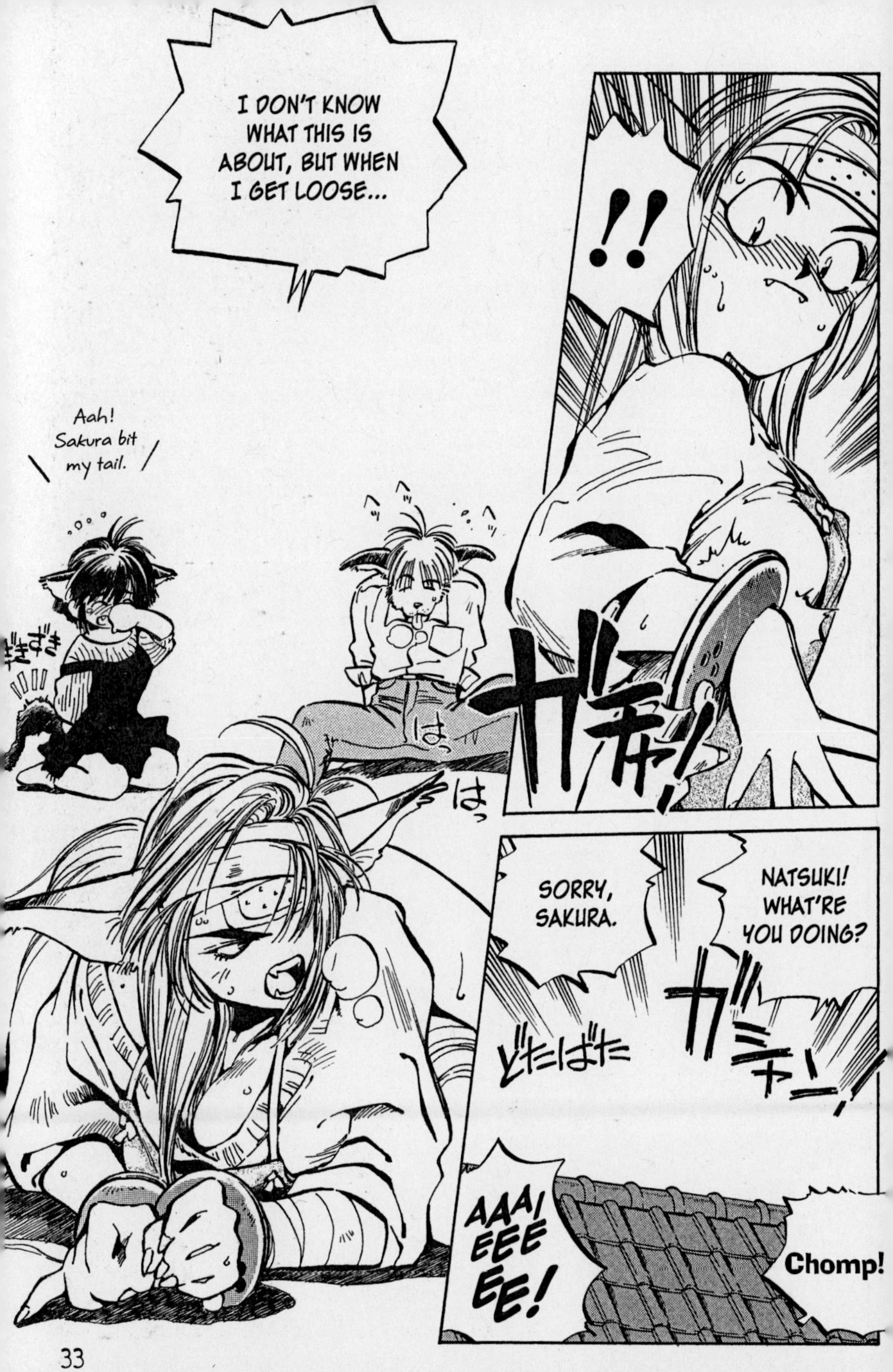
!!
ガチャ!
NATSUKI! WHAT'RE YOU DOING?
SORRY, SAKURA.
ガシャン!
どたばた
Chomp!
AAAIEEEEEE!
I DON'T KNOW WHAT THIS IS ABOUT, BUT WHEN I GET LOOSE...
Aah! Sakura bit my tail.
ずきずき
はっ
はっ

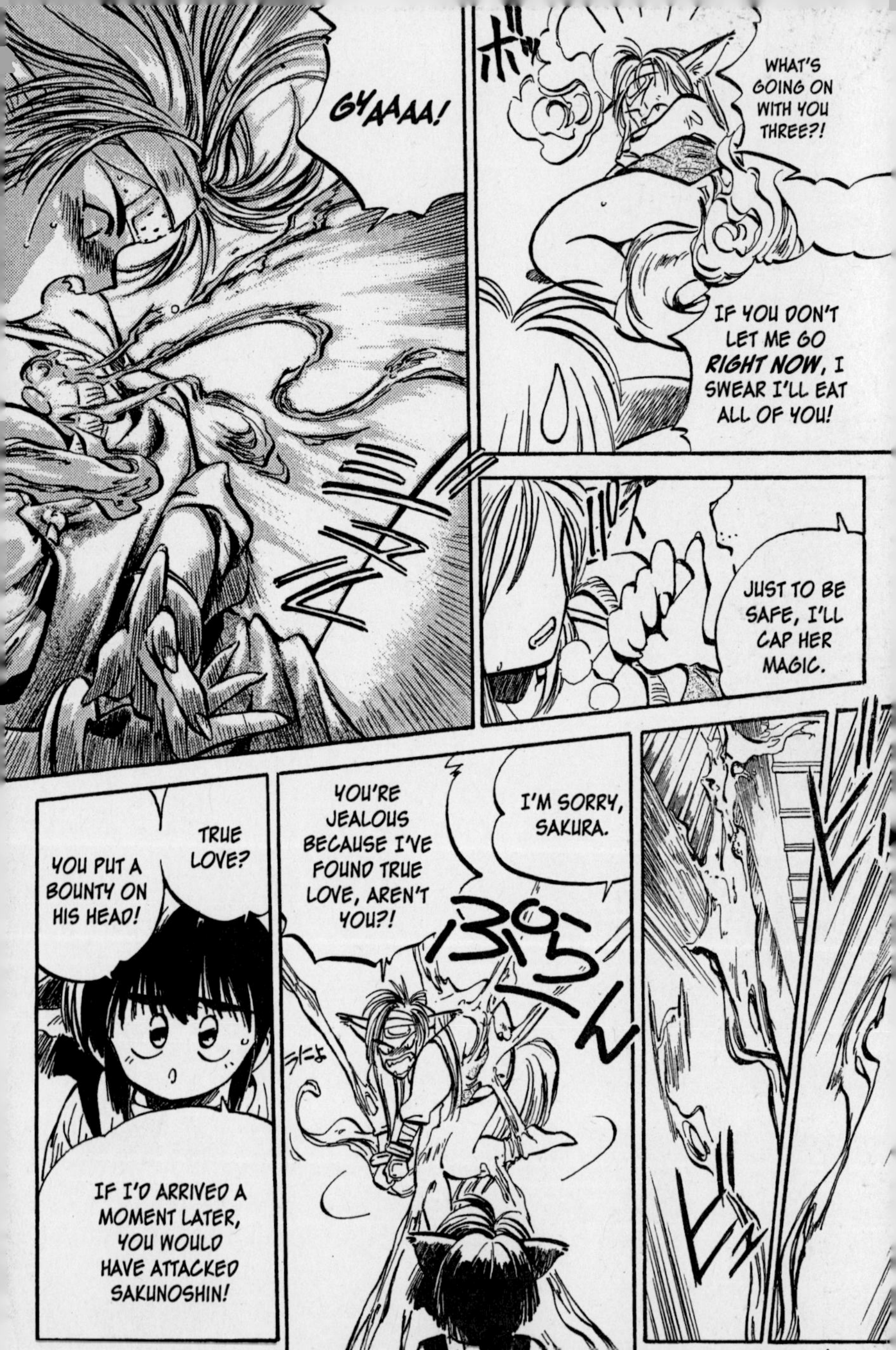
WHAT'S GOING ON WITH YOU THREE?!
IF YOU DON'T LET ME GO RIGHT NOW, I SWEAR I'LL EAT ALL OF YOU!
JUST TO BE SAFE, I'LL CAP HER MAGIC.
GYAAAA!
I'M SORRY, SAKURA.
YOU'RE JEALOUS BECAUSE I'VE FOUND TRUE LOVE, AREN'T YOU?!
TRUE LOVE?
YOU PUT A BOUNTY ON HIS HEAD!
IF I'D ARRIVED A MOMENT LATER, YOU WOULD HAVE ATTACKED SAKUNOSHIN!

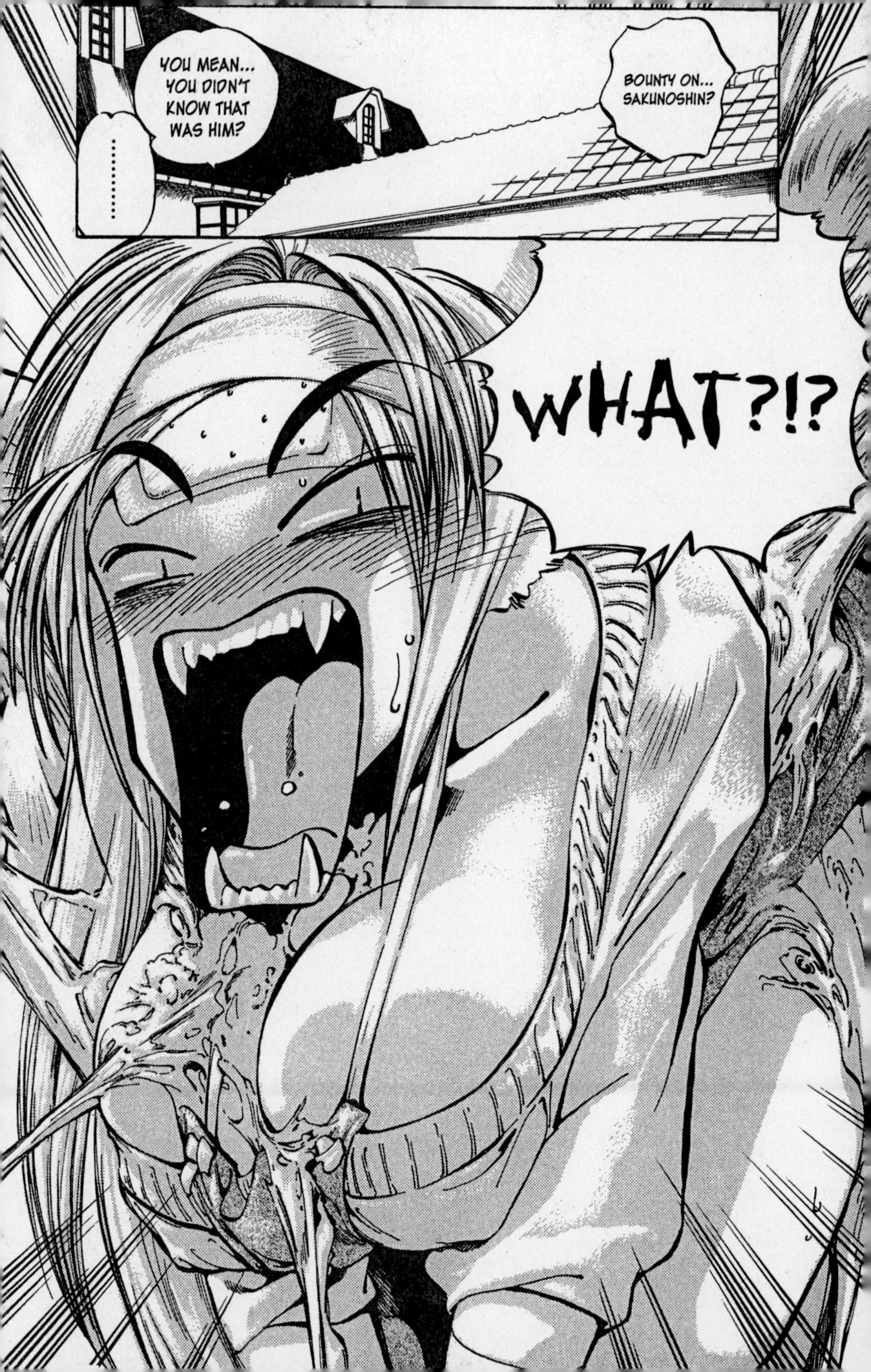
BOUNTY ON... SAKUNOSHIN?
YOU MEAN... YOU DIDN'T KNOW THAT WAS HIM?
......
WHAT?!?

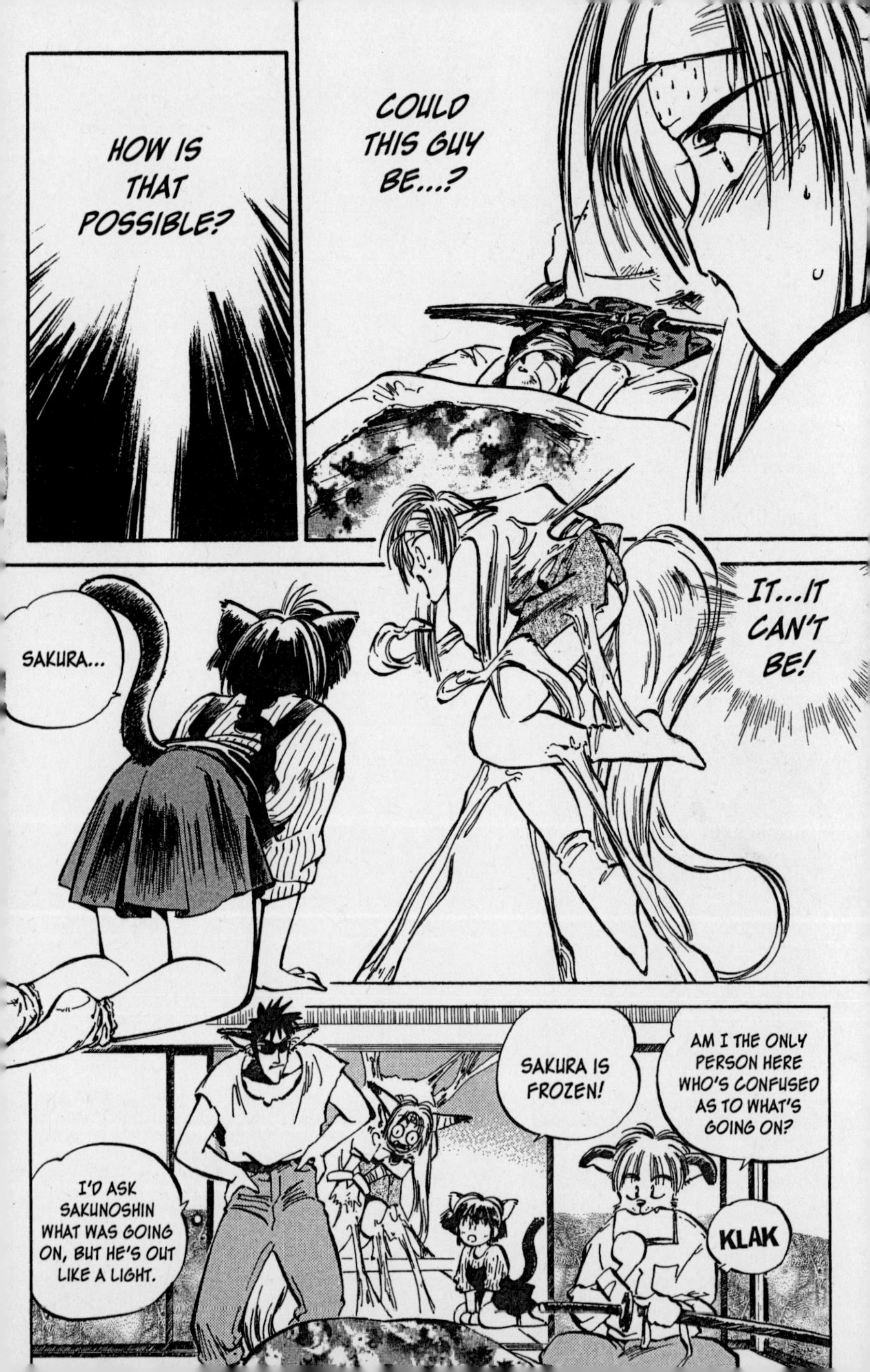
COULD THIS GUY BE...?
HOW IS THAT POSSIBLE?
IT...IT CAN'T BE!
SAKURA...
AM I THE ONLY PERSON HERE WHO'S CONFUSED AS TO WHAT'S GOING ON?
SAKURA IS FROZEN!
KLAK
I'D ASK SAKUNOSHIN WHAT WAS GOING ON, BUT HE'S OUT LIKE A LIGHT.

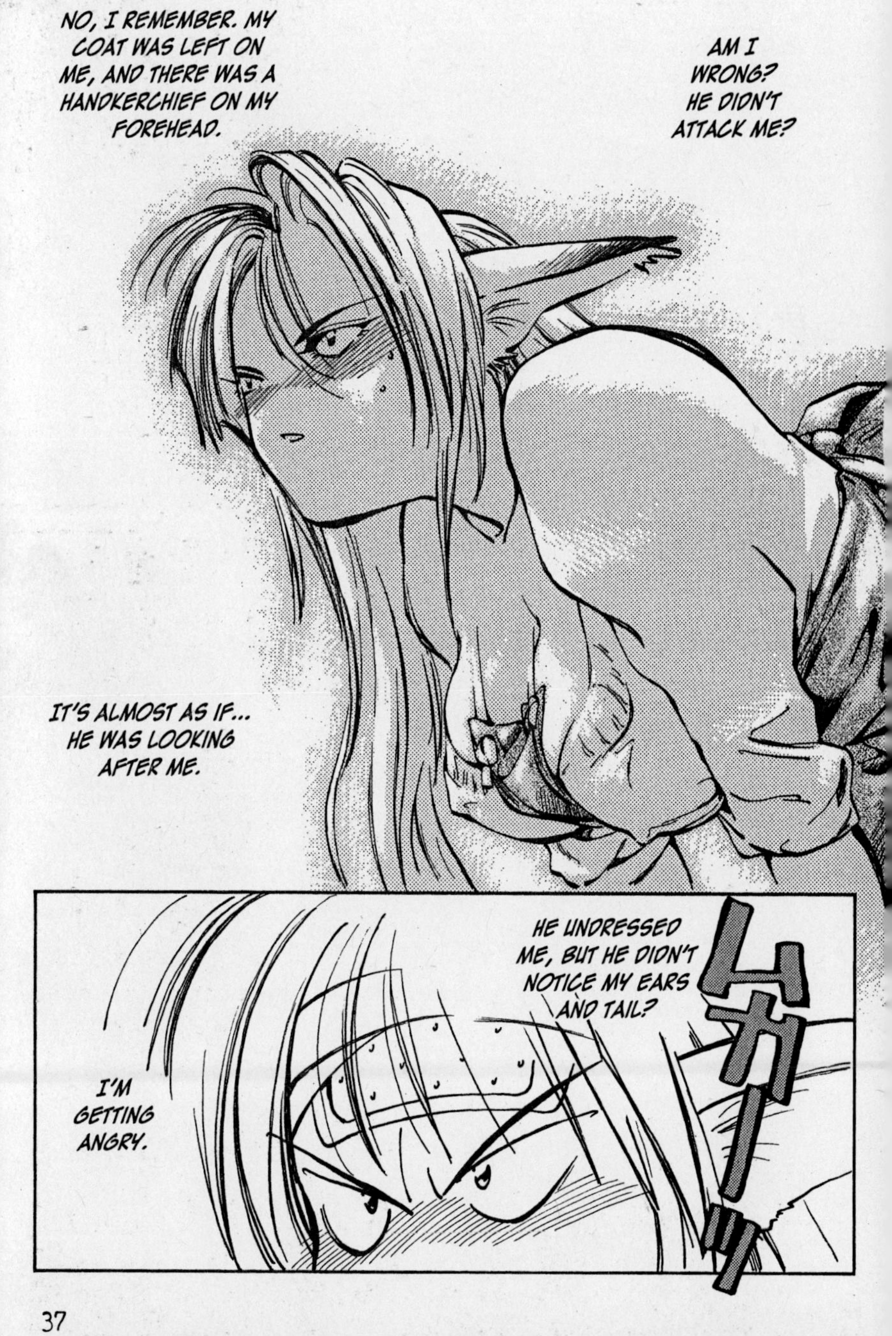

AM I WRONG? HE DIDN'T ATTACK ME?
NO, I REMEMBER. MY COAT WAS LEFT ON ME, AND THERE WAS A HANDKERCHIEF ON MY FOREHEAD.
IT'S ALMOST AS IF... HE WAS LOOKING AFTER ME.
HE UNDRESSED ME, BUT HE DIDN'T NOTICE MY EARS AND TAIL?
ムカーッ
I'M GETTING ANGRY.

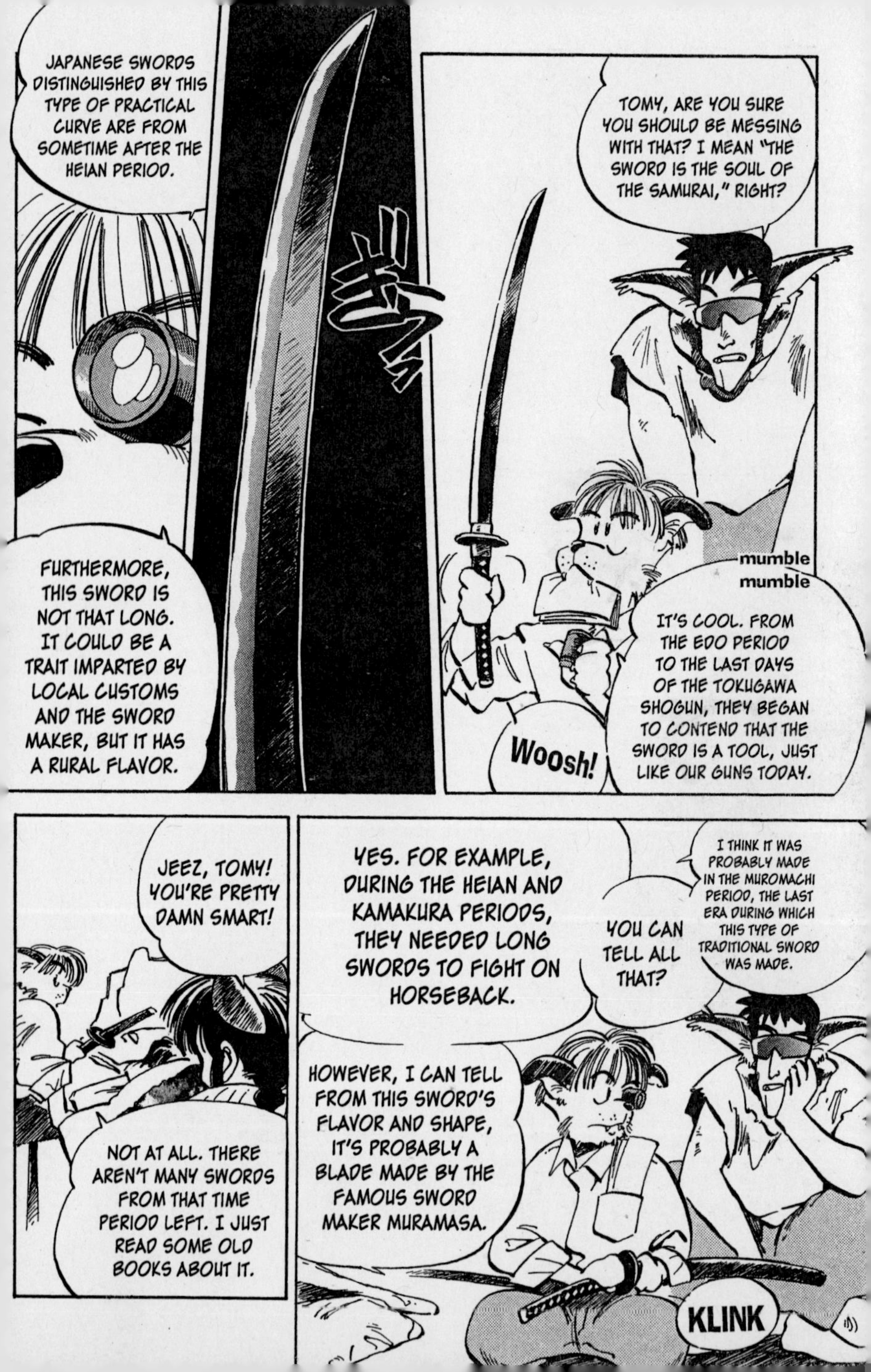
TOMY, ARE YOU SURE YOU SHOULD BE MESSING WITH THAT? I MEAN "THE SWORD IS THE SOUL OF THE SAMURAI," RIGHT?
mumble mumble
IT'S COOL. FROM THE EDO PERIOD TO THE LAST DAYS OF THE TOKUGAWA SHOGUN, THEY BEGAN TO CONTEND THAT THE SWORD IS A TOOL, JUST LIKE OUR GUNS TODAY.
Woosh!
JAPANESE SWORDS DISTINGUISHED BY THIS TYPE OF PRACTICAL CURVE ARE FROM SOMETIME AFTER THE HEIAN PERIOD.
FURTHERMORE, THIS SWORD IS NOT THAT LONG. IT COULD BE A TRAIT IMPARTED BY LOCAL CUSTOMS AND THE SWORD MAKER, BUT IT HAS A RURAL FLAVOR.
I THINK IT WAS PROBABLY MADE IN THE MUROMACHI PERIOD, THE LAST ERA DURING WHICH THIS TYPE OF TRADITIONAL SWORD WAS MADE.
YOU CAN TELL ALL THAT?
YES. FOR EXAMPLE, DURING THE HEIAN AND KAMAKURA PERIODS, THEY NEEDED LONG SWORDS TO FIGHT ON HORSEBACK.
HOWEVER, I CAN TELL FROM THIS SWORD'S FLAVOR AND SHAPE, IT'S PROBABLY A BLADE MADE BY THE FAMOUS SWORD MAKER MURAMASA.
KLINK
JEEZ, TOMY! YOU'RE PRETTY DAMN SMART!
NOT AT ALL. THERE AREN'T MANY SWORDS FROM THAT TIME PERIOD LEFT. I JUST READ SOME OLD BOOKS ABOUT IT.

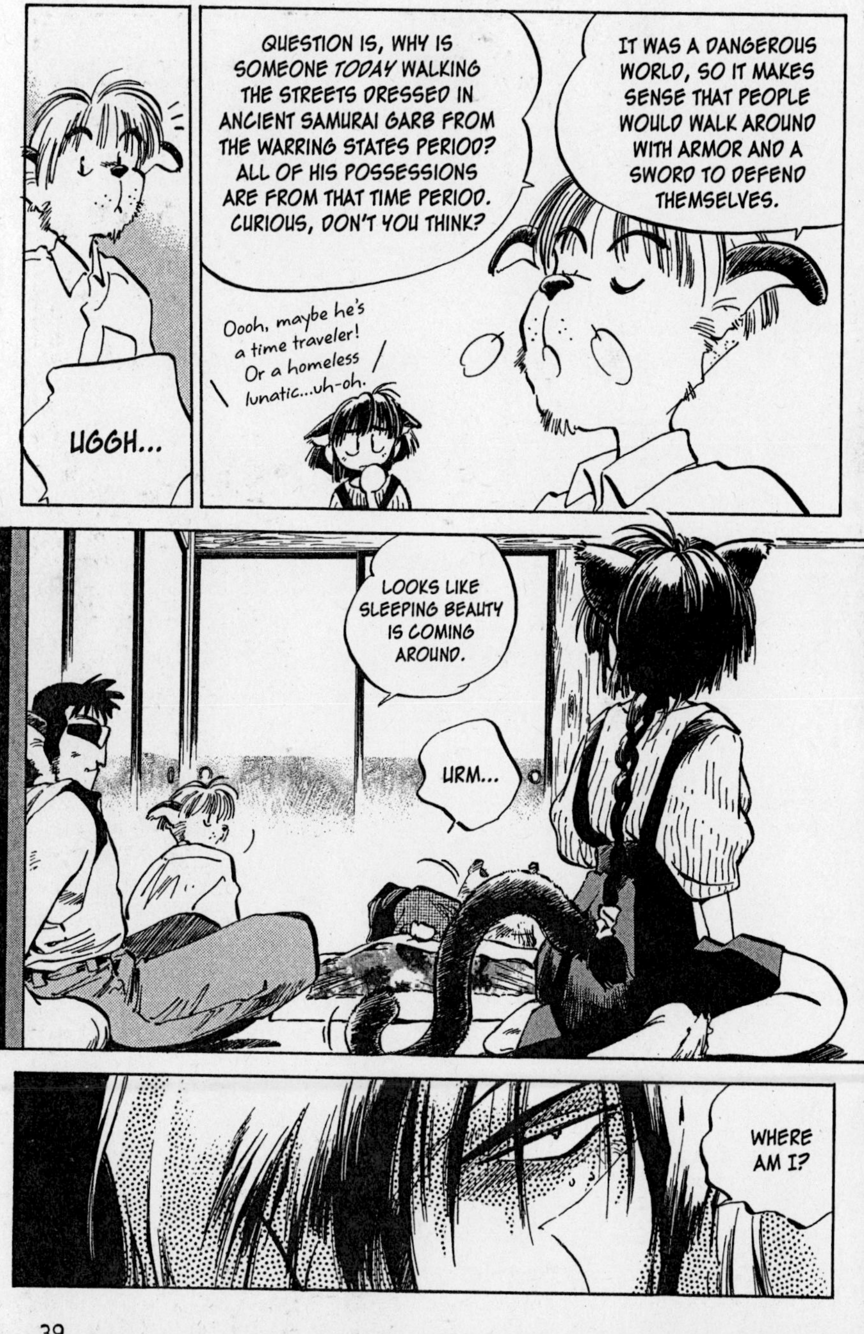
IT WAS A DANGEROUS WORLD, SO IT MAKES SENSE THAT PEOPLE WOULD WALK AROUND WITH ARMOR AND A SWORD TO DEFEND THEMSELVES.
QUESTION IS, WHY IS SOMEONE *TODAY* WALKING THE STREETS DRESSED IN ANCIENT SAMURAI GARB FROM THE WARRING STATES PERIOD? ALL OF HIS POSSESSIONS ARE FROM THAT TIME PERIOD. CURIOUS, DON'T YOU THINK?
Oooh, maybe he's a time traveler! Or a homeless lunatic...uh-oh.
UGGH...
LOOKS LIKE SLEEPING BEAUTY IS COMING AROUND.
URM...
WHERE AM I?

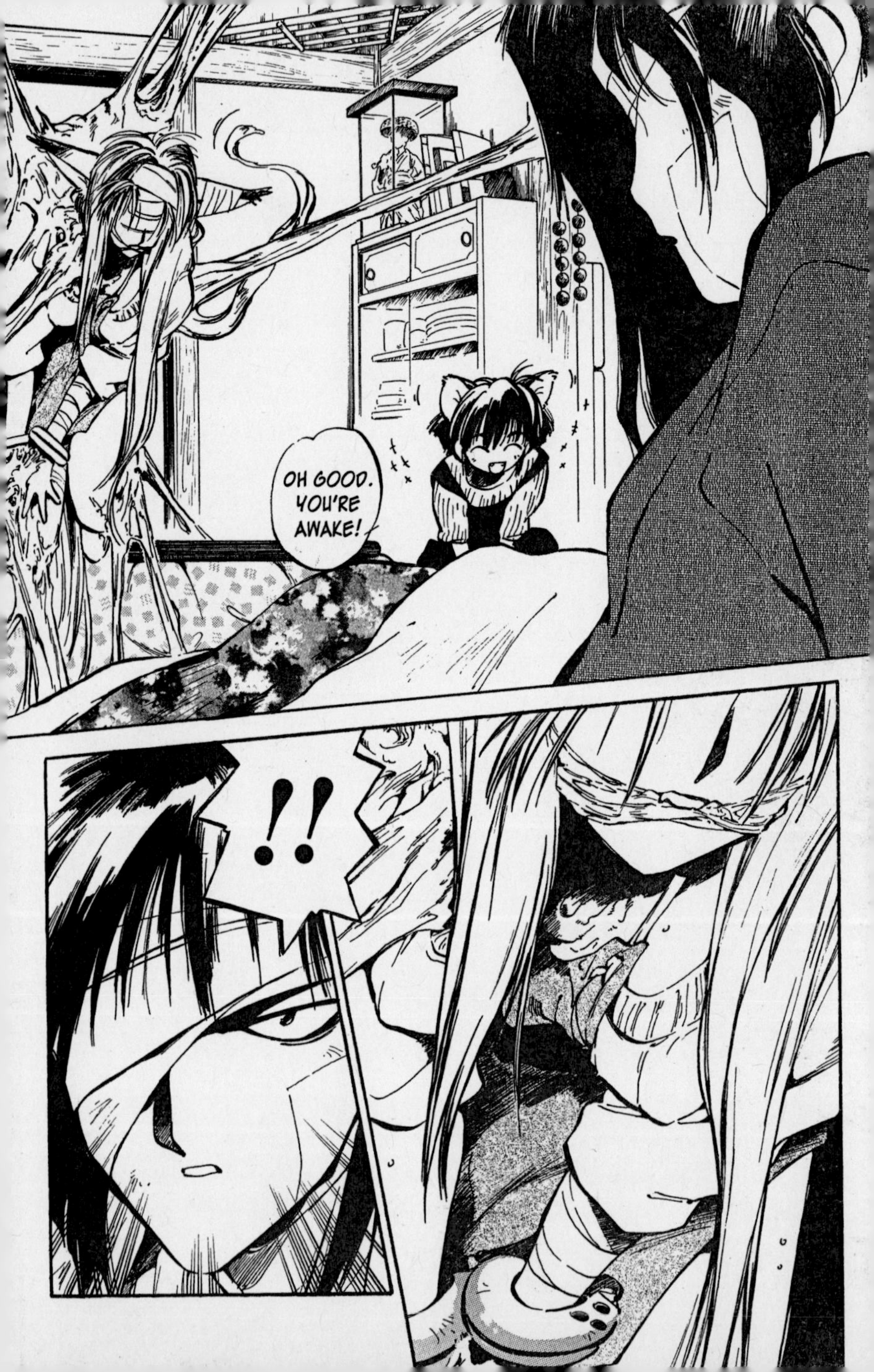
OH GOOD. YOU'RE AWAKE!
!!

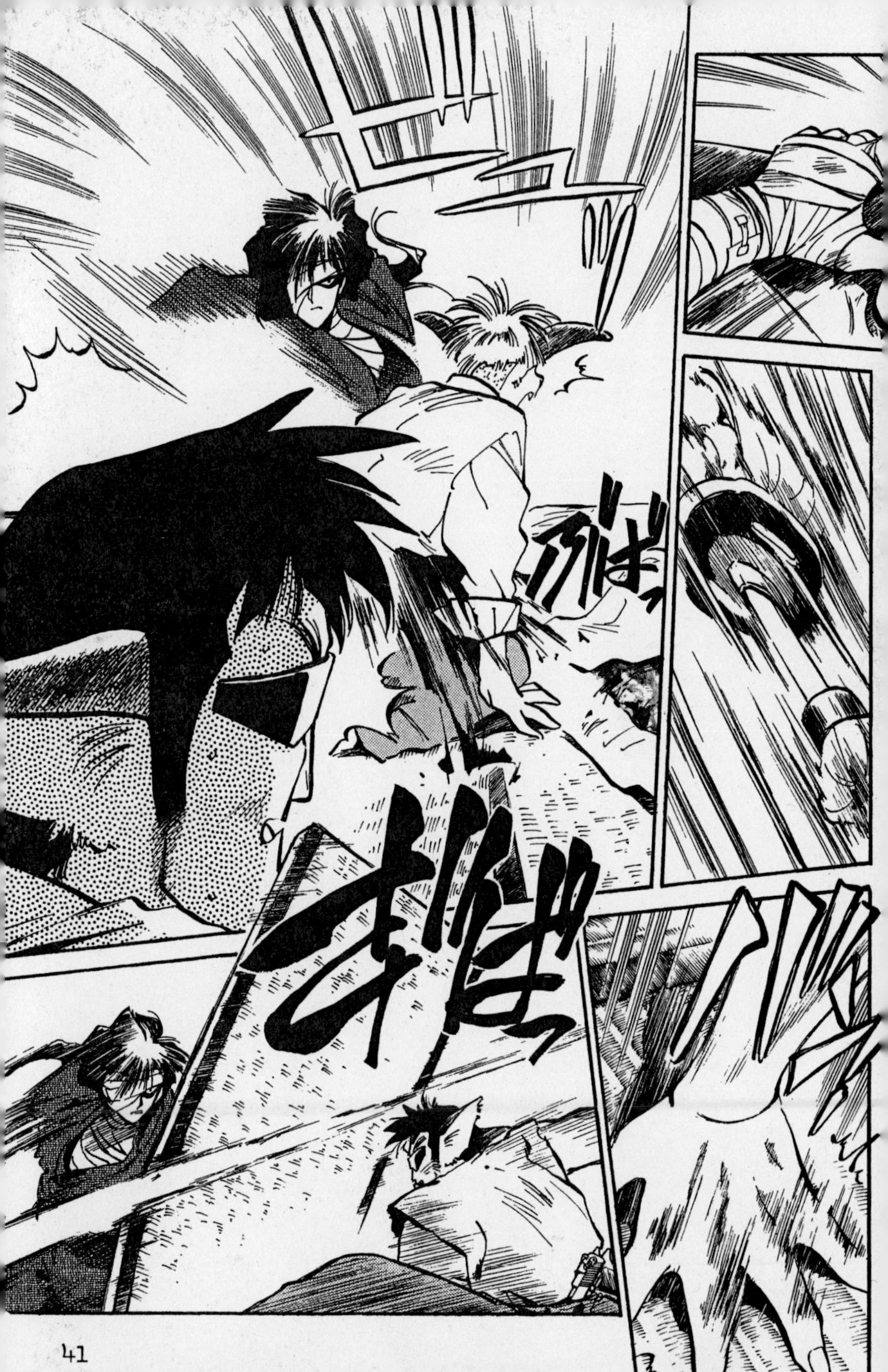
がばっ

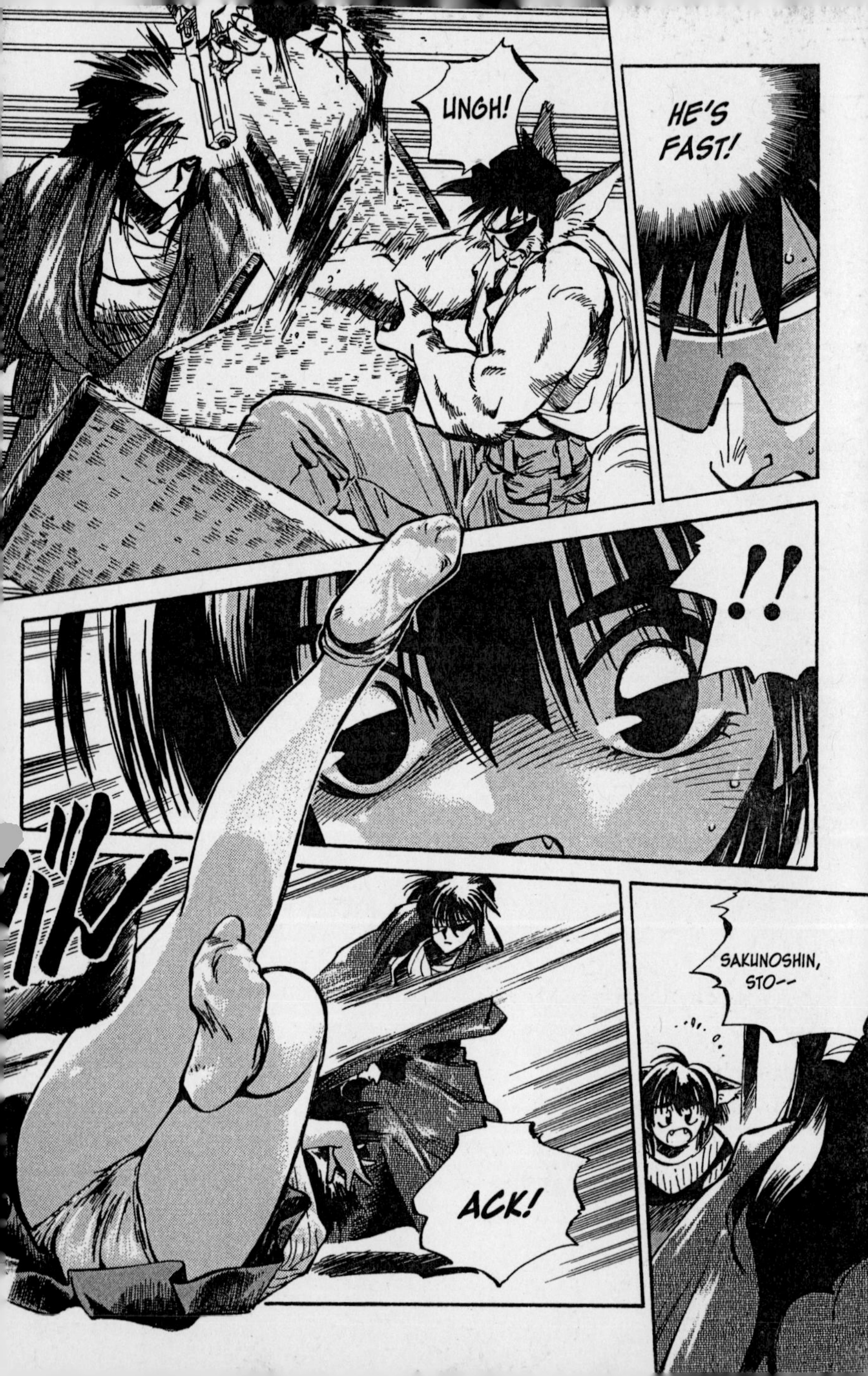
HE'S FAST!
UNGH!
!!
SAKUNOSHIN, STO--
ACK!

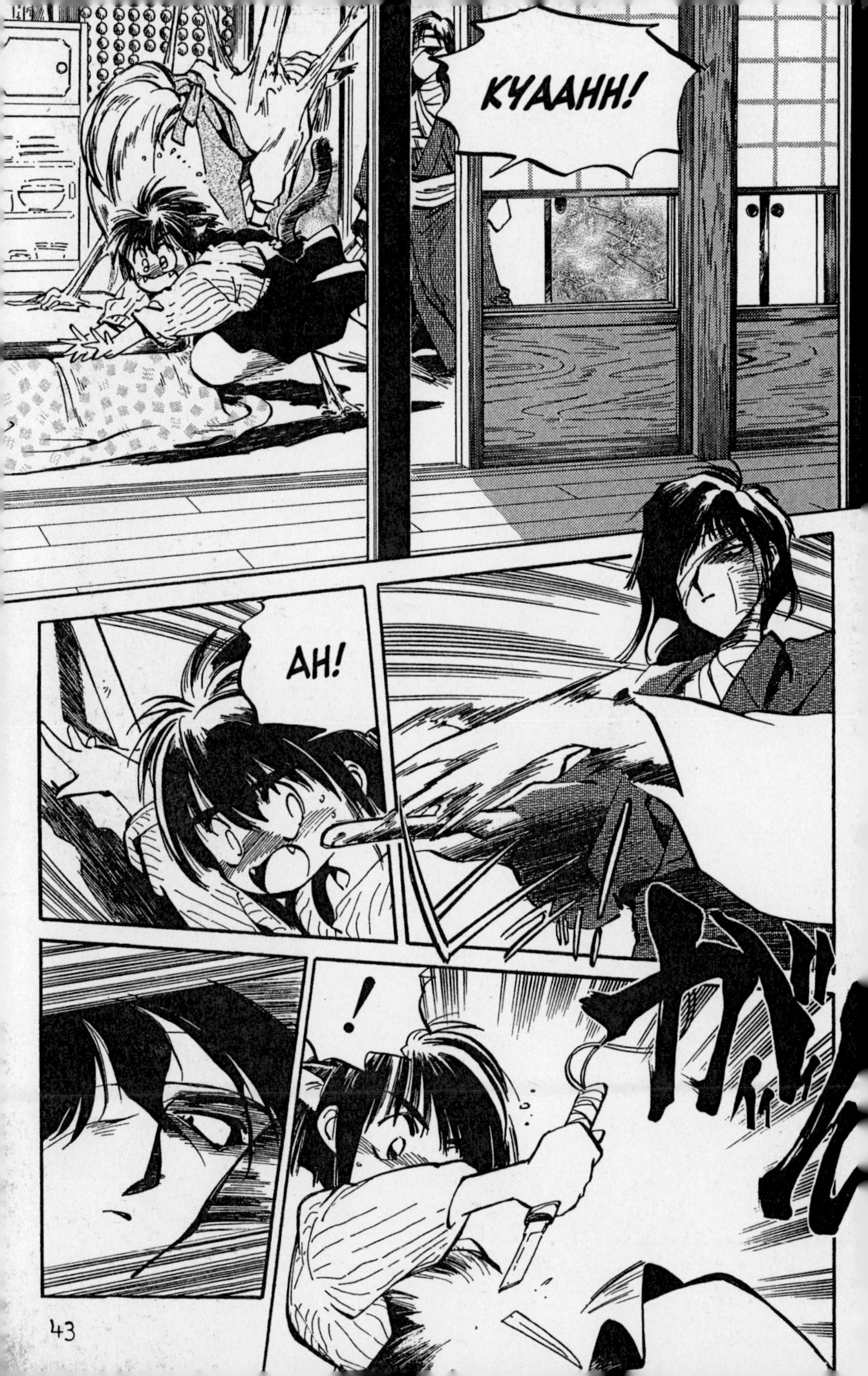
KYAAHH!
AH!
!

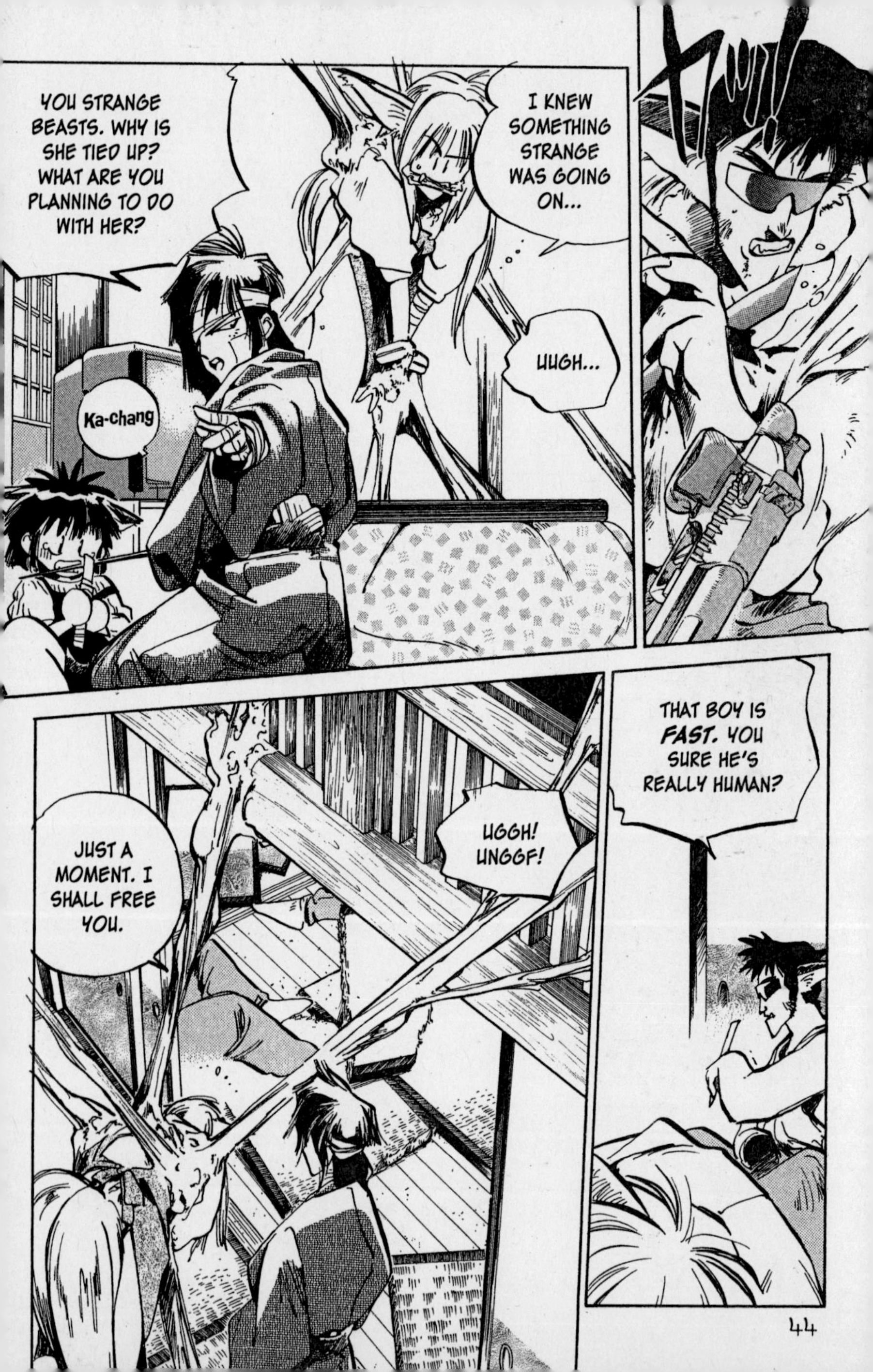
I KNEW SOMETHING STRANGE WAS GOING ON...
YOU STRANGE BEASTS. WHY IS SHE TIED UP? WHAT ARE YOU PLANNING TO DO WITH HER?
UUGH...
Ka-chang
THAT BOY IS FAST. YOU SURE HE'S REALLY HUMAN?
UGGH! UNGGF!
JUST A MOMENT. I SHALL FREE YOU.

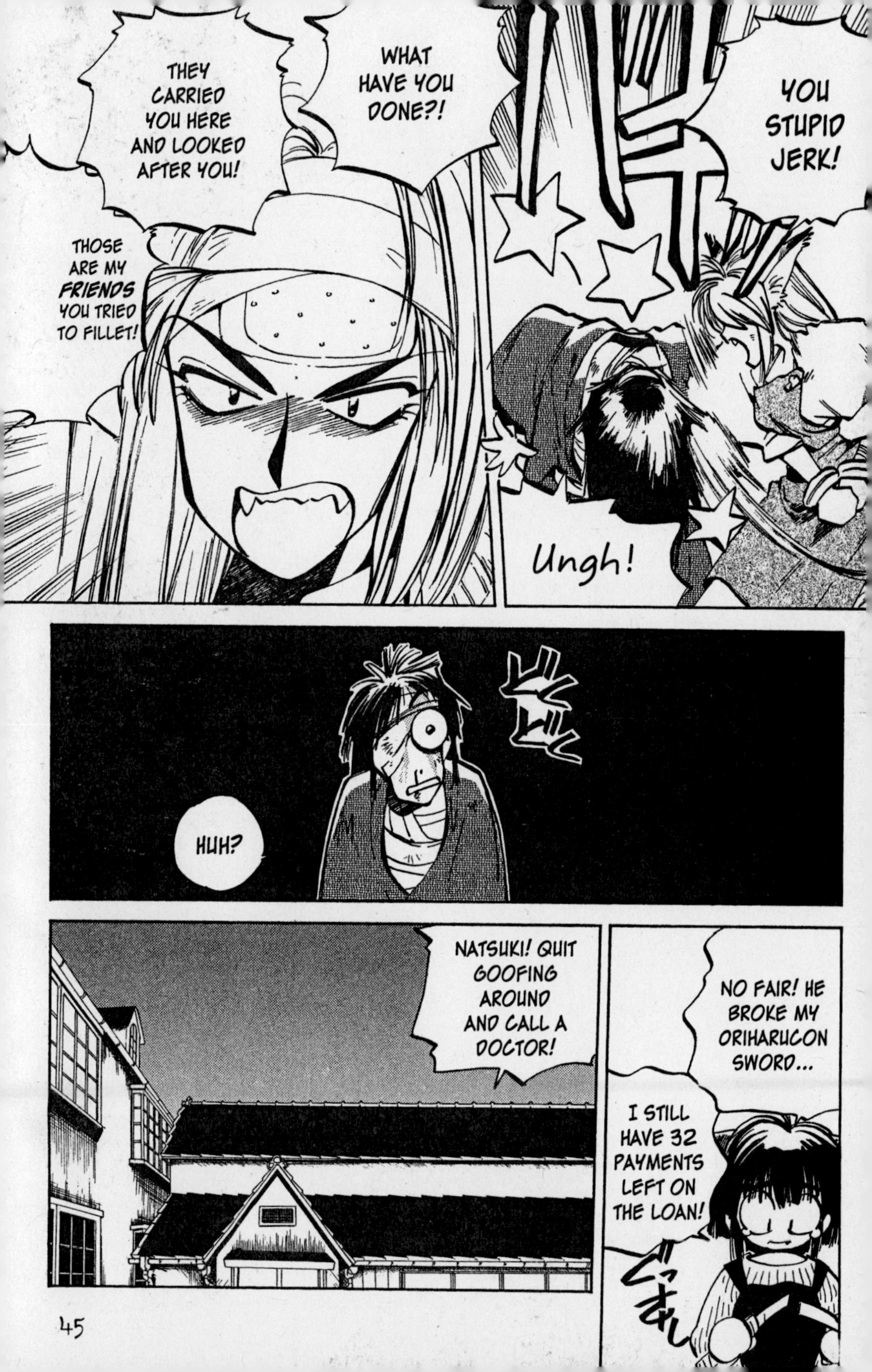
YOU STUPID JERK!
Ungh!
WHAT HAVE YOU DONE?!
THEY CARRIED YOU HERE AND LOOKED AFTER YOU!
THOSE ARE MY *FRIENDS* YOU TRIED TO FILLET!
HUH?
NO FAIR! HE BROKE MY ORIHARUCON SWORD...
I STILL HAVE 32 PAYMENTS LEFT ON THE LOAN!
NATSUKI! QUIT GOOFING AROUND AND CALL A DOCTOR!

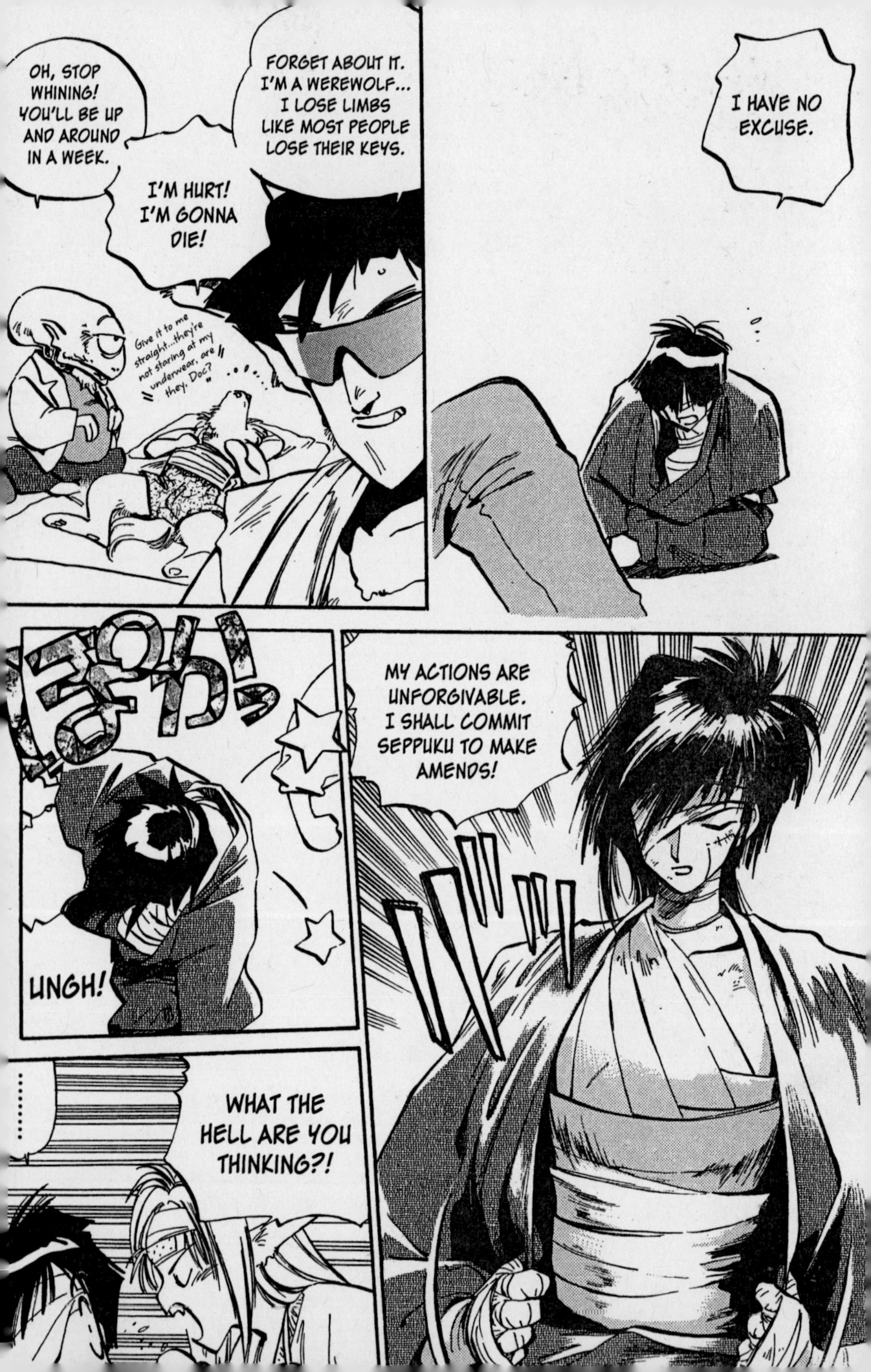
I HAVE NO EXCUSE.
FORGET ABOUT IT. I'M A WEREWOLF... I LOSE LIMBS LIKE MOST PEOPLE LOSE THEIR KEYS.
OH, STOP WHINING! YOU'LL BE UP AND AROUND IN A WEEK.
I'M HURT! I'M GONNA DIE!
Give it to me straight...they're not staring at my underwear, are they, Doc?
MY ACTIONS ARE UNFORGIVABLE. I SHALL COMMIT SEPPUKU TO MAKE AMENDS!
UNGH!
WHAT THE HELL ARE YOU THINKING?!
......

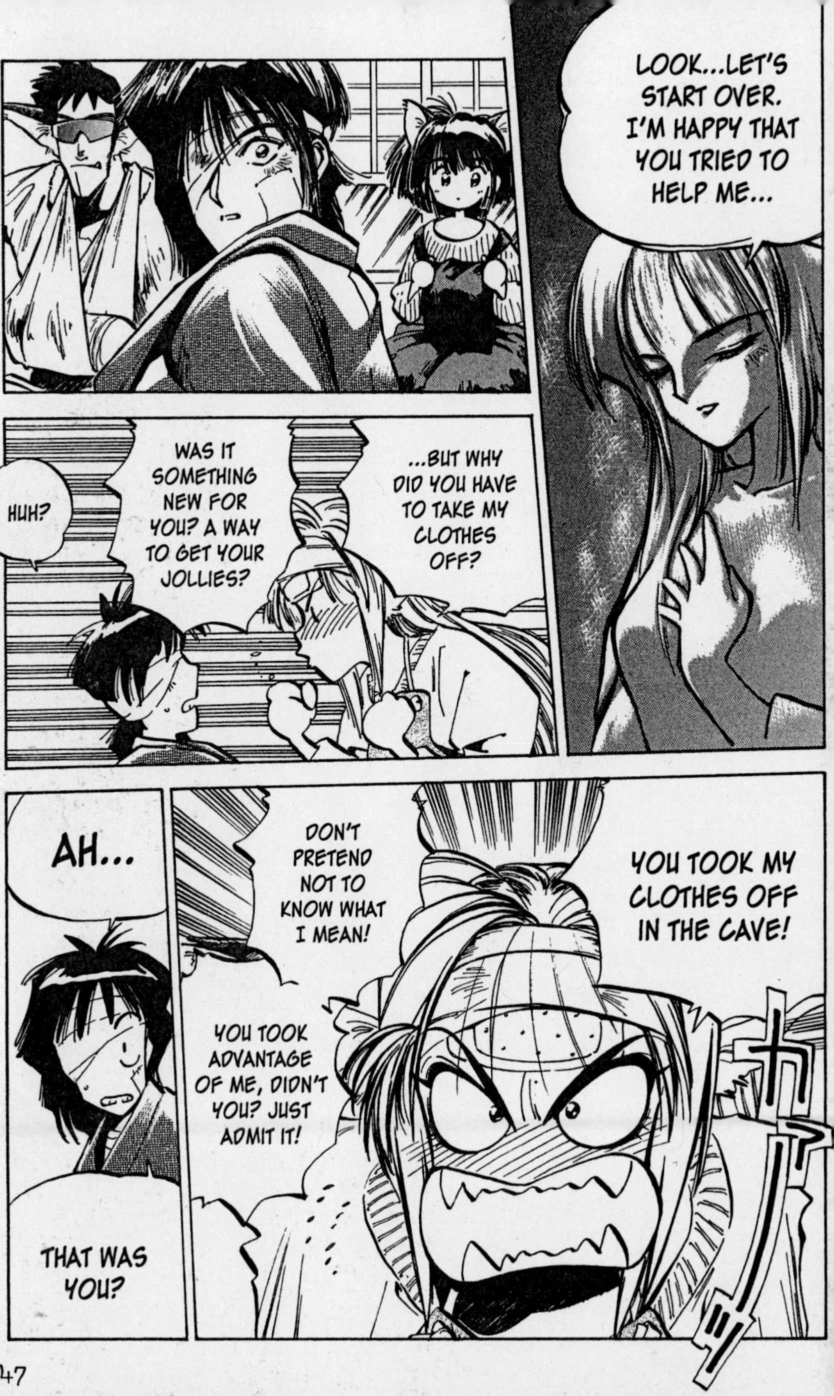
LOOK...LET'S START OVER. I'M HAPPY THAT YOU TRIED TO HELP ME...
...BUT WHY DID YOU HAVE TO TAKE MY CLOTHES OFF?
WAS IT SOMETHING NEW FOR YOU? A WAY TO GET YOUR JOLLIES?
HUH?
YOU TOOK MY CLOTHES OFF IN THE CAVE!
DON'T PRETEND NOT TO KNOW WHAT I MEAN!
YOU TOOK ADVANTAGE OF ME, DIDN'T YOU? JUST ADMIT IT!
AH...
THAT WAS YOU?

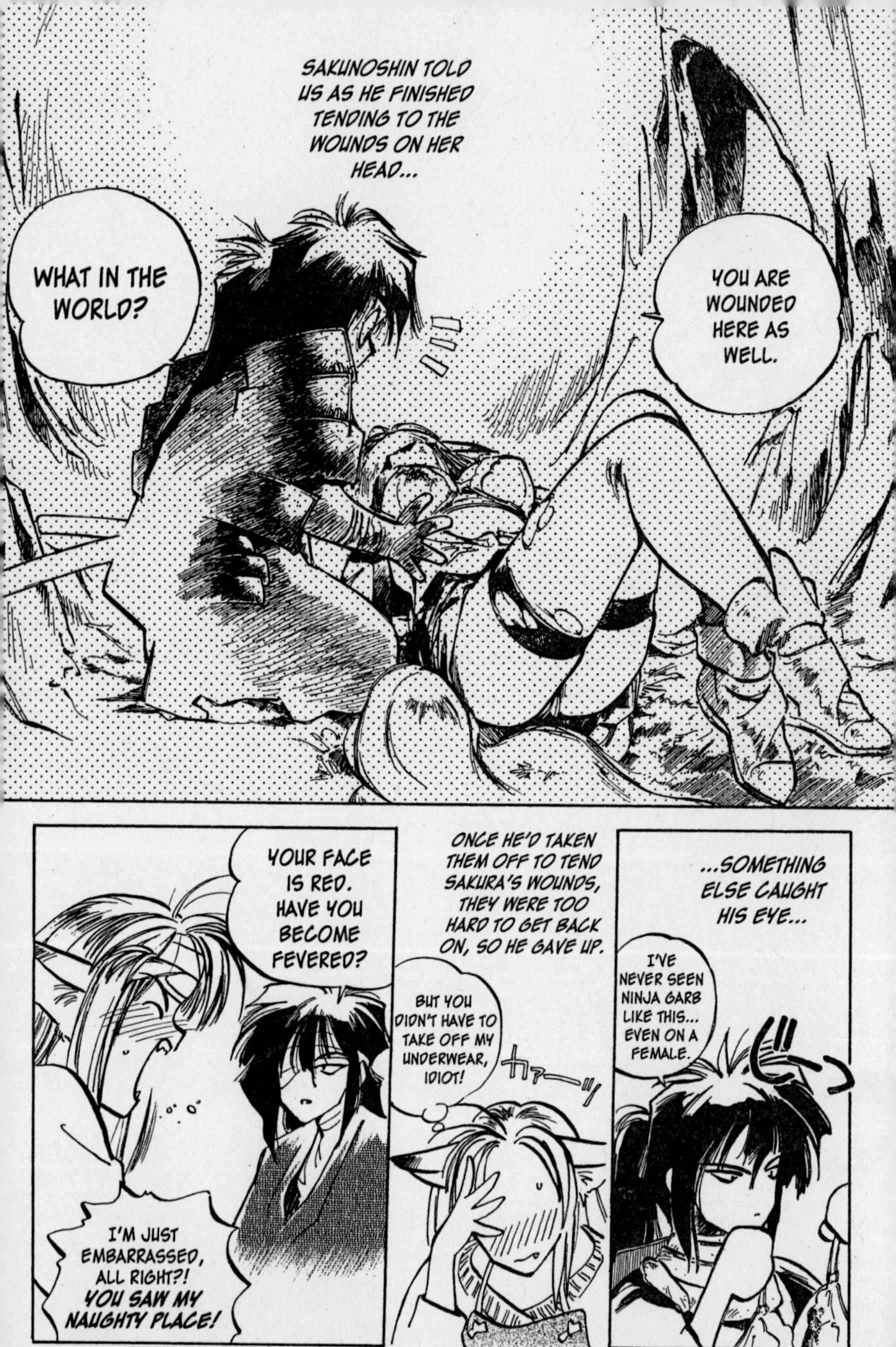
SAKUNOSHIN TOLD US AS HE FINISHED TENDING TO THE WOUNDS ON HER HEAD...
YOU ARE WOUNDED HERE AS WELL.
WHAT IN THE WORLD?
...SOMETHING ELSE CAUGHT HIS EYE...
I'VE NEVER SEEN NINJA GARB LIKE THIS... EVEN ON A FEMALE.
ONCE HE'D TAKEN THEM OFF TO TEND SAKURA'S WOUNDS, THEY WERE TOO HARD TO GET BACK ON, SO HE GAVE UP.
BUT YOU DIDN'T HAVE TO TAKE OFF MY UNDERWEAR, IDIOT!
YOUR FACE IS RED. HAVE YOU BECOME FEVERED?
I'M JUST EMBARRASSED, ALL RIGHT?! YOU SAW MY NAUGHTY PLACE!

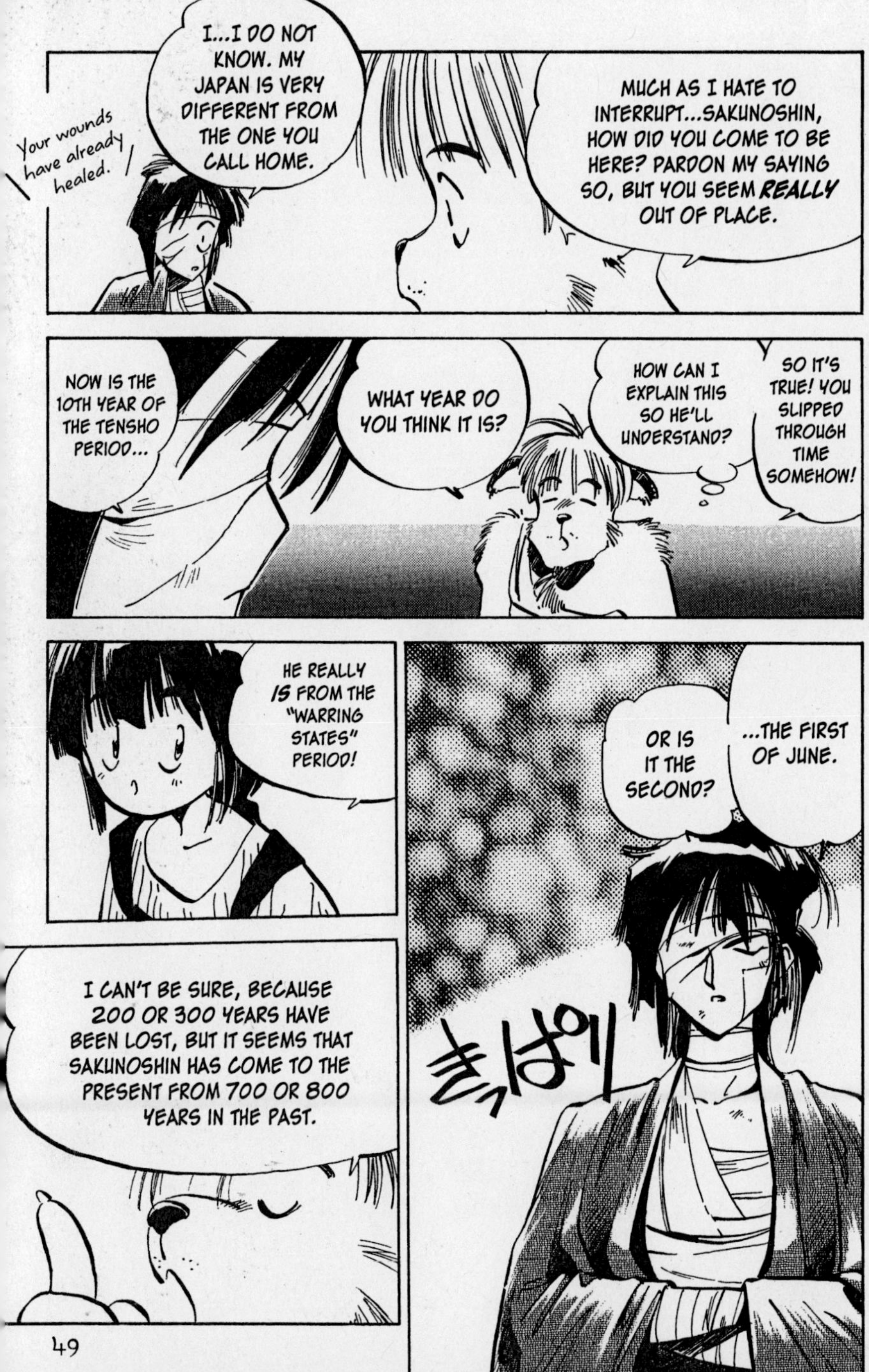
MUCH AS I HATE TO INTERRUPT...SAKUNOSHIN, HOW DID YOU COME TO BE HERE? PARDON MY SAYING SO, BUT YOU SEEM *REALLY* OUT OF PLACE.
I...I DO NOT KNOW. MY JAPAN IS VERY DIFFERENT FROM THE ONE YOU CALL HOME.
Your wounds have already healed.
SO IT'S TRUE! YOU SLIPPED THROUGH TIME SOMEHOW!
HOW CAN I EXPLAIN THIS SO HE'LL UNDERSTAND?
WHAT YEAR DO YOU THINK IT IS?
NOW IS THE 10TH YEAR OF THE TENSHO PERIOD...
...THE FIRST OF JUNE.
OR IS IT THE SECOND?
きっぱり
HE REALLY *IS* FROM THE "WARRING STATES" PERIOD!
I CAN'T BE SURE, BECAUSE 200 OR 300 YEARS HAVE BEEN LOST, BUT IT SEEMS THAT SAKUNOSHIN HAS COME TO THE PRESENT FROM 700 OR 800 YEARS IN THE PAST.

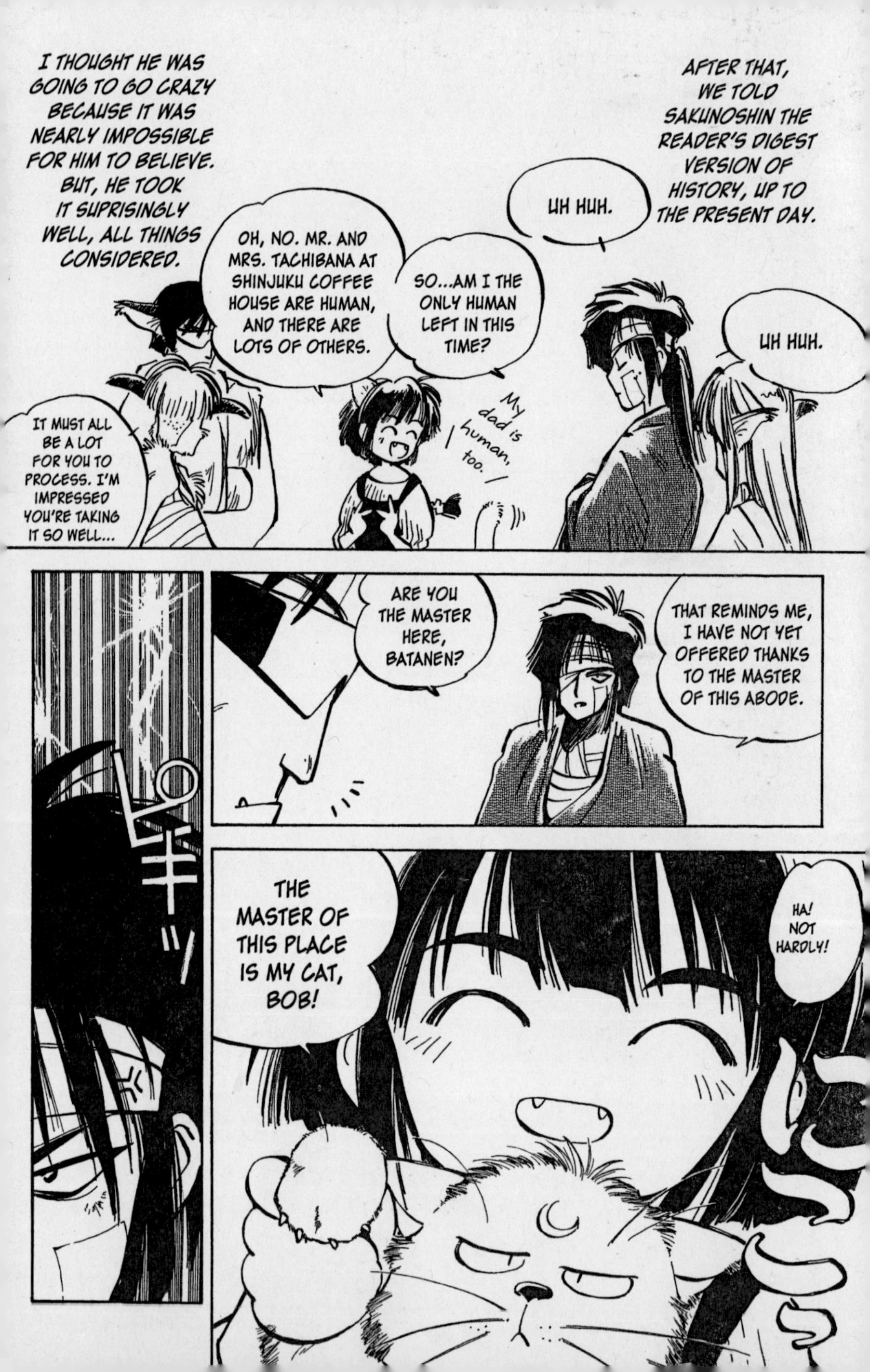
AFTER THAT, WE TOLD SAKUNOSHIN THE READER'S DIGEST VERSION OF HISTORY, UP TO THE PRESENT DAY.
UH HUH.
UH HUH.
SO...AM I THE ONLY HUMAN LEFT IN THIS TIME?
OH, NO. MR. AND MRS. TACHIBANA AT SHINJUKU COFFEE HOUSE ARE HUMAN, AND THERE ARE LOTS OF OTHERS.
My dad is human, too.
I THOUGHT HE WAS GOING TO GO CRAZY BECAUSE IT WAS NEARLY IMPOSSIBLE FOR HIM TO BELIEVE. BUT, HE TOOK IT SUPRISINGLY WELL, ALL THINGS CONSIDERED.
IT MUST ALL BE A LOT FOR YOU TO PROCESS. I'M IMPRESSED YOU'RE TAKING IT SO WELL...
THAT REMINDS ME, I HAVE NOT YET OFFERED THANKS TO THE MASTER OF THIS ABODE.
ARE YOU THE MASTER HERE, BATANEN?
HA! NOT HARDLY!
THE MASTER OF THIS PLACE IS MY CAT, BOB!

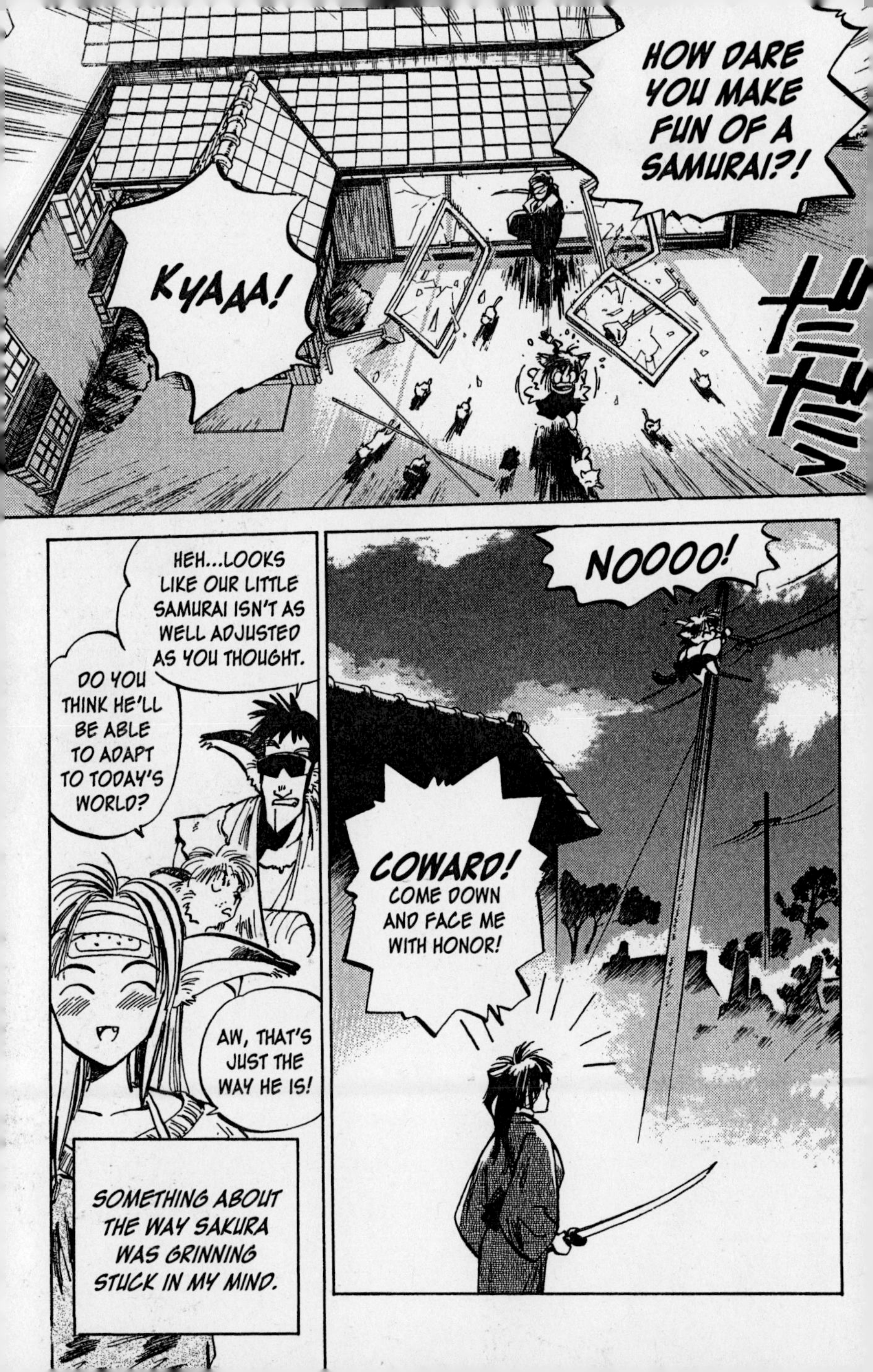
HOW DARE YOU MAKE FUN OF A SAMURAI?!
KYAAA!
NOOOO!
COWARD! COME DOWN AND FACE ME WITH HONOR!
HEH...LOOKS LIKE OUR LITTLE SAMURAI ISN'T AS WELL ADJUSTED AS YOU THOUGHT.
DO YOU THINK HE'LL BE ABLE TO ADAPT TO TODAY'S WORLD?
AW, THAT'S JUST THE WAY HE IS!
SOMETHING ABOUT THE WAY SAKURA WAS GRINNING STUCK IN MY MIND.

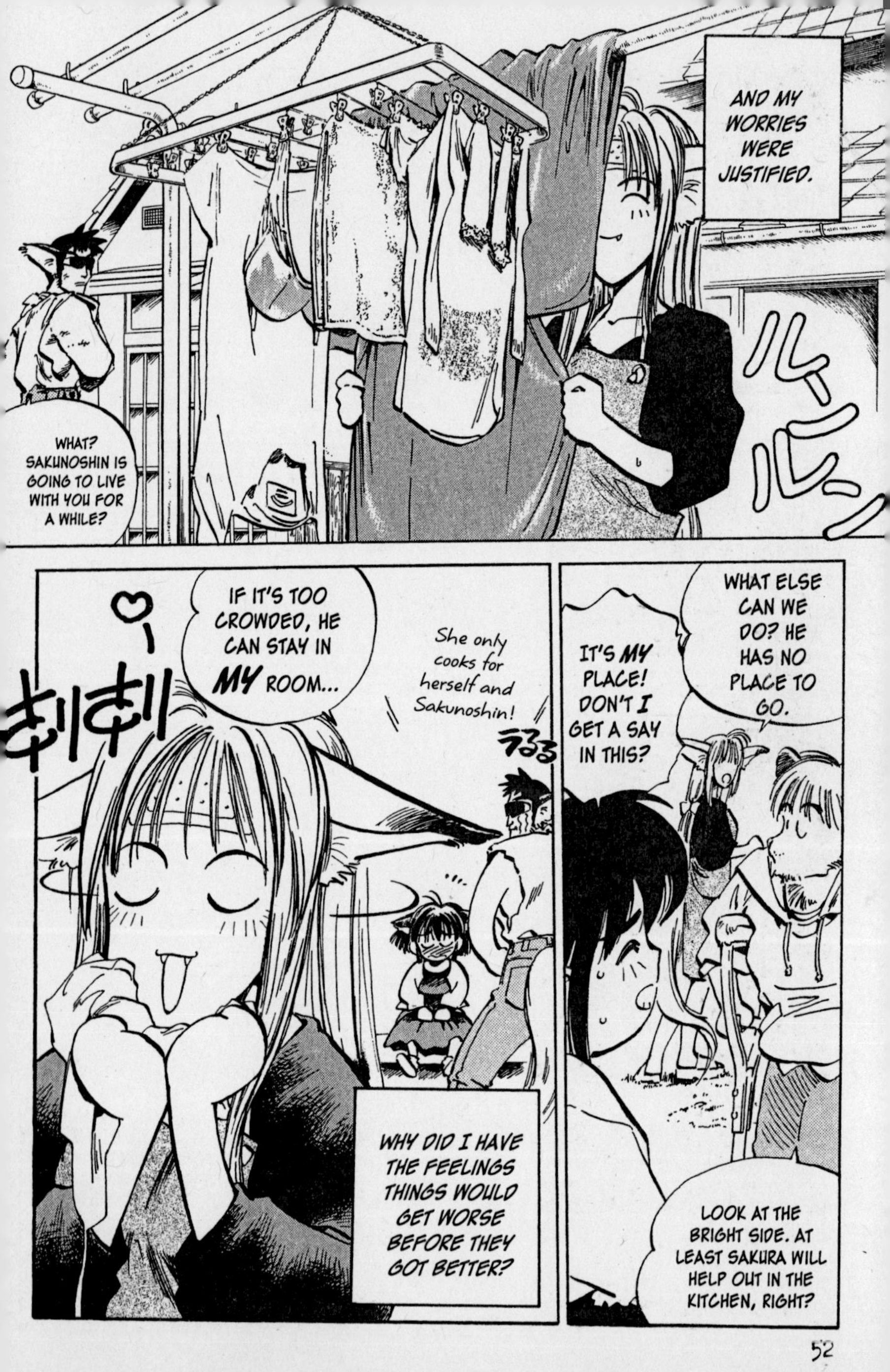
AND MY WORRIES WERE JUSTIFIED.
ルンルン
WHAT? SAKUNOSHIN IS GOING TO LIVE WITH YOU FOR A WHILE?
WHAT ELSE CAN WE DO? HE HAS NO PLACE TO GO.
IT'S MY PLACE! DON'T I GET A SAY IN THIS?
LOOK AT THE BRIGHT SIDE. AT LEAST SAKURA WILL HELP OUT IN THE KITCHEN, RIGHT?
IF IT'S TOO CROWDED, HE CAN STAY IN MY ROOM...
She only cooks for herself and Sakunoshin!
うるる
WHY DID I HAVE THE FEELINGS THINGS WOULD GET WORSE BEFORE THEY GOT BETTER?

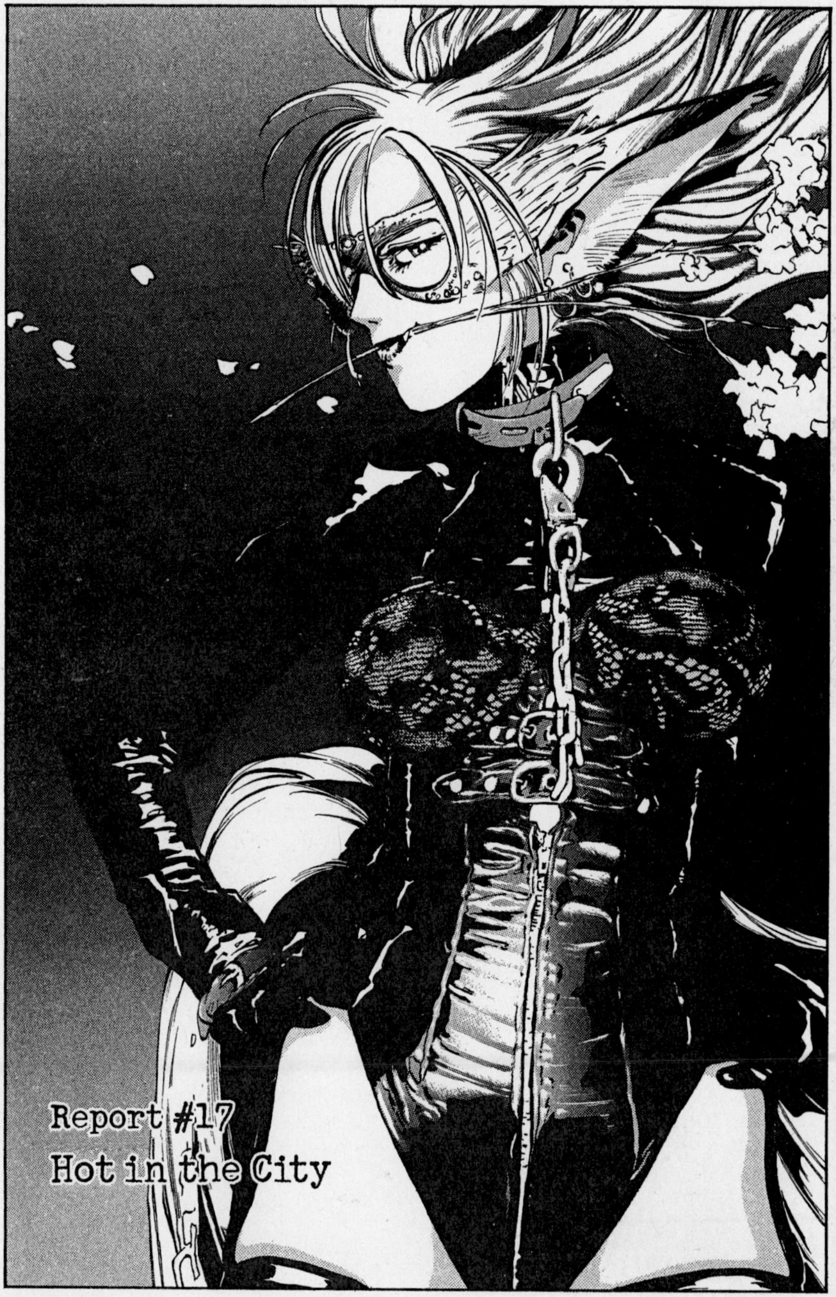
Report #17
Hot in the City

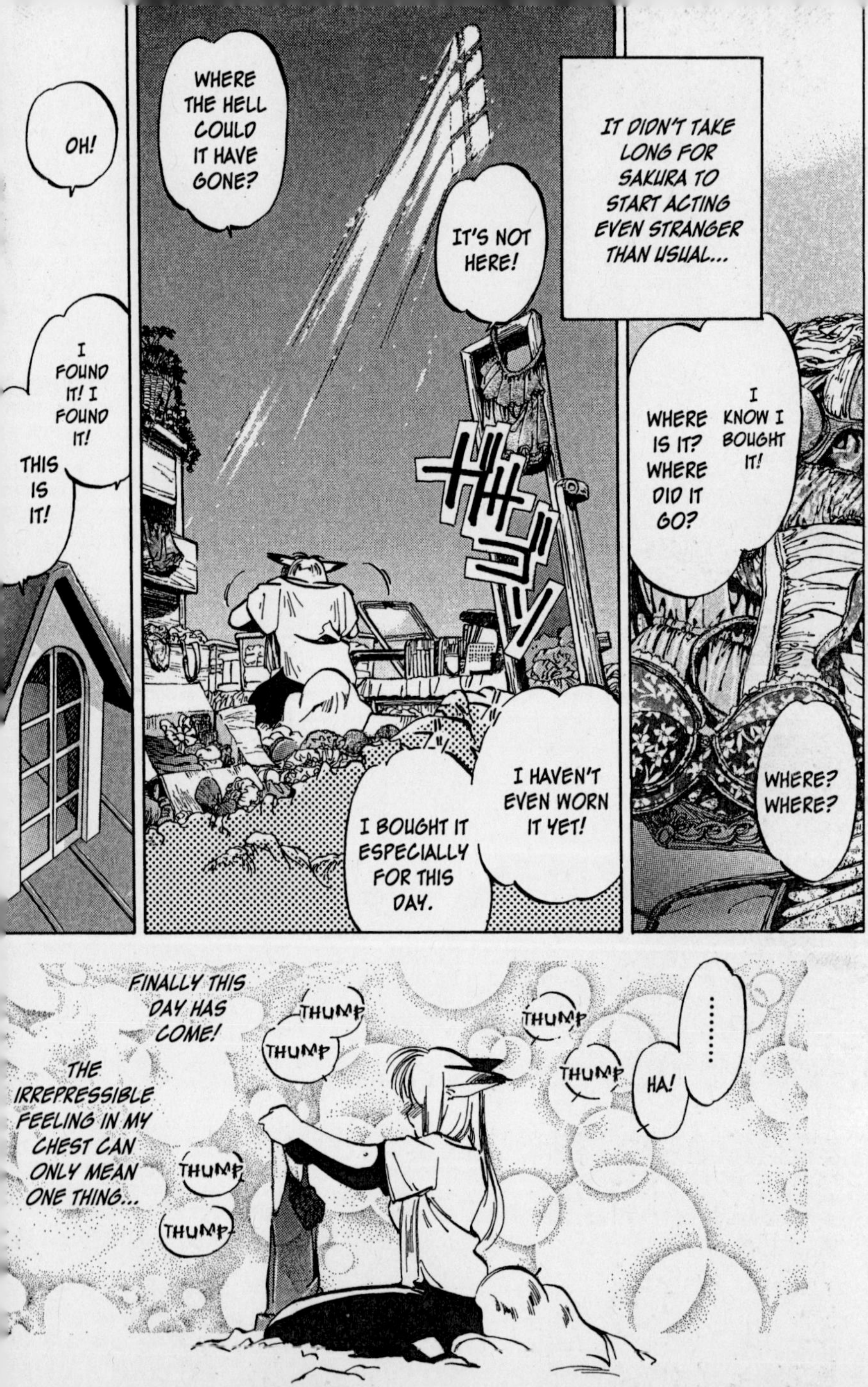
IT DIDN'T TAKE LONG FOR SAKURA TO START ACTING EVEN STRANGER THAN USUAL...
I KNOW I BOUGHT IT!
WHERE IS IT? WHERE DID IT GO?
WHERE? WHERE?
IT'S NOT HERE!
WHERE THE HELL COULD IT HAVE GONE?
I HAVEN'T EVEN WORN IT YET!
I BOUGHT IT ESPECIALLY FOR THIS DAY.
OH!
I FOUND IT! I FOUND IT!
THIS IS IT!
....
HA!
THUMP
THUMP
THUMP
THUMP
FINALLY THIS DAY HAS COME!
THE IRREPRESSIBLE FEELING IN MY CHEST CAN ONLY MEAN ONE THING...
THUMP
THUMP

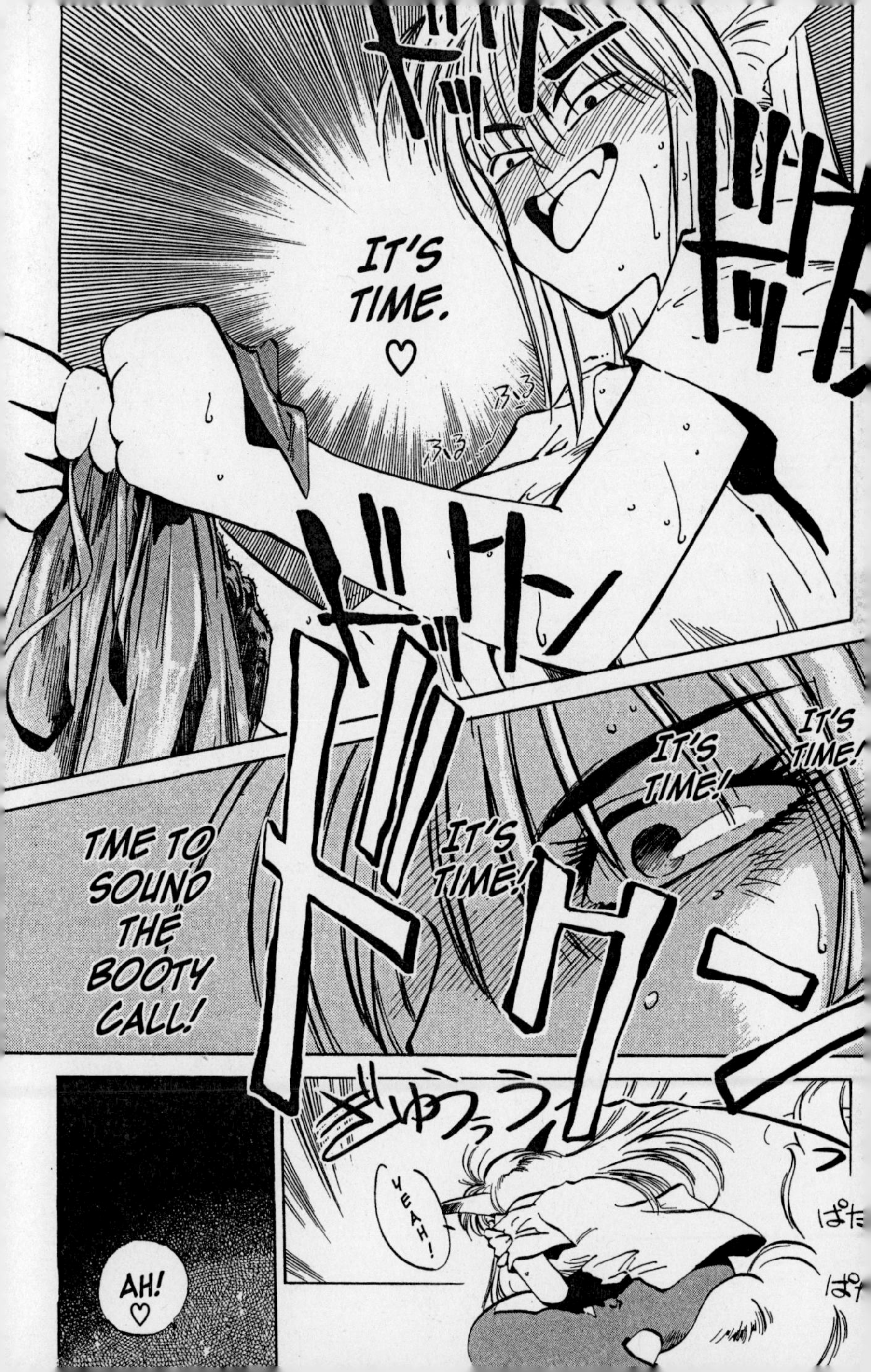
IT'S TIME. ♡
IT'S TIME!
IT'S TIME!
IT'S TIME!
TME TO SOUND THE BOOTY CALL!
YEAH!
AH! ♡

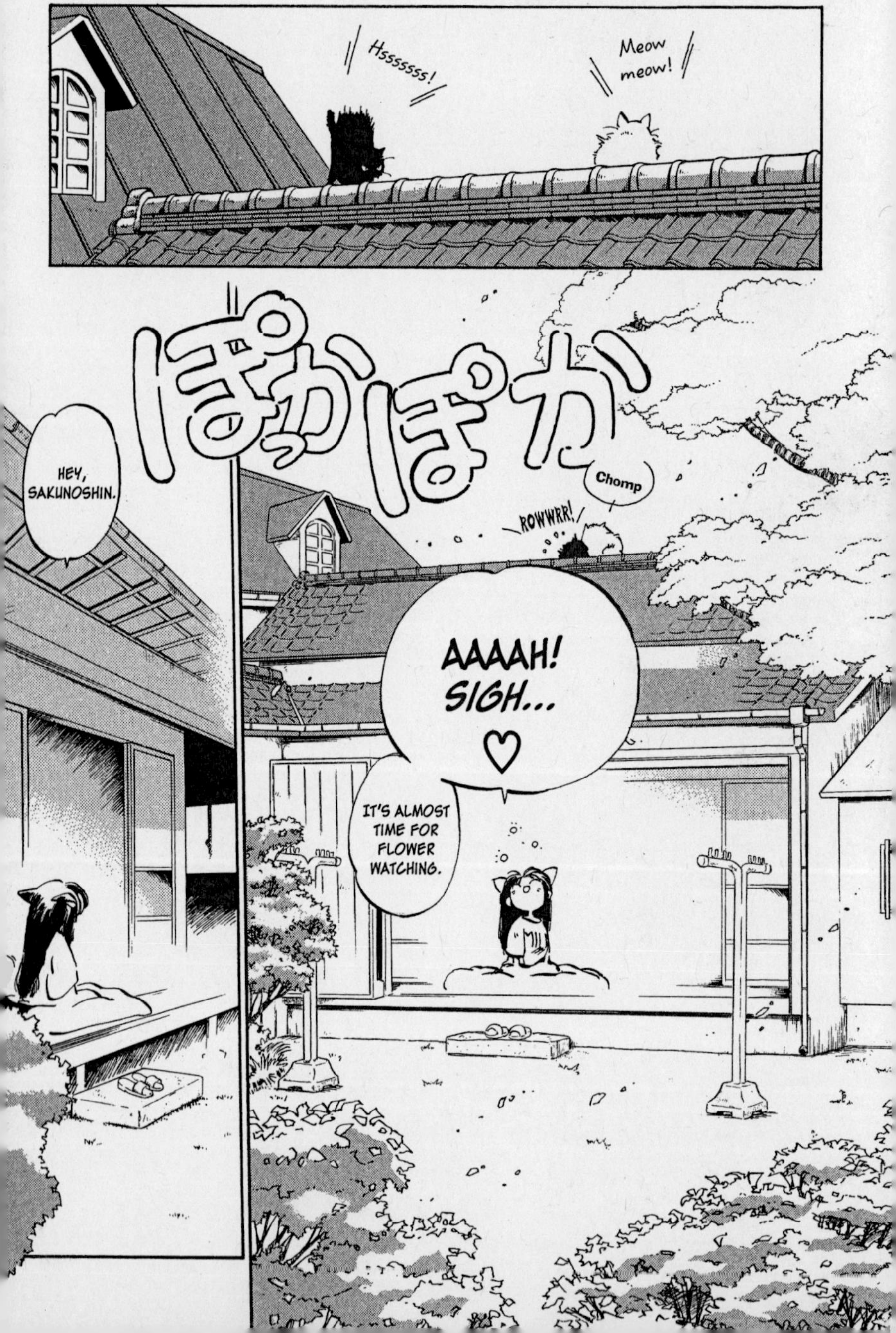
Meow meow!
Hsssssss!
ぽかぽか
Chomp
ROWWRR!
AAAAH! SIGH... ♡
IT'S ALMOST TIME FOR FLOWER WATCHING.
HEY, SAKUNOSHIN.

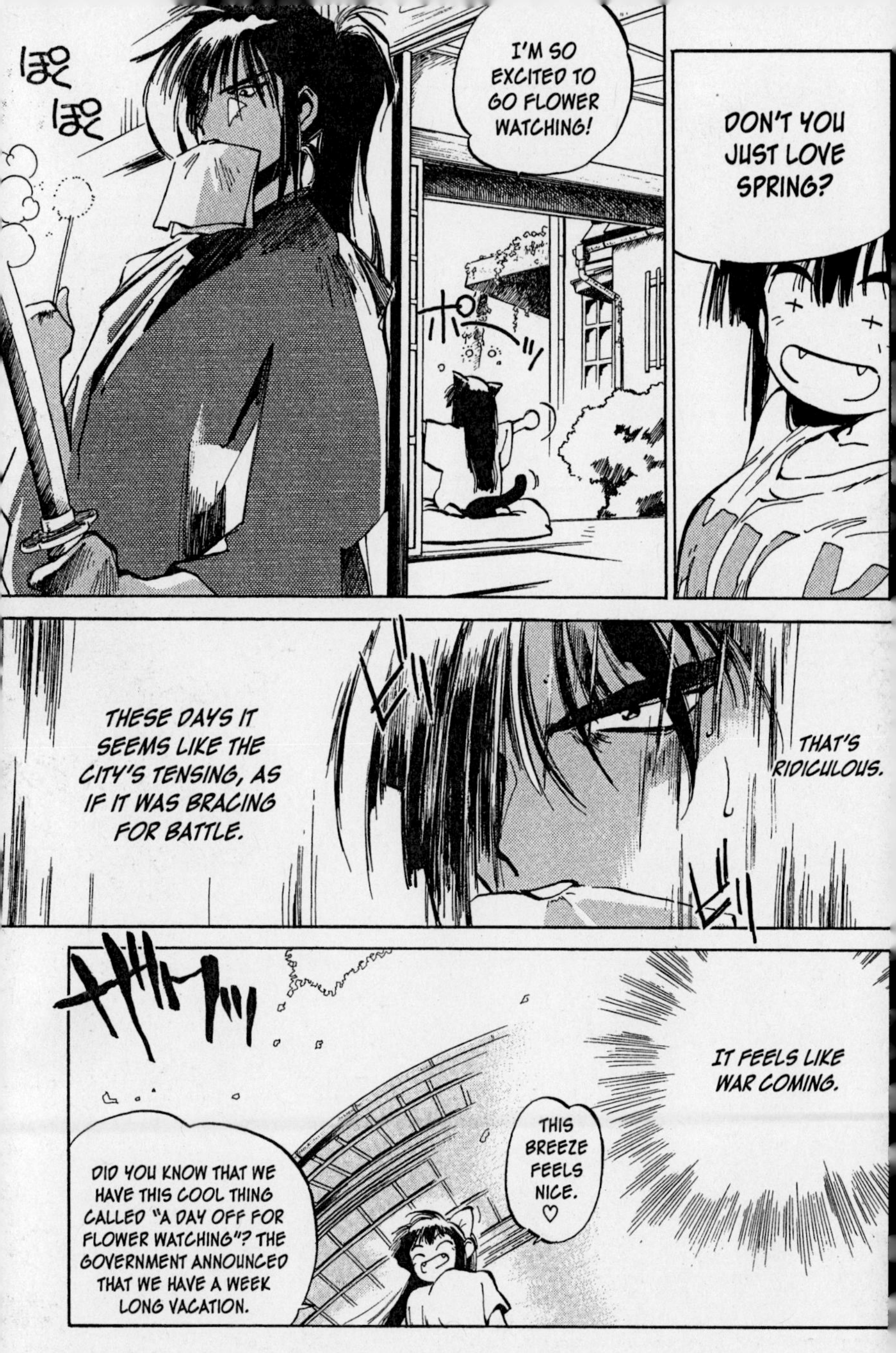
DON'T YOU JUST LOVE SPRING?
I'M SO EXCITED TO GO FLOWER WATCHING!
ぽくぽく
THAT'S RIDICULOUS.
THESE DAYS IT SEEMS LIKE THE CITY'S TENSING, AS IF IT WAS BRACING FOR BATTLE.
IT FEELS LIKE WAR COMING.
THIS BREEZE FEELS NICE. ♡
DID YOU KNOW THAT WE HAVE THIS COOL THING CALLED "A DAY OFF FOR FLOWER WATCHING"? THE GOVERNMENT ANNOUNCED THAT WE HAVE A WEEK LONG VACATION.

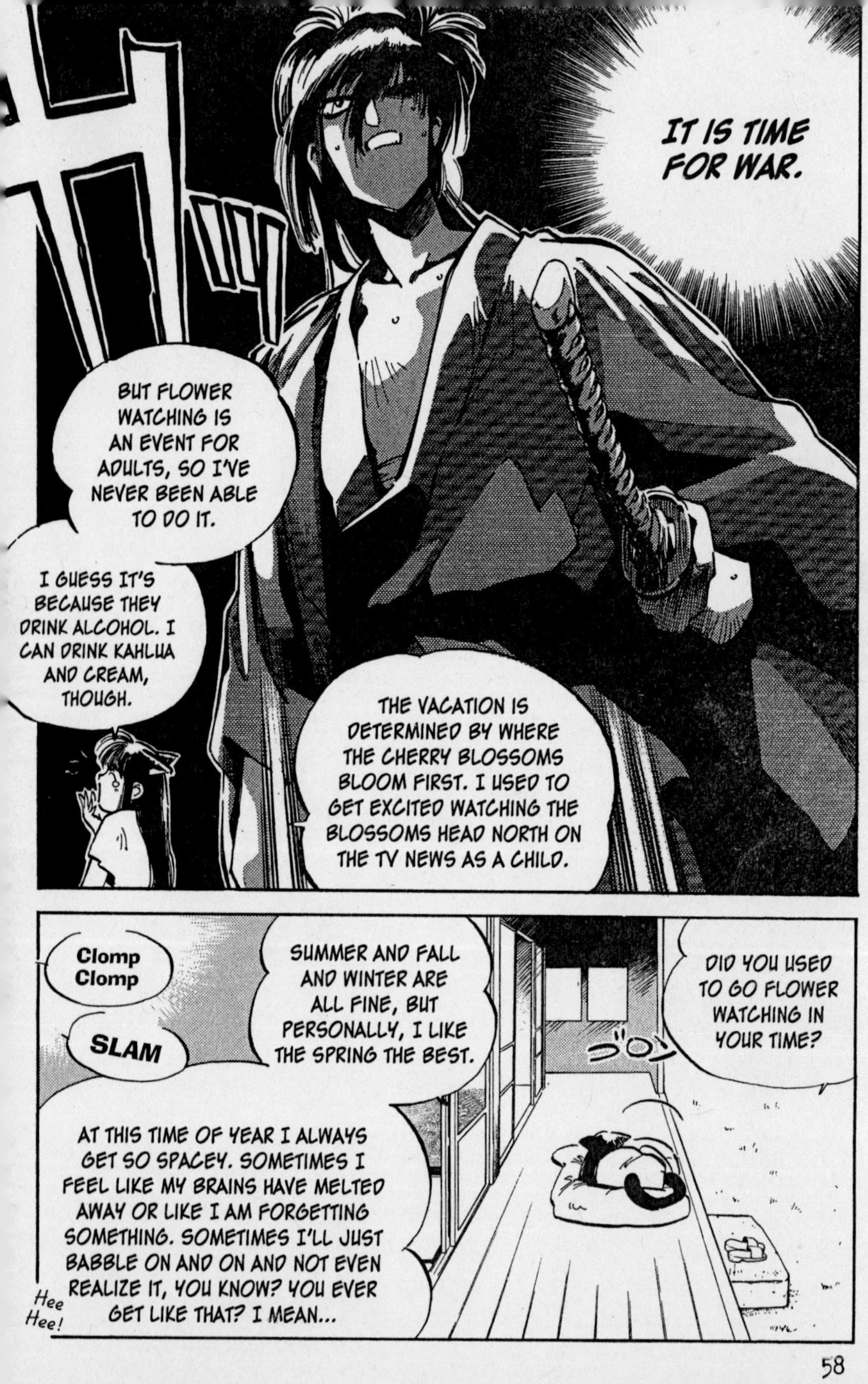
IT IS TIME FOR WAR.
THE VACATION IS DETERMINED BY WHERE THE CHERRY BLOSSOMS BLOOM FIRST. I USED TO GET EXCITED WATCHING THE BLOSSOMS HEAD NORTH ON THE TV NEWS AS A CHILD.
BUT FLOWER WATCHING IS AN EVENT FOR ADULTS, SO I'VE NEVER BEEN ABLE TO DO IT.
I GUESS IT'S BECAUSE THEY DRINK ALCOHOL. I CAN DRINK KAHLUA AND CREAM, THOUGH.
DID YOU USED TO GO FLOWER WATCHING IN YOUR TIME?
SUMMER AND FALL AND WINTER ARE ALL FINE, BUT PERSONALLY, I LIKE THE SPRING THE BEST.
Clomp Clomp
SLAM
AT THIS TIME OF YEAR I ALWAYS GET SO SPACEY. SOMETIMES I FEEL LIKE MY BRAINS HAVE MELTED AWAY OR LIKE I AM FORGETTING SOMETHING. SOMETIMES I'LL JUST BABBLE ON AND ON AND NOT EVEN REALIZE IT, YOU KNOW? YOU EVER GET LIKE THAT? I MEAN...
Hee Hee!

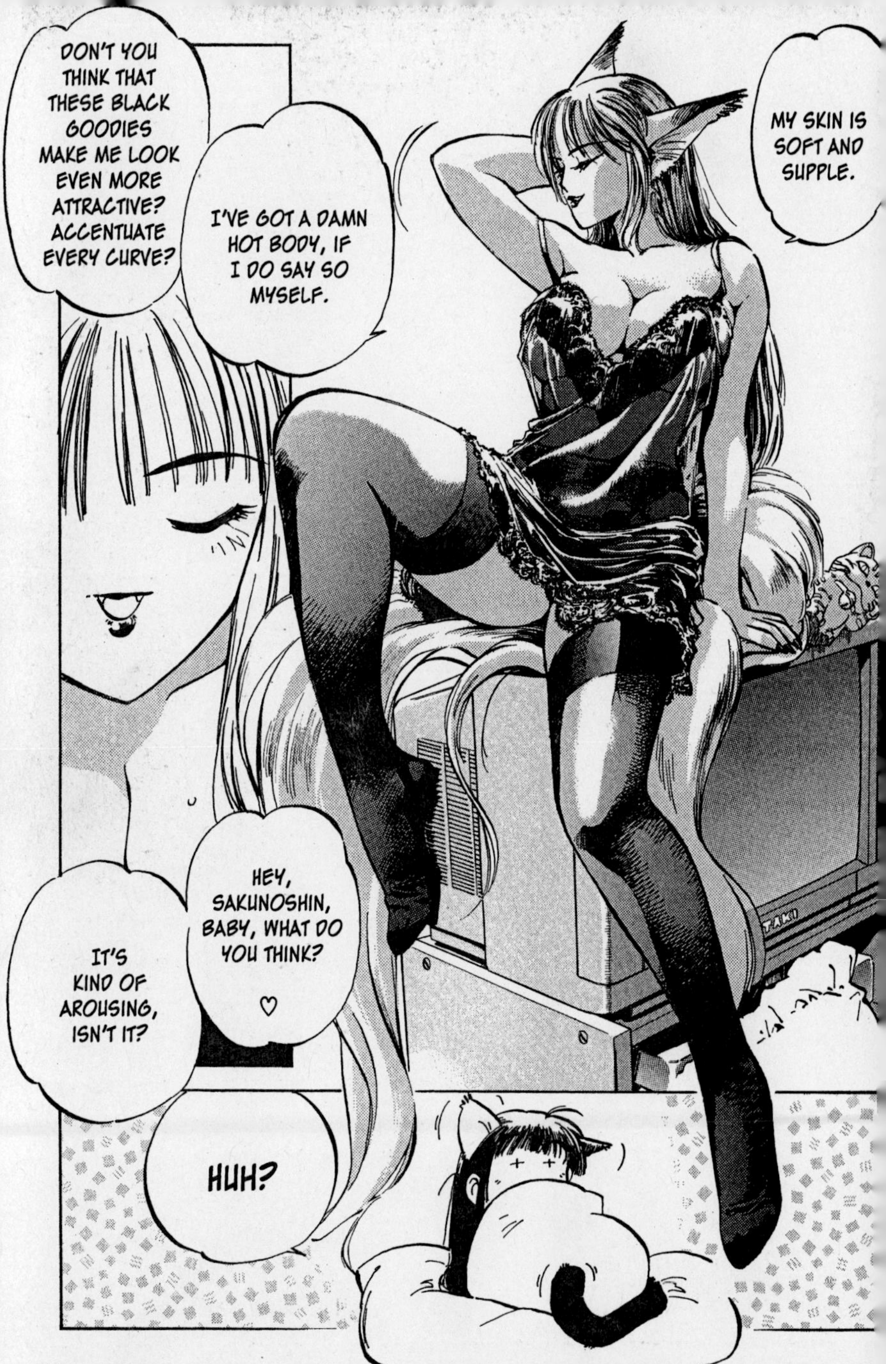
MY SKIN IS SOFT AND SUPPLE.
I'VE GOT A DAMN HOT BODY, IF I DO SAY SO MYSELF.
DON'T YOU THINK THAT THESE BLACK GOODIES MAKE ME LOOK EVEN MORE ATTRACTIVE? ACCENTUATE EVERY CURVE?
HEY, SAKUNOSHIN, BABY, WHAT DO YOU THINK? ♡
IT'S KIND OF AROUSING, ISN'T IT?
HUH?

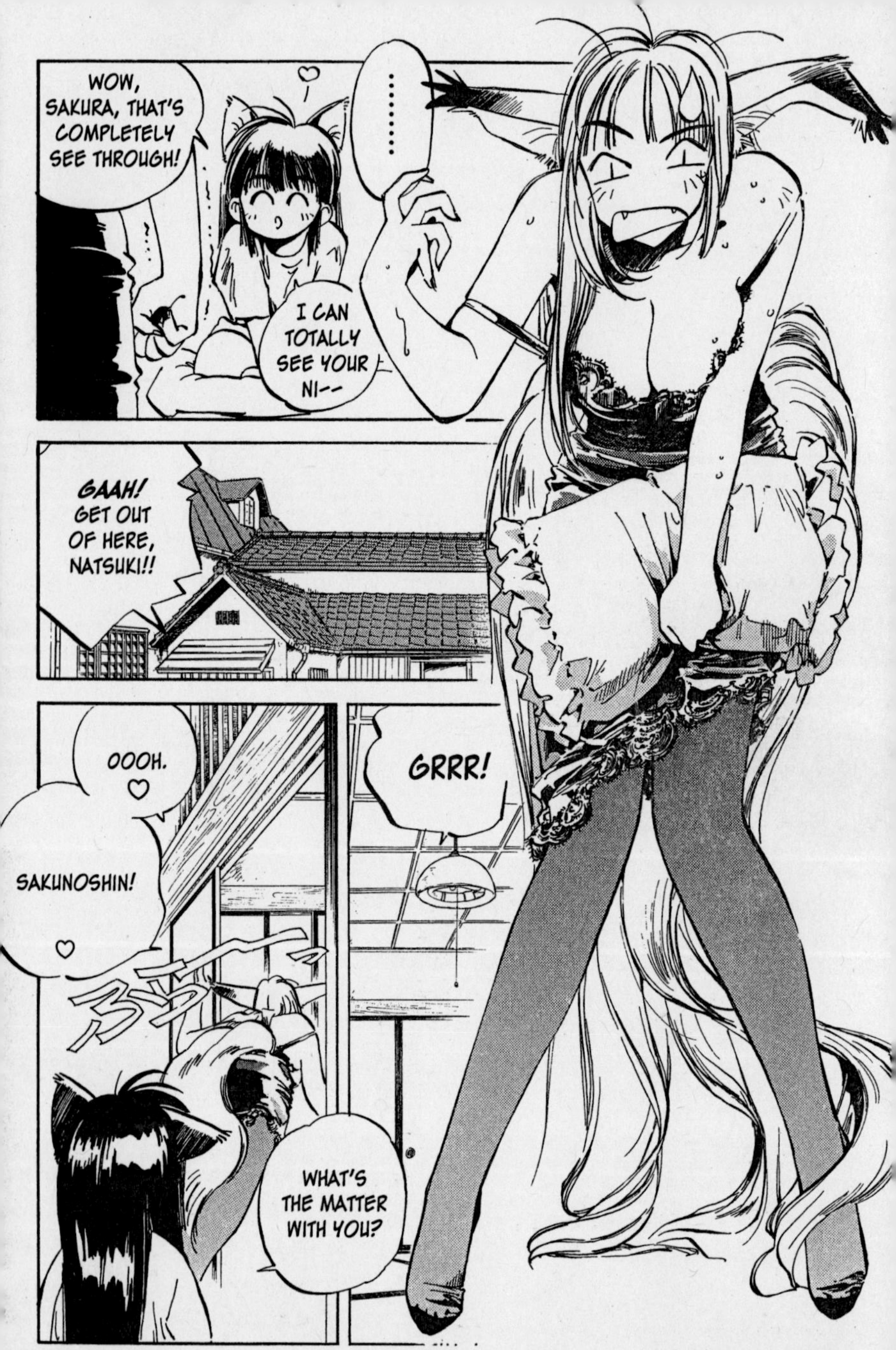
......
WOW, SAKURA, THAT'S COMPLETELY SEE THROUGH!
I CAN TOTALLY SEE YOUR NI--
GAAH! GET OUT OF HERE, NATSUKI!!
GRRR!
OOOH. ♡
SAKUNOSHIN! ♡
WHAT'S THE MATTER WITH YOU?

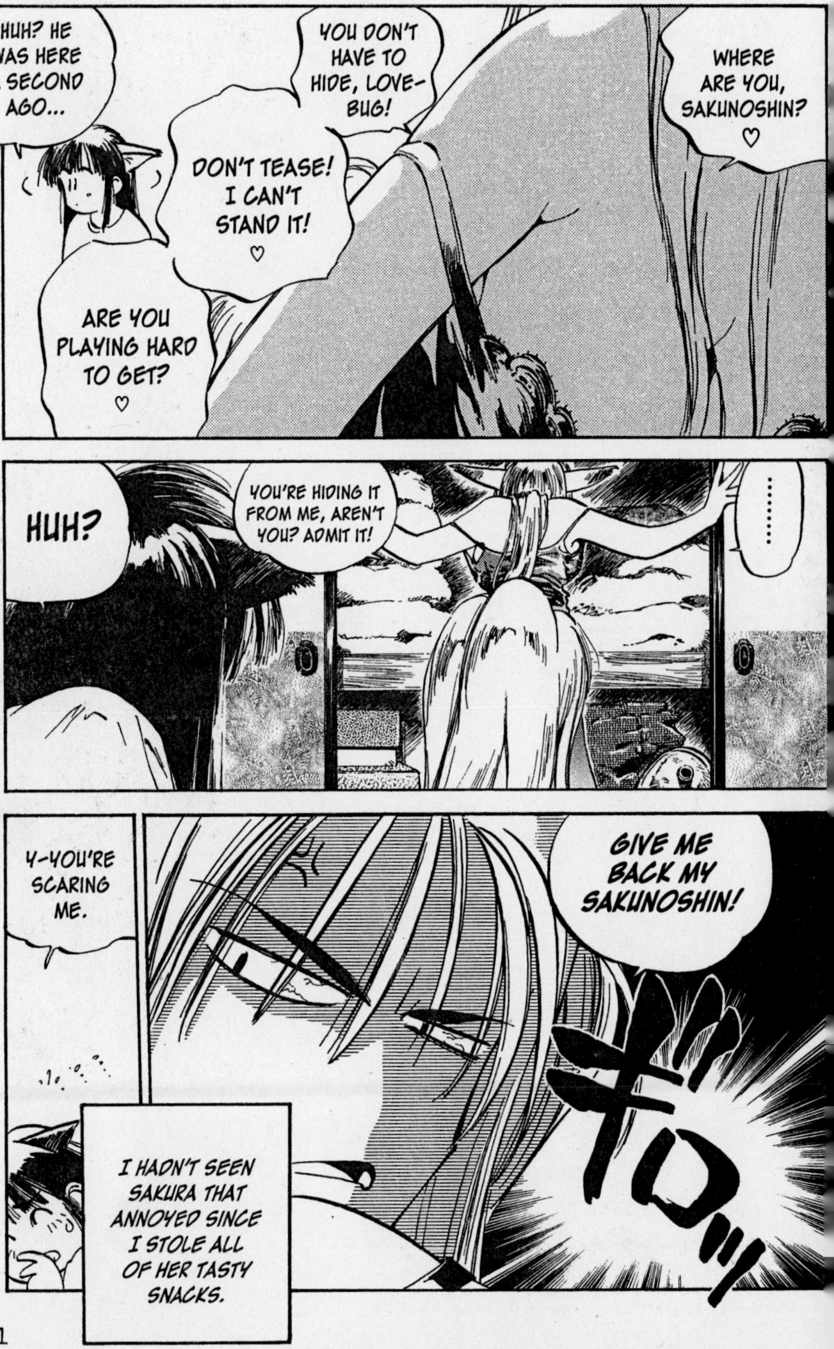
WHERE ARE YOU, SAKUNOSHIN? ♡
YOU DON'T HAVE TO HIDE, LOVE-BUG!
HUH? HE WAS HERE A SECOND AGO...
DON'T TEASE! I CAN'T STAND IT! ♡
ARE YOU PLAYING HARD TO GET? ♡
......
YOU'RE HIDING IT FROM ME, AREN'T YOU? ADMIT IT!
HUH?
GIVE ME BACK MY SAKUNOSHIN!
ギロッ!!
I HADN'T SEEN SAKURA THAT ANNOYED SINCE I STOLE ALL OF HER TASTY SNACKS.
Y-YOU'RE SCARING ME.

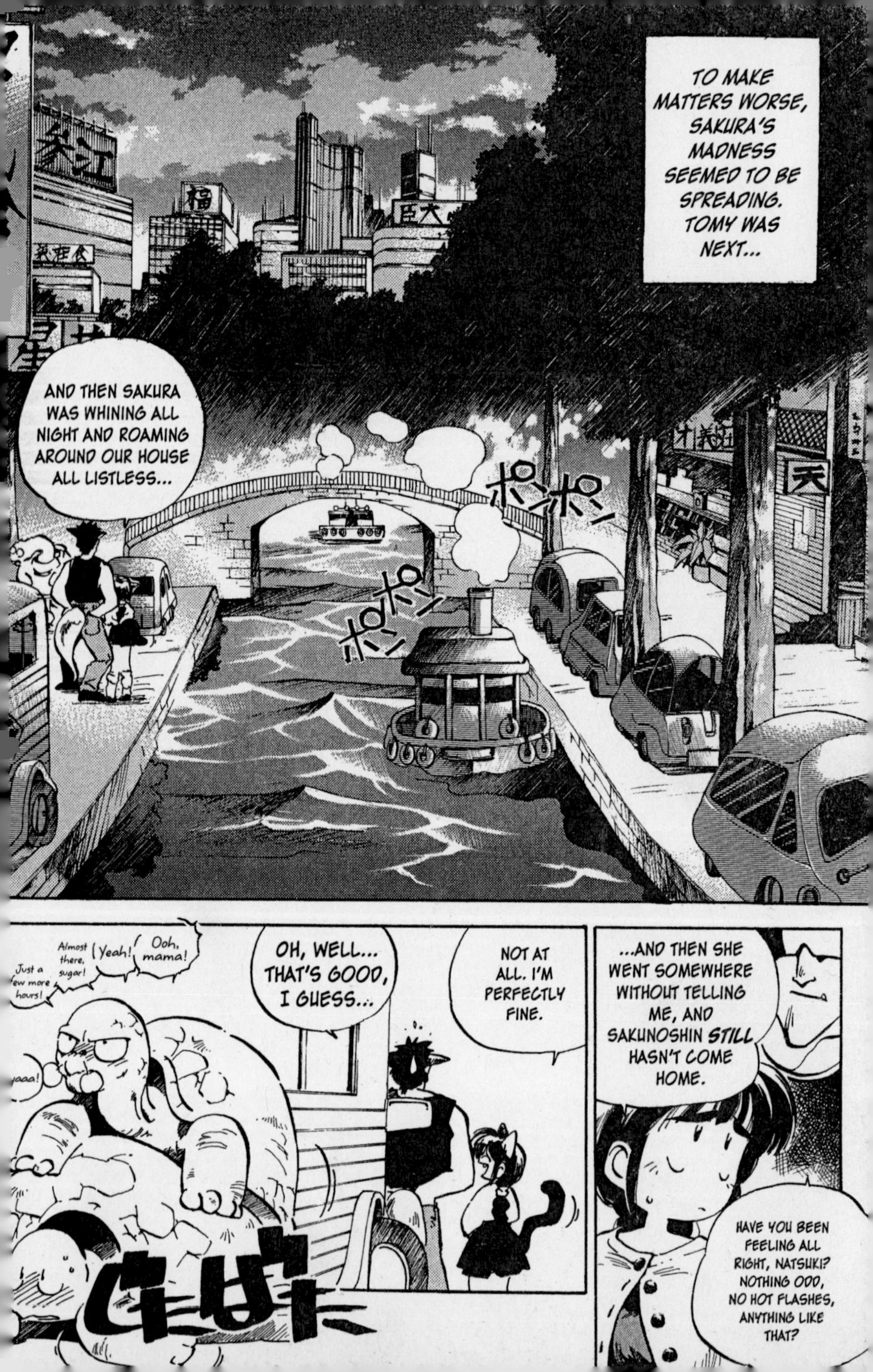
TO MAKE MATTERS WORSE, SAKURA'S MADNESS SEEMED TO BE SPREADING. TOMY WAS NEXT...
ポンポン
ポンポン
AND THEN SAKURA WAS WHINING ALL NIGHT AND ROAMING AROUND OUR HOUSE ALL LISTLESS...
...AND THEN SHE WENT SOMEWHERE WITHOUT TELLING ME, AND SAKUNOSHIN STILL HASN'T COME HOME.
HAVE YOU BEEN FEELING ALL RIGHT, NATSUKI? NOTHING ODD, NO HOT FLASHES, ANYTHING LIKE THAT?
NOT AT ALL. I'M PERFECTLY FINE.
OH, WELL... THAT'S GOOD, I GUESS...
Ooh, mama!
Yeah!
Almost there, sugar!
Just a few more hours!

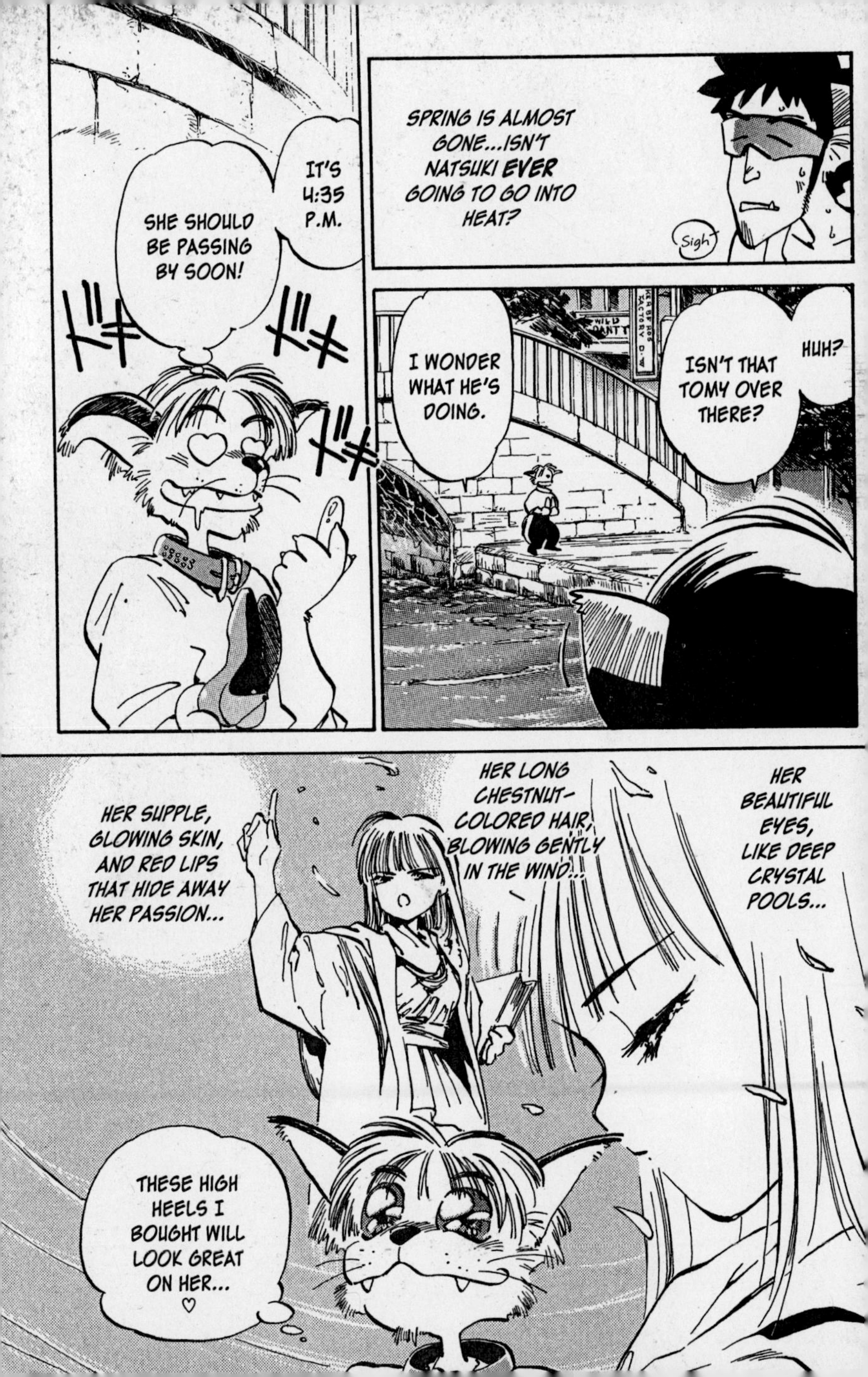
SPRING IS ALMOST GONE...ISN'T NATSUKI EVER GOING TO GO INTO HEAT?
Sigh
HUH?
ISN'T THAT TOMY OVER THERE?
I WONDER WHAT HE'S DOING.
IT'S 4:35 P.M.
SHE SHOULD BE PASSING BY SOON!
ドキ
ドキ
ドキ
HER BEAUTIFUL EYES, LIKE DEEP CRYSTAL POOLS...
HER LONG CHESTNUT-COLORED HAIR, BLOWING GENTLY IN THE WIND...
HER SUPPLE, GLOWING SKIN, AND RED LIPS THAT HIDE AWAY HER PASSION...
THESE HIGH HEELS I BOUGHT WILL LOOK GREAT ON HER... ♡

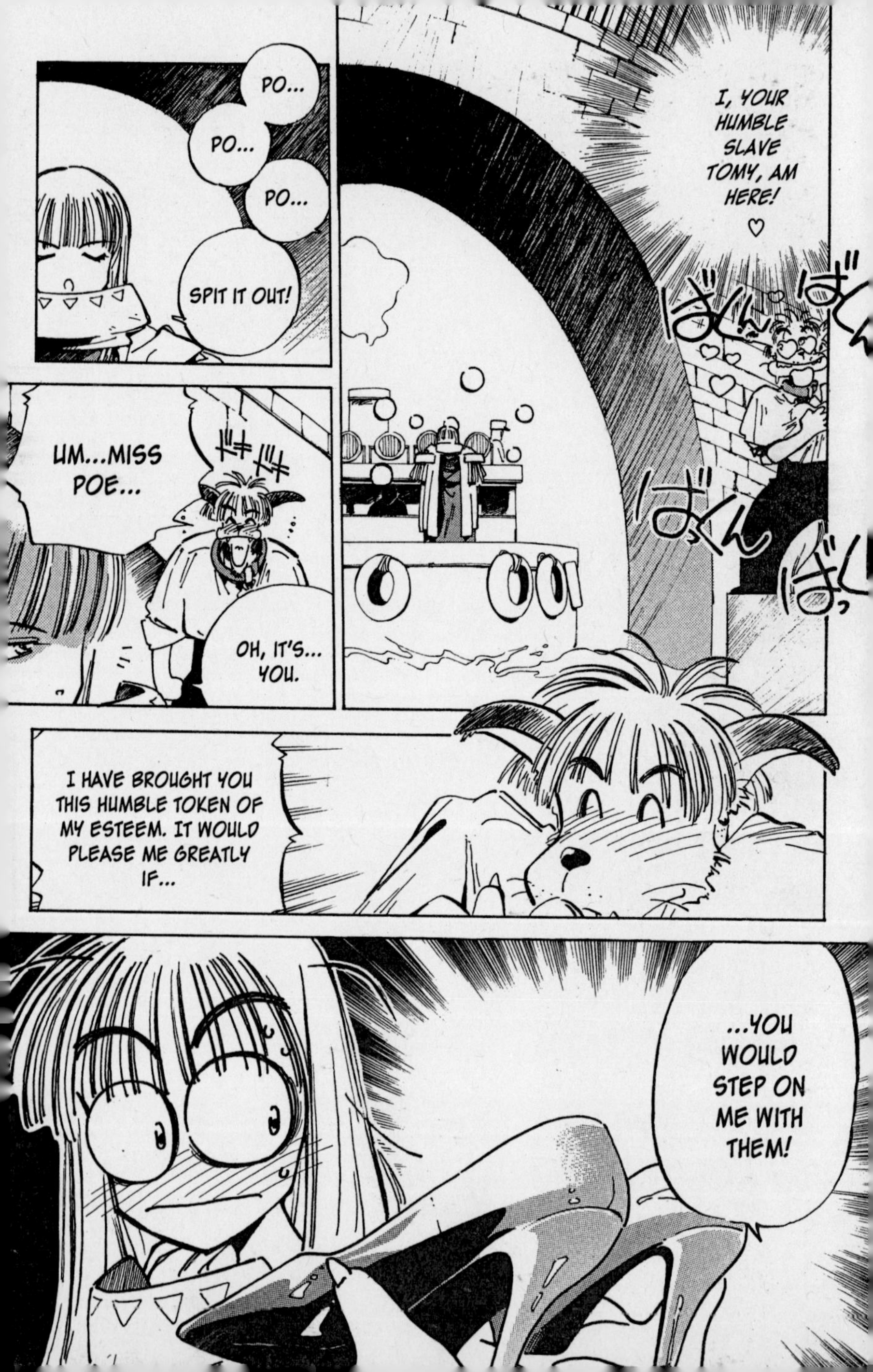
I, YOUR HUMBLE SLAVE TOMY, AM HERE! ♡
ばくん ばくん
ばくん ばくっ
PO...
PO...
PO...
SPIT IT OUT!
ドキドキ
UM...MISS POE...
OH, IT'S... YOU.
I HAVE BROUGHT YOU THIS HUMBLE TOKEN OF MY ESTEEM. IT WOULD PLEASE ME GREATLY IF...
...YOU WOULD STEP ON ME WITH THEM!

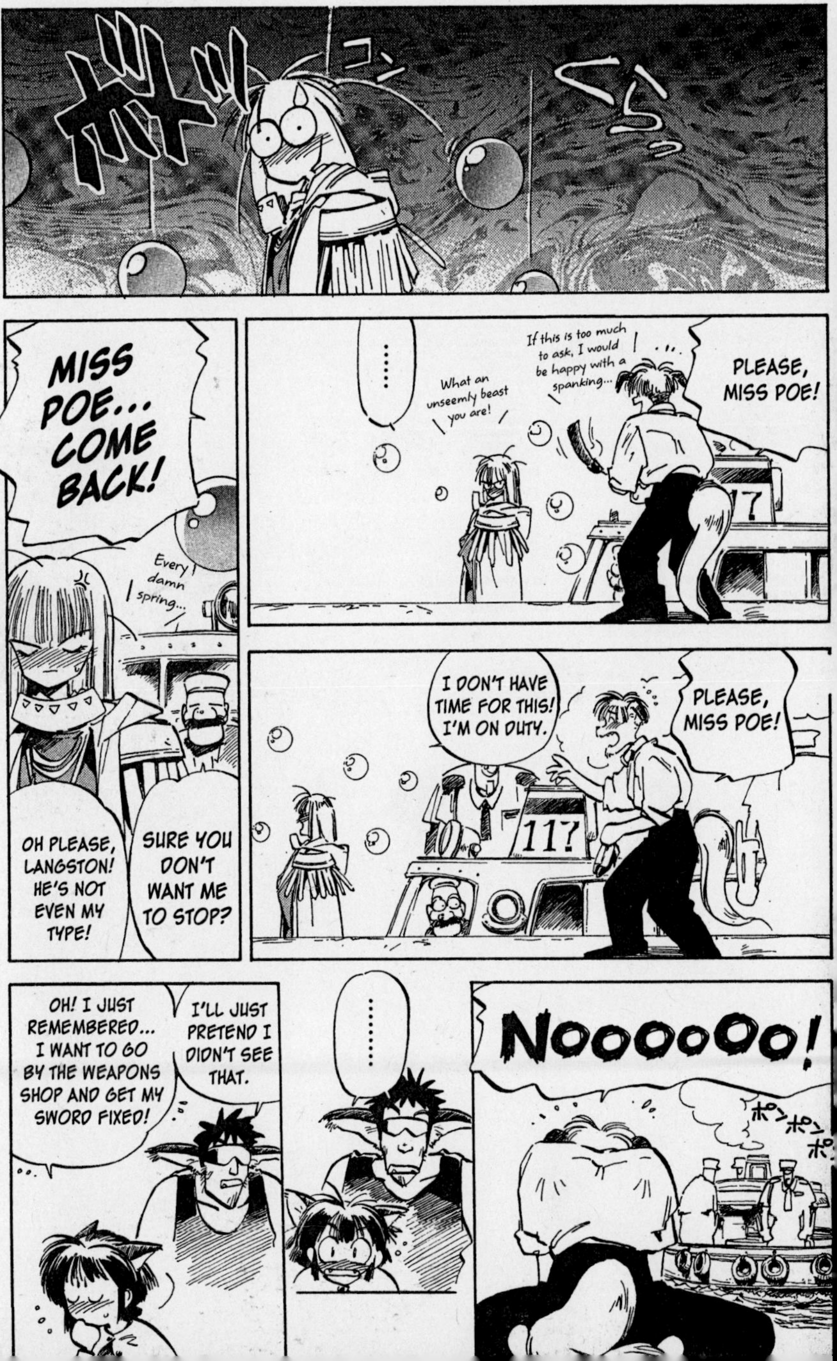
くらっ
コン
ボキッ
PLEASE, MISS POE!
If this is too much to ask, I would be happy with a spanking...
What an unseemly beast you are!
......
PLEASE, MISS POE!
I DON'T HAVE TIME FOR THIS! I'M ON DUTY.
MISS POE... COME BACK!
Every damn spring...
SURE YOU DON'T WANT ME TO STOP?
OH PLEASE, LANGSTON! HE'S NOT EVEN MY TYPE!
NOOOOOO!
ポンポンポ
......
I'LL JUST PRETEND I DIDN'T SEE THAT.
OH! I JUST REMEMBERED... I WANT TO GO BY THE WEAPONS SHOP AND GET MY SWORD FIXED!

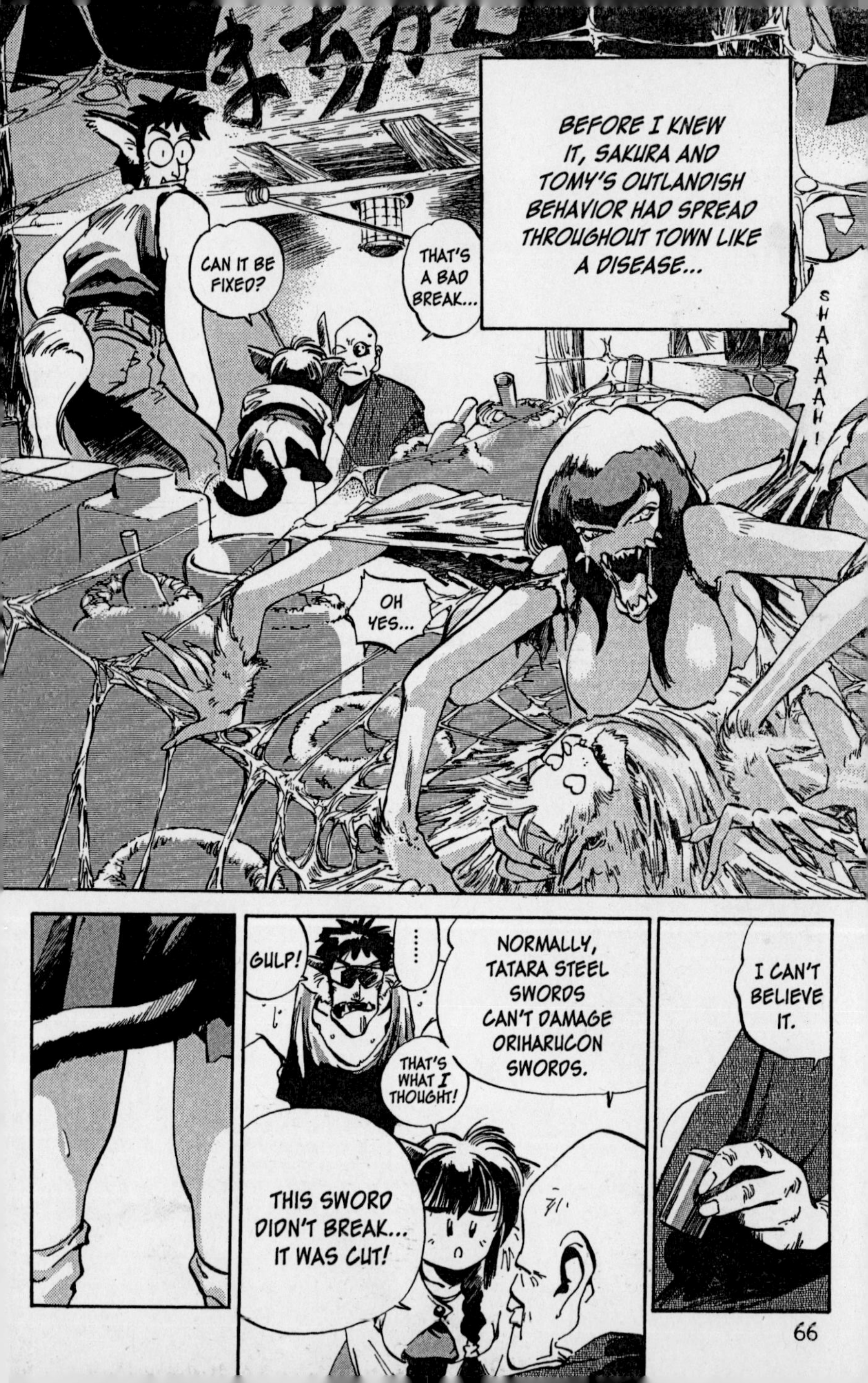

CAN IT BE FIXED?
THAT'S A BAD BREAK...
BEFORE I KNEW IT, SAKURA AND TOMY'S OUTLANDISH BEHAVIOR HAD SPREAD THROUGHOUT TOWN LIKE A DISEASE...
SHAAAAAH!
OH YES...
GULP!
......
NORMALLY, TATARA STEEL SWORDS CAN'T DAMAGE ORIHARUCON SWORDS.
THAT'S WHAT *I* THOUGHT!
THIS SWORD DIDN'T BREAK... IT WAS CUT!
I CAN'T BELIEVE IT.

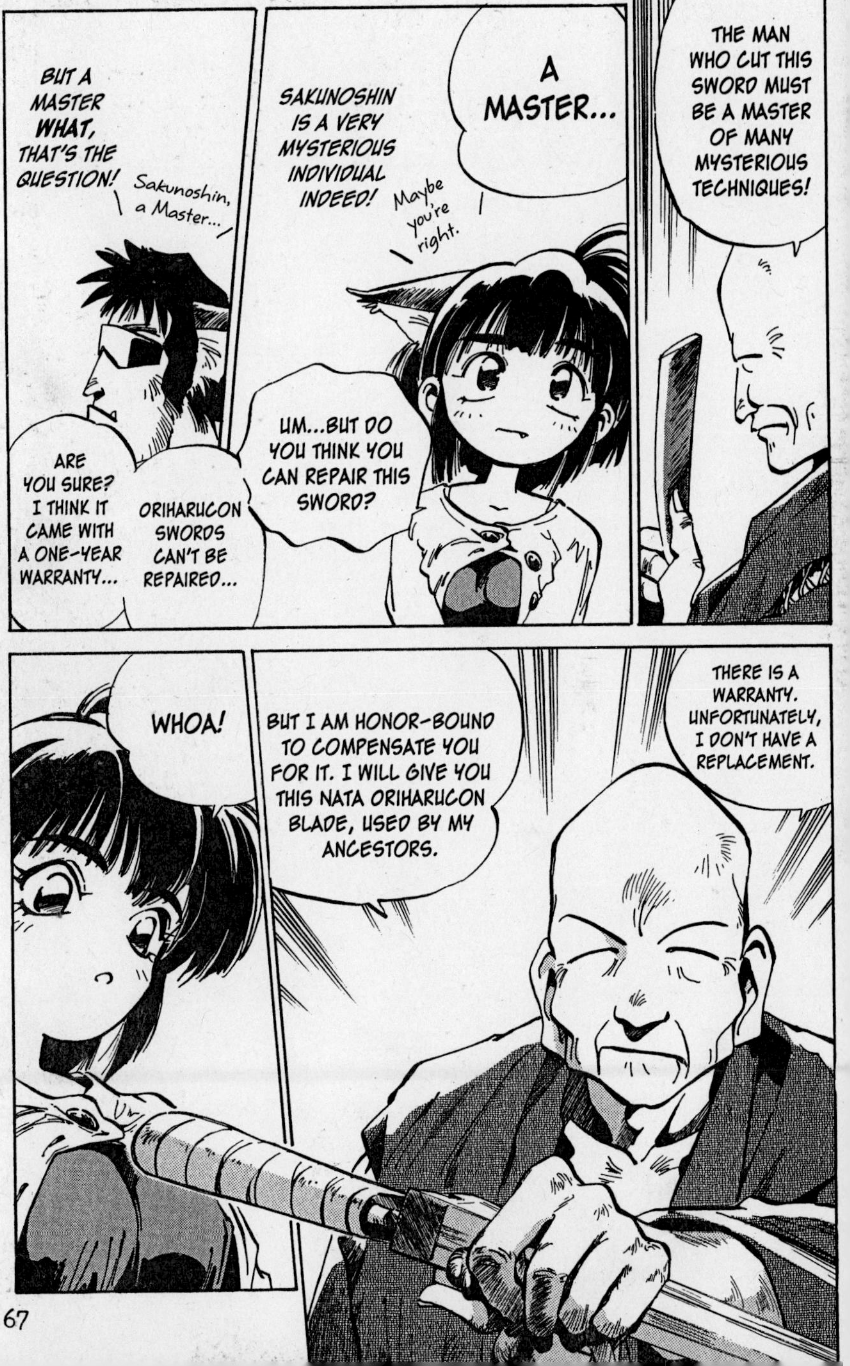
THE MAN WHO CUT THIS SWORD MUST BE A MASTER OF MANY MYSTERIOUS TECHNIQUES!
A MASTER...
SAKUNOSHIN IS A VERY MYSTERIOUS INDIVIDUAL INDEED!
Maybe you're right.
UM...BUT DO YOU THINK YOU CAN REPAIR THIS SWORD?
BUT A MASTER WHAT, THAT'S THE QUESTION!
Sakunoshin, a Master...
ORIHARUCON SWORDS CAN'T BE REPAIRED...
ARE YOU SURE? I THINK IT CAME WITH A ONE-YEAR WARRANTY...
THERE IS A WARRANTY. UNFORTUNATELY, I DON'T HAVE A REPLACEMENT.
BUT I AM HONOR-BOUND TO COMPENSATE YOU FOR IT. I WILL GIVE YOU THIS NATA ORIHARUCON BLADE, USED BY MY ANCESTORS.
WHOA!

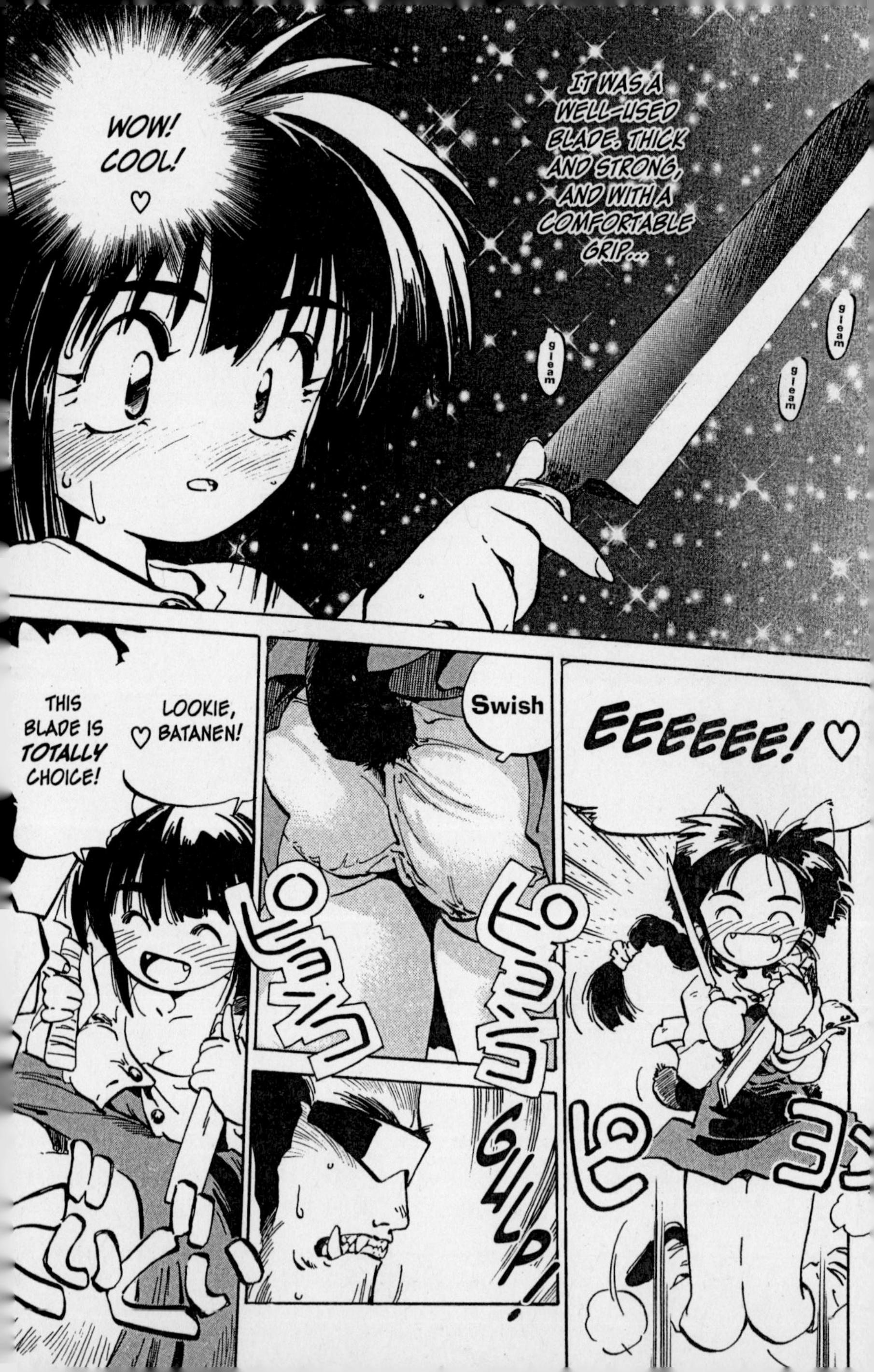
IT WAS A WELL-USED BLADE. THICK AND STRONG, AND WITH A COMFORTABLE GRIP...
gleam
gleam
gleam
WOW! COOL! ♥
EEEEEEE! ♥
Swish
GULP!
LOOKIE, BATANEN! ♥
THIS BLADE IS TOTALLY CHOICE!

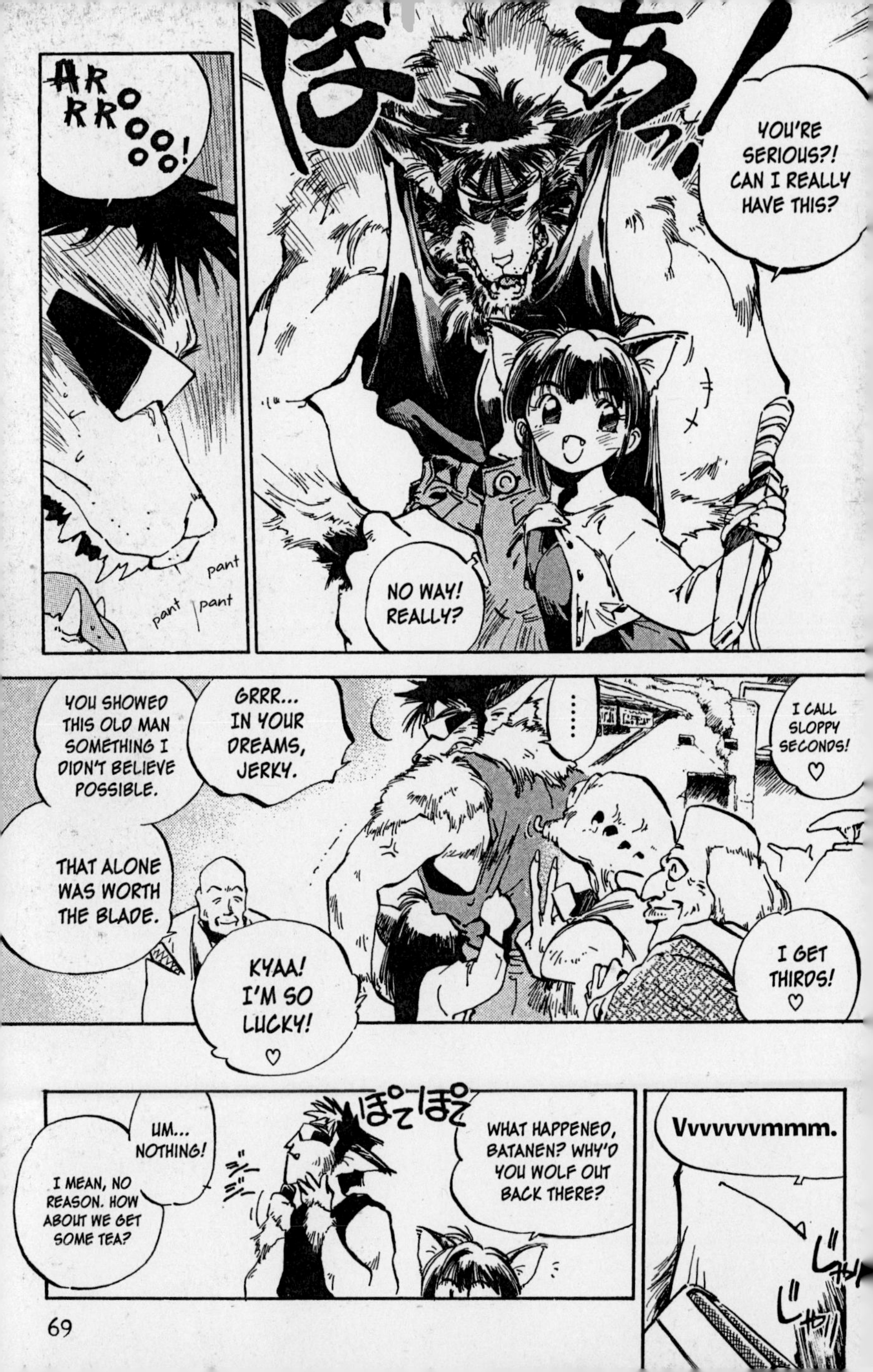
ぼあっ!
YOU'RE SERIOUS?! CAN I REALLY HAVE THIS?
NO WAY! REALLY?
ARRROOOOO!
pant
pant
pant
I CALL SLOPPY SECONDS! ♡
I GET THIRDS! ♡
......
GRRR... IN YOUR DREAMS, JERKY.
YOU SHOWED THIS OLD MAN SOMETHING I DIDN'T BELIEVE POSSIBLE.
THAT ALONE WAS WORTH THE BLADE.
KYAA! I'M SO LUCKY! ♡
Vvvvvvvmmm.
ぽてぽて
WHAT HAPPENED, BATANEN? WHY'D YOU WOLF OUT BACK THERE?
UM... NOTHING!
I MEAN, NO REASON. HOW ABOUT WE GET SOME TEA?

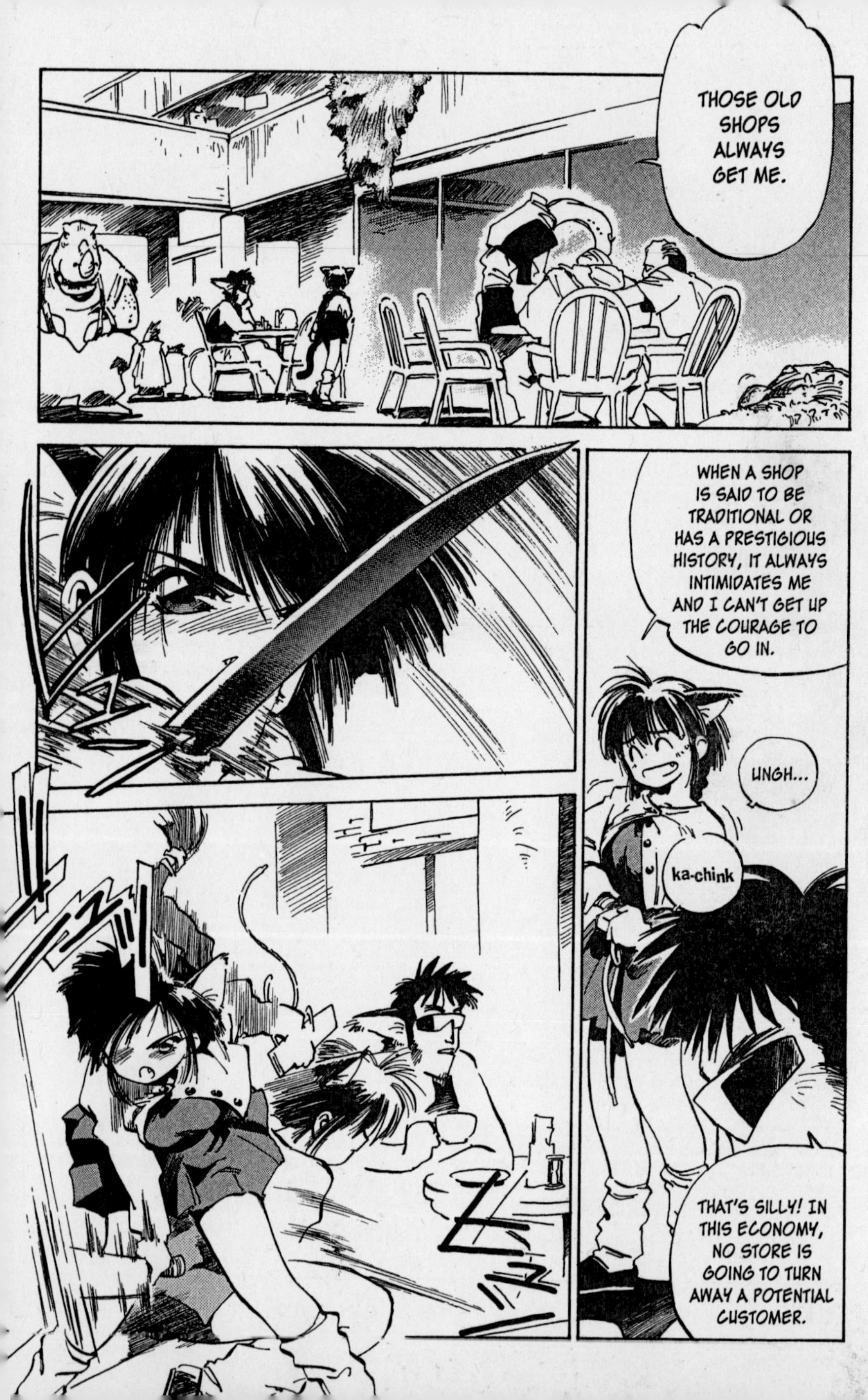
THOSE OLD SHOPS ALWAYS GET ME.
WHEN A SHOP IS SAID TO BE TRADITIONAL OR HAS A PRESTIGIOUS HISTORY, IT ALWAYS INTIMIDATES ME AND I CAN'T GET UP THE COURAGE TO GO IN.
UNGH...
ka-chink
THAT'S SILLY! IN THIS ECONOMY, NO STORE IS GOING TO TURN AWAY A POTENTIAL CUSTOMER.

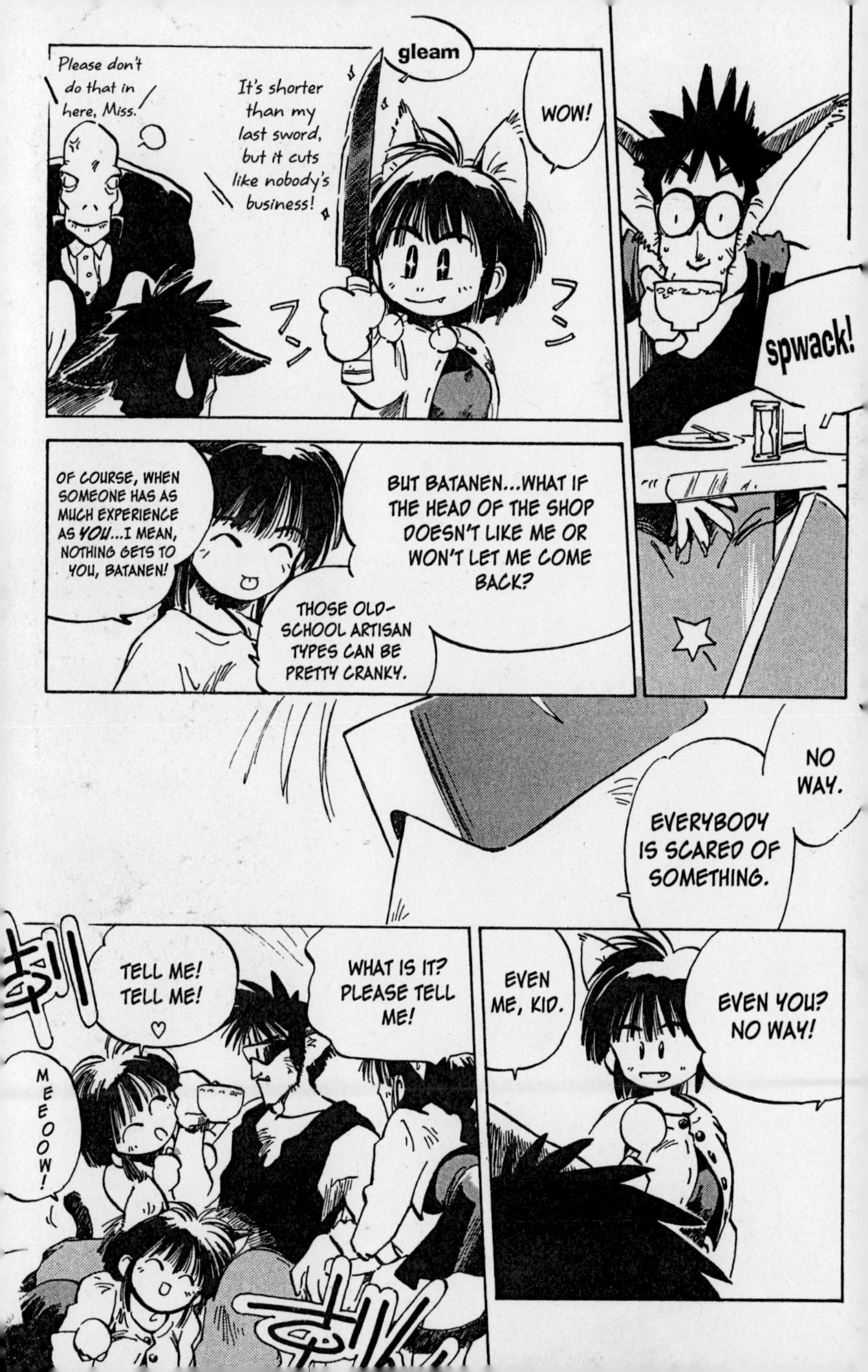
spwack!
gleam
WOW!
It's shorter than my last sword, but it cuts like nobody's business!
Please don't do that in here, Miss.
BUT BATANEN...WHAT IF THE HEAD OF THE SHOP DOESN'T LIKE ME OR WON'T LET ME COME BACK?
THOSE OLD-SCHOOL ARTISAN TYPES CAN BE PRETTY CRANKY.
OF COURSE, WHEN SOMEONE HAS AS MUCH EXPERIENCE AS YOU...I MEAN, NOTHING GETS TO YOU, BATANEN!
NO WAY.
EVERYBODY IS SCARED OF SOMETHING.
EVEN YOU? NO WAY!
EVEN ME, KID.
WHAT IS IT? PLEASE TELL ME!
TELL ME! TELL ME! ♡
MEEOOW!

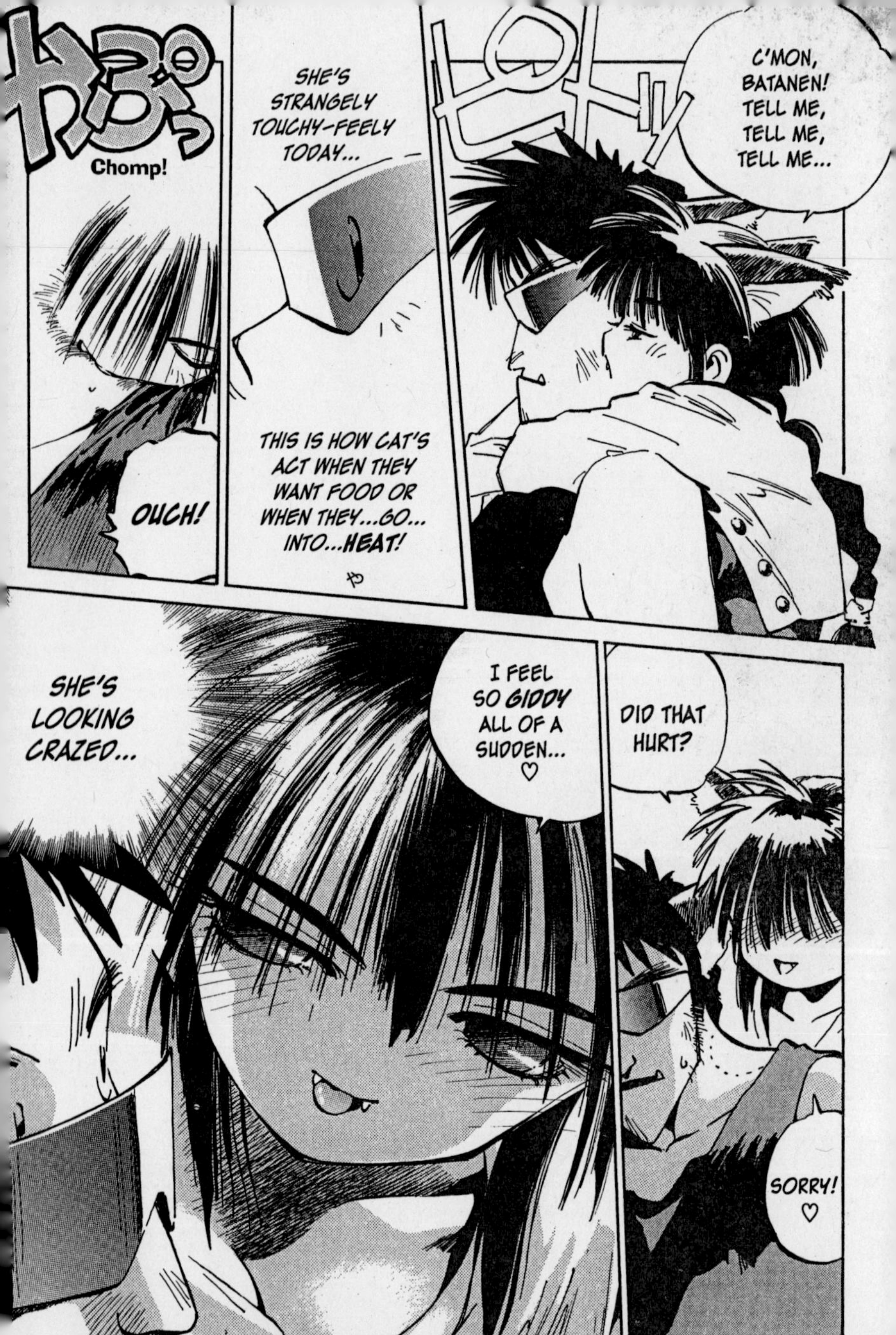
C'MON, BATANEN! TELL ME, TELL ME, TELL ME...
SHE'S STRANGELY TOUCHY-FEELY TODAY...
THIS IS HOW CAT'S ACT WHEN THEY WANT FOOD OR WHEN THEY...GO... INTO...HEAT!
Chomp!
OUCH!
DID THAT HURT?
SORRY! ♡
I FEEL SO GIDDY ALL OF A SUDDEN... ♡
SHE'S LOOKING CRAZED...

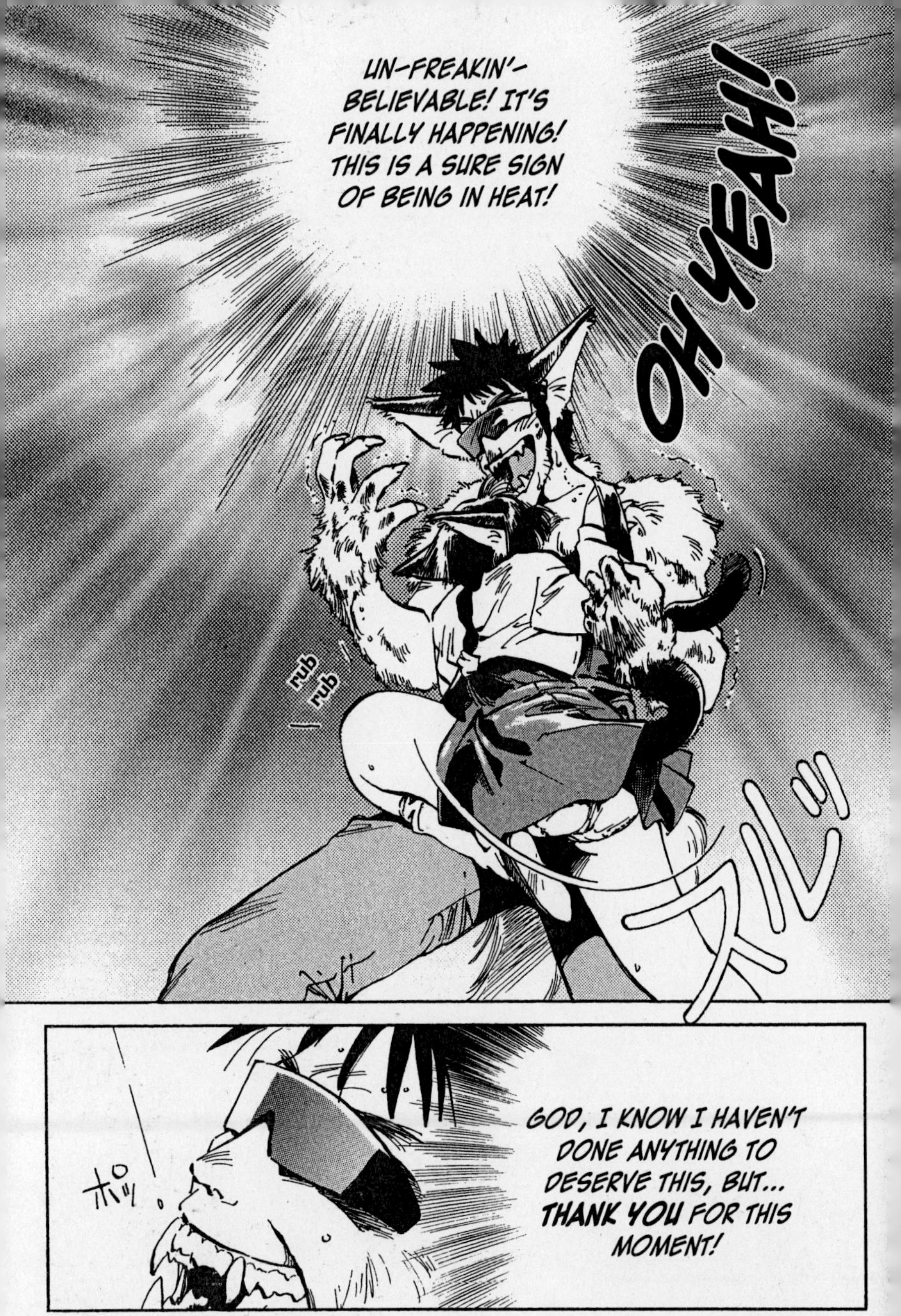
UN-FREAKIN'-BELIEVABLE! IT'S FINALLY HAPPENING! THIS IS A SURE SIGN OF BEING IN HEAT!
OH YEAH!!
ズルッ
rub rub
GOD, I KNOW I HAVEN'T DONE ANYTHING TO DESERVE THIS, BUT... **THANK YOU** FOR THIS MOMENT!
ポッ

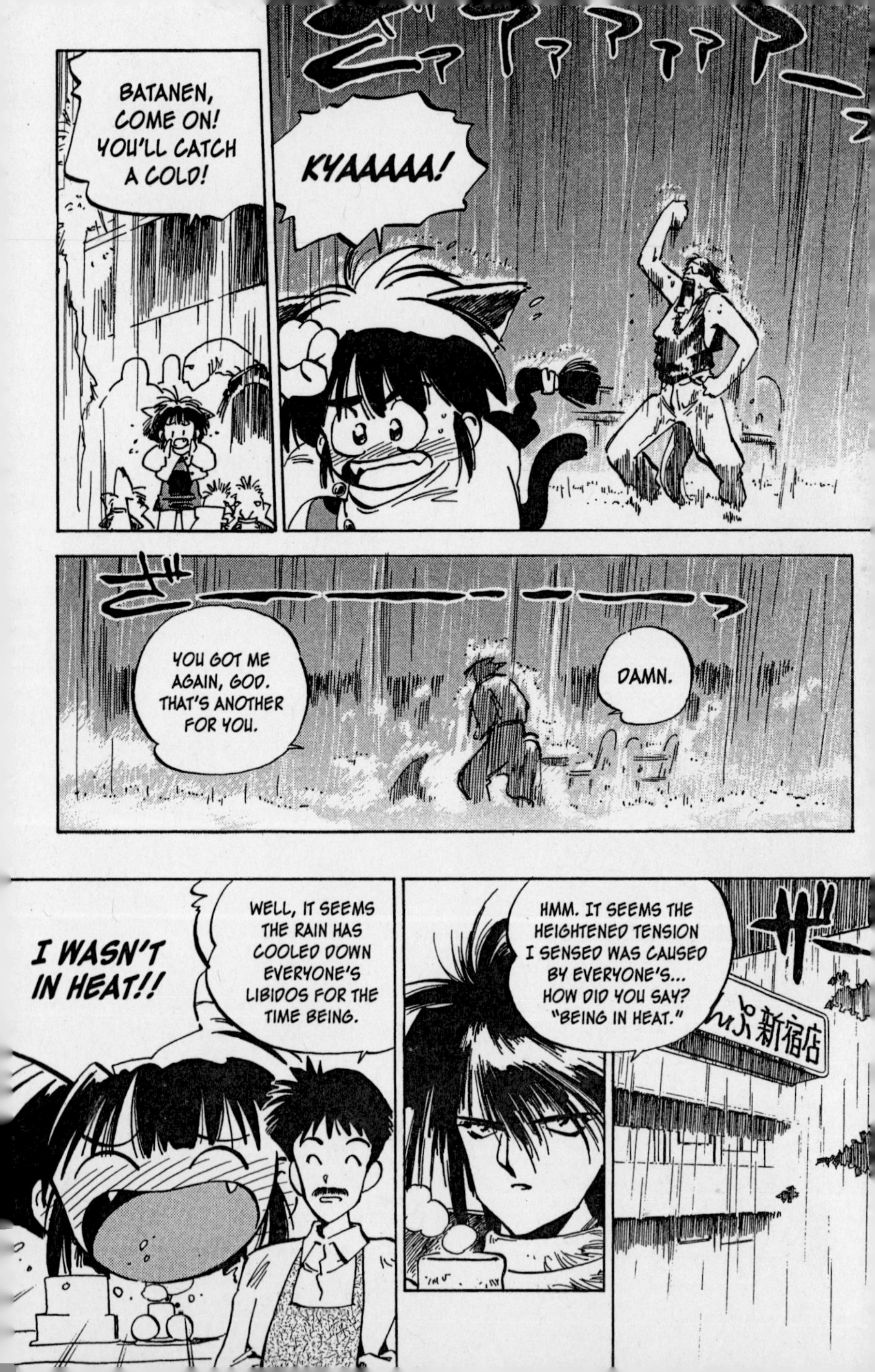
ザァァァァァアーッ
KYAAAAA!
BATANEN, COME ON! YOU'LL CATCH A COLD!
ざーーーーーーッ
DAMN.
YOU GOT ME AGAIN, GOD. THAT'S ANOTHER FOR YOU.
ザー
んぷ新宿店
HMM. IT SEEMS THE HEIGHTENED TENSION I SENSED WAS CAUSED BY EVERYONE'S... HOW DID YOU SAY? "BEING IN HEAT."
WELL, IT SEEMS THE RAIN HAS COOLED DOWN EVERYONE'S LIBIDOS FOR THE TIME BEING.
I WASN'T IN HEAT!!

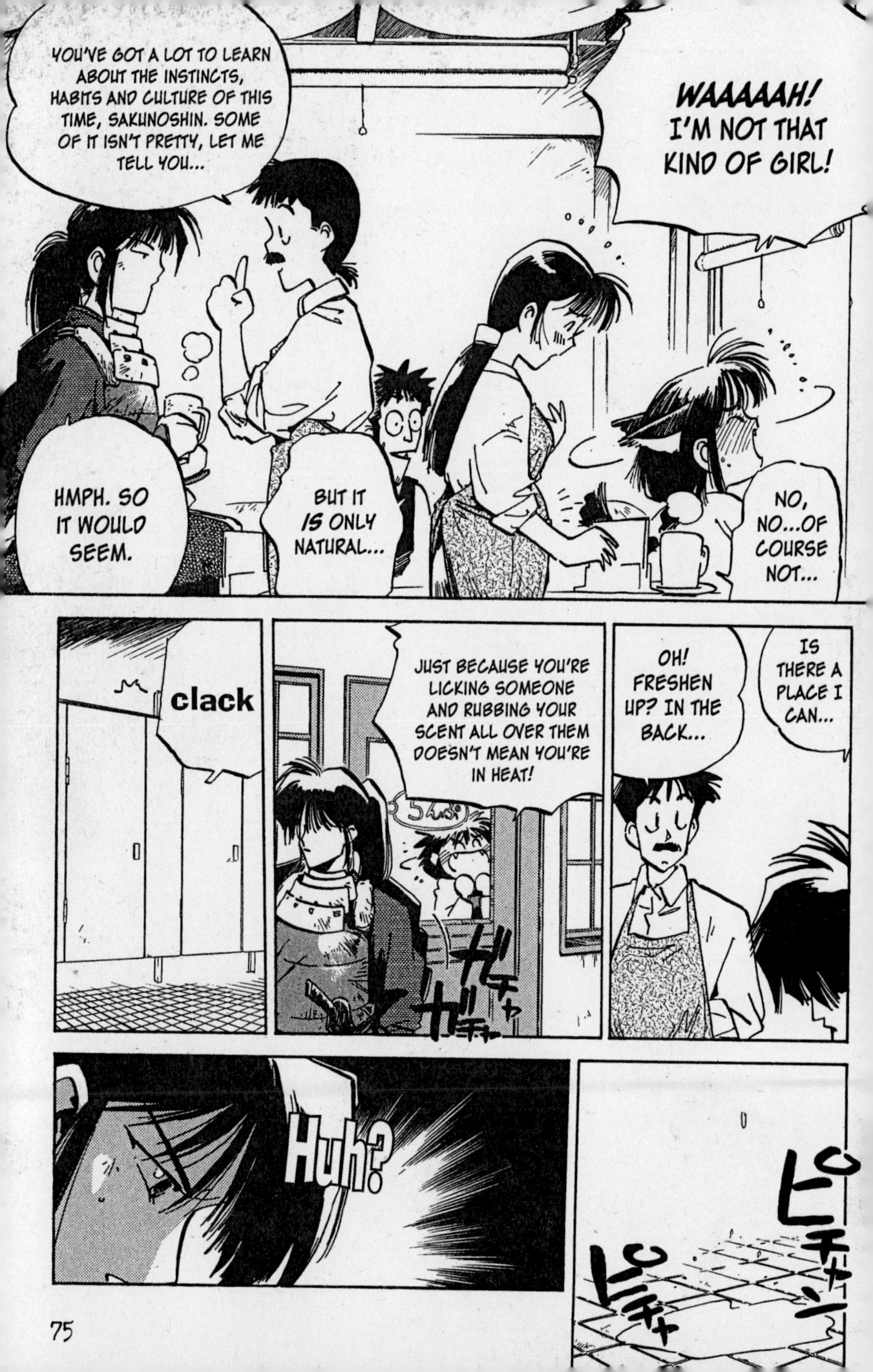
WAAAAAH! I'M NOT THAT KIND OF GIRL!
NO, NO...OF COURSE NOT...
YOU'VE GOT A LOT TO LEARN ABOUT THE INSTINCTS, HABITS AND CULTURE OF THIS TIME, SAKUNOSHIN. SOME OF IT ISN'T PRETTY, LET ME TELL YOU...
BUT IT IS ONLY NATURAL...
HMPH. SO IT WOULD SEEM.
IS THERE A PLACE I CAN...
OH! FRESHEN UP? IN THE BACK...
JUST BECAUSE YOU'RE LICKING SOMEONE AND RUBBING YOUR SCENT ALL OVER THEM DOESN'T MEAN YOU'RE IN HEAT!
ガチャ
ガチャ
clack
ピチャン
ピチャ
Huh?

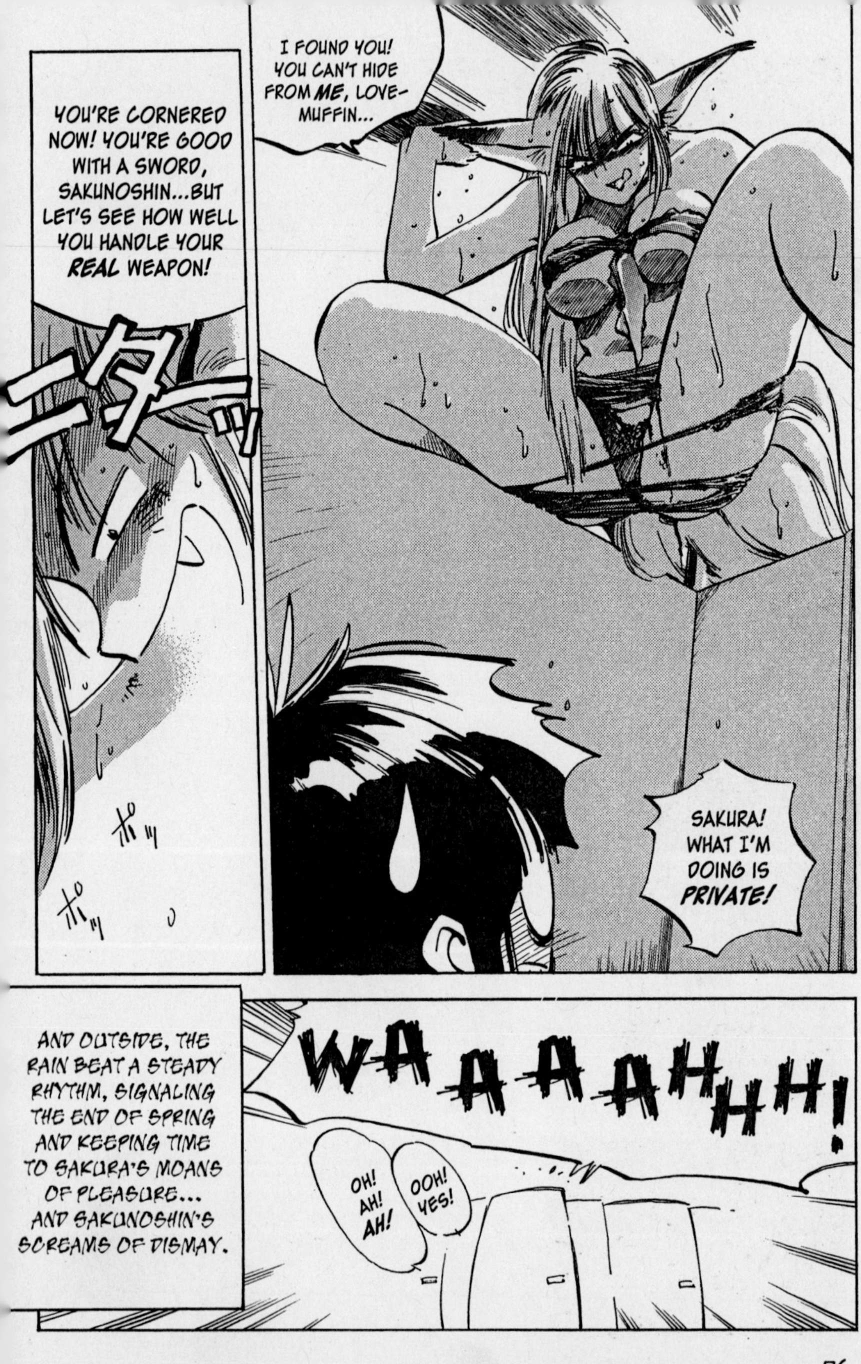
I FOUND YOU! YOU CAN'T HIDE FROM *ME*, LOVE-MUFFIN...
SAKURA! WHAT I'M DOING IS *PRIVATE!*
YOU'RE CORNERED NOW! YOU'RE GOOD WITH A SWORD, SAKUNOSHIN...BUT LET'S SEE HOW WELL YOU HANDLE YOUR *REAL* WEAPON!
WAAAAHHH!
OOH! YES!
OH! AH! AH!
AND OUTSIDE, THE RAIN BEAT A STEADY RHYTHM, SIGNALING THE END OF SPRING AND KEEPING TIME TO SAKURA'S MOANS OF PLEASURE... AND SAKUNOSHIN'S SCREAMS OF DISMAY.

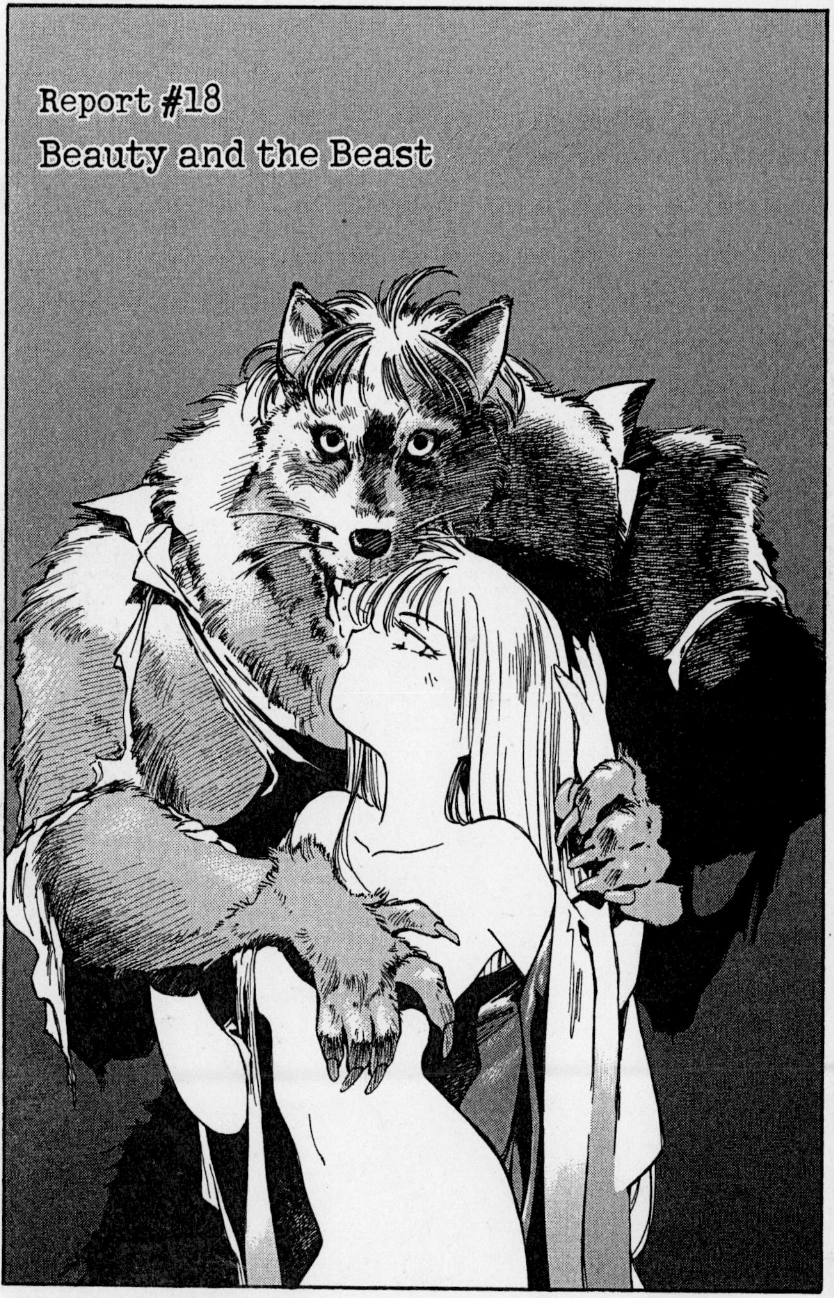
Report #18
Beauty and the Beast

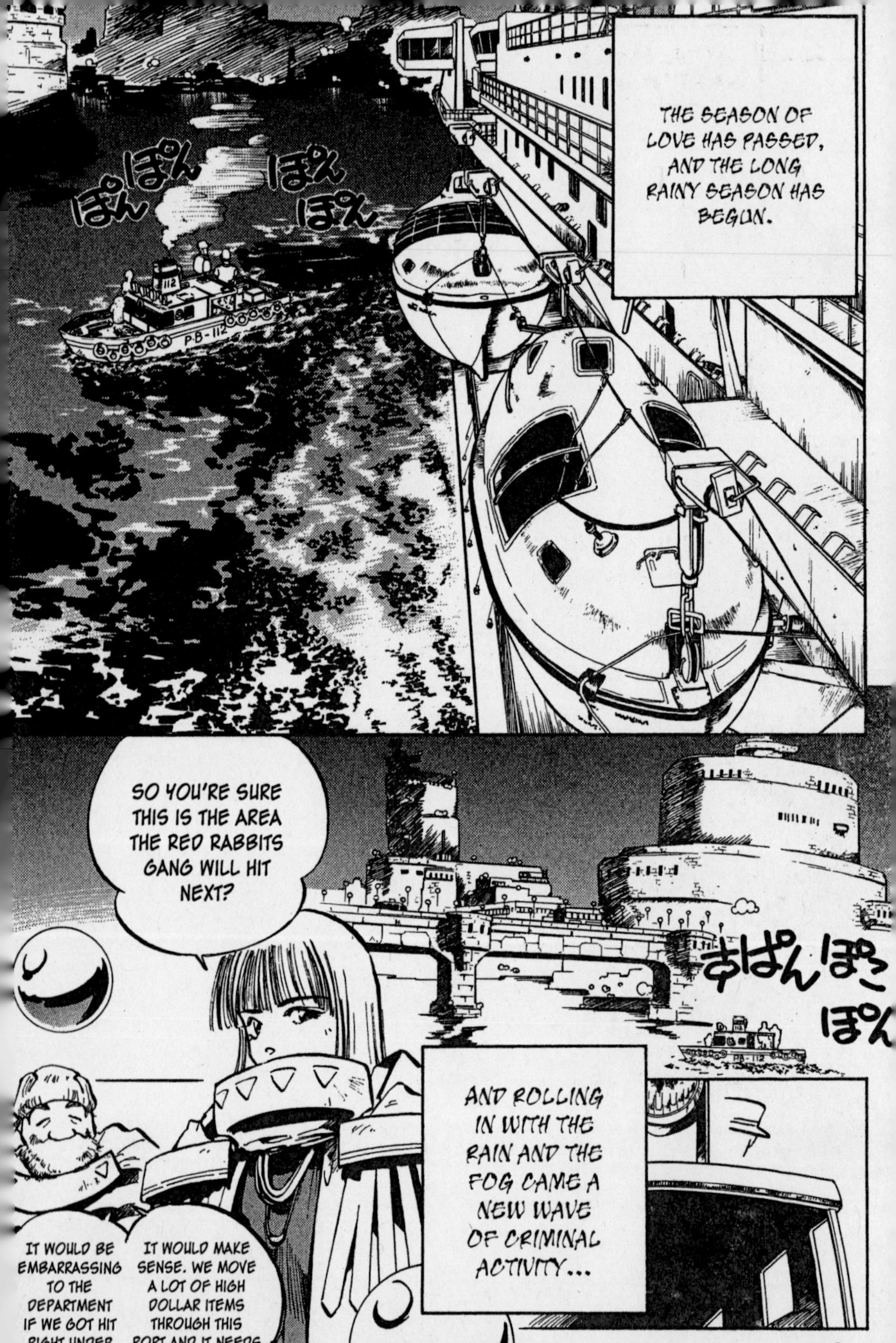
THE SEASON OF LOVE HAS PASSED, AND THE LONG RAINY SEASON HAS BEGUN.
ぽん ぽん
ぽん ぽん
ぱん ぽこ ぽん
AND ROLLING IN WITH THE RAIN AND THE FOG CAME A NEW WAVE OF CRIMINAL ACTIVITY...
SO YOU'RE SURE THIS IS THE AREA THE RED RABBITS GANG WILL HIT NEXT?
IT WOULD MAKE SENSE. WE MOVE A LOT OF HIGH DOLLAR ITEMS THROUGH THIS PORT AND IT NEEDS PROTECTING.
IT WOULD BE EMBARRASSING TO THE DEPARTMENT IF WE GOT HIT RIGHT UNDER OUR NOSE.

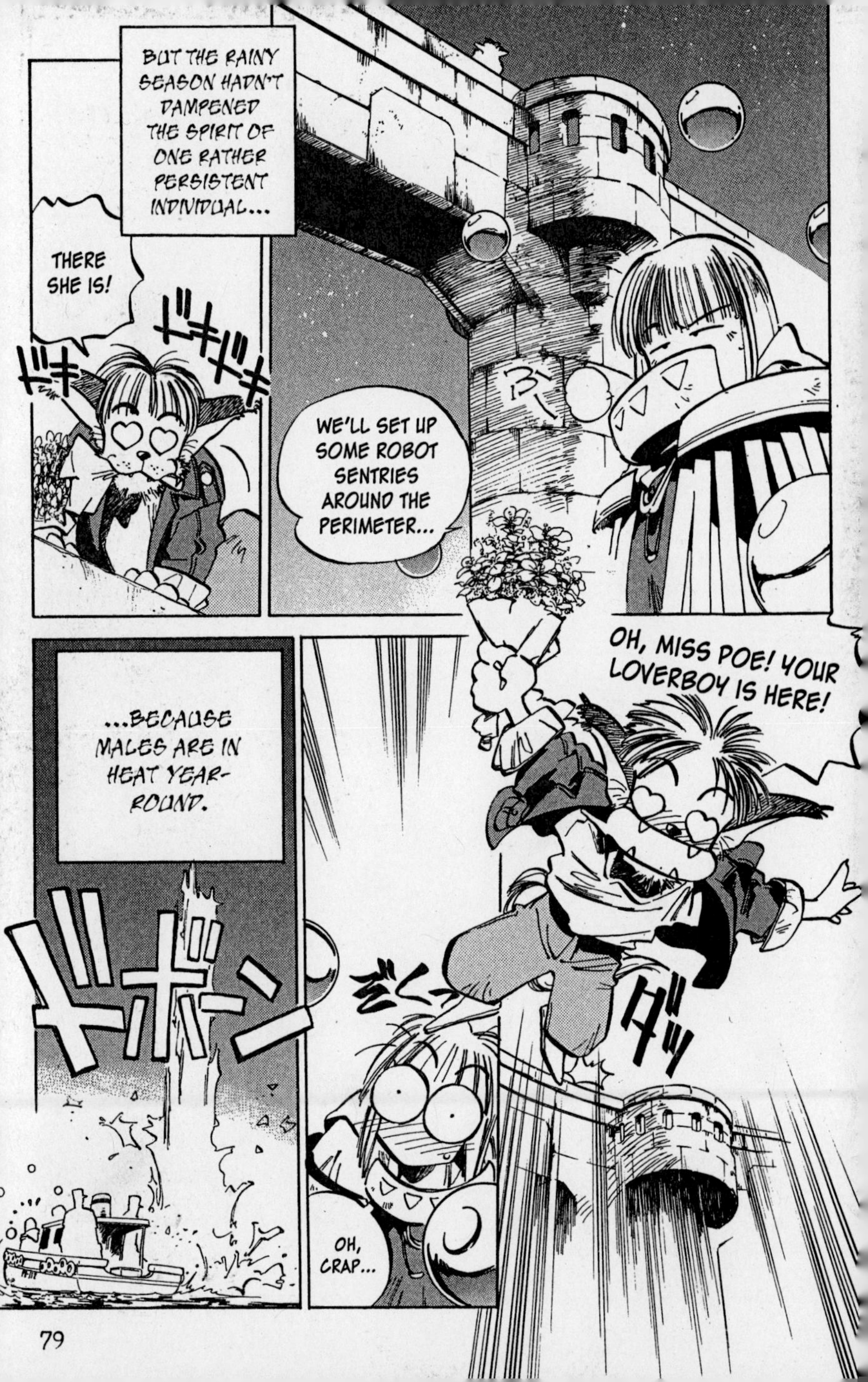
BUT THE RAINY SEASON HADN'T DAMPENED THE SPIRIT OF ONE RATHER PERSISTENT INDIVIDUAL...
WE'LL SET UP SOME ROBOT SENTRIES AROUND THE PERIMETER...
THERE SHE IS!
ドキドキ
ドキ
OH, MISS POE! YOUR LOVERBOY IS HERE!
ダッ
ぎくっ
OH, CRAP...
...BECAUSE MALES ARE IN HEAT YEAR-ROUND.
ドボーン

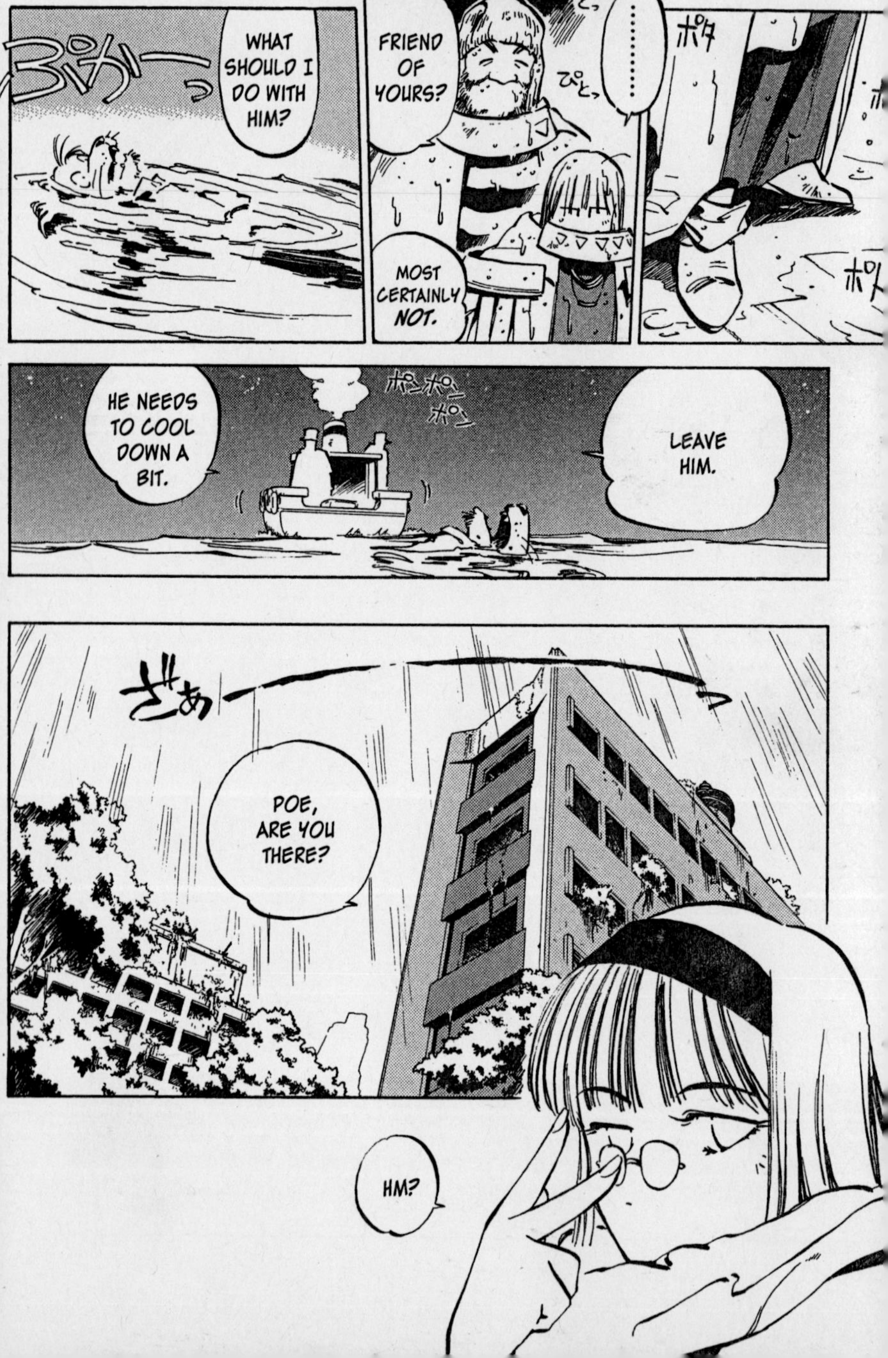

ポタ
……
ぴとっ
ぴとっ
FRIEND OF YOURS?
MOST CERTAINLY NOT.
WHAT SHOULD I DO WITH HIM?
ぷかーっ
LEAVE HIM.
ポンポン
ポン
HE NEEDS TO COOL DOWN A BIT.
ざあーー
ポタっ
POE, ARE YOU THERE?
HM?

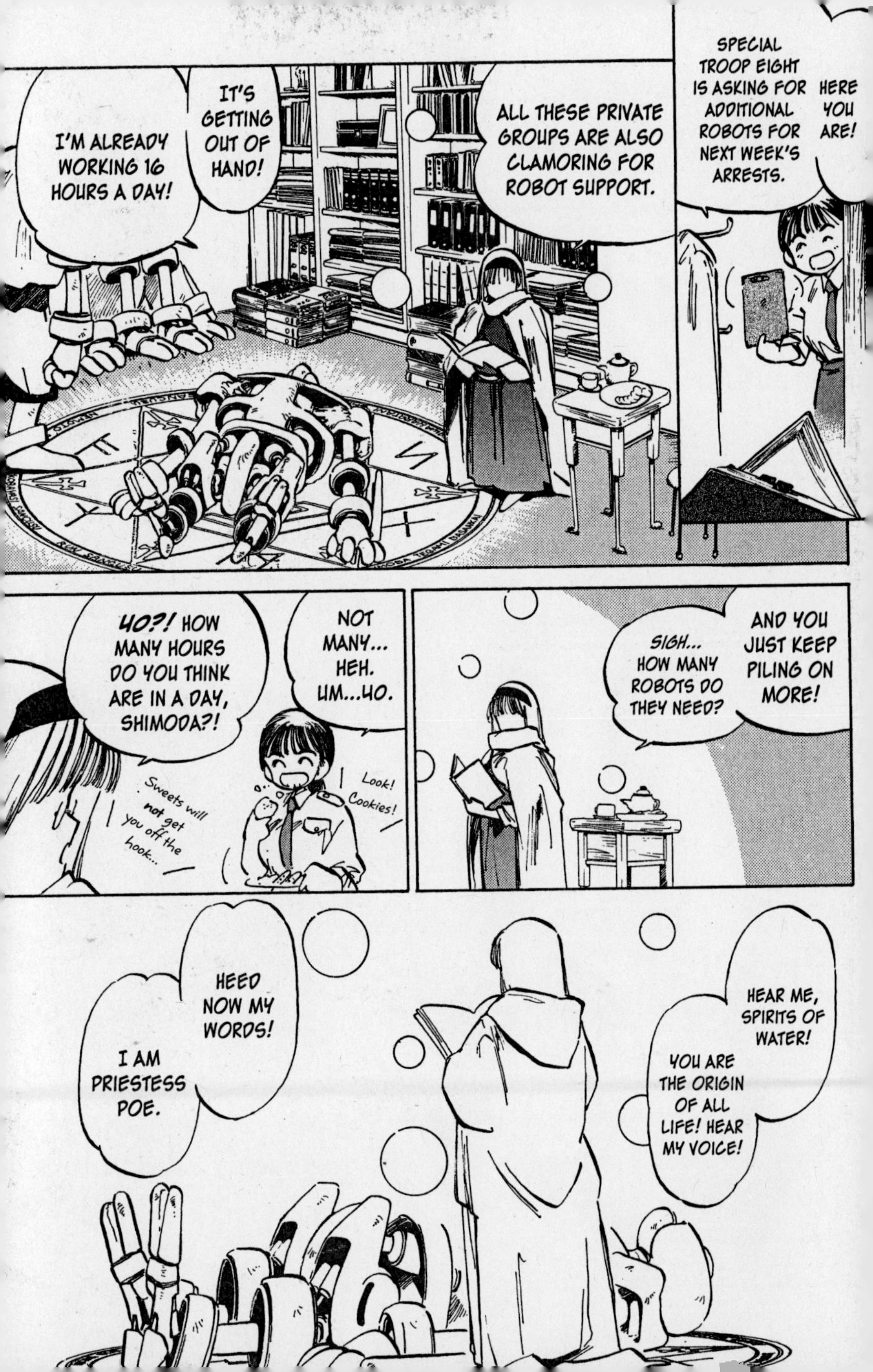
HERE YOU ARE!
SPECIAL TROOP EIGHT IS ASKING FOR ADDITIONAL ROBOTS FOR NEXT WEEK'S ARRESTS.
ALL THESE PRIVATE GROUPS ARE ALSO CLAMORING FOR ROBOT SUPPORT.
IT'S GETTING OUT OF HAND!
I'M ALREADY WORKING 16 HOURS A DAY!
AND YOU JUST KEEP PILING ON MORE!
SIGH... HOW MANY ROBOTS DO THEY NEED?
NOT MANY... HEH. UM...40.
Look! Cookies!
40?! HOW MANY HOURS DO YOU THINK ARE IN A DAY, SHIMODA?!
Sweets will not get you off the hook...
HEAR ME, SPIRITS OF WATER!
YOU ARE THE ORIGIN OF ALL LIFE! HEAR MY VOICE!
HEED NOW MY WORDS!
I AM PRIESTESS POE.

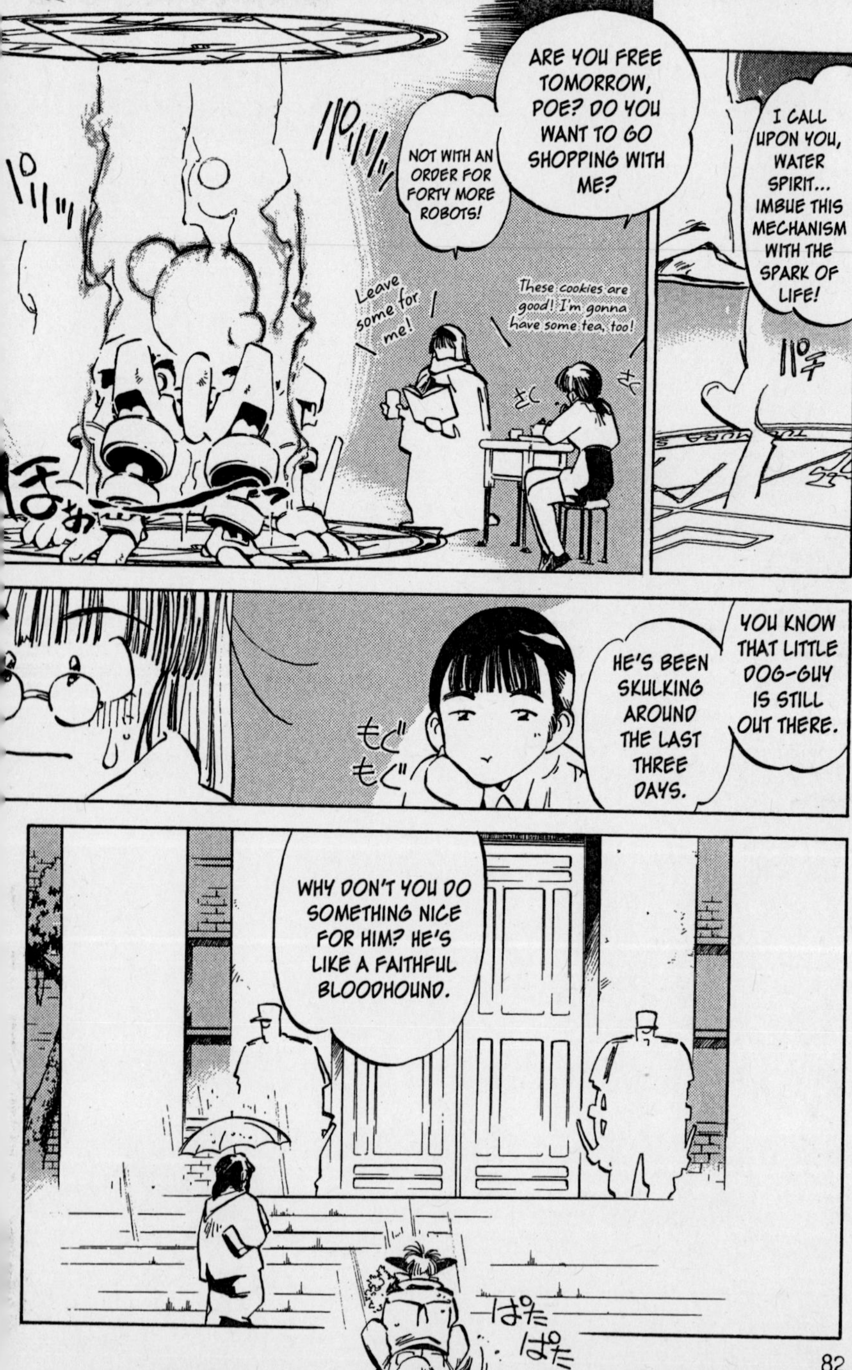
I CALL UPON YOU, WATER SPIRIT... IMBUE THIS MECHANISM WITH THE SPARK OF LIFE!
ARE YOU FREE TOMORROW, POE? DO YOU WANT TO GO SHOPPING WITH ME?
NOT WITH AN ORDER FOR FORTY MORE ROBOTS!
These cookies are good! I'm gonna have some tea, too!
Leave some for me!
YOU KNOW THAT LITTLE DOG-GUY IS STILL OUT THERE.
HE'S BEEN SKULKING AROUND THE LAST THREE DAYS.
もぐもぐ
WHY DON'T YOU DO SOMETHING NICE FOR HIM? HE'S LIKE A FAITHFUL BLOODHOUND.
ぱたぱた

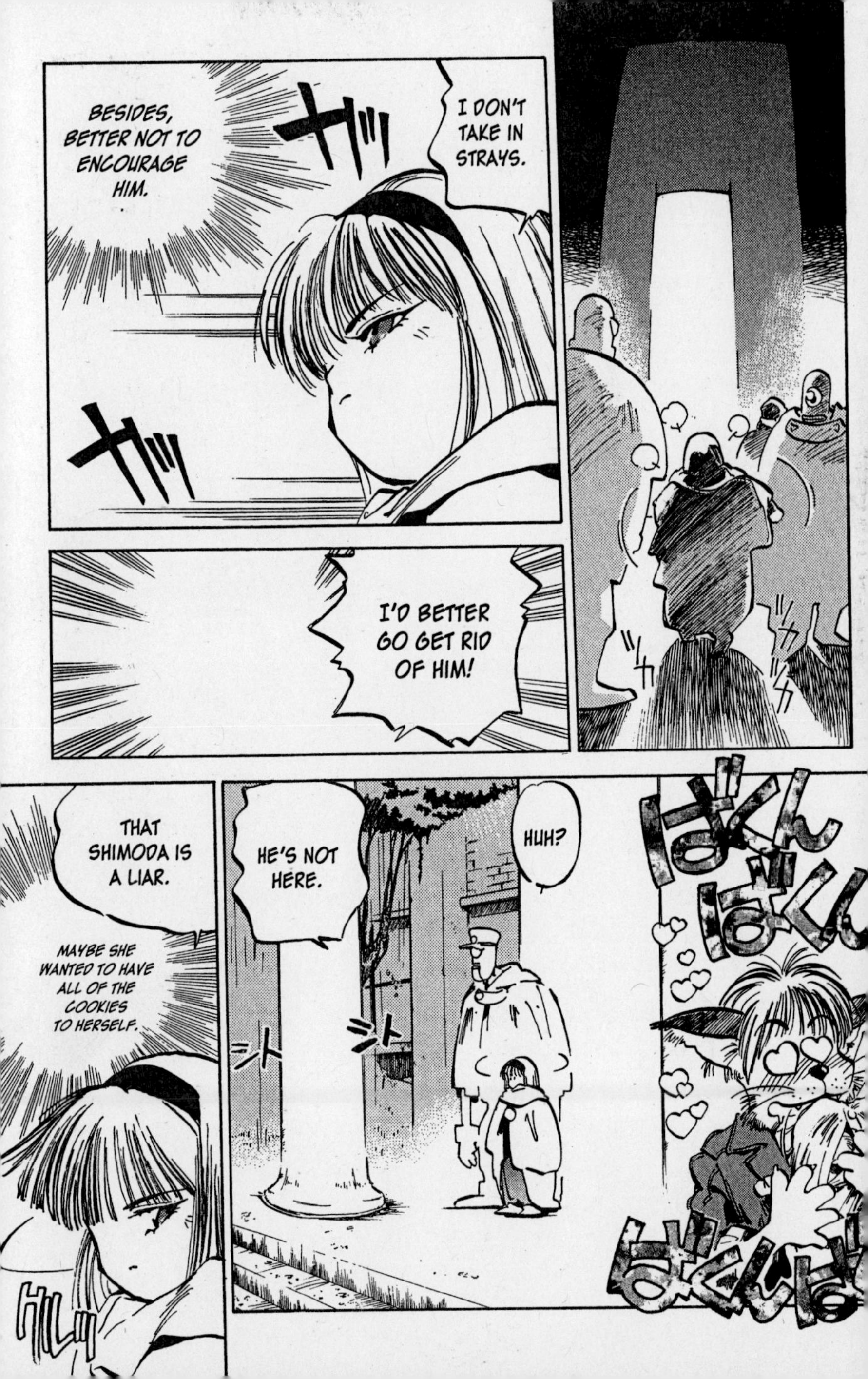
I DON'T TAKE IN STRAYS.
BESIDES, BETTER NOT TO ENCOURAGE HIM.
I'D BETTER GO GET RID OF HIM!
HUH?
HE'S NOT HERE.
THAT SHIMODA IS A LIAR.
MAYBE SHE WANTED TO HAVE ALL OF THE COOKIES TO HERSELF.

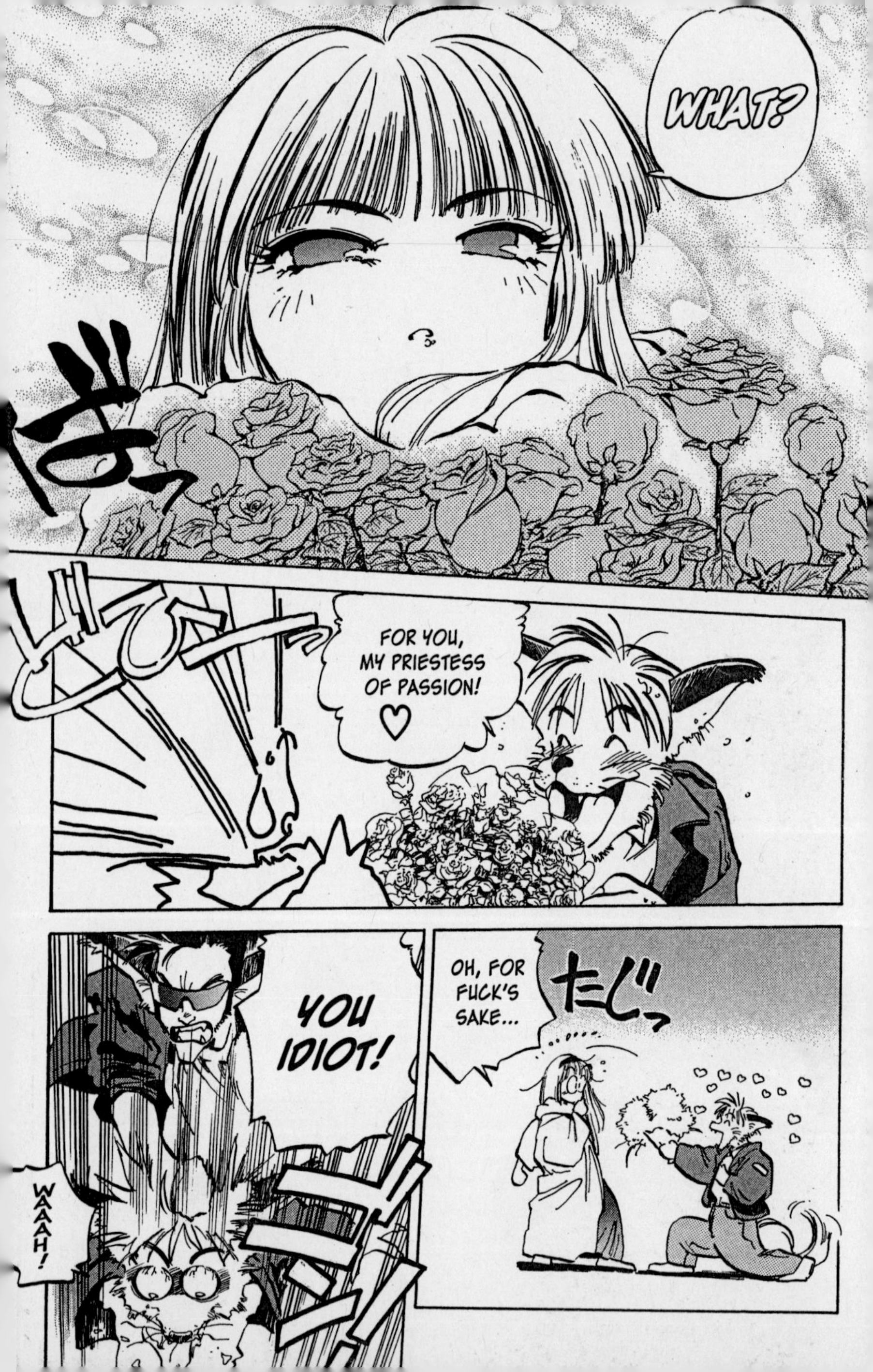
WHAT?
FOR YOU, MY PRIESTESS OF PASSION! ♡
OH, FOR FUCK'S SAKE...
YOU IDIOT!
WAAAH!

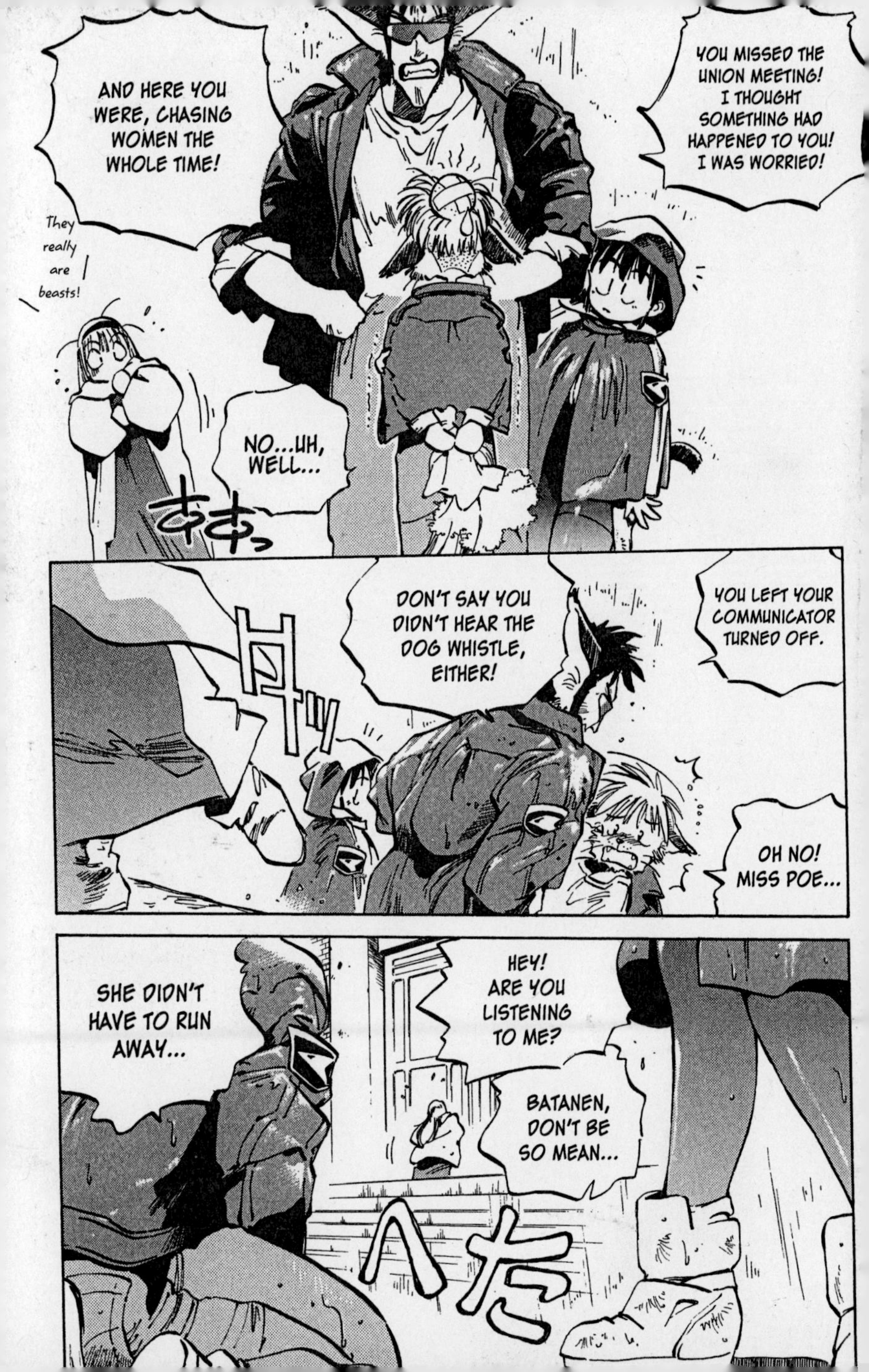
YOU MISSED THE UNION MEETING! I THOUGHT SOMETHING HAD HAPPENED TO YOU! I WAS WORRIED!
AND HERE YOU WERE, CHASING WOMEN THE WHOLE TIME!
They really are beasts!
NO...UH, WELL...
YOU LEFT YOUR COMMUNICATOR TURNED OFF.
DON'T SAY YOU DIDN'T HEAR THE DOG WHISTLE, EITHER!
ハッ
OH NO! MISS POE...
HEY! ARE YOU LISTENING TO ME?
BATANEN, DON'T BE SO MEAN...
へた
SHE DIDN'T HAVE TO RUN AWAY...

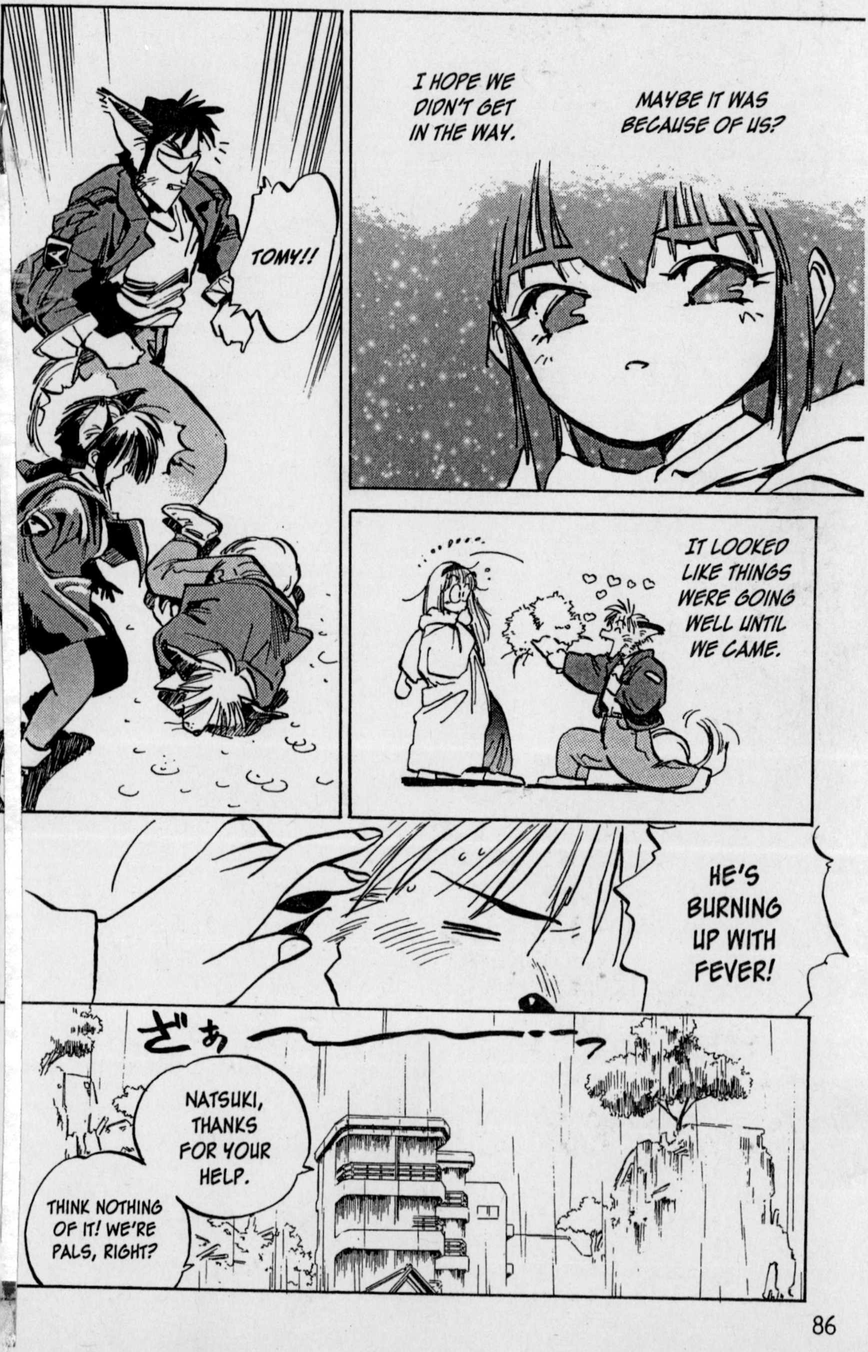
MAYBE IT WAS BECAUSE OF US?
I HOPE WE DIDN'T GET IN THE WAY.
IT LOOKED LIKE THINGS WERE GOING WELL UNTIL WE CAME.
TOMY!!
HE'S BURNING UP WITH FEVER!
ざぁーーーっ
NATSUKI, THANKS FOR YOUR HELP.
THINK NOTHING OF IT! WE'RE PALS, RIGHT?

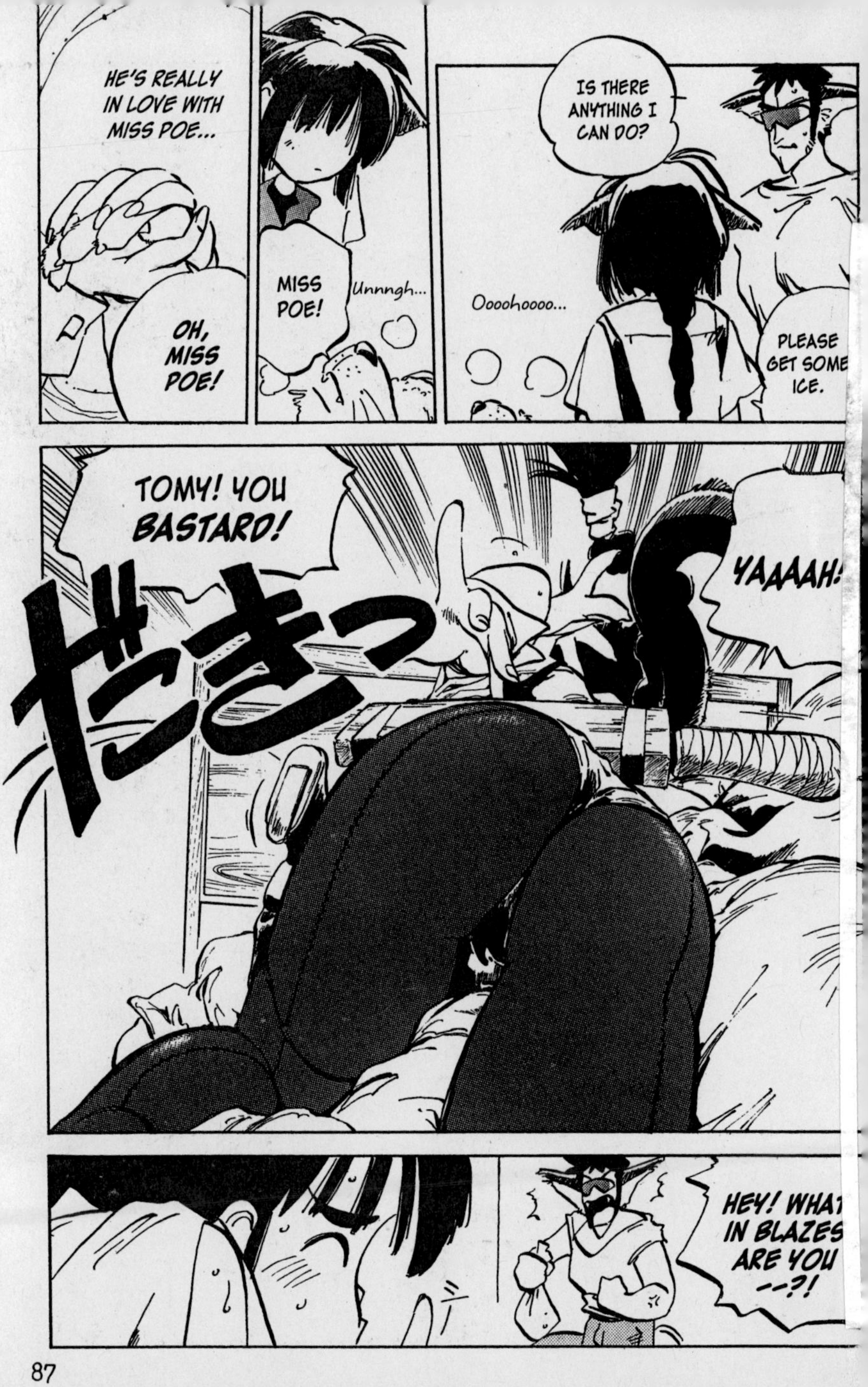
IS THERE ANYTHING I CAN DO?
PLEASE GET SOME ICE.
Ooooh oooo...
MISS POE!
Unnngh...
HE'S REALLY IN LOVE WITH MISS POE...
OH, MISS POE!
YAAAAH!
TOMY! YOU BASTARD!
だきっ
HEY! WHAT IN BLAZES ARE YOU --?!

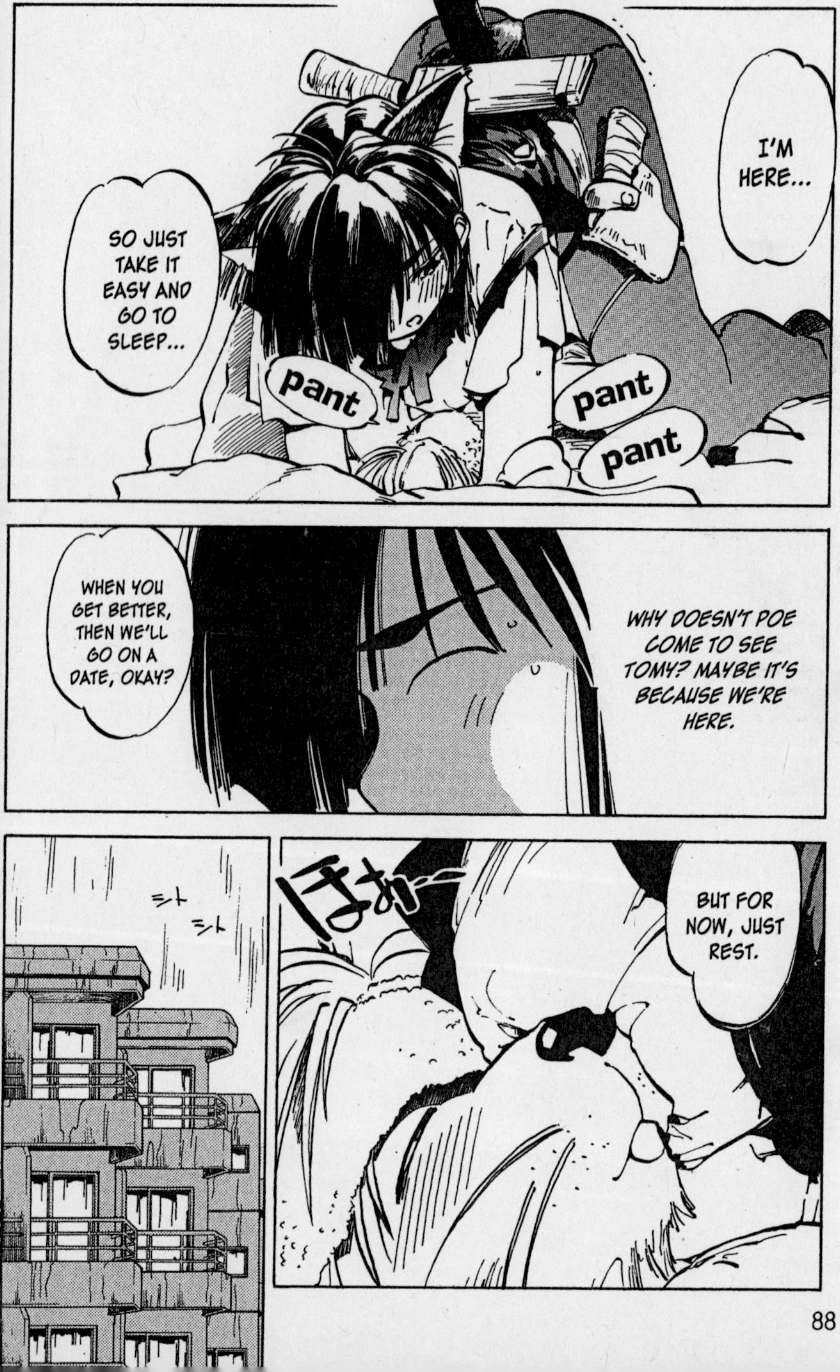
I'M HERE...
SO JUST TAKE IT EASY AND GO TO SLEEP...
pant
pant
pant
WHY DOESN'T POE COME TO SEE TOMY? MAYBE IT'S BECAUSE WE'RE HERE.
WHEN YOU GET BETTER, THEN WE'LL GO ON A DATE, OKAY?
BUT FOR NOW, JUST REST.
シト
シト

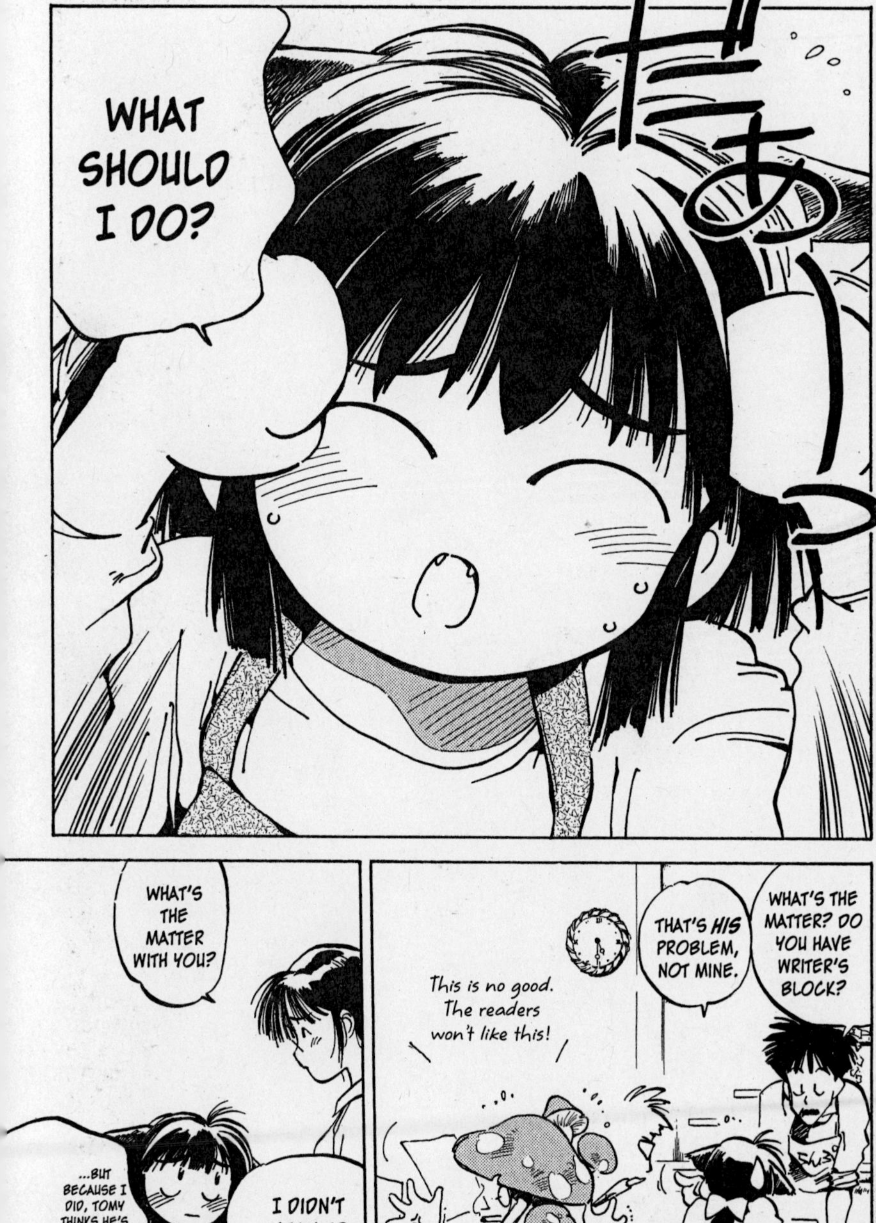
だあ〜っ?
WHAT SHOULD I DO?
WHAT'S THE MATTER? DO YOU HAVE WRITER'S BLOCK?
THAT'S *HIS* PROBLEM, NOT MINE.
This is no good. The readers won't like this!
WHAT'S THE MATTER WITH YOU?
I DIDN'T MEAN TO LIE...
...BUT BECAUSE I DID, TOMY THINKS HE'S GOING ON A DATE WITH POE!

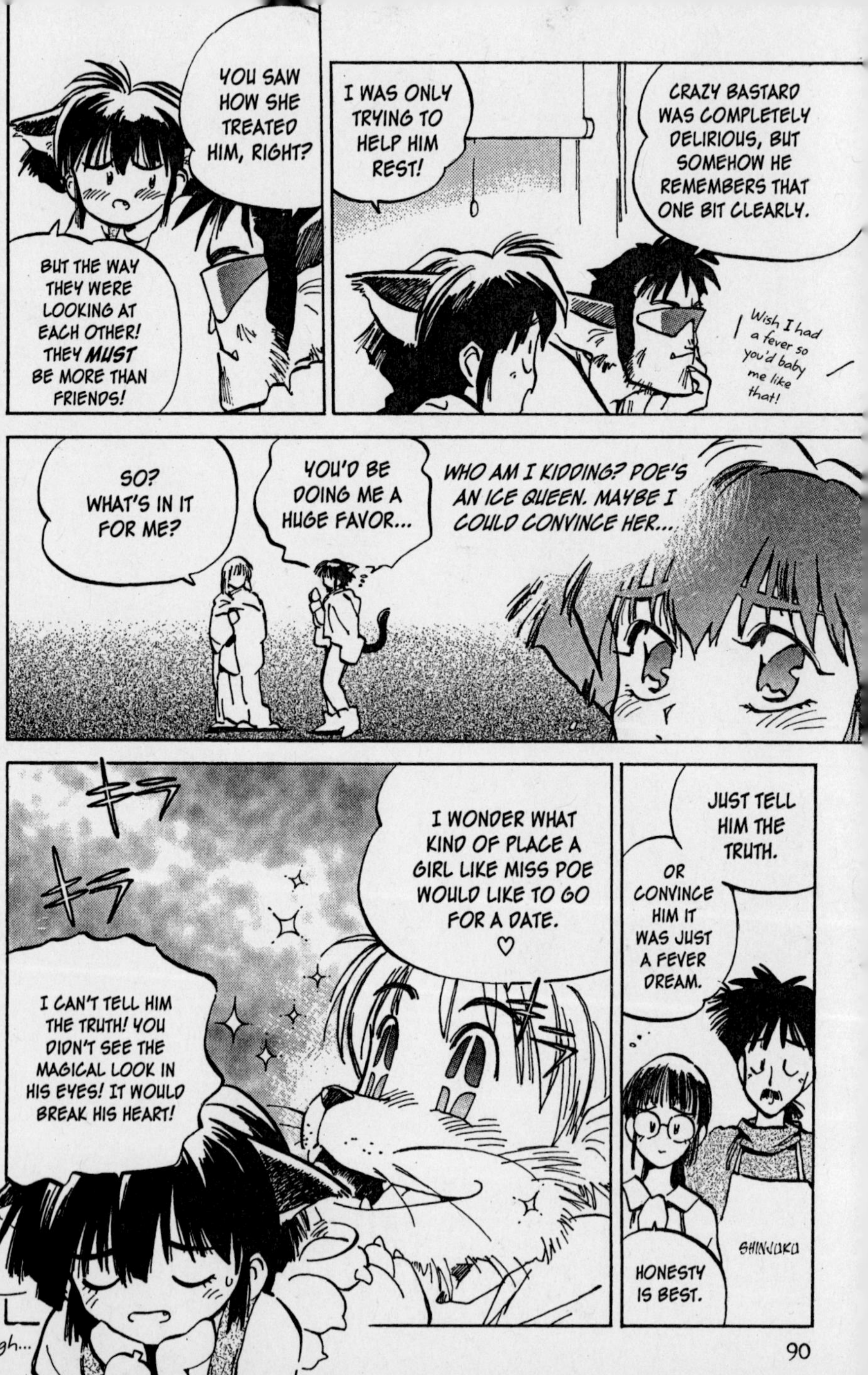
CRAZY BASTARD WAS COMPLETELY DELIRIOUS, BUT SOMEHOW HE REMEMBERS THAT ONE BIT CLEARLY.
I WAS ONLY TRYING TO HELP HIM REST!
Wish I had a fever so you'd baby me like that!
YOU SAW HOW SHE TREATED HIM, RIGHT?
BUT THE WAY THEY WERE LOOKING AT EACH OTHER! THEY *MUST* BE MORE THAN FRIENDS!
WHO AM I KIDDING? POE'S AN ICE QUEEN. MAYBE I COULD CONVINCE HER...
YOU'D BE DOING ME A HUGE FAVOR...
SO? WHAT'S IN IT FOR ME?
JUST TELL HIM THE TRUTH.
OR CONVINCE HIM IT WAS JUST A FEVER DREAM.
SHINJUKU
HONESTY IS BEST.
I WONDER WHAT KIND OF PLACE A GIRL LIKE MISS POE WOULD LIKE TO GO FOR A DATE. ♡
I CAN'T TELL HIM THE TRUTH! YOU DIDN'T SEE THE MAGICAL LOOK IN HIS EYES! IT WOULD BREAK HIS HEART!
Sigh...

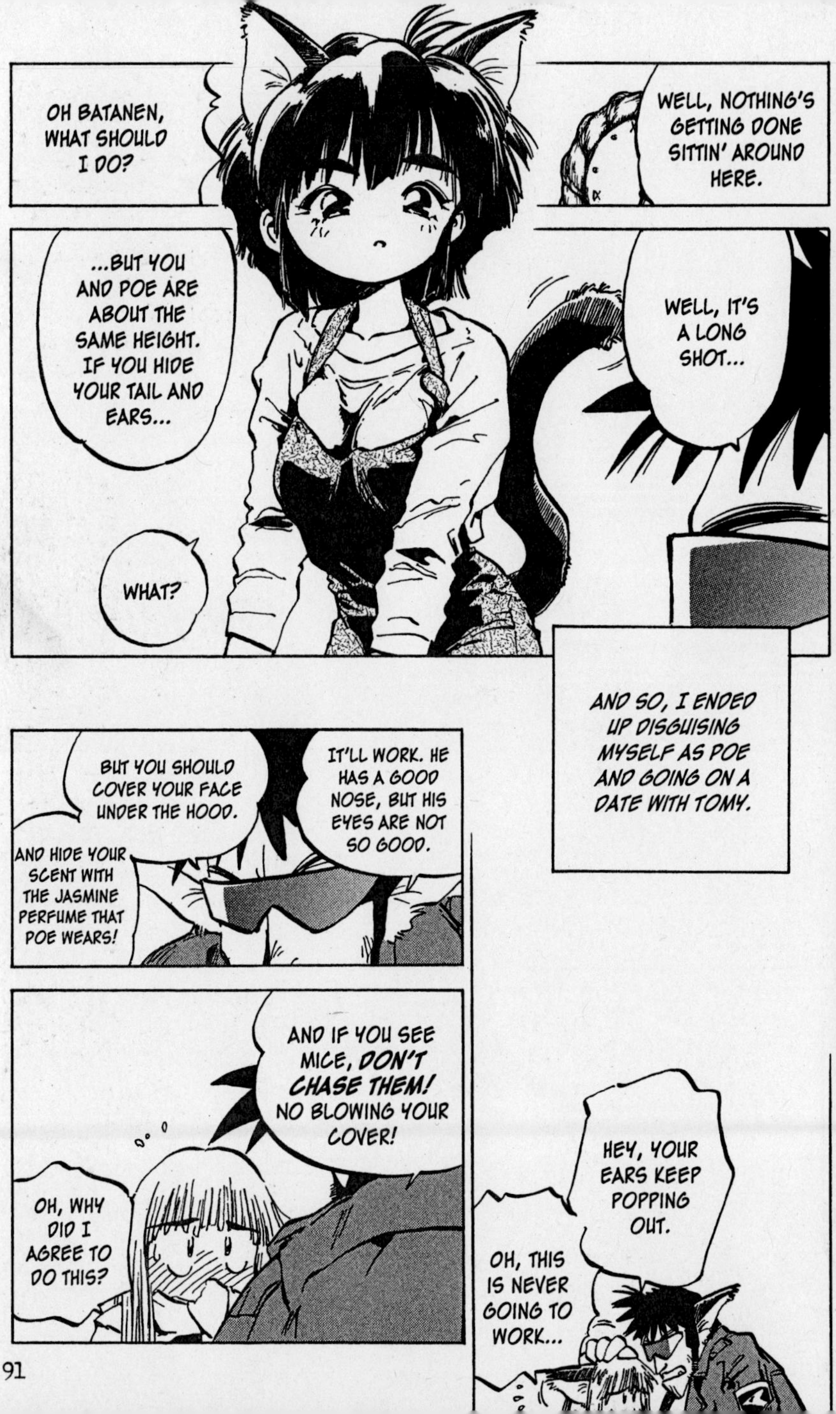
WELL, NOTHING'S GETTING DONE SITTIN' AROUND HERE.
OH BATANEN, WHAT SHOULD I DO?
WELL, IT'S A LONG SHOT...
...BUT YOU AND POE ARE ABOUT THE SAME HEIGHT. IF YOU HIDE YOUR TAIL AND EARS...
WHAT?
AND SO, I ENDED UP DISGUISING MYSELF AS POE AND GOING ON A DATE WITH TOMY.
IT'LL WORK. HE HAS A GOOD NOSE, BUT HIS EYES ARE NOT SO GOOD.
BUT YOU SHOULD COVER YOUR FACE UNDER THE HOOD.
AND HIDE YOUR SCENT WITH THE JASMINE PERFUME THAT POE WEARS!
AND IF YOU SEE MICE, DON'T CHASE THEM! NO BLOWING YOUR COVER!
OH, WHY DID I AGREE TO DO THIS?
HEY, YOUR EARS KEEP POPPING OUT.
OH, THIS IS NEVER GOING TO WORK...

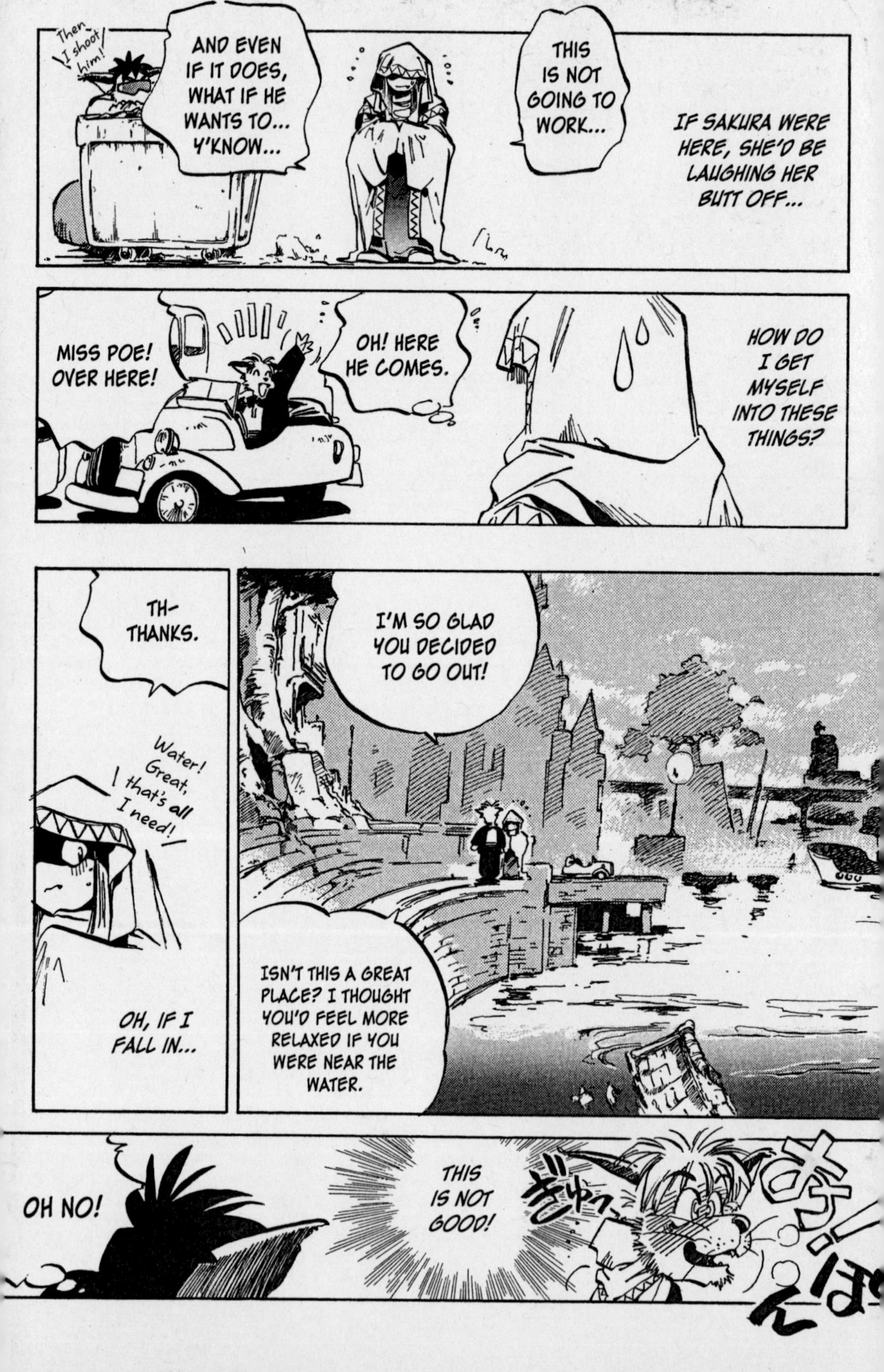
IF SAKURA WERE HERE, SHE'D BE LAUGHING HER BUTT OFF...
THIS IS NOT GOING TO WORK...
AND EVEN IF IT DOES, WHAT IF HE WANTS TO... Y'KNOW...
Then I shoot him!
HOW DO I GET MYSELF INTO THESE THINGS?
OH! HERE HE COMES.
MISS POE! OVER HERE!
I'M SO GLAD YOU DECIDED TO GO OUT!
ISN'T THIS A GREAT PLACE? I THOUGHT YOU'D FEEL MORE RELAXED IF YOU WERE NEAR THE WATER.
TH-THANKS.
Water! Great, that's all I need!
OH, IF I FALL IN...
THIS IS NOT GOOD!
OH NO!

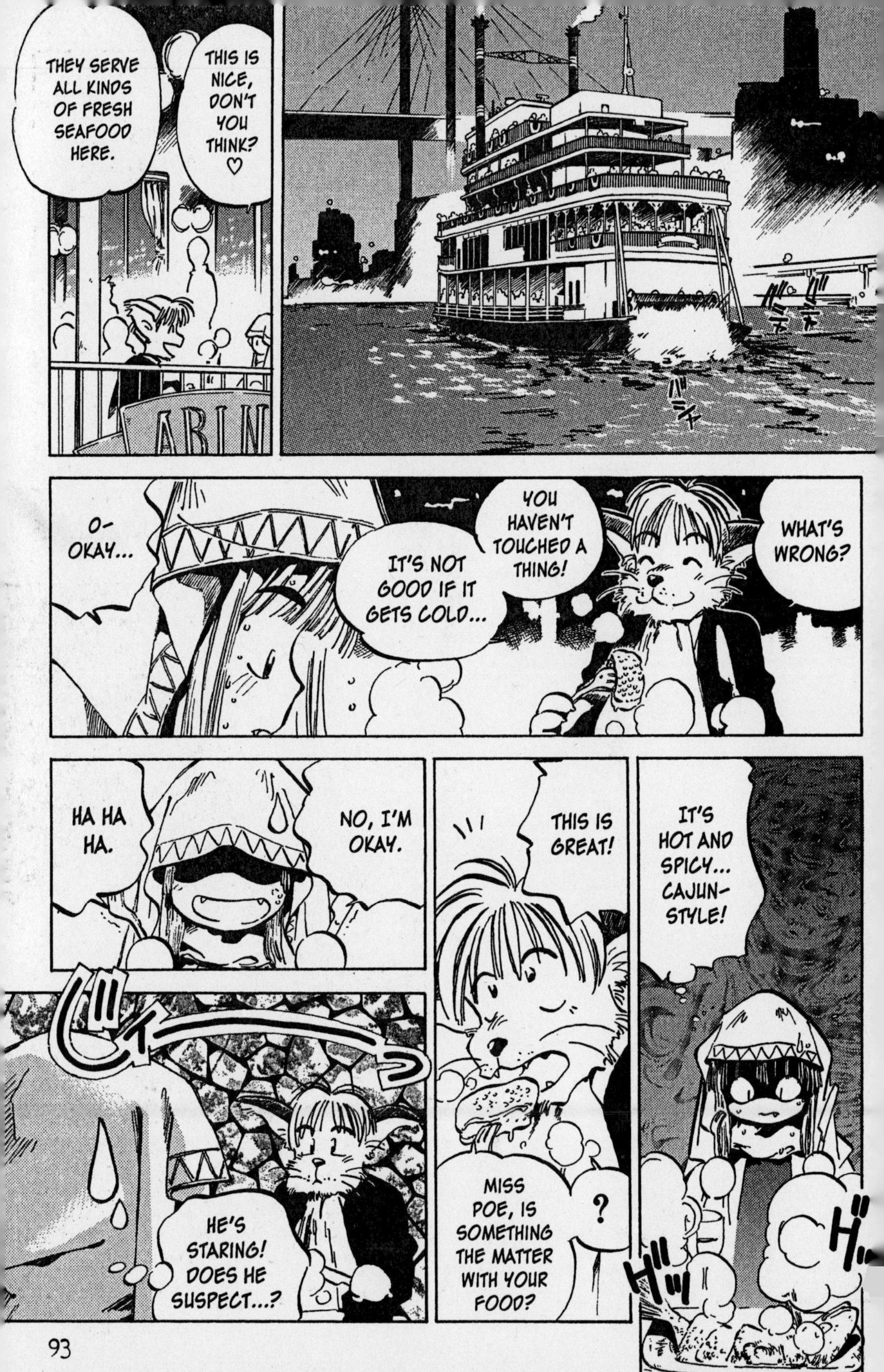
THIS IS NICE, DON'T YOU THINK? ♡
THEY SERVE ALL KINDS OF FRESH SEAFOOD HERE.
WHAT'S WRONG?
YOU HAVEN'T TOUCHED A THING!
IT'S NOT GOOD IF IT GETS COLD...
O- OKAY...
IT'S HOT AND SPICY... CAJUN-STYLE!
THIS IS GREAT!
?
MISS POE, IS SOMETHING THE MATTER WITH YOUR FOOD?
NO, I'M OKAY.
HA HA HA.
HE'S STARING! DOES HE SUSPECT...?

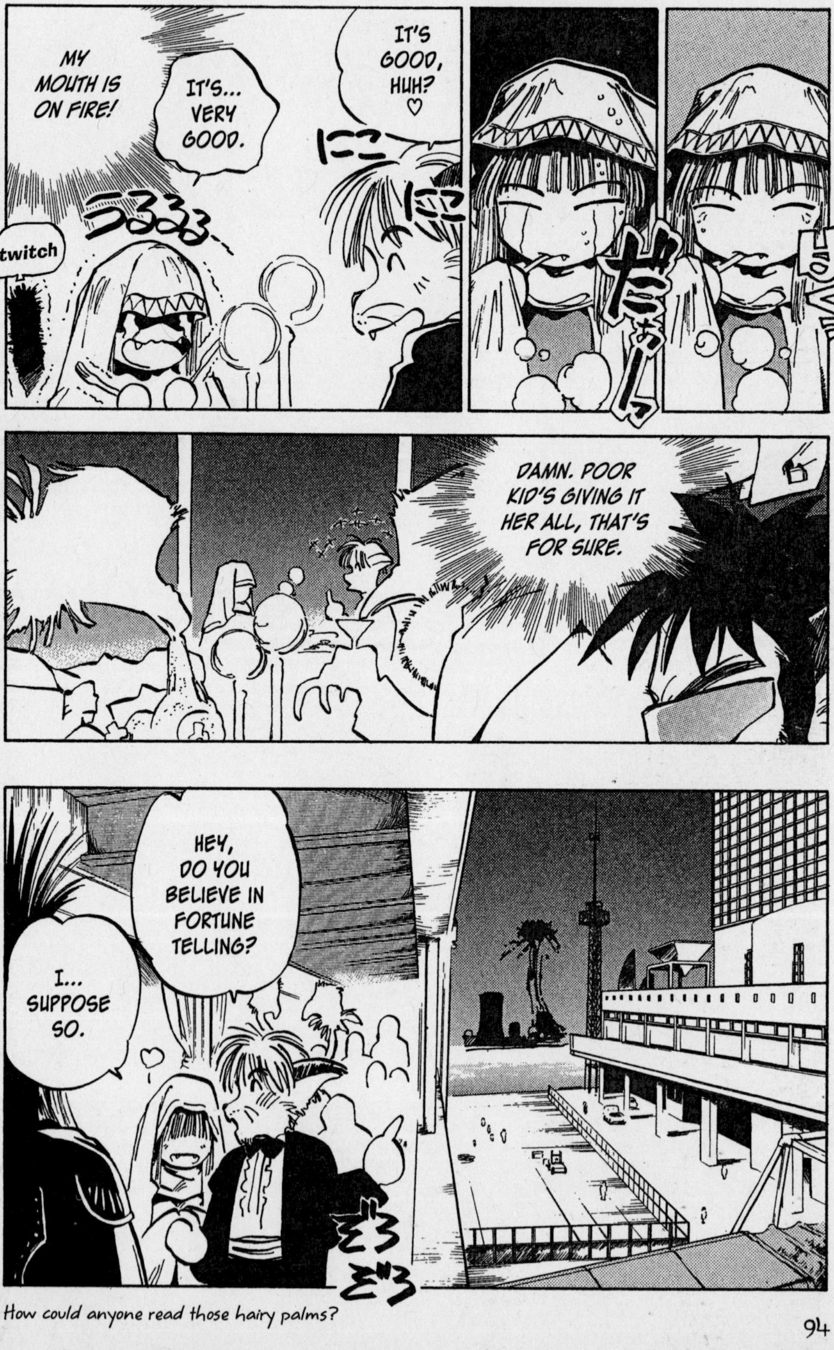
ぱくっ
だあーっ
IT'S GOOD, HUH? ♡
にこ
にこ
IT'S... VERY GOOD.
MY MOUTH IS ON FIRE!
うるるる
twitch
DAMN. POOR KID'S GIVING IT HER ALL, THAT'S FOR SURE.
HEY, DO YOU BELIEVE IN FORTUNE TELLING?
I... SUPPOSE SO.
ぞろ
ぞろ

How could anyone read those hairy palms?

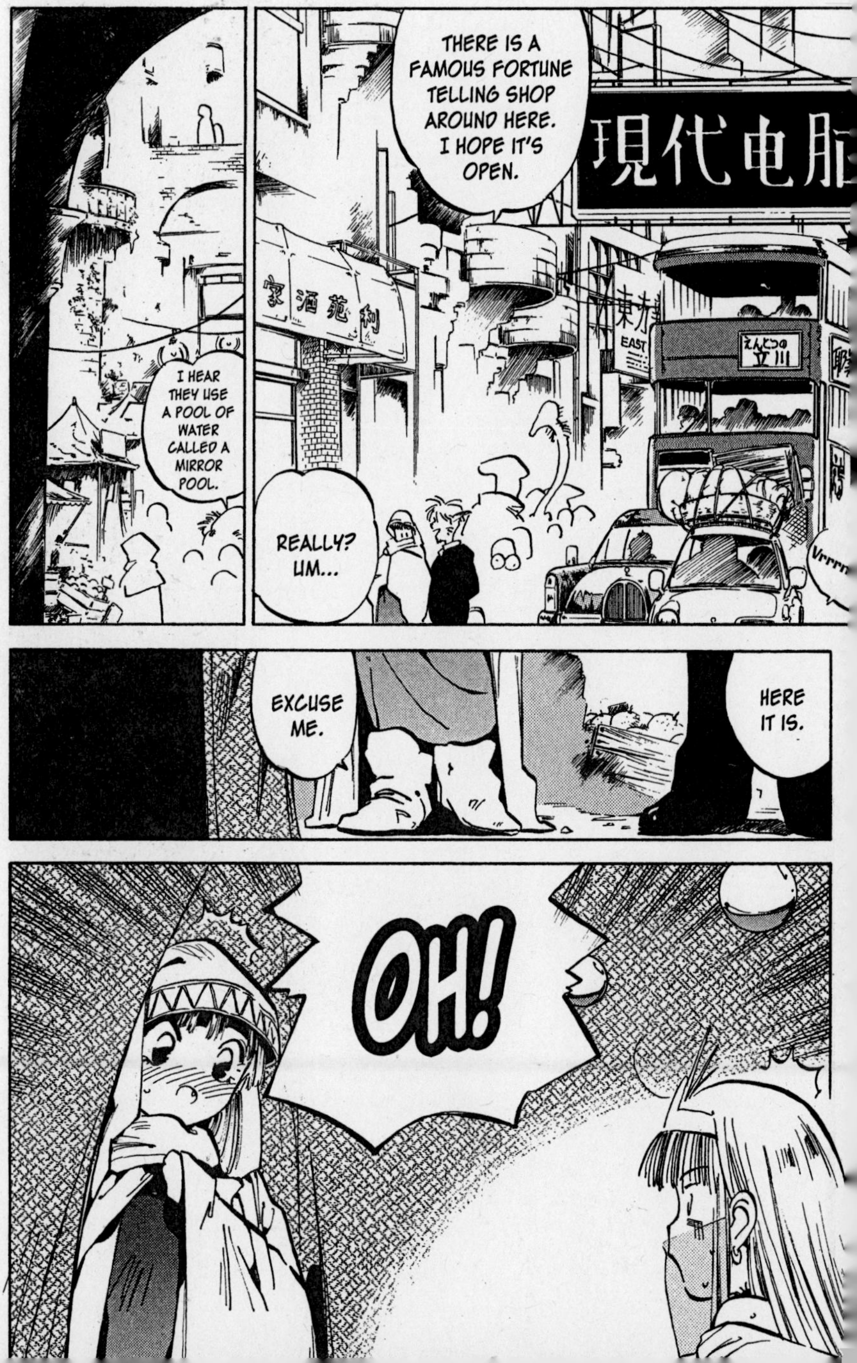

現代电脑
THERE IS A FAMOUS FORTUNE TELLING SHOP AROUND HERE. I HOPE IT'S OPEN.
REALLY? UM...
I HEAR THEY USE A POOL OF WATER CALLED A MIRROR POOL.
HERE IT IS.
EXCUSE ME.
OH!

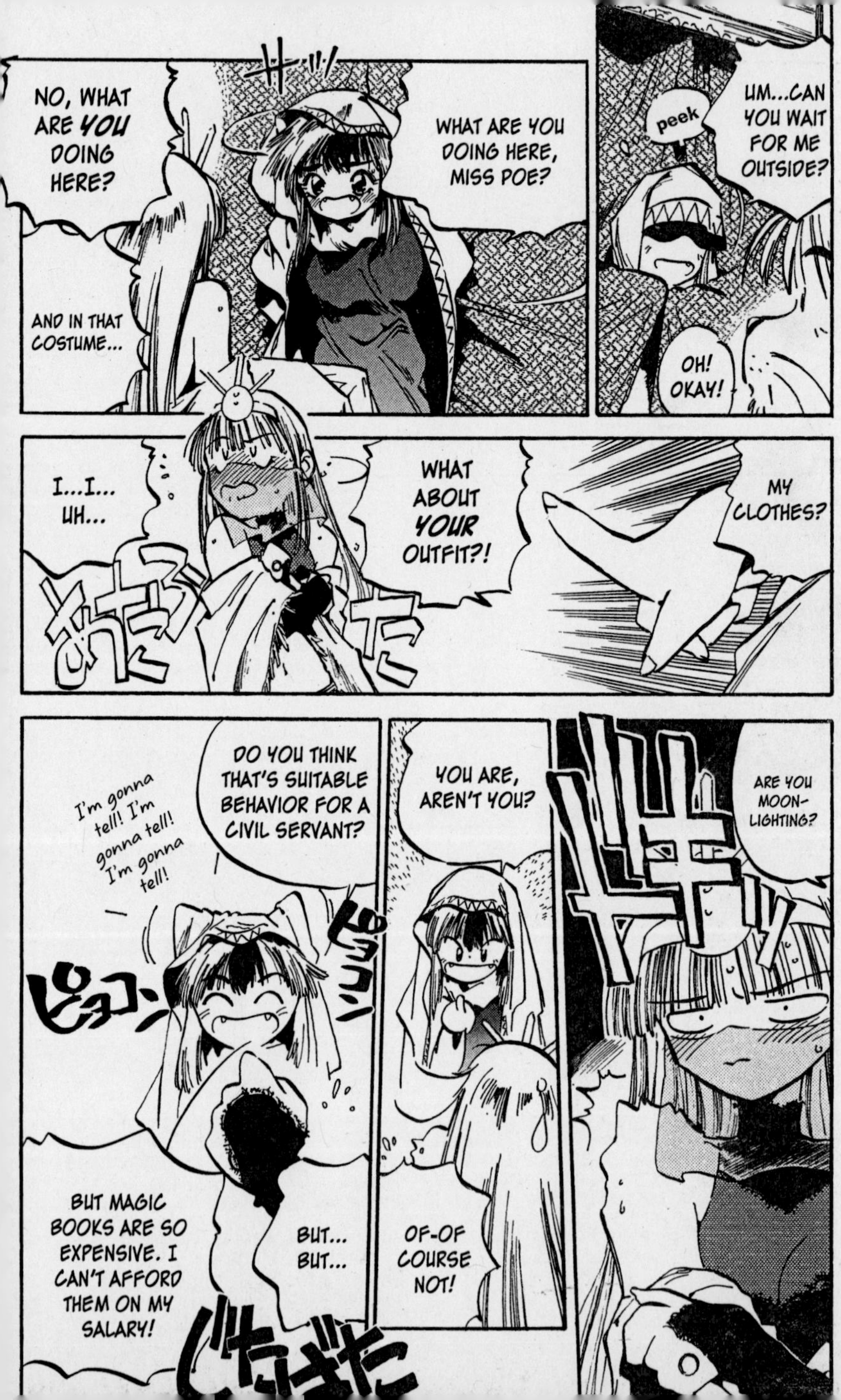
peek
UM...CAN YOU WAIT FOR ME OUTSIDE?
OH! OKAY!
WHAT ARE YOU DOING HERE, MISS POE?
NO, WHAT ARE **YOU** DOING HERE?
AND IN THAT COSTUME...
MY CLOTHES?
WHAT ABOUT **YOUR** OUTFIT?!
I...I... UH...
ARE YOU MOON-LIGHTING?
YOU ARE, AREN'T YOU?
OF-OF COURSE NOT!
DO YOU THINK THAT'S SUITABLE BEHAVIOR FOR A CIVIL SERVANT?
I'm gonna tell! I'm gonna tell! I'm gonna tell!
BUT... BUT...
BUT MAGIC BOOKS ARE SO EXPENSIVE. I CAN'T AFFORD THEM ON MY SALARY!

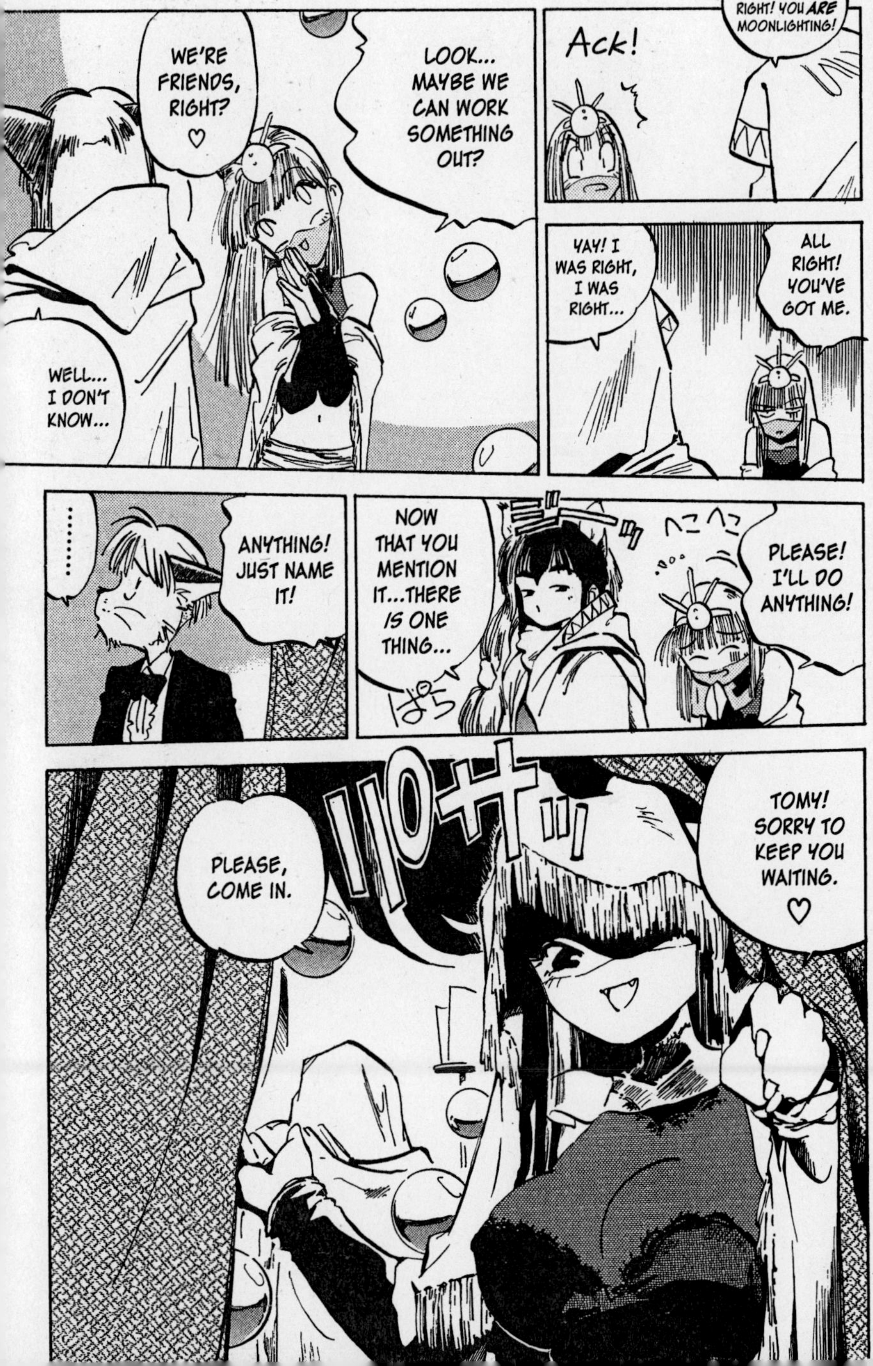
SO I WAS RIGHT! YOU ARE MOONLIGHTING!
Ack!
ALL RIGHT! YOU'VE GOT ME.
YAY! I WAS RIGHT, I WAS RIGHT...
LOOK... MAYBE WE CAN WORK SOMETHING OUT?
WE'RE FRIENDS, RIGHT? ♡
WELL... I DON'T KNOW...
PLEASE! I'LL DO ANYTHING!
NOW THAT YOU MENTION IT...THERE IS ONE THING...
ANYTHING! JUST NAME IT!
......
TOMY! SORRY TO KEEP YOU WAITING. ♡
PLEASE, COME IN.

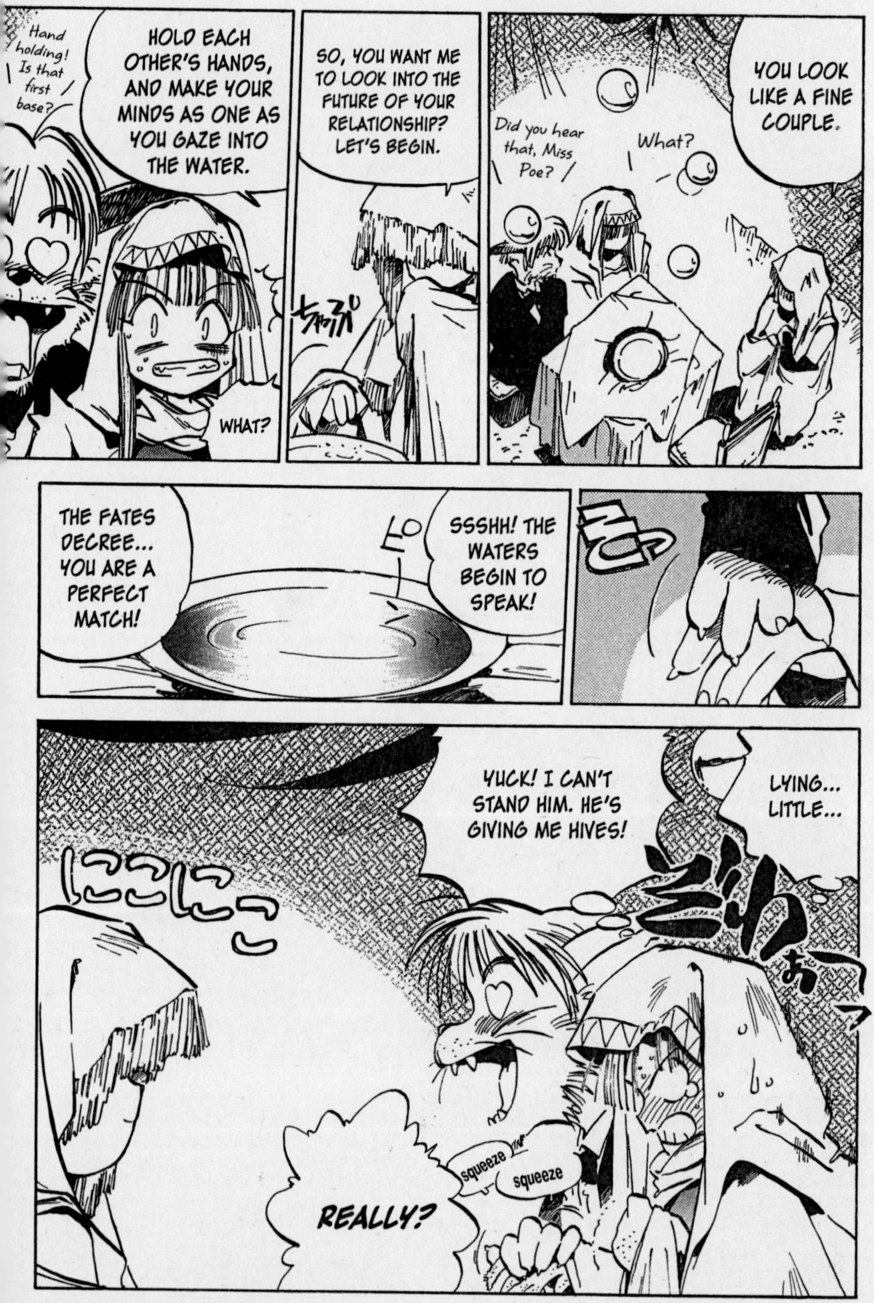
YOU LOOK LIKE A FINE COUPLE.
What?
Did you hear that, Miss Poe?
SO, YOU WANT ME TO LOOK INTO THE FUTURE OF YOUR RELATIONSHIP? LET'S BEGIN.
HOLD EACH OTHER'S HANDS, AND MAKE YOUR MINDS AS ONE AS YOU GAZE INTO THE WATER.
Hand holding! Is that first base?
WHAT?
SSSHH! THE WATERS BEGIN TO SPEAK!
THE FATES DECREE... YOU ARE A PERFECT MATCH!
LYING... LITTLE...
YUCK! I CAN'T STAND HIM. HE'S GIVING ME HIVES!
にこにこ
squeeze
squeeze
REALLY?

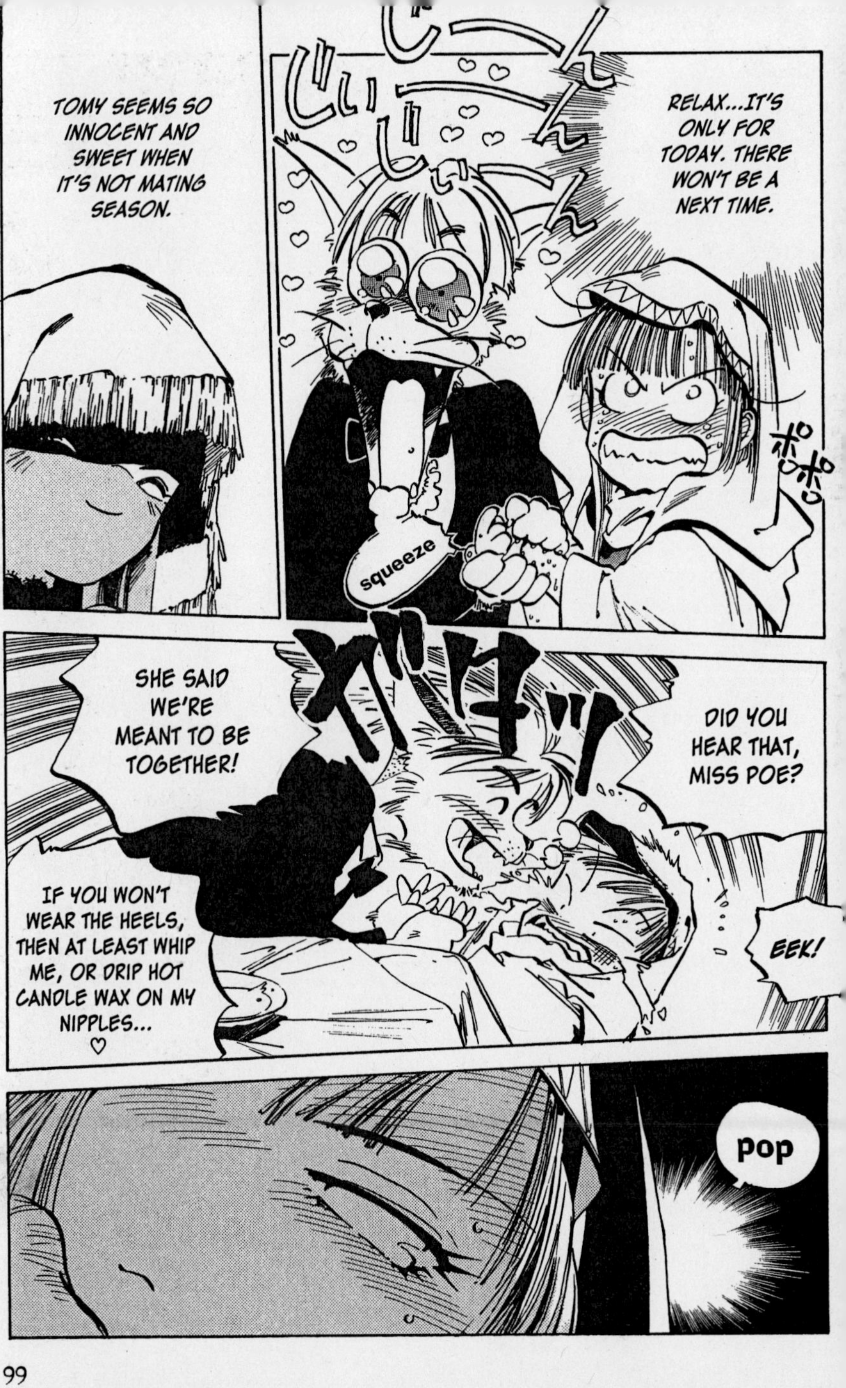
RELAX...IT'S ONLY FOR TODAY. THERE WON'T BE A NEXT TIME.
squeeze
TOMY SEEMS SO INNOCENT AND SWEET WHEN IT'S NOT MATING SEASON.
DID YOU HEAR THAT, MISS POE?
SHE SAID WE'RE MEANT TO BE TOGETHER!
EEK!
IF YOU WON'T WEAR THE HEELS, THEN AT LEAST WHIP ME, OR DRIP HOT CANDLE WAX ON MY NIPPLES... ♡
pop

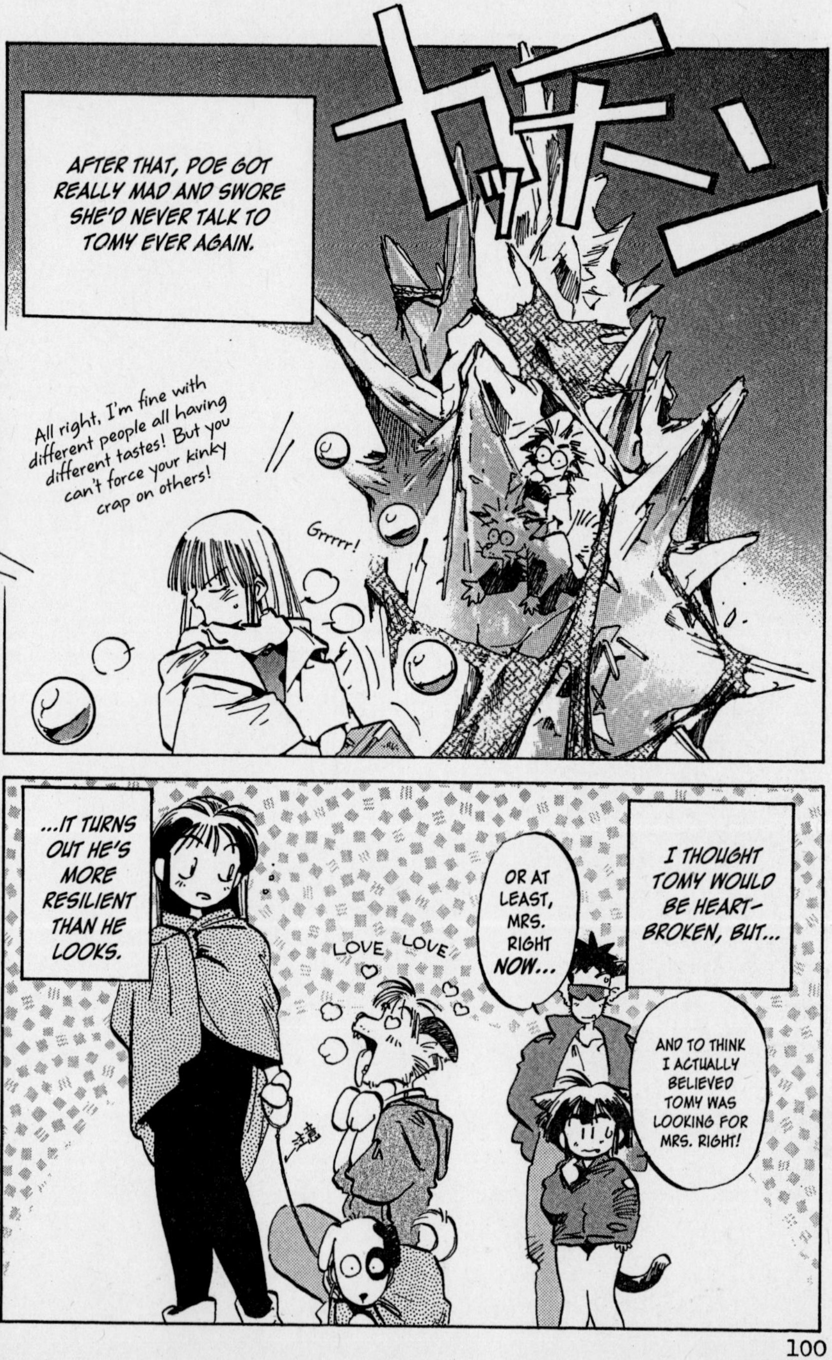

カッチーン
AFTER THAT, POE GOT REALLY MAD AND SWORE SHE'D NEVER TALK TO TOMY EVER AGAIN.
Grrrrr!
All right, I'm fine with different people all having different tastes! But you can't force your kinky crap on others!
I THOUGHT TOMY WOULD BE HEART-BROKEN, BUT...
AND TO THINK I ACTUALLY BELIEVED TOMY WAS LOOKING FOR MRS. RIGHT!
OR AT LEAST, MRS. RIGHT NOW...
LOVE LOVE
...IT TURNS OUT HE'S MORE RESILIENT THAN HE LOOKS.
注意

Report #19
The Bitch is Back

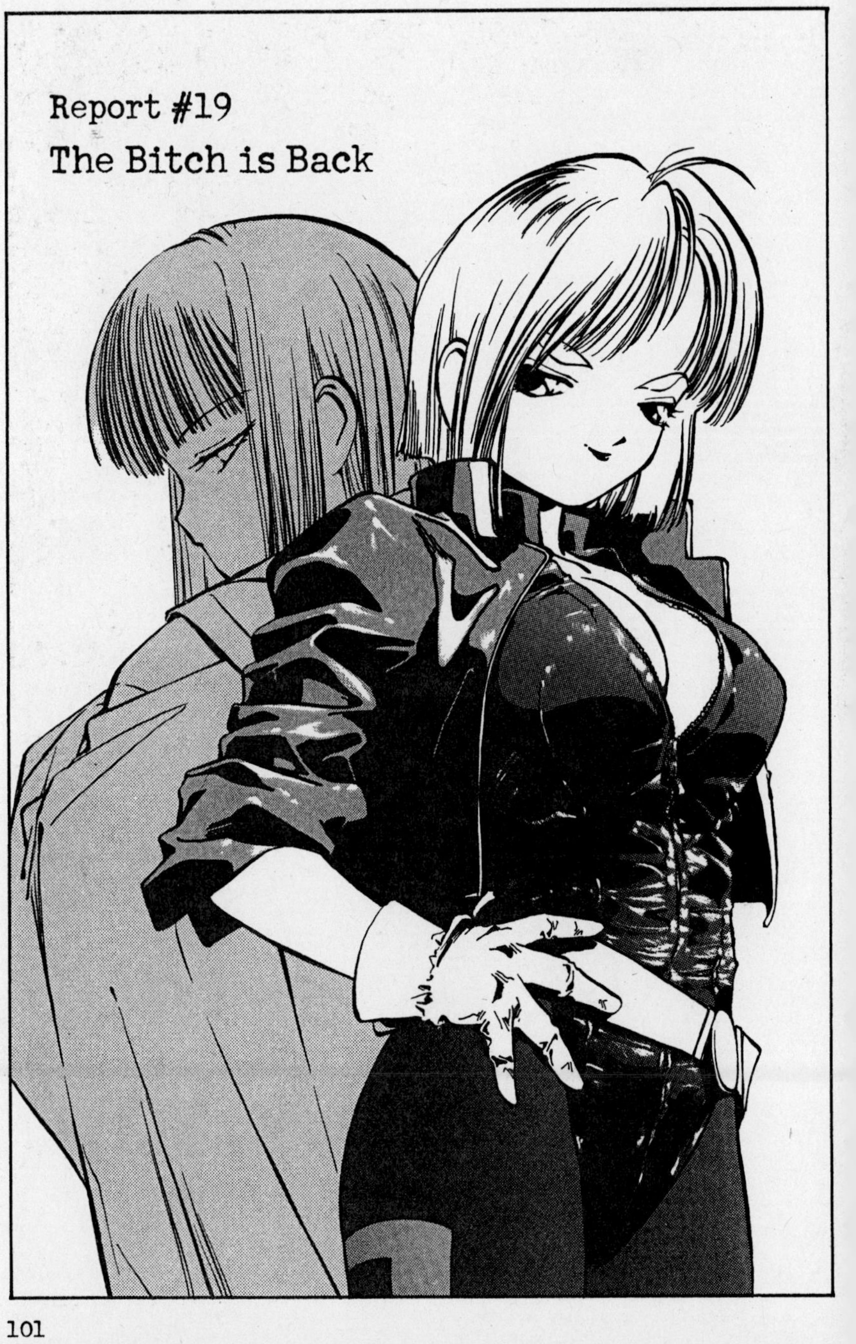

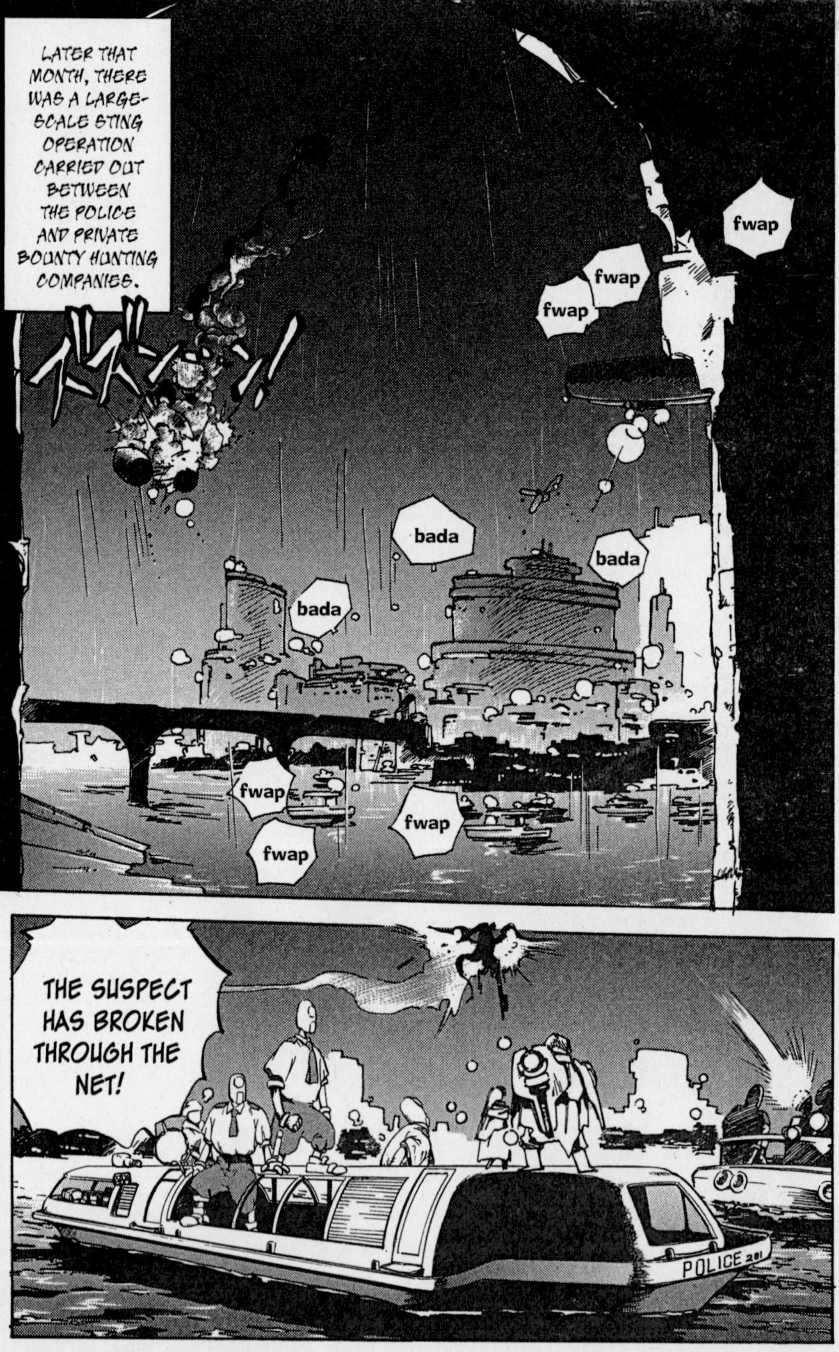
LATER THAT MONTH, THERE WAS A LARGE-SCALE STING OPERATION CARRIED OUT BETWEEN THE POLICE AND PRIVATE BOUNTY HUNTING COMPANIES.
fwap
fwap
fwap
bada
bada
bada
fwap
fwap
fwap
THE SUSPECT HAS BROKEN THROUGH THE NET!
POLICE 281

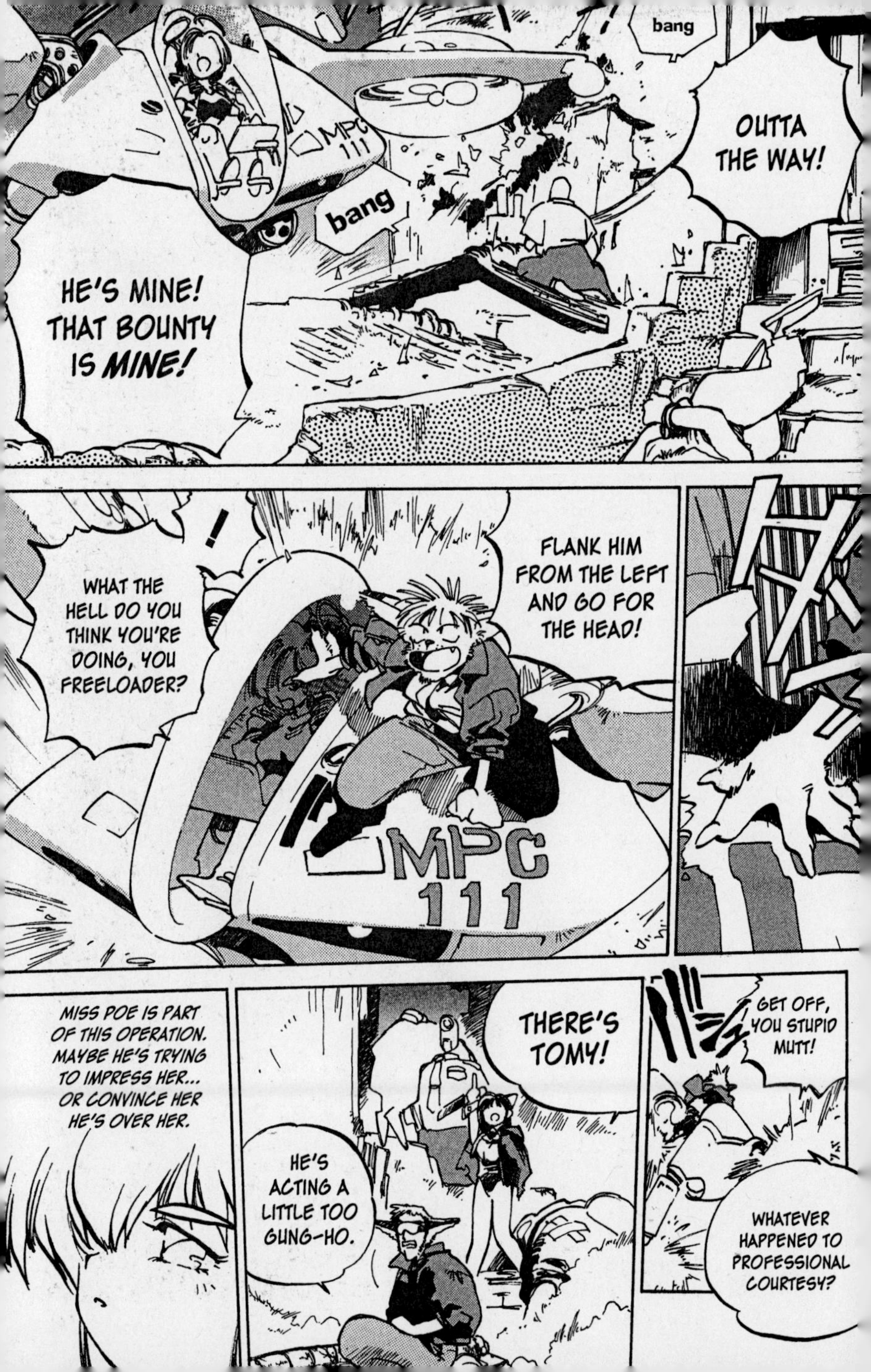
bang
OUTTA THE WAY!
bang
HE'S MINE! THAT BOUNTY IS *MINE!*
FLANK HIM FROM THE LEFT AND GO FOR THE HEAD!
!
WHAT THE HELL DO YOU THINK YOU'RE DOING, YOU FREELOADER?
MPC 111
GET OFF, YOU STUPID MUTT!
WHATEVER HAPPENED TO PROFESSIONAL COURTESY?
THERE'S TOMY!
HE'S ACTING A LITTLE TOO GUNG-HO.
MISS POE IS PART OF THIS OPERATION. MAYBE HE'S TRYING TO IMPRESS HER... OR CONVINCE HER HE'S OVER HER.

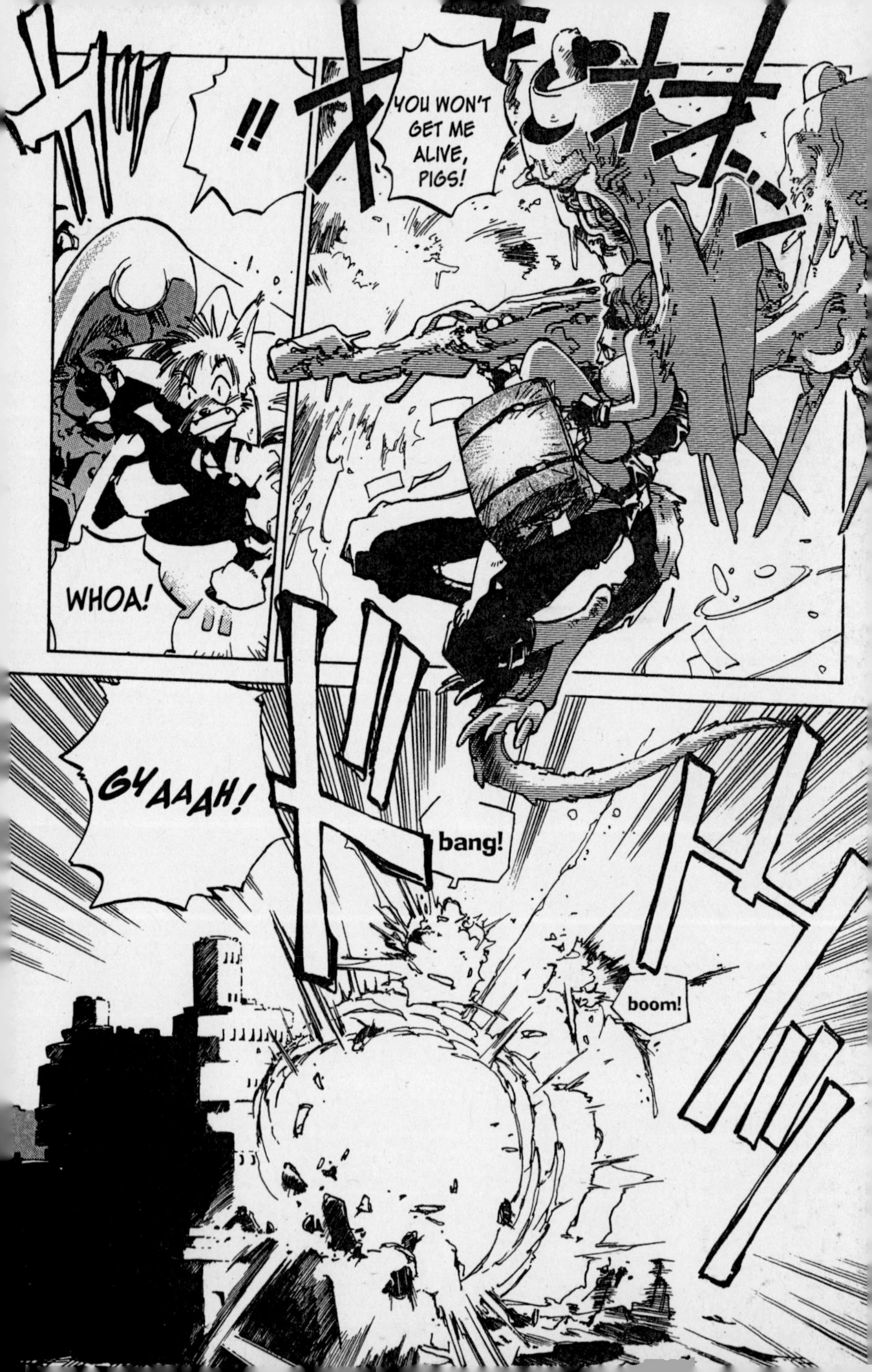
YOU WON'T GET ME ALIVE, PIGS!
!!
WHOA!
GYAAAH!
bang!
boom!

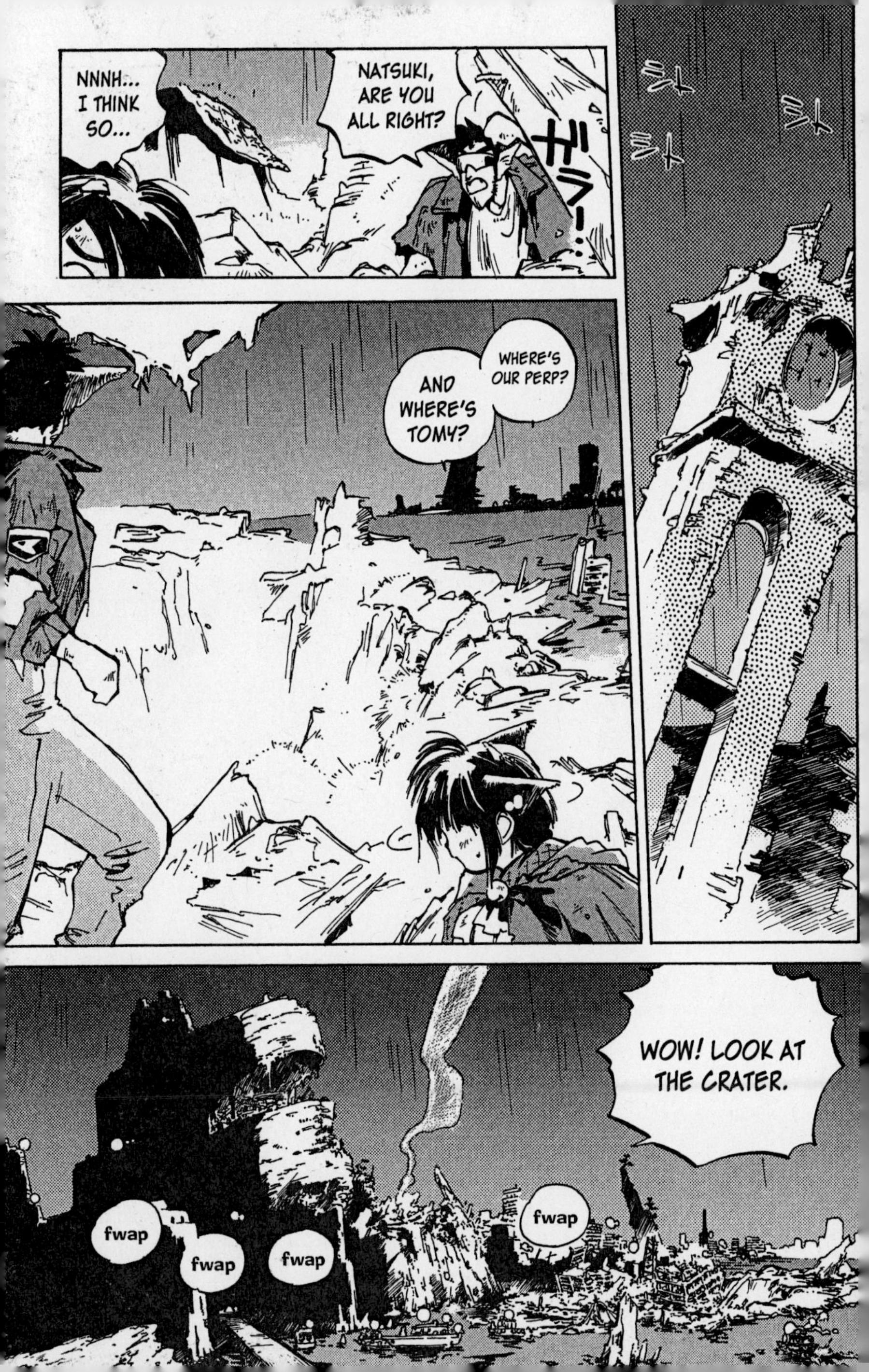
シト
シト
シト
NATSUKI, ARE YOU ALL RIGHT?
ガラー…
NNNH... I THINK SO...
WHERE'S OUR PERP?
AND WHERE'S TOMY?
WOW! LOOK AT THE CRATER.
fwap
fwap
fwap
fwap

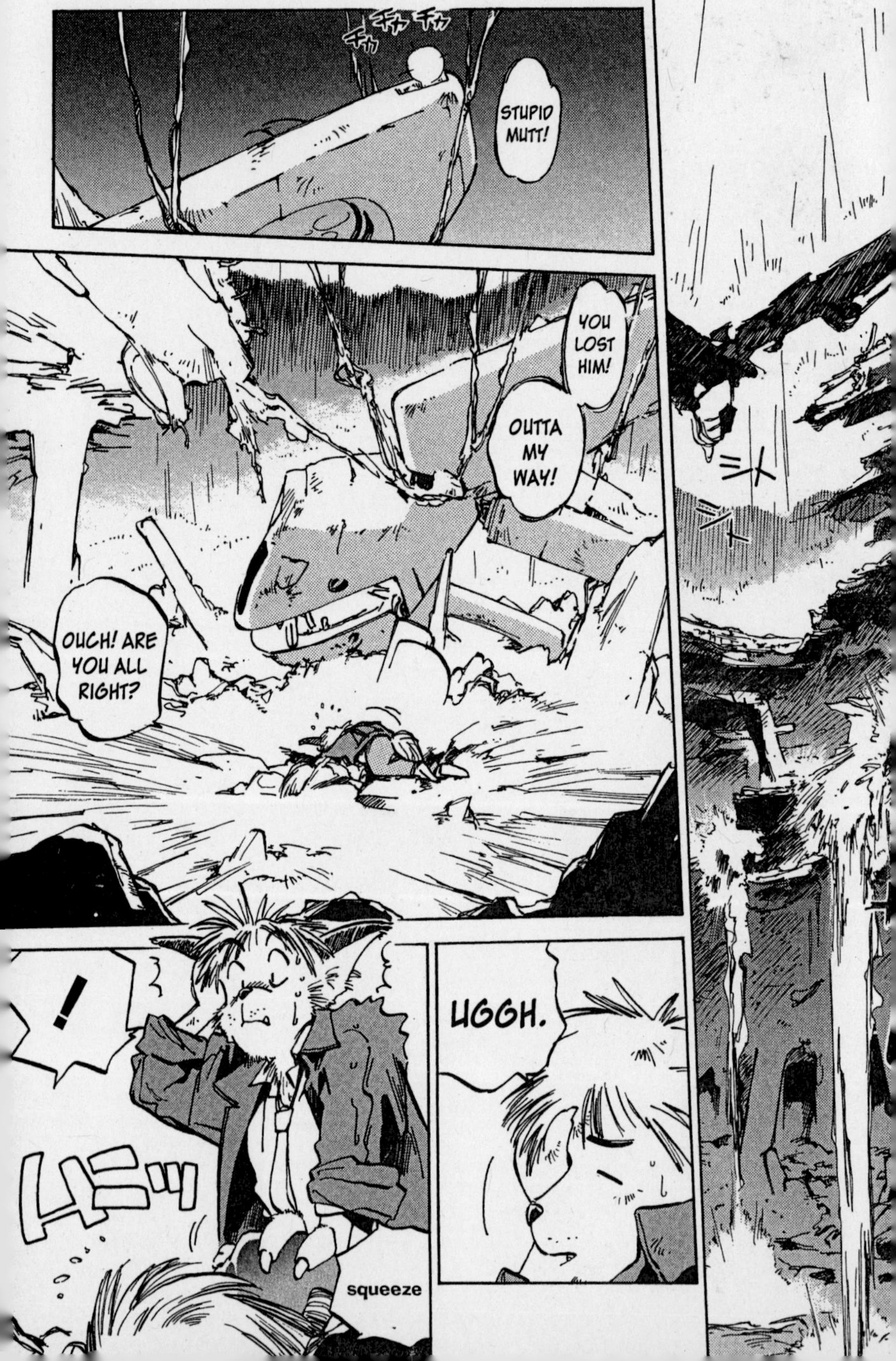
チュ チュ チュ
STUPID MUTT!
YOU LOST HIM!
OUTTA MY WAY!
OUCH! ARE YOU ALL RIGHT?
UGGH.
!
ムニッ
squeeze

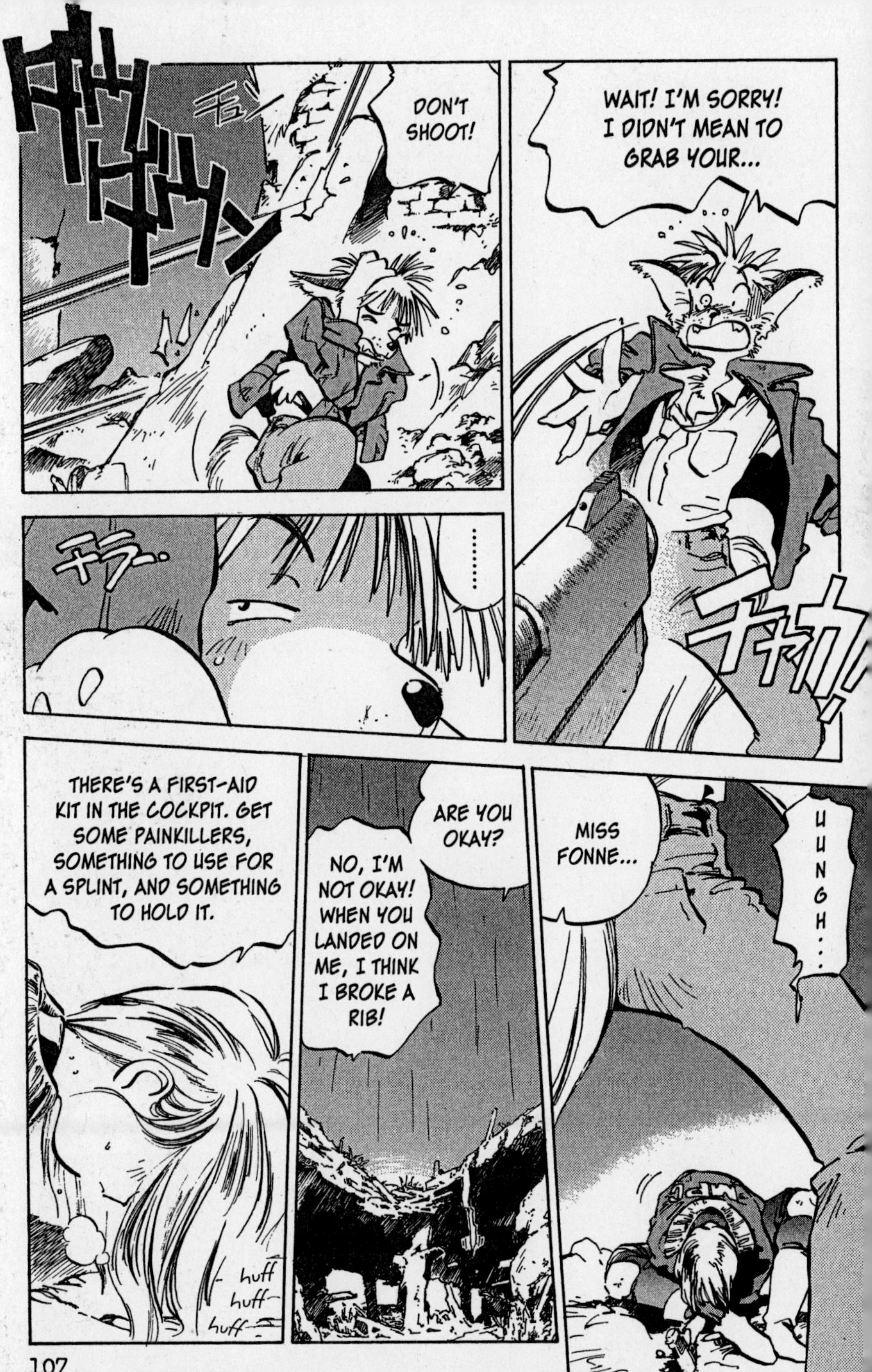
WAIT! I'M SORRY! I DIDN'T MEAN TO GRAB YOUR...
DON'T SHOOT!
......
UUNGH...
MISS FONNE...
ARE YOU OKAY?
NO, I'M NOT OKAY! WHEN YOU LANDED ON ME, I THINK I BROKE A RIB!
THERE'S A FIRST-AID KIT IN THE COCKPIT. GET SOME PAINKILLERS, SOMETHING TO USE FOR A SPLINT, AND SOMETHING TO HOLD IT.
huff huff huff

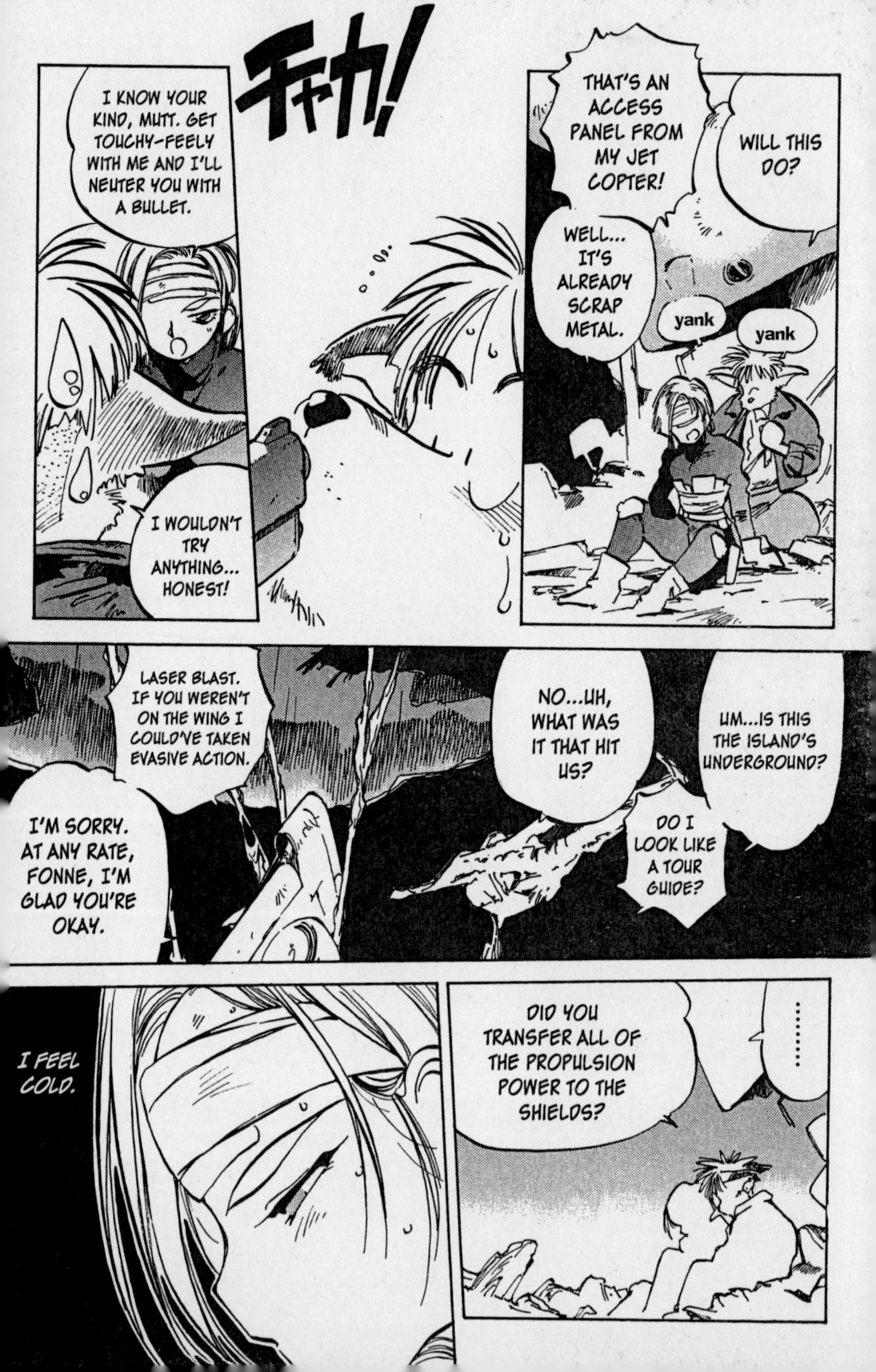
WILL THIS DO?
THAT'S AN ACCESS PANEL FROM MY JET COPTER!
WELL... IT'S ALREADY SCRAP METAL.
yank
yank
チャカ!
I KNOW YOUR KIND, MUTT. GET TOUCHY-FEELY WITH ME AND I'LL NEUTER YOU WITH A BULLET.
I WOULDN'T TRY ANYTHING... HONEST!
UM...IS THIS THE ISLAND'S UNDERGROUND?
DO I LOOK LIKE A TOUR GUIDE?
NO...UH, WHAT WAS IT THAT HIT US?
LASER BLAST. IF YOU WEREN'T ON THE WING I COULD'VE TAKEN EVASIVE ACTION.
I'M SORRY. AT ANY RATE, FONNE, I'M GLAD YOU'RE OKAY.
....
DID YOU TRANSFER ALL OF THE PROPULSION POWER TO THE SHIELDS?
I FEEL COLD.

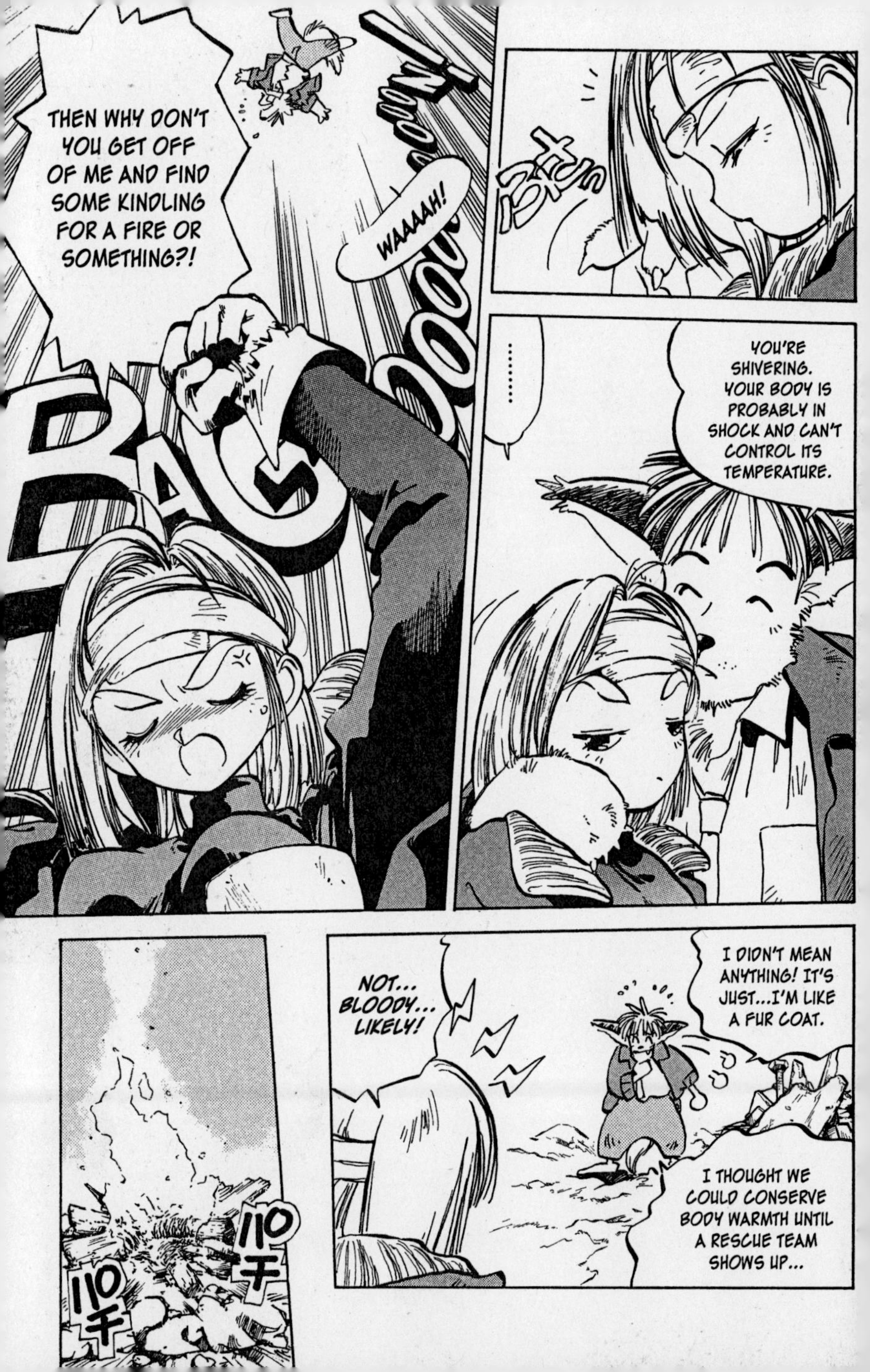
YOU'RE SHIVERING. YOUR BODY IS PROBABLY IN SHOCK AND CAN'T CONTROL ITS TEMPERATURE.
......
THEN WHY DON'T YOU GET OFF OF ME AND FIND SOME KINDLING FOR A FIRE OR SOMETHING?!
DAG
WAAAAH!
NOOOOOOOO!
I DIDN'T MEAN ANYTHING! IT'S JUST...I'M LIKE A FUR COAT.
I THOUGHT WE COULD CONSERVE BODY WARMTH UNTIL A RESCUE TEAM SHOWS UP...
NOT... BLOODY... LIKELY!
パチ
パチ

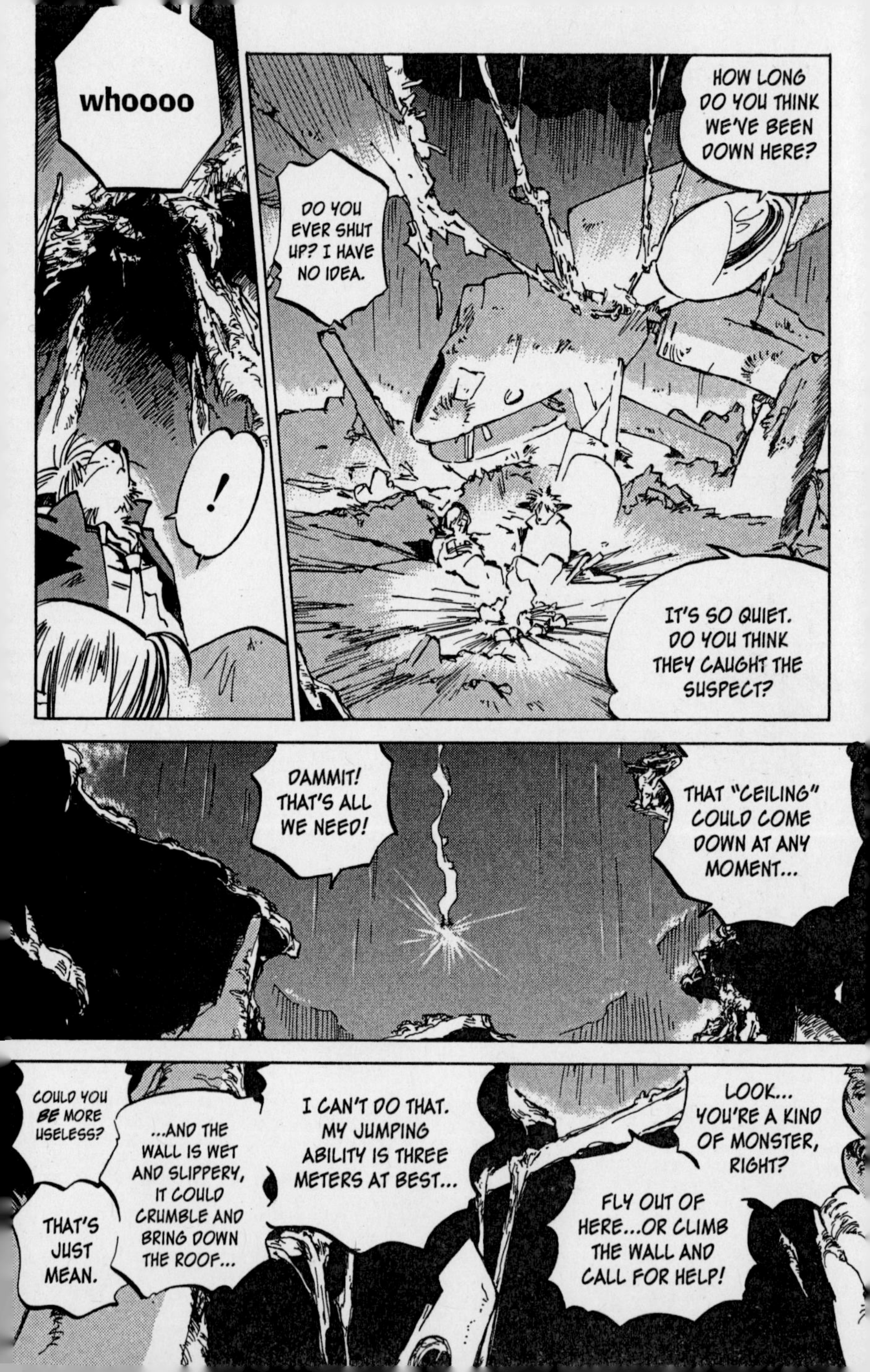
HOW LONG DO YOU THINK WE'VE BEEN DOWN HERE?
DO YOU EVER SHUT UP? I HAVE NO IDEA.
IT'S SO QUIET. DO YOU THINK THEY CAUGHT THE SUSPECT?
whoooo
!
THAT "CEILING" COULD COME DOWN AT ANY MOMENT...
DAMMIT! THAT'S ALL WE NEED!
LOOK... YOU'RE A KIND OF MONSTER, RIGHT?
FLY OUT OF HERE...OR CLIMB THE WALL AND CALL FOR HELP!
I CAN'T DO THAT. MY JUMPING ABILITY IS THREE METERS AT BEST...
...AND THE WALL IS WET AND SLIPPERY, IT COULD CRUMBLE AND BRING DOWN THE ROOF...
COULD YOU *BE* MORE USELESS?
THAT'S JUST MEAN.

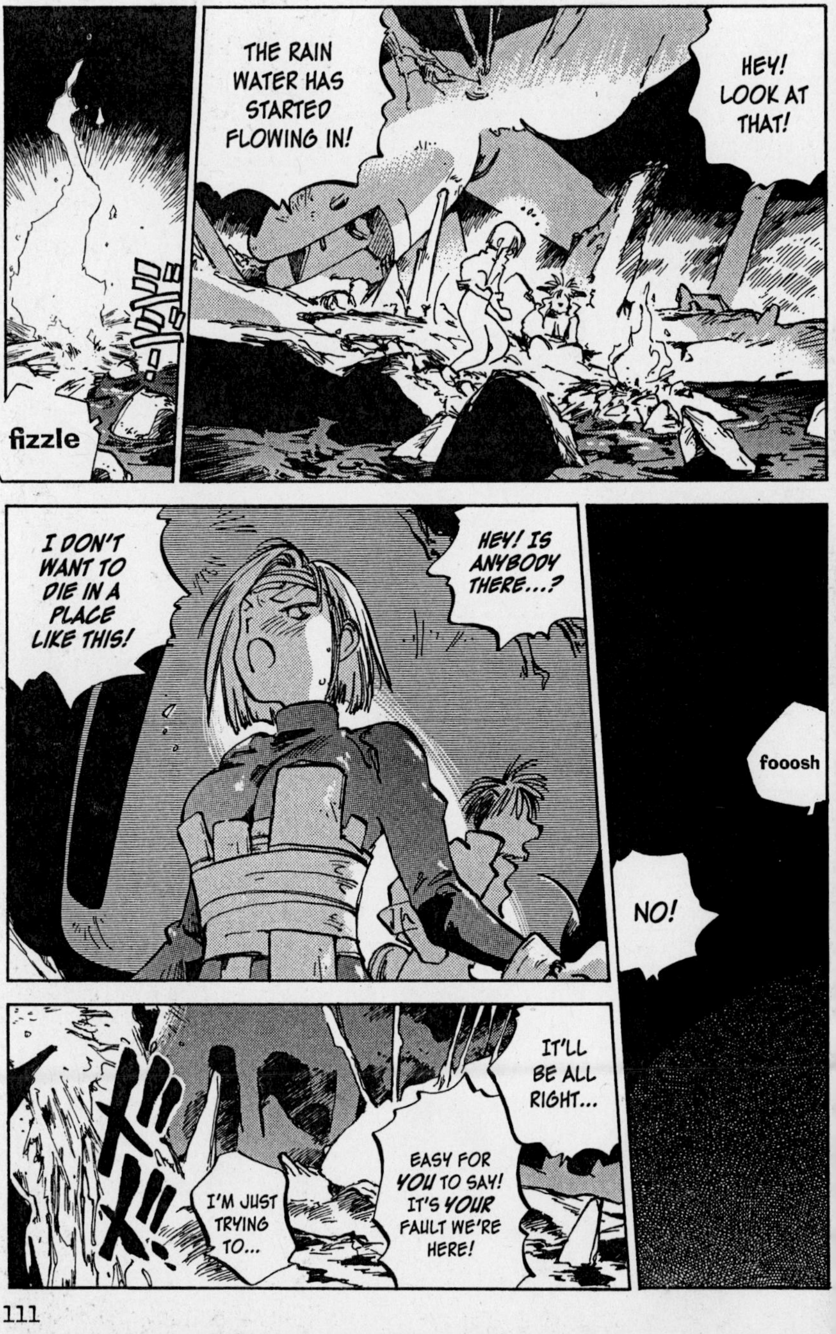
HEY! LOOK AT THAT!
THE RAIN WATER HAS STARTED FLOWING IN!
fizzle
fooosh
NO!
HEY! IS ANYBODY THERE...?
I DON'T WANT TO DIE IN A PLACE LIKE THIS!
IT'LL BE ALL RIGHT...
EASY FOR YOU TO SAY! IT'S YOUR FAULT WE'RE HERE!
I'M JUST TRYING TO...

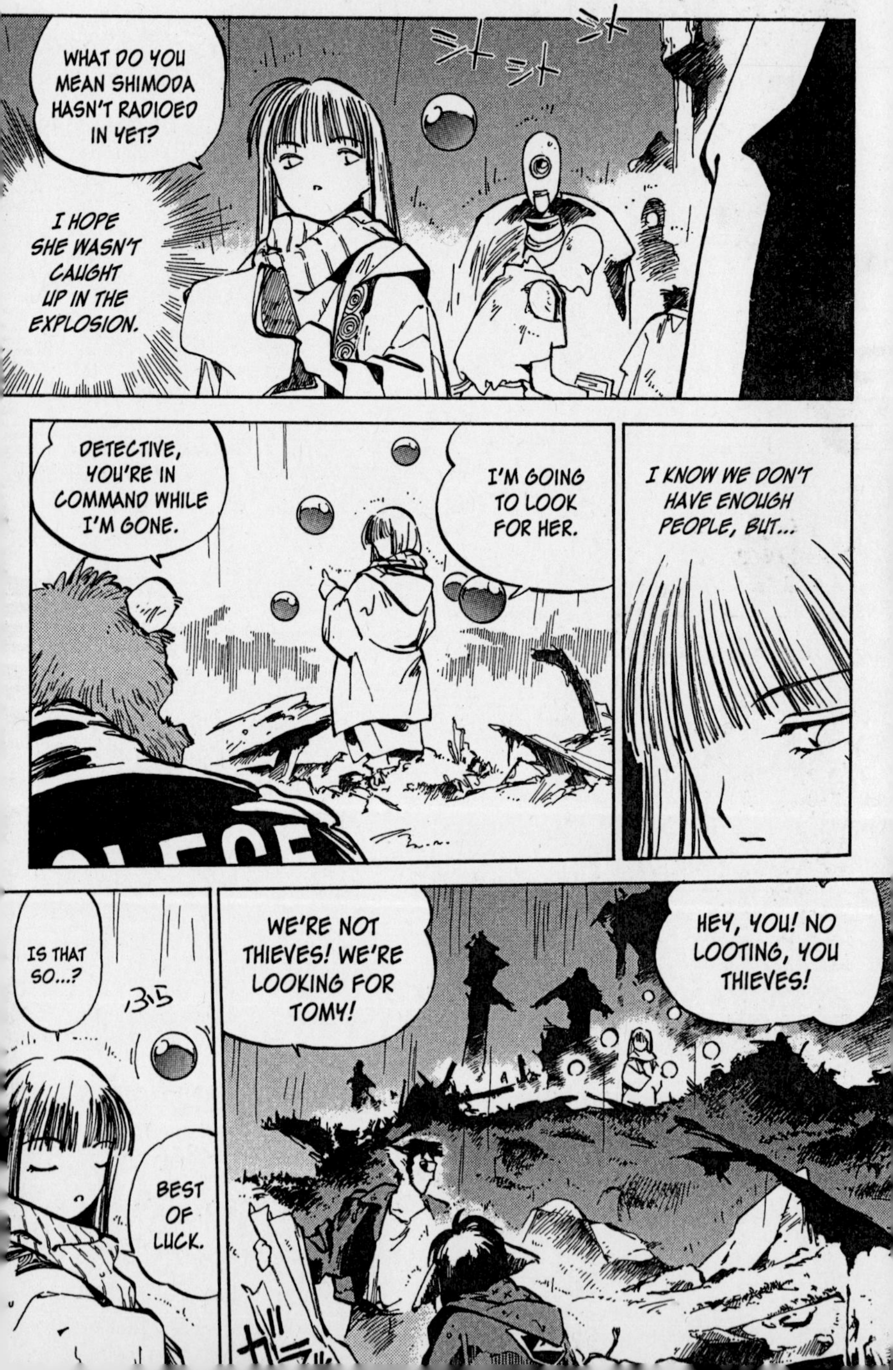
シト シト シト シト
WHAT DO YOU MEAN SHIMODA HASN'T RADIOED IN YET?
I HOPE SHE WASN'T CAUGHT UP IN THE EXPLOSION.
I KNOW WE DON'T HAVE ENOUGH PEOPLE, BUT...
I'M GOING TO LOOK FOR HER.
DETECTIVE, YOU'RE IN COMMAND WHILE I'M GONE.
HEY, YOU! NO LOOTING, YOU THIEVES!
WE'RE NOT THIEVES! WE'RE LOOKING FOR TOMY!
IS THAT SO...?
ふら
BEST OF LUCK.

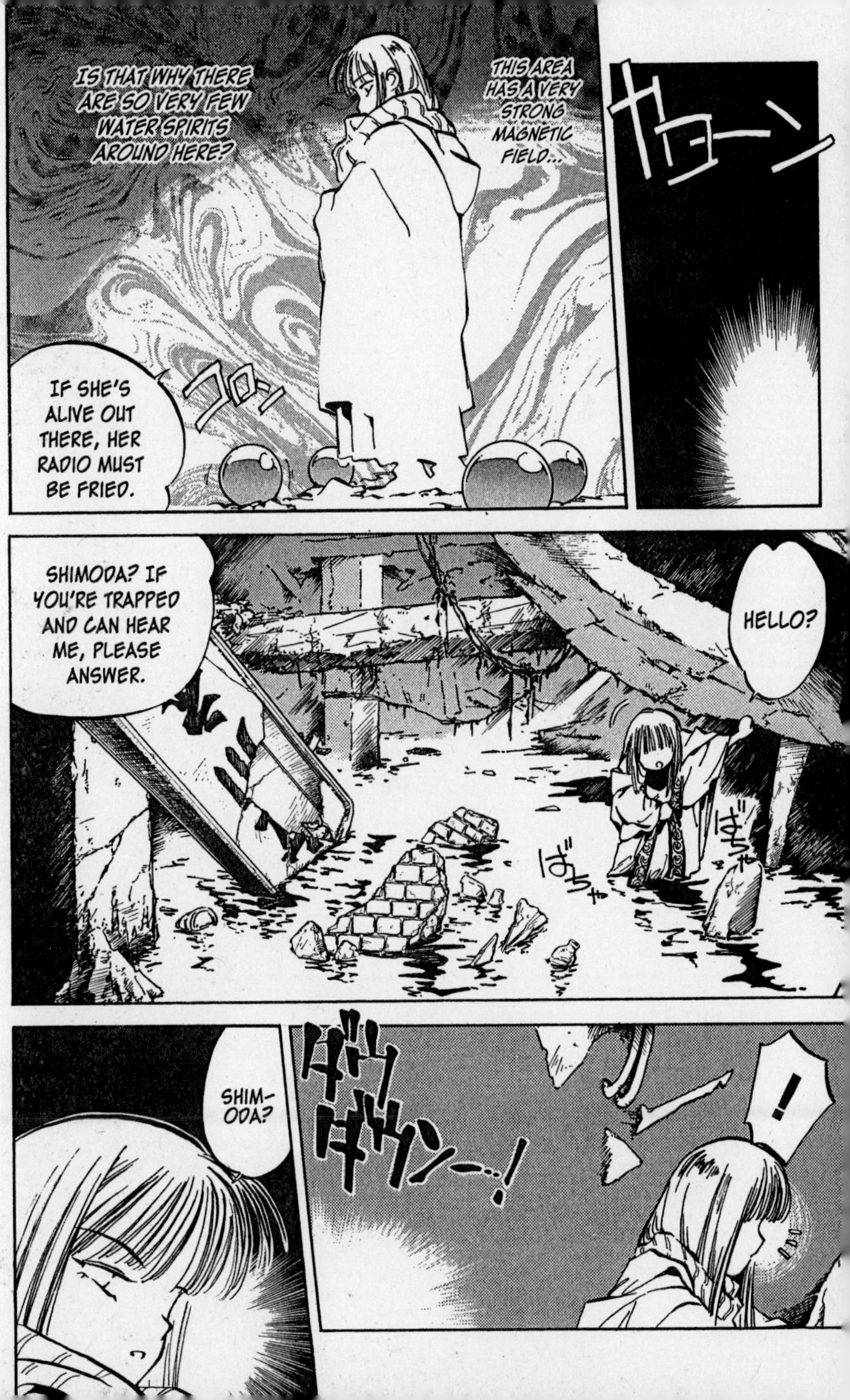
THIS AREA HAS A VERY STRONG MAGNETIC FIELD...
IS THAT WHY THERE ARE SO VERY FEW WATER SPIRITS AROUND HERE?
IF SHE'S ALIVE OUT THERE, HER RADIO MUST BE FRIED.
HELLO?
SHIMODA? IF YOU'RE TRAPPED AND CAN HEAR ME, PLEASE ANSWER.
!
SHIM-ODA?

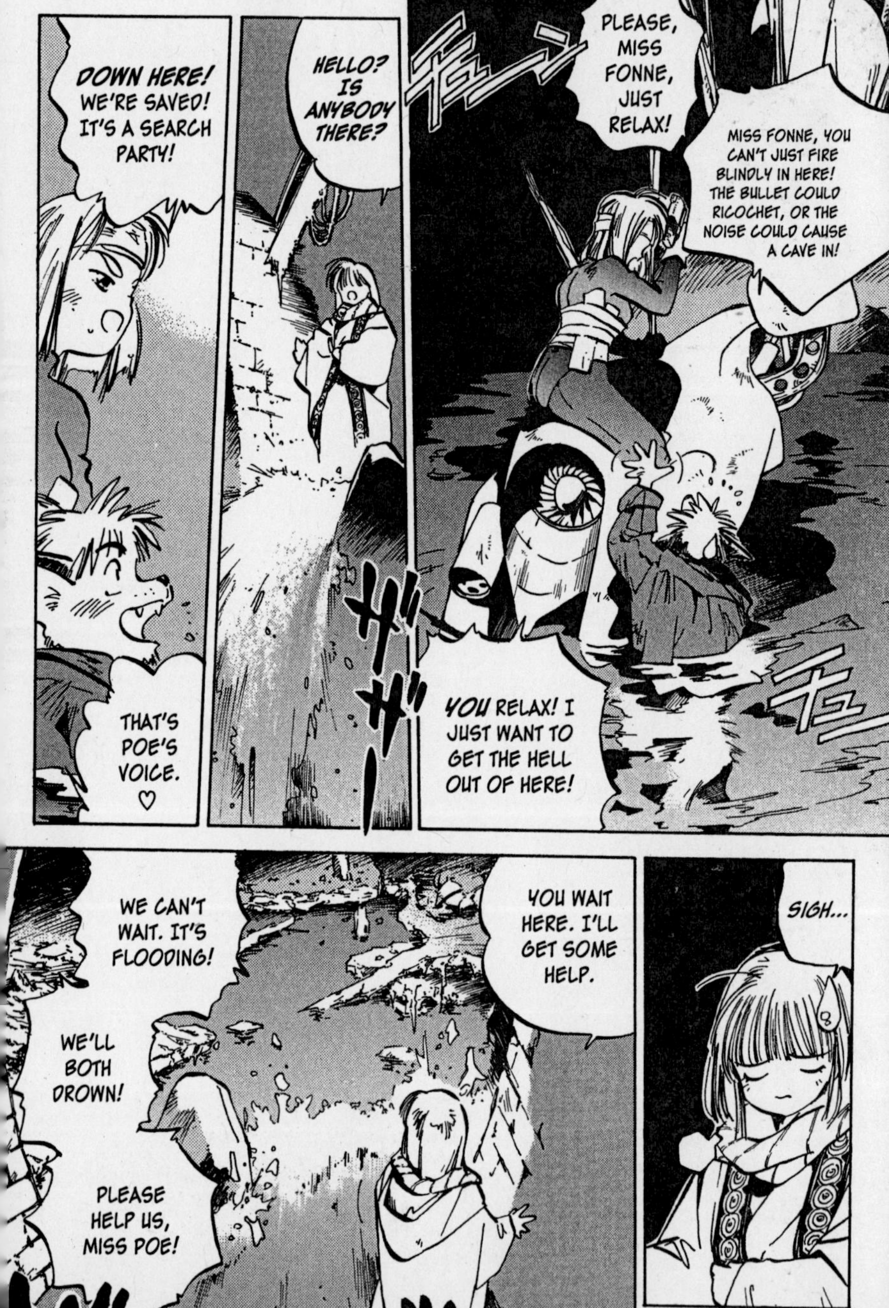
MISS FONNE, YOU CAN'T JUST FIRE BLINDLY IN HERE! THE BULLET COULD RICOCHET, OR THE NOISE COULD CAUSE A CAVE IN!
PLEASE, MISS FONNE, JUST RELAX!
YOU RELAX! I JUST WANT TO GET THE HELL OUT OF HERE!
HELLO? IS ANYBODY THERE?
DOWN HERE! WE'RE SAVED! IT'S A SEARCH PARTY!
THAT'S POE'S VOICE. ♡
SIGH...
YOU WAIT HERE. I'LL GET SOME HELP.
WE CAN'T WAIT. IT'S FLOODING!
WE'LL BOTH DROWN!
PLEASE HELP US, MISS POE!

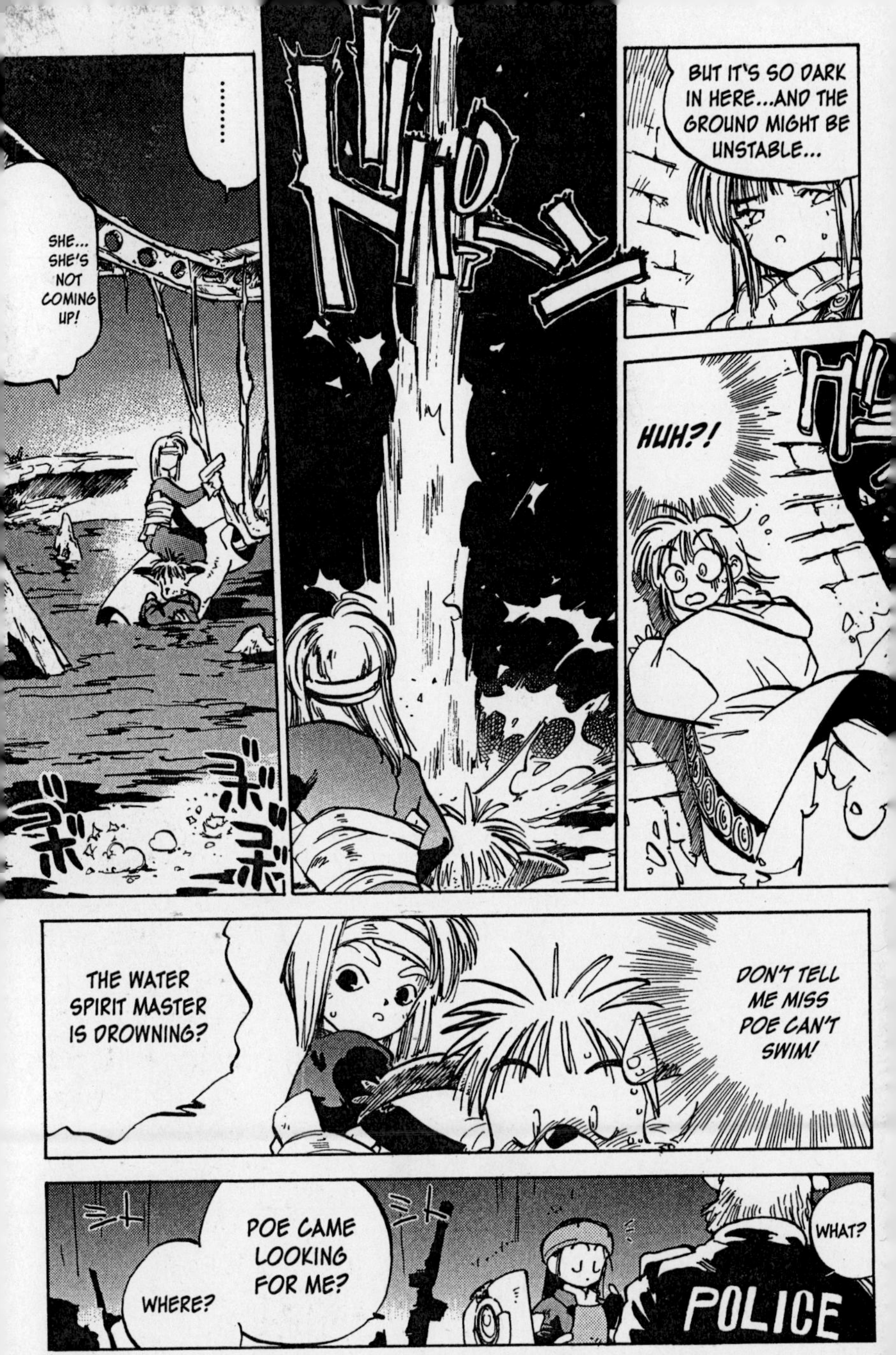
BUT IT'S SO DARK IN HERE...AND THE GROUND MIGHT BE UNSTABLE...
HUH?!
......
SHE... SHE'S NOT COMING UP!
DON'T TELL ME MISS POE CAN'T SWIM!
THE WATER SPIRIT MASTER IS DROWNING?
WHAT?
POLICE
POE CAME LOOKING FOR ME?
WHERE?

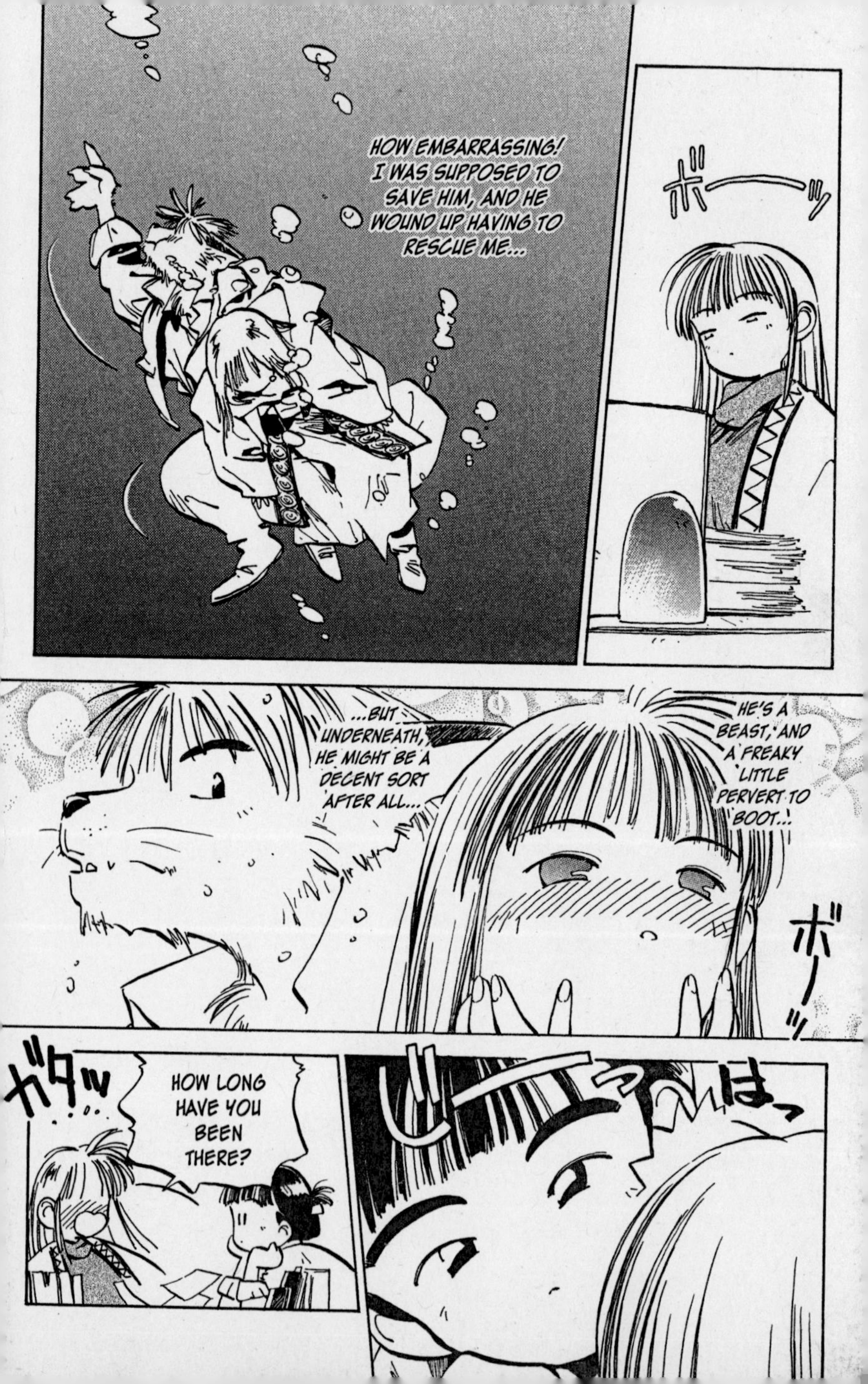
ボーーーッ
HOW EMBARRASSING! I WAS SUPPOSED TO SAVE HIM, AND HE WOUND UP HAVING TO RESCUE ME...
HE'S A BEAST, AND A FREAKY LITTLE PERVERT TO BOOT...
...BUT UNDERNEATH, HE MIGHT BE A DECENT SORT AFTER ALL...
ボーッ
ガタッ
HOW LONG HAVE YOU BEEN THERE?

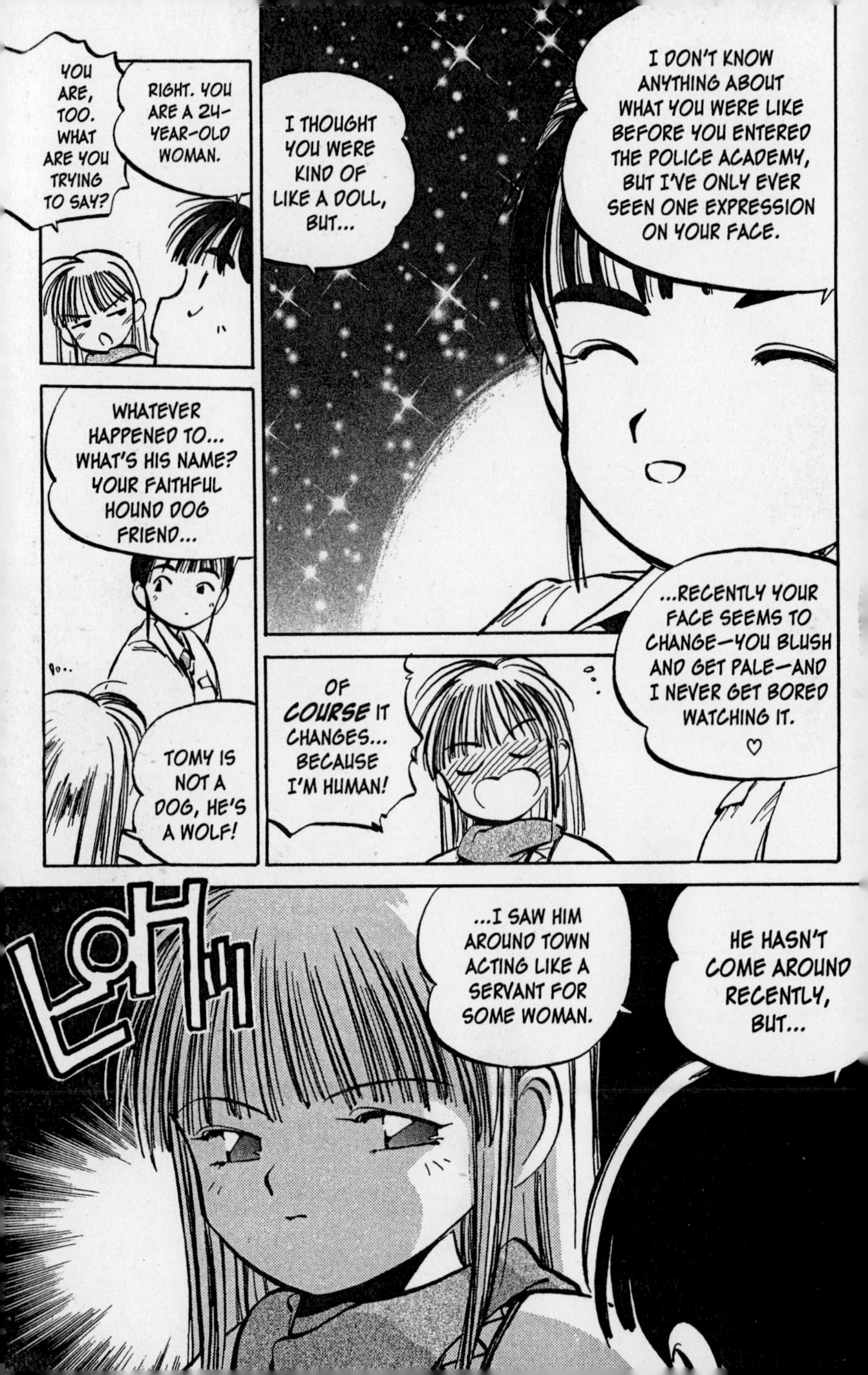
I DON'T KNOW ANYTHING ABOUT WHAT YOU WERE LIKE BEFORE YOU ENTERED THE POLICE ACADEMY, BUT I'VE ONLY EVER SEEN ONE EXPRESSION ON YOUR FACE.
I THOUGHT YOU WERE KIND OF LIKE A DOLL, BUT...
...RECENTLY YOUR FACE SEEMS TO CHANGE—YOU BLUSH AND GET PALE—AND I NEVER GET BORED WATCHING IT. ♡
OF *COURSE* IT CHANGES... BECAUSE I'M HUMAN!
RIGHT. YOU ARE A 24-YEAR-OLD WOMAN.
YOU ARE, TOO. WHAT ARE YOU TRYING TO SAY?
WHATEVER HAPPENED TO... WHAT'S HIS NAME? YOUR FAITHFUL HOUND DOG FRIEND...
TOMY IS NOT A DOG, HE'S A WOLF!
HE HASN'T COME AROUND RECENTLY, BUT...
...I SAW HIM AROUND TOWN ACTING LIKE A SERVANT FOR SOME WOMAN.

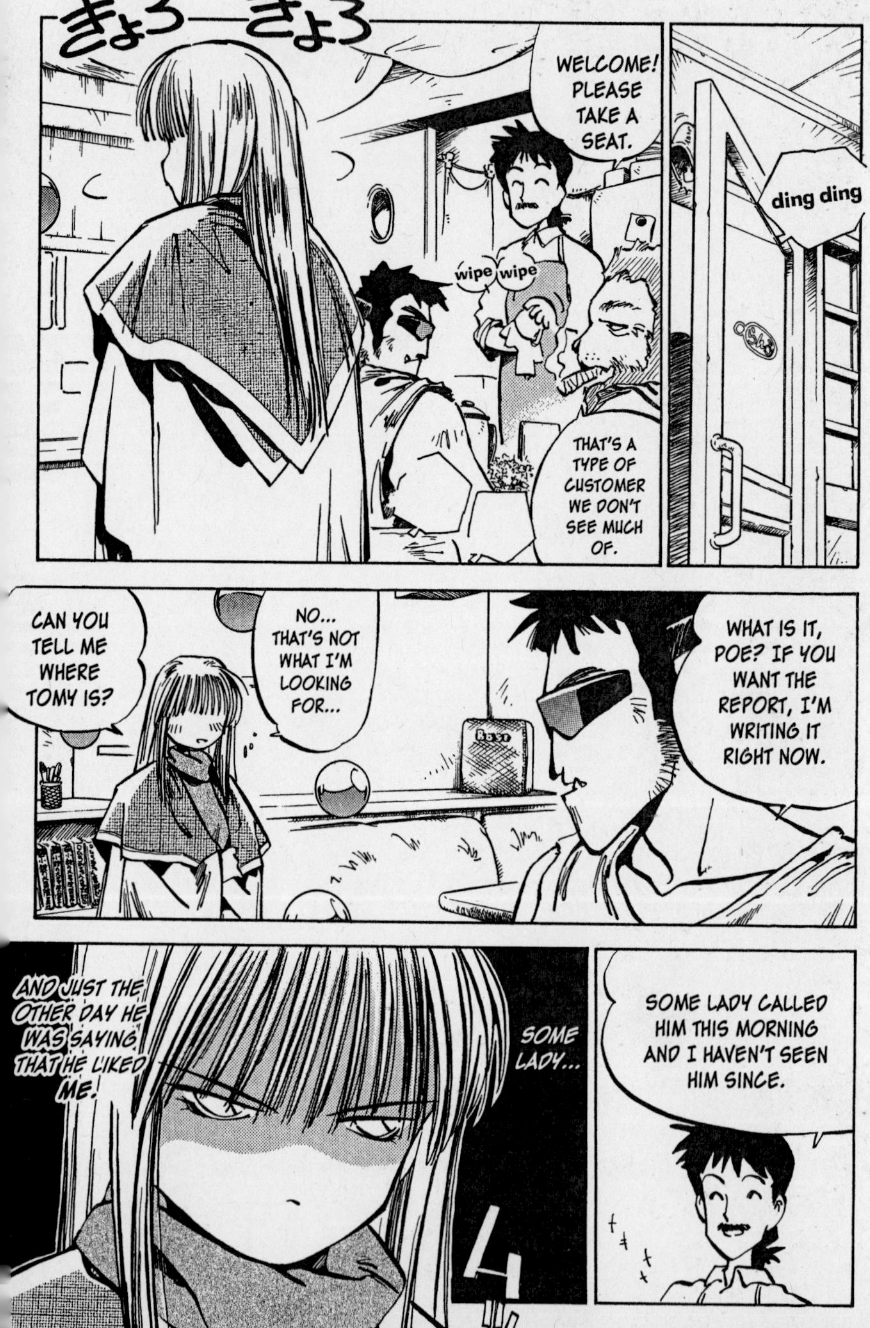
ding ding
きょろ きょろ
WELCOME! PLEASE TAKE A SEAT.
wipe wipe
THAT'S A TYPE OF CUSTOMER WE DON'T SEE MUCH OF.
WHAT IS IT, POE? IF YOU WANT THE REPORT, I'M WRITING IT RIGHT NOW.
NO... THAT'S NOT WHAT I'M LOOKING FOR...
CAN YOU TELL ME WHERE TOMY IS?
SOME LADY CALLED HIM THIS MORNING AND I HAVEN'T SEEN HIM SINCE.
SOME LADY...
AND JUST THE OTHER DAY HE WAS SAYING THAT HE LIKED ME!

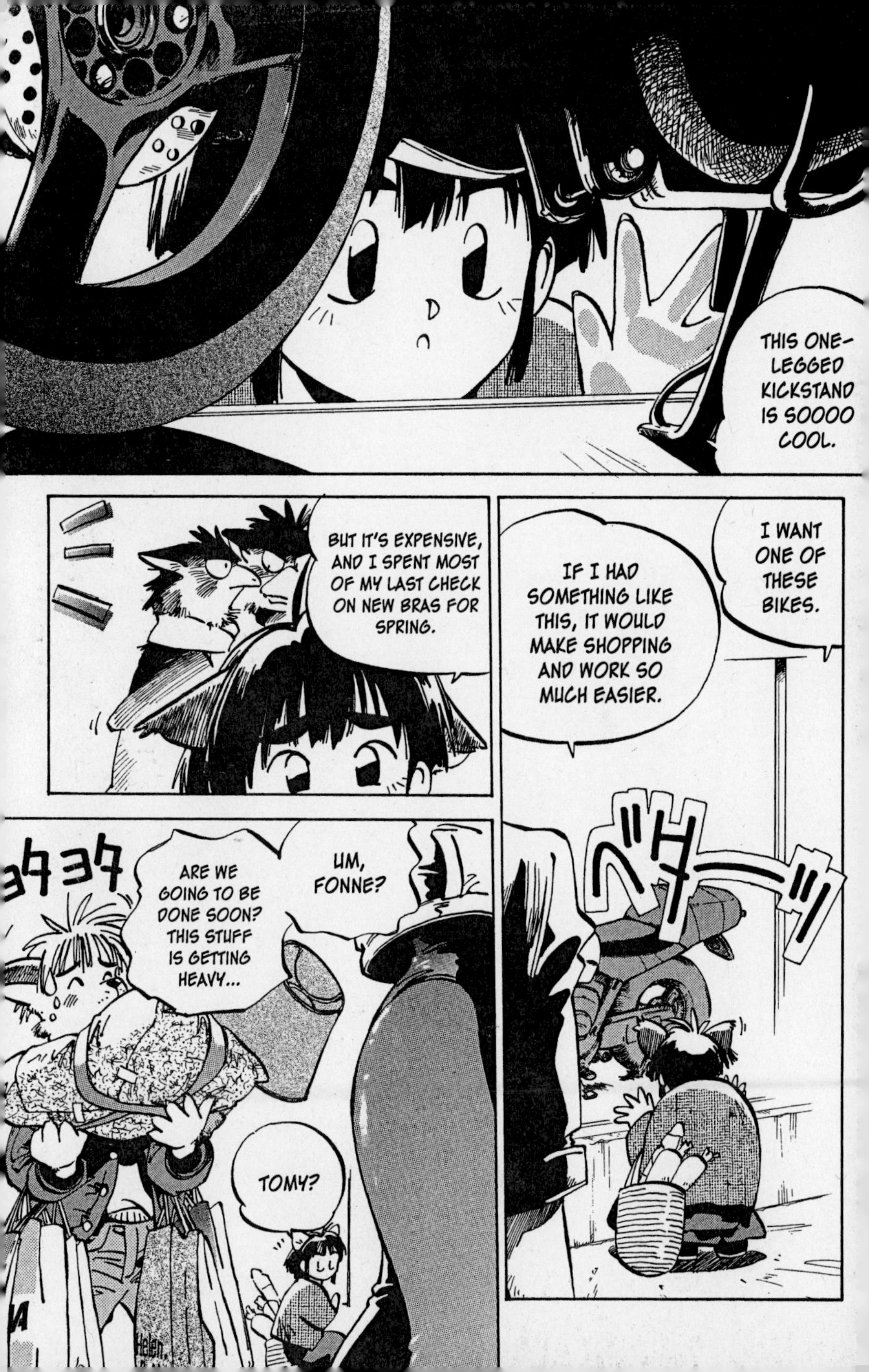
THIS ONE-LEGGED KICKSTAND IS SOOOO COOL.
I WANT ONE OF THESE BIKES.
IF I HAD SOMETHING LIKE THIS, IT WOULD MAKE SHOPPING AND WORK SO MUCH EASIER.
BUT IT'S EXPENSIVE, AND I SPENT MOST OF MY LAST CHECK ON NEW BRAS FOR SPRING.
ベターッ
UM, FONNE?
ARE WE GOING TO BE DONE SOON? THIS STUFF IS GETTING HEAVY...
TOMY?

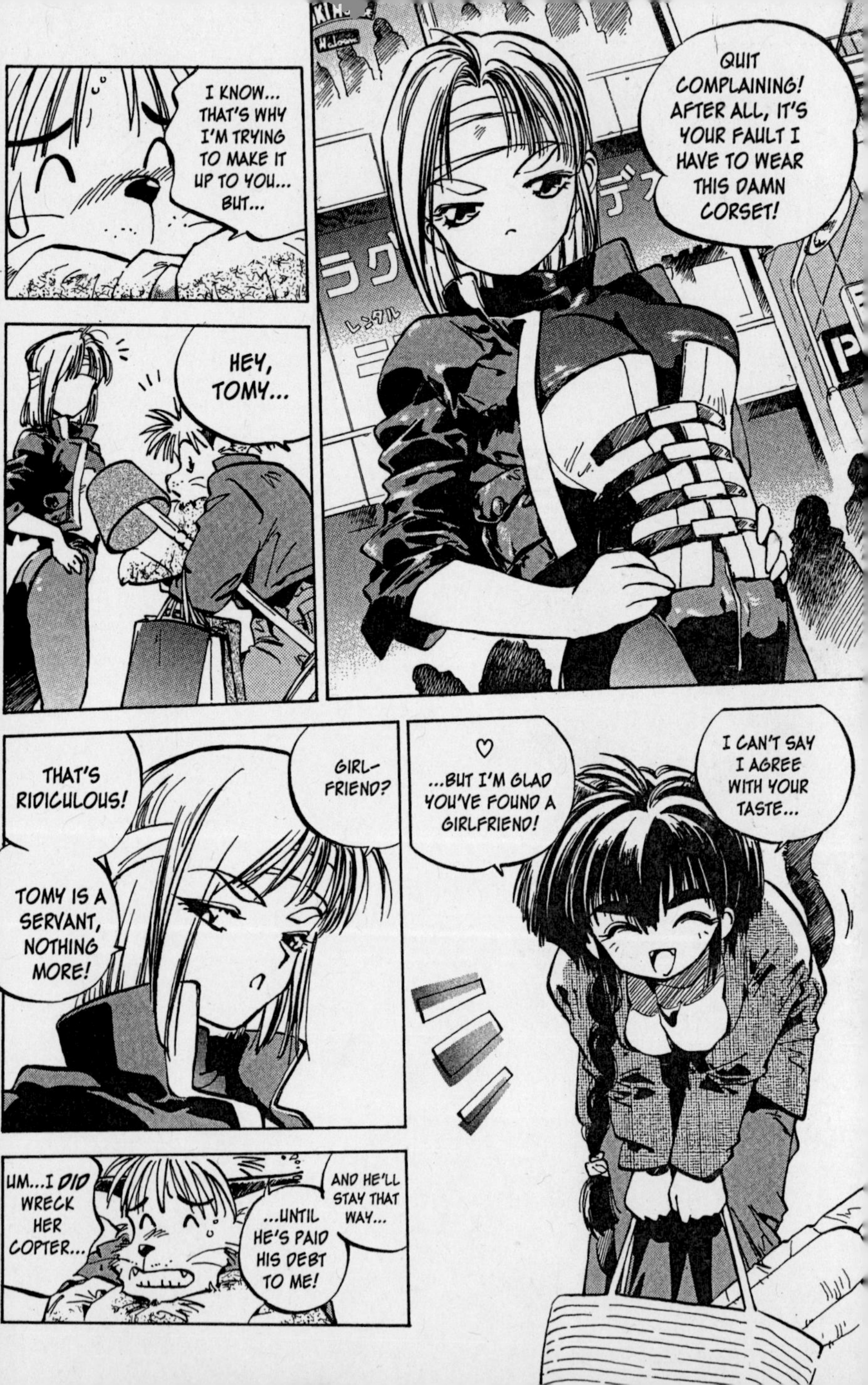
QUIT COMPLAINING! AFTER ALL, IT'S YOUR FAULT I HAVE TO WEAR THIS DAMN CORSET!
I KNOW... THAT'S WHY I'M TRYING TO MAKE IT UP TO YOU... BUT...
HEY, TOMY...
I CAN'T SAY I AGREE WITH YOUR TASTE...
♡ ...BUT I'M GLAD YOU'VE FOUND A GIRLFRIEND!
GIRL-FRIEND?
THAT'S RIDICULOUS!
TOMY IS A SERVANT, NOTHING MORE!
AND HE'LL STAY THAT WAY...
...UNTIL HE'S PAID HIS DEBT TO ME!
UM...I *DID* WRECK HER COPTER...

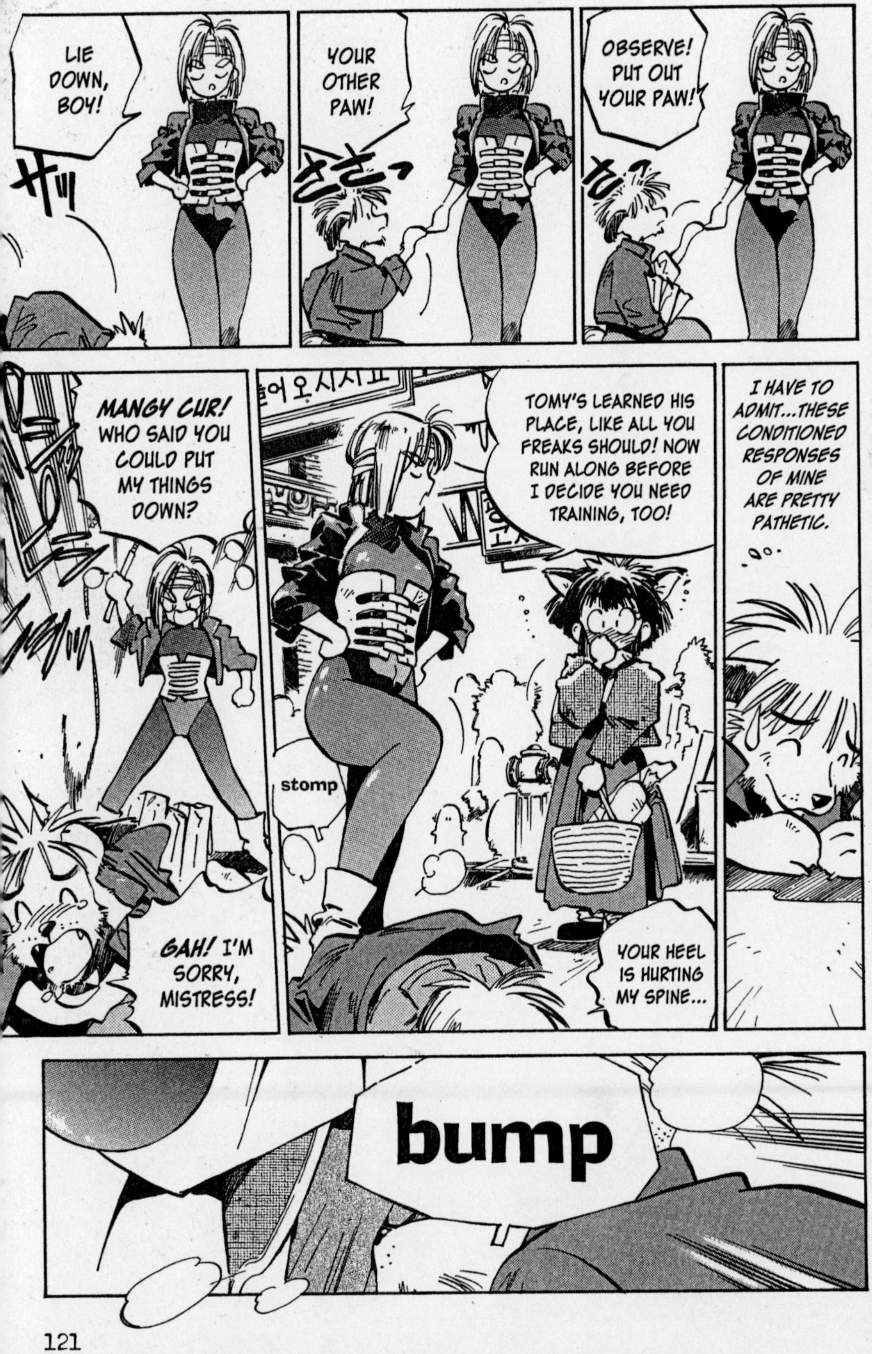
OBSERVE! PUT OUT YOUR PAW!
YOUR OTHER PAW!
LIE DOWN, BOY!
I HAVE TO ADMIT...THESE CONDITIONED RESPONSES OF MINE ARE PRETTY PATHETIC.
TOMY'S LEARNED HIS PLACE, LIKE ALL YOU FREAKS SHOULD! NOW RUN ALONG BEFORE I DECIDE YOU NEED TRAINING, TOO!
stomp
YOUR HEEL IS HURTING MY SPINE...
MANGY CUR! WHO SAID YOU COULD PUT MY THINGS DOWN?
GAH! I'M SORRY, MISTRESS!
bump

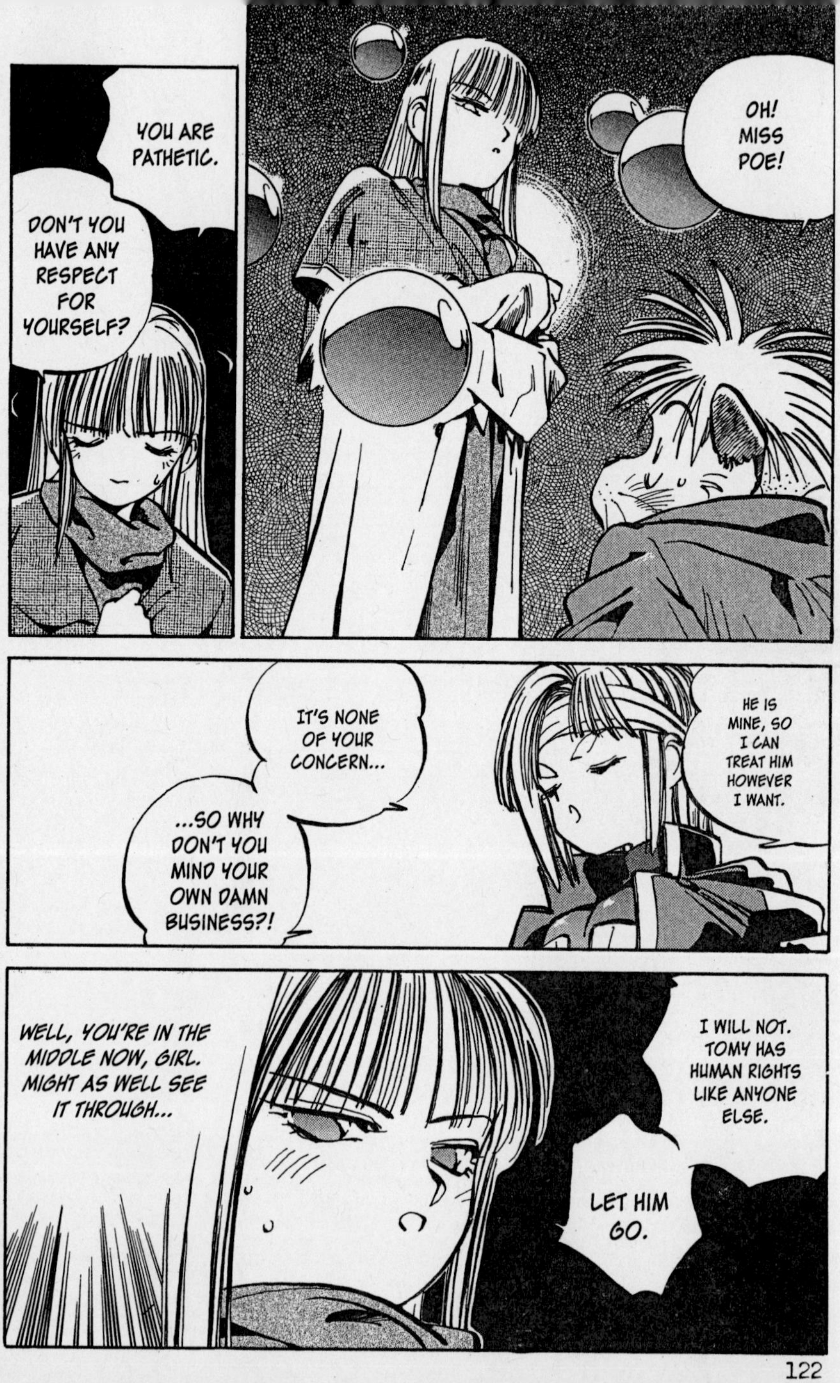
OH! MISS POE!
YOU ARE PATHETIC.
DON'T YOU HAVE ANY RESPECT FOR YOURSELF?
HE IS MINE, SO I CAN TREAT HIM HOWEVER I WANT.
IT'S NONE OF YOUR CONCERN...
...SO WHY DON'T YOU MIND YOUR OWN DAMN BUSINESS?!
I WILL NOT. TOMY HAS HUMAN RIGHTS LIKE ANYONE ELSE.
LET HIM GO.
WELL, YOU'RE IN THE MIDDLE NOW, GIRL. MIGHT AS WELL SEE IT THROUGH...

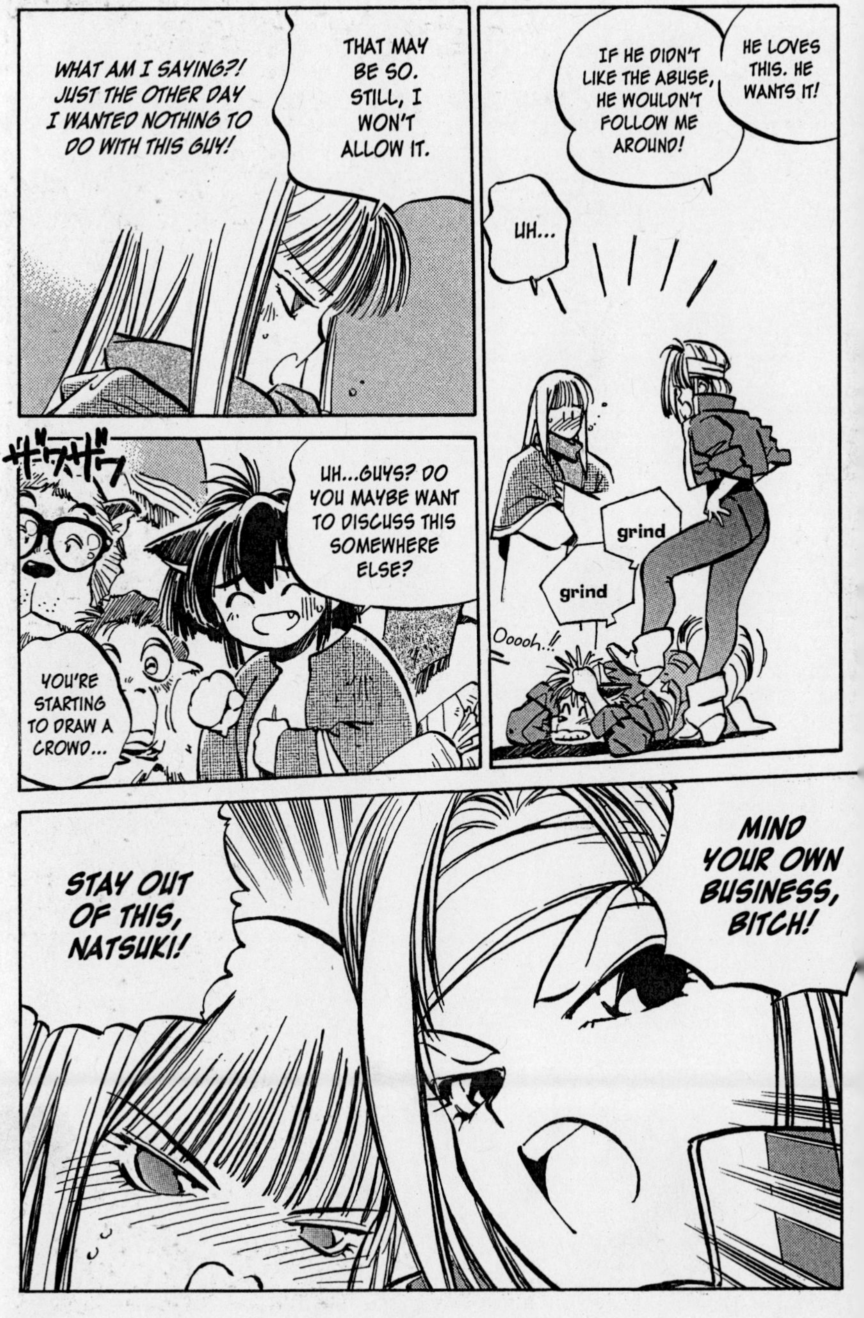
HE LOVES THIS. HE WANTS IT!
IF HE DIDN'T LIKE THE ABUSE, HE WOULDN'T FOLLOW ME AROUND!
UH...
grind
grind
Ooooh..!!
THAT MAY BE SO. STILL, I WON'T ALLOW IT.
WHAT AM I SAYING?! JUST THE OTHER DAY I WANTED NOTHING TO DO WITH THIS GUY!
UH...GUYS? DO YOU MAYBE WANT TO DISCUSS THIS SOMEWHERE ELSE?
ザワザワ
YOU'RE STARTING TO DRAW A CROWD...
MIND YOUR OWN BUSINESS, BITCH!
STAY OUT OF THIS, NATSUKI!

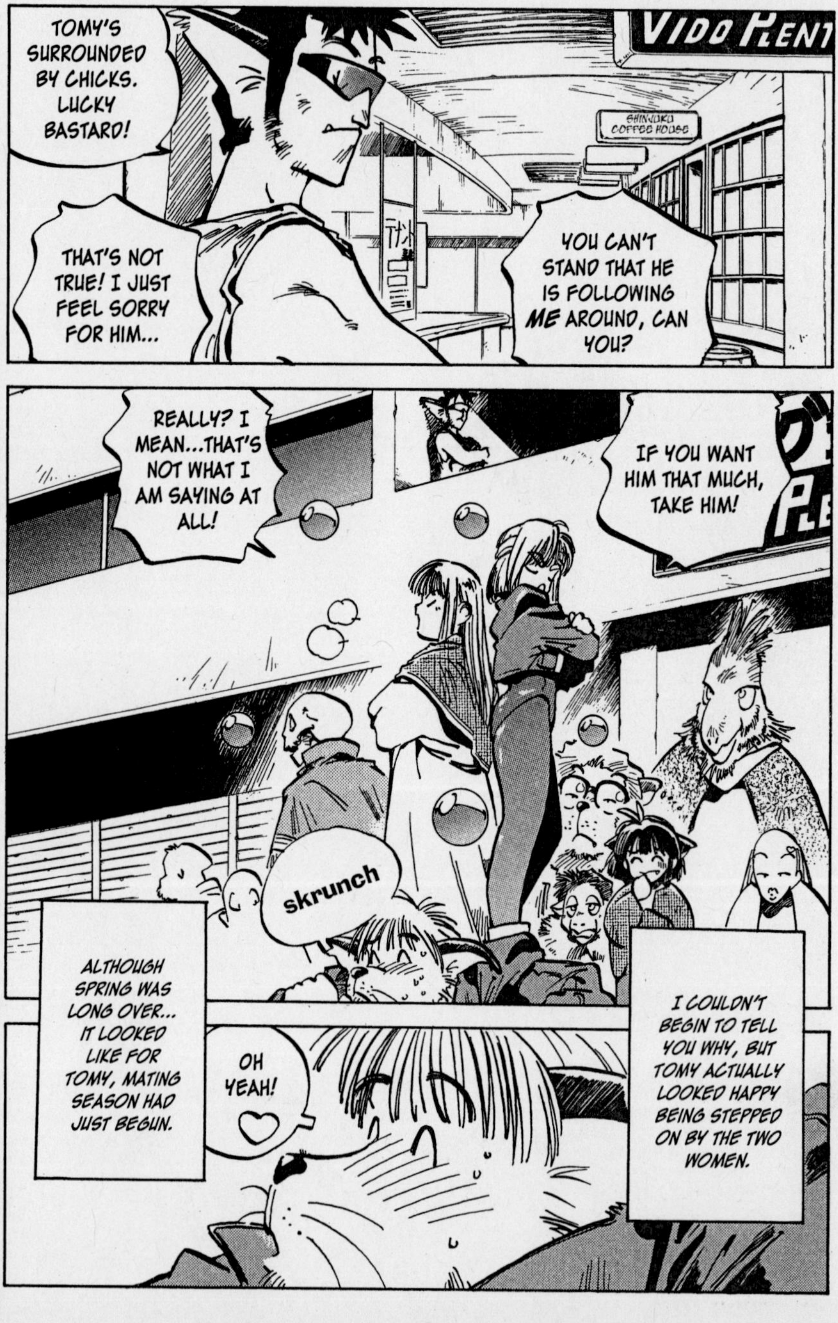

SHINJUKU COFFEE HOUSE
TOMY'S SURROUNDED BY CHICKS. LUCKY BASTARD!
YOU CAN'T STAND THAT HE IS FOLLOWING ME AROUND, CAN YOU?
THAT'S NOT TRUE! I JUST FEEL SORRY FOR HIM...
IF YOU WANT HIM THAT MUCH, TAKE HIM!
REALLY? I MEAN...THAT'S NOT WHAT I AM SAYING AT ALL!
skrunch
I COULDN'T BEGIN TO TELL YOU WHY, BUT TOMY ACTUALLY LOOKED HAPPY BEING STEPPED ON BY THE TWO WOMEN.
OH YEAH!
ALTHOUGH SPRING WAS LONG OVER... IT LOOKED LIKE FOR TOMY, MATING SEASON HAD JUST BEGUN.

Report #20
Baby Blues

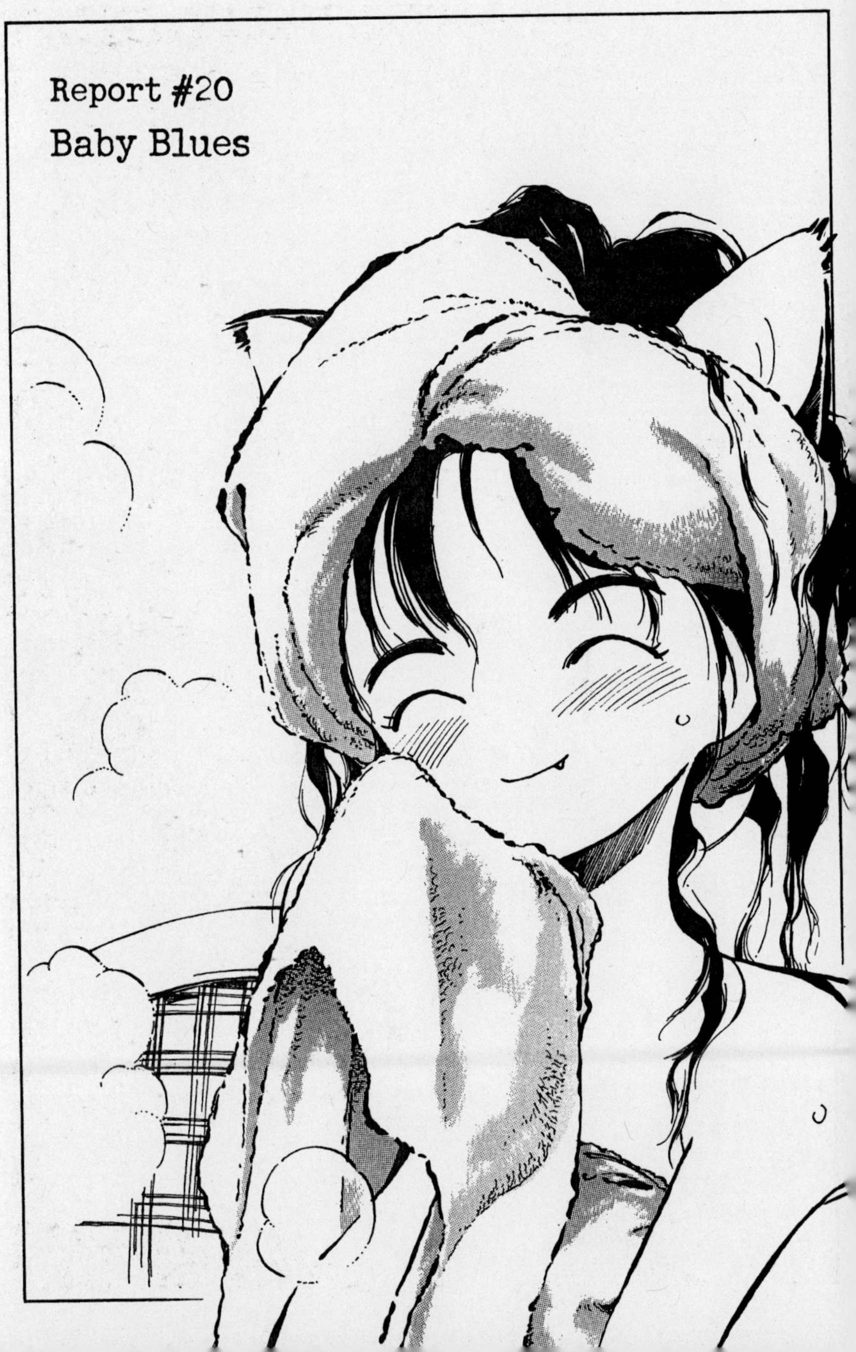

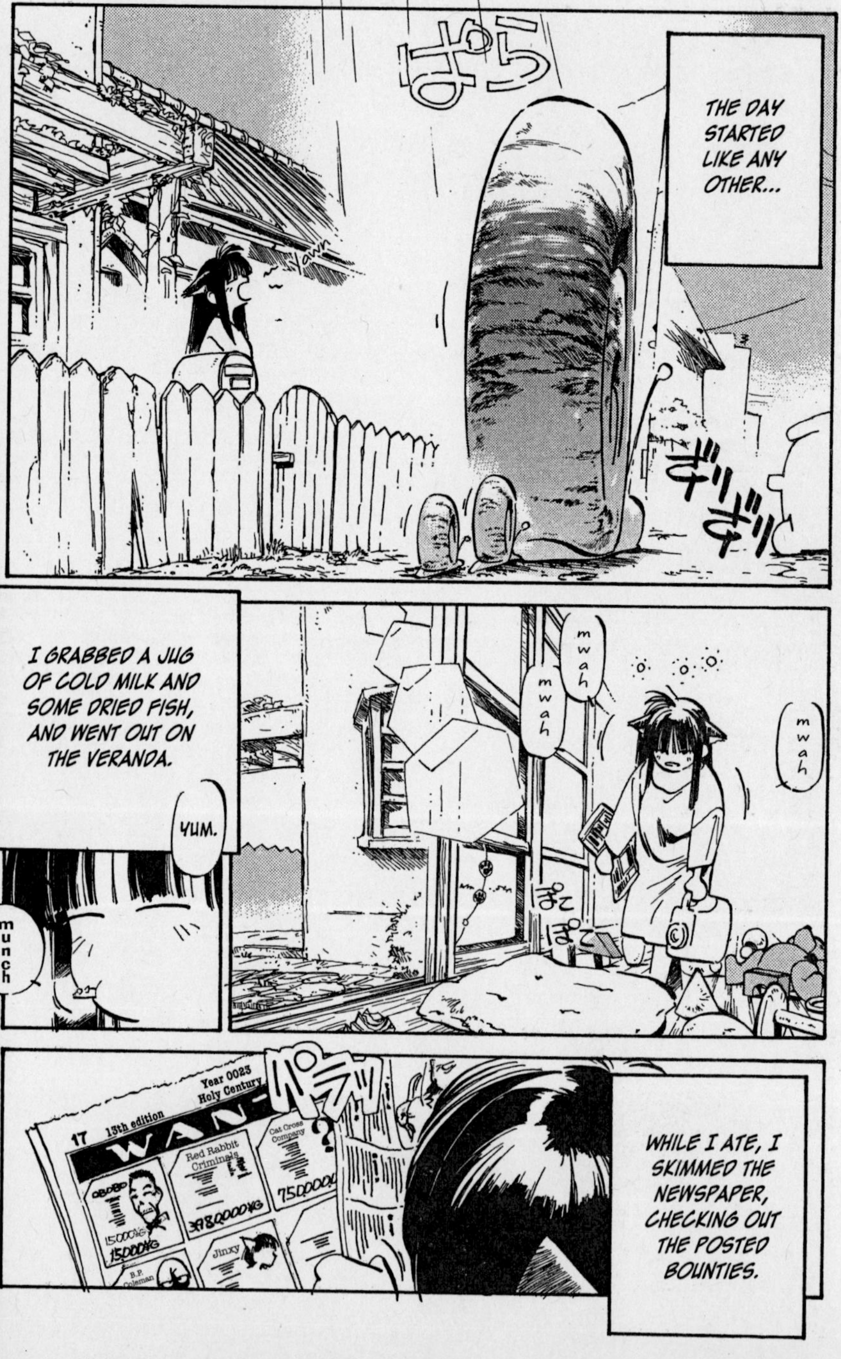
THE DAY STARTED LIKE ANY OTHER...
ぱら
yawn
ずりずり
mwah
mwah
mwah
ぽてぽて
I GRABBED A JUG OF COLD MILK AND SOME DRIED FISH, AND WENT OUT ON THE VERANDA.
YUM.
munch
WHILE I ATE, I SKIMMED THE NEWSPAPER, CHECKING OUT THE POSTED BOUNTIES.
パラッ
Year 0023 Holy Century
17 13th edition
WAN-
Cat Cross Company
Red Rabbit Criminals
Jinxy
B.P. Coleman

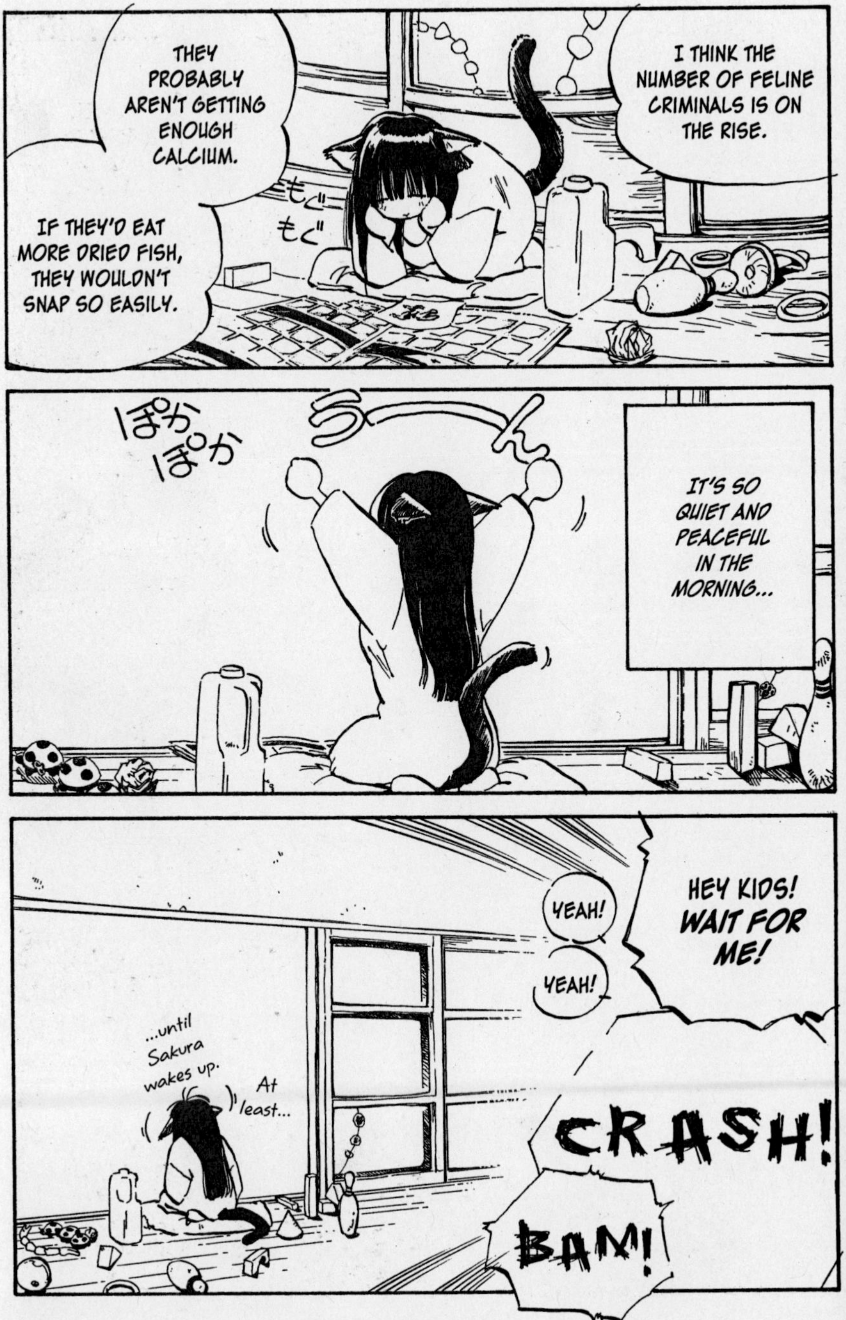
I THINK THE NUMBER OF FELINE CRIMINALS IS ON THE RISE.
もぐもぐ
THEY PROBABLY AREN'T GETTING ENOUGH CALCIUM.
IF THEY'D EAT MORE DRIED FISH, THEY WOULDN'T SNAP SO EASILY.
IT'S SO QUIET AND PEACEFUL IN THE MORNING...
うーん
ぽかぽか
HEY KIDS! WAIT FOR ME!
YEAH!
YEAH!
CRASH!
BAM!
At least...
...until Sakura wakes up.

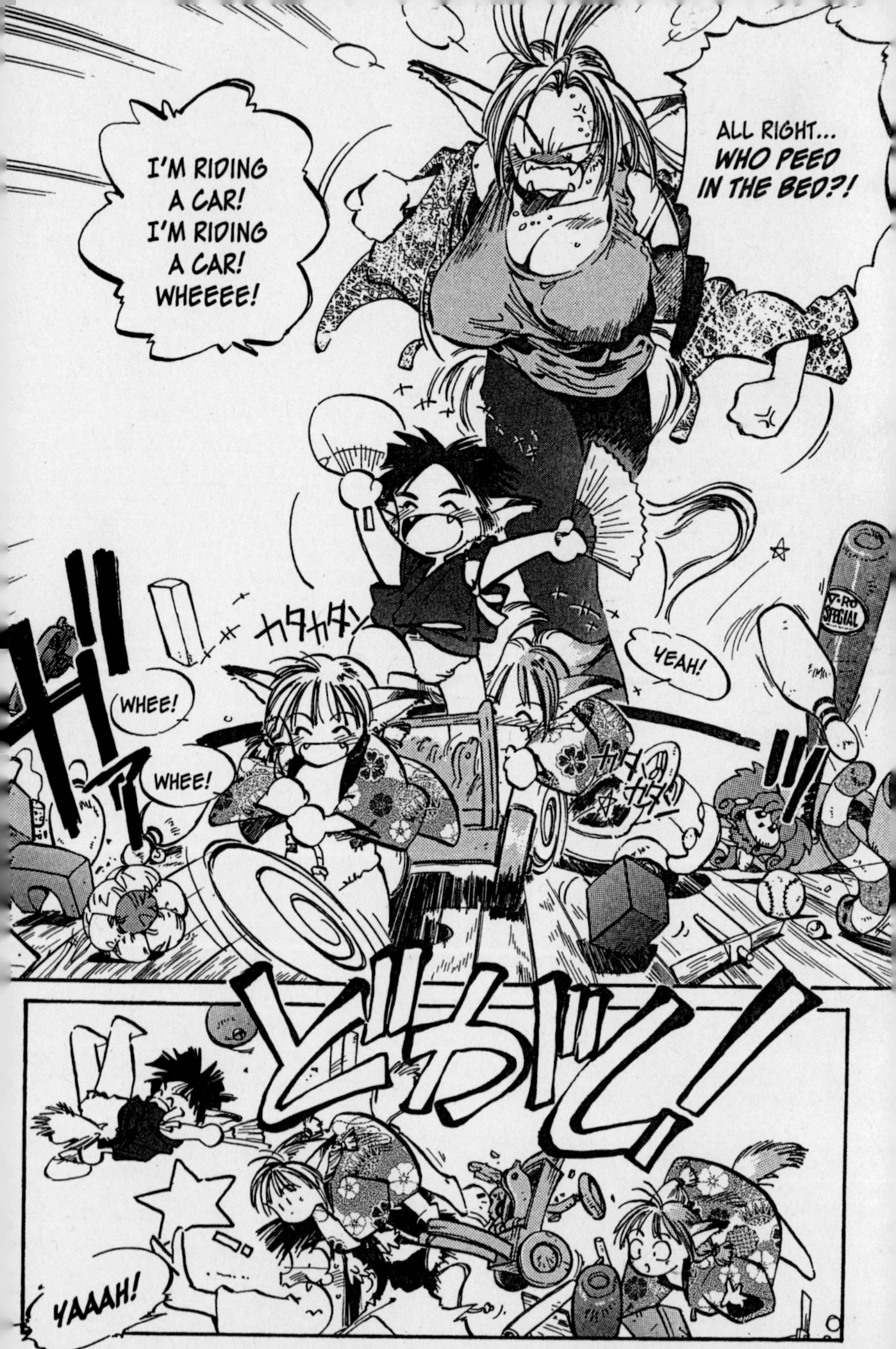
ALL RIGHT... WHO PEED IN THE BED?!
I'M RIDING A CAR! I'M RIDING A CAR! WHEEEE!
YEAH!
カタカタン
WHEE!
WHEE!
YAAAH!

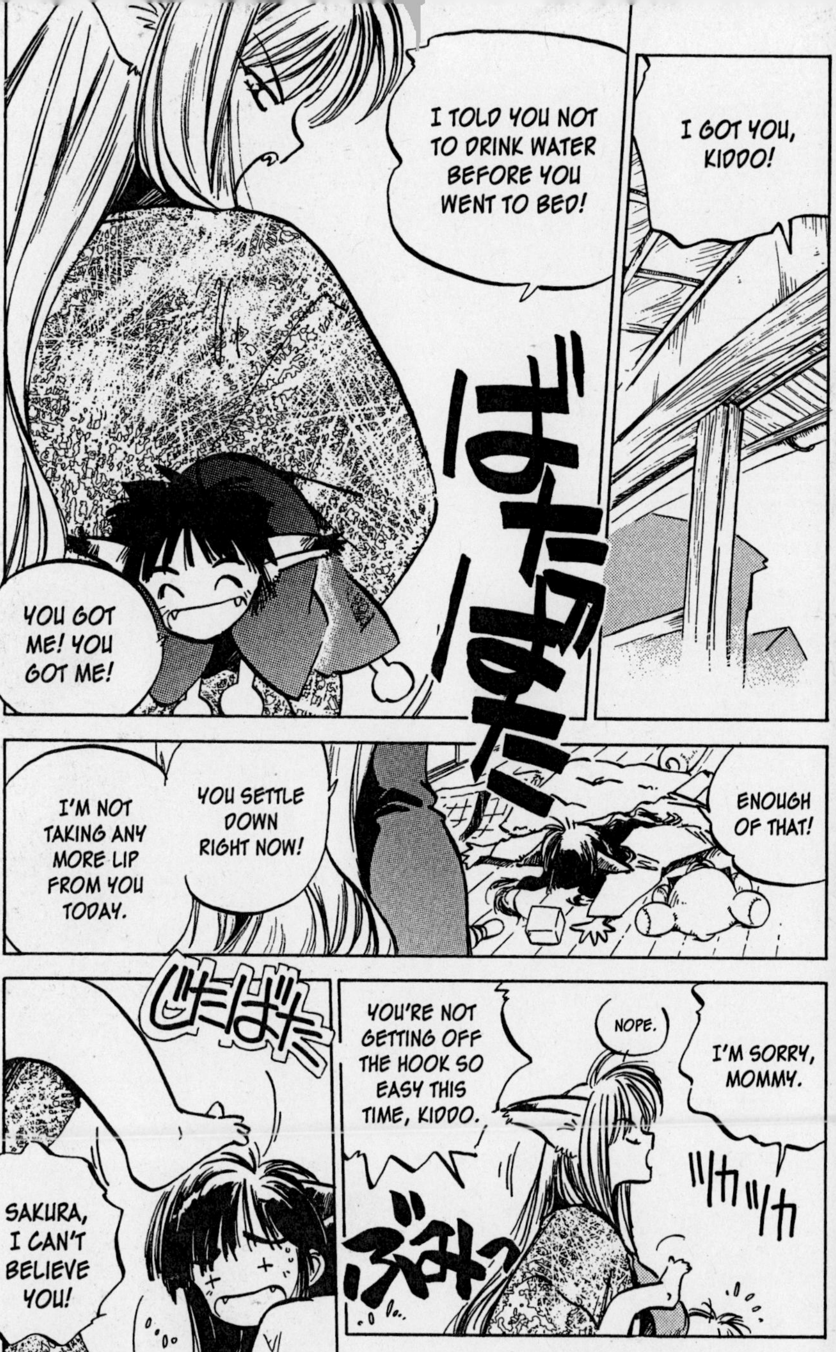
I GOT YOU, KIDDO!
I TOLD YOU NOT TO DRINK WATER BEFORE YOU WENT TO BED!
YOU GOT ME! YOU GOT ME!
ENOUGH OF THAT!
YOU SETTLE DOWN RIGHT NOW!
I'M NOT TAKING ANY MORE LIP FROM YOU TODAY.
I'M SORRY, MOMMY.
NOPE.
YOU'RE NOT GETTING OFF THE HOOK SO EASY THIS TIME, KIDDO.
ツカツカ
ぶみっ
じたばた
SAKURA, I CAN'T BELIEVE YOU!

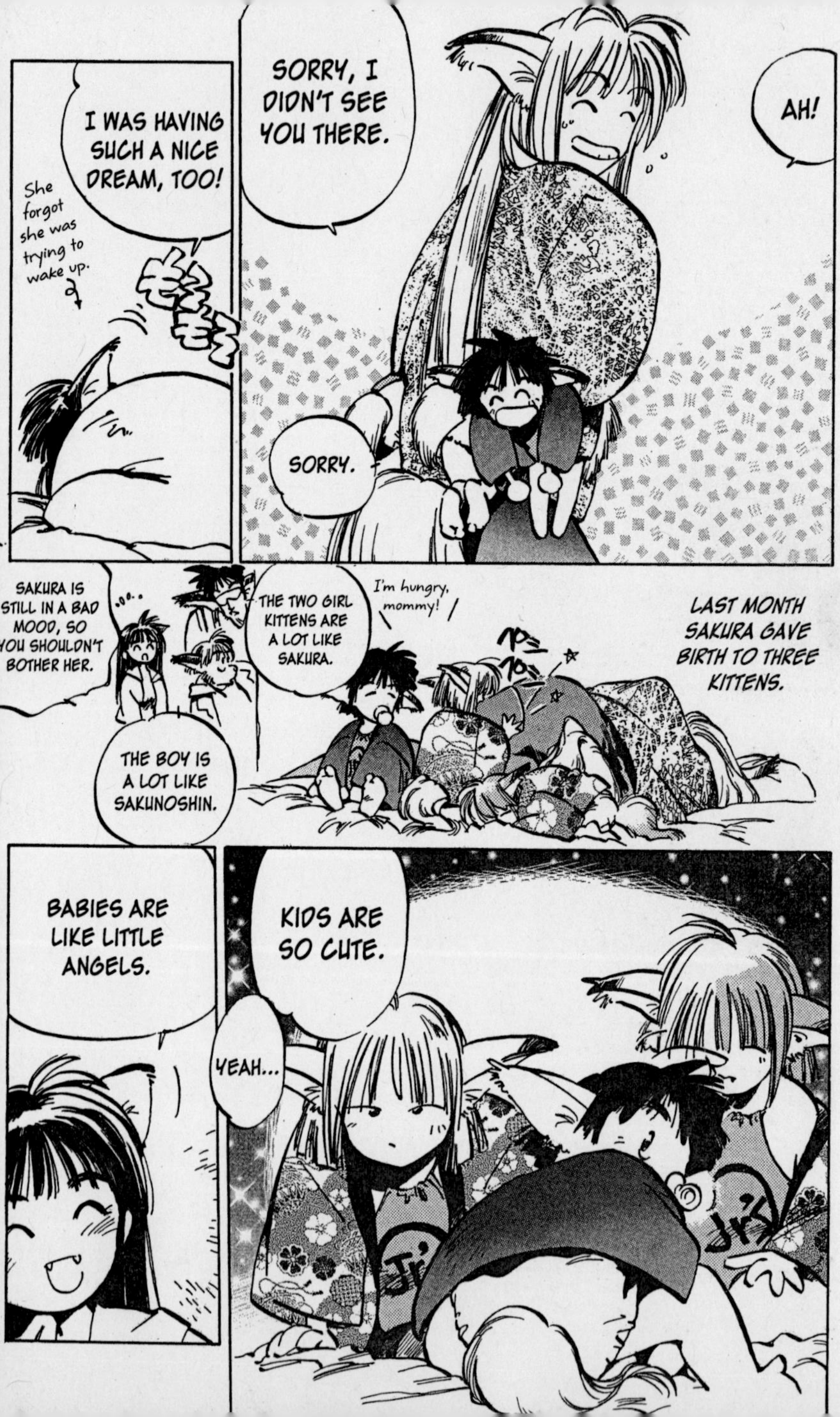
AH!
SORRY, I DIDN'T SEE YOU THERE.
SORRY.
I WAS HAVING SUCH A NICE DREAM, TOO!
She forgot she was trying to wake up.
LAST MONTH SAKURA GAVE BIRTH TO THREE KITTENS.
I'm hungry, mommy!
THE TWO GIRL KITTENS ARE A LOT LIKE SAKURA.
THE BOY IS A LOT LIKE SAKUNOSHIN.
SAKURA IS STILL IN A BAD MOOD, SO YOU SHOULDN'T BOTHER HER.
KIDS ARE SO CUTE.
YEAH...
BABIES ARE LIKE LITTLE ANGELS.

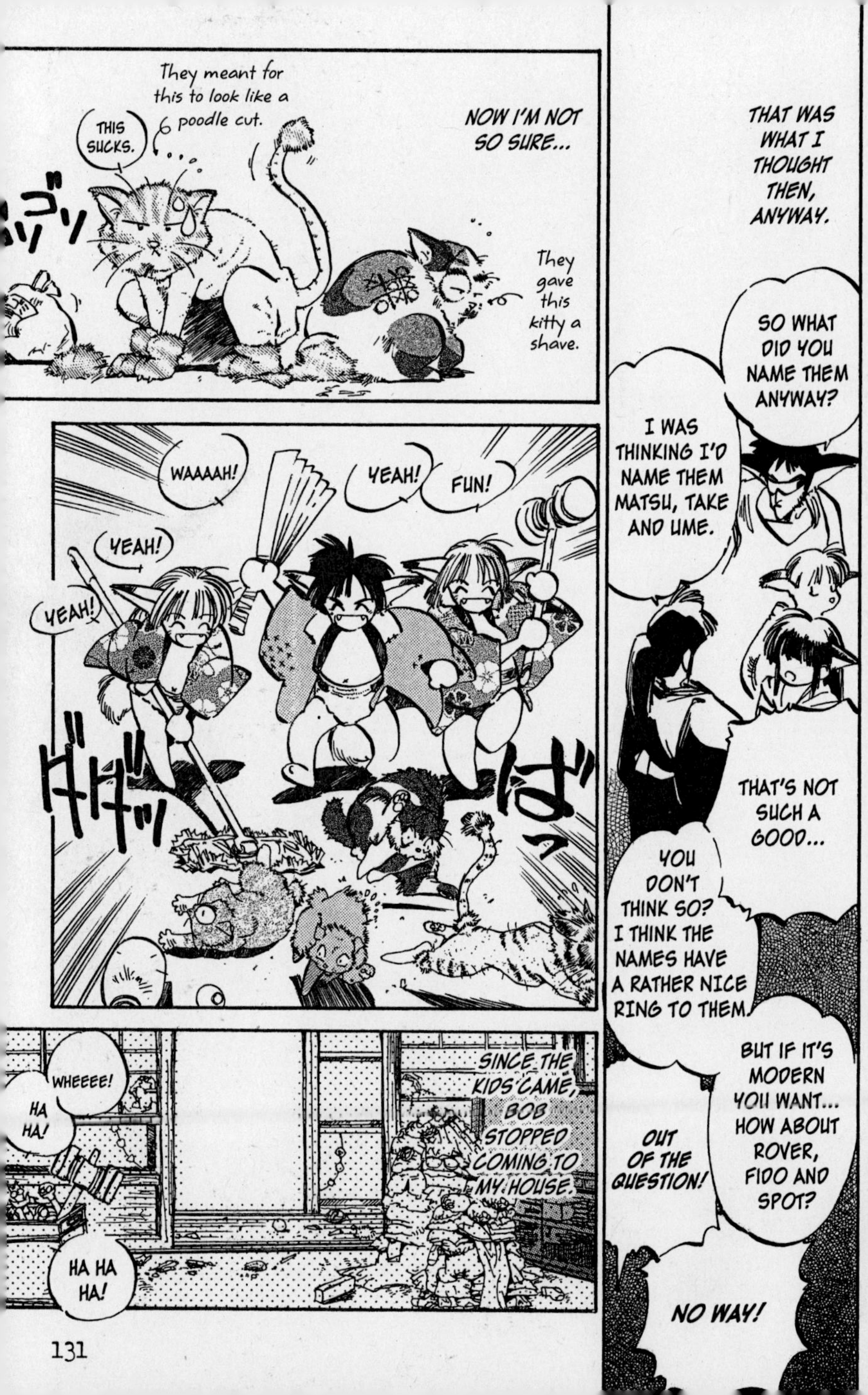
THAT WAS WHAT I THOUGHT THEN, ANYWAY.
SO WHAT DID YOU NAME THEM ANYWAY?
I WAS THINKING I'D NAME THEM MATSU, TAKE AND UME.
THAT'S NOT SUCH A GOOD...
YOU DON'T THINK SO? I THINK THE NAMES HAVE A RATHER NICE RING TO THEM.
BUT IF IT'S MODERN YOU WANT... HOW ABOUT ROVER, FIDO AND SPOT?
OUT OF THE QUESTION!
NO WAY!
NOW I'M NOT SO SURE...
They gave this kitty a shave.
They meant for this to look like a poodle cut.
THIS SUCKS.
FUN!
YEAH!
WAAAAH!
YEAH!
YEAH!
ばっ
ダダッ
SINCE THE KIDS CAME, BOB STOPPED COMING TO MY HOUSE.
WHEEEE!
HA HA!
HA HA HA!

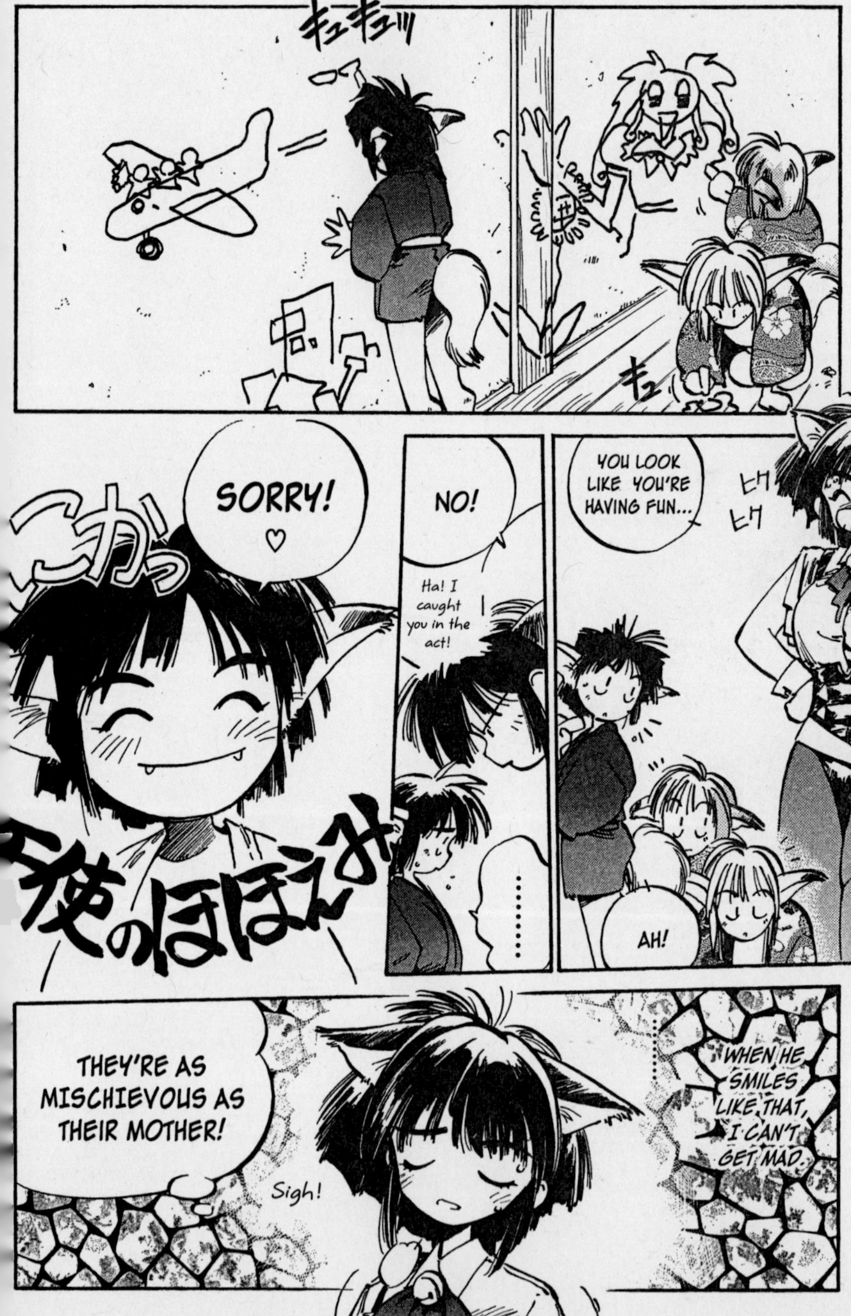
キュキュッ
キュ
YOU LOOK LIKE YOU'RE HAVING FUN...
ヒク ヒク
AH!
NO!
Ha! I caught you in the act!
......
SORRY! ♡
にかっ
使のほほえみ
WHEN HE SMILES LIKE THAT, I CAN'T GET MAD.
THEY'RE AS MISCHIEVOUS AS THEIR MOTHER!
Sigh!

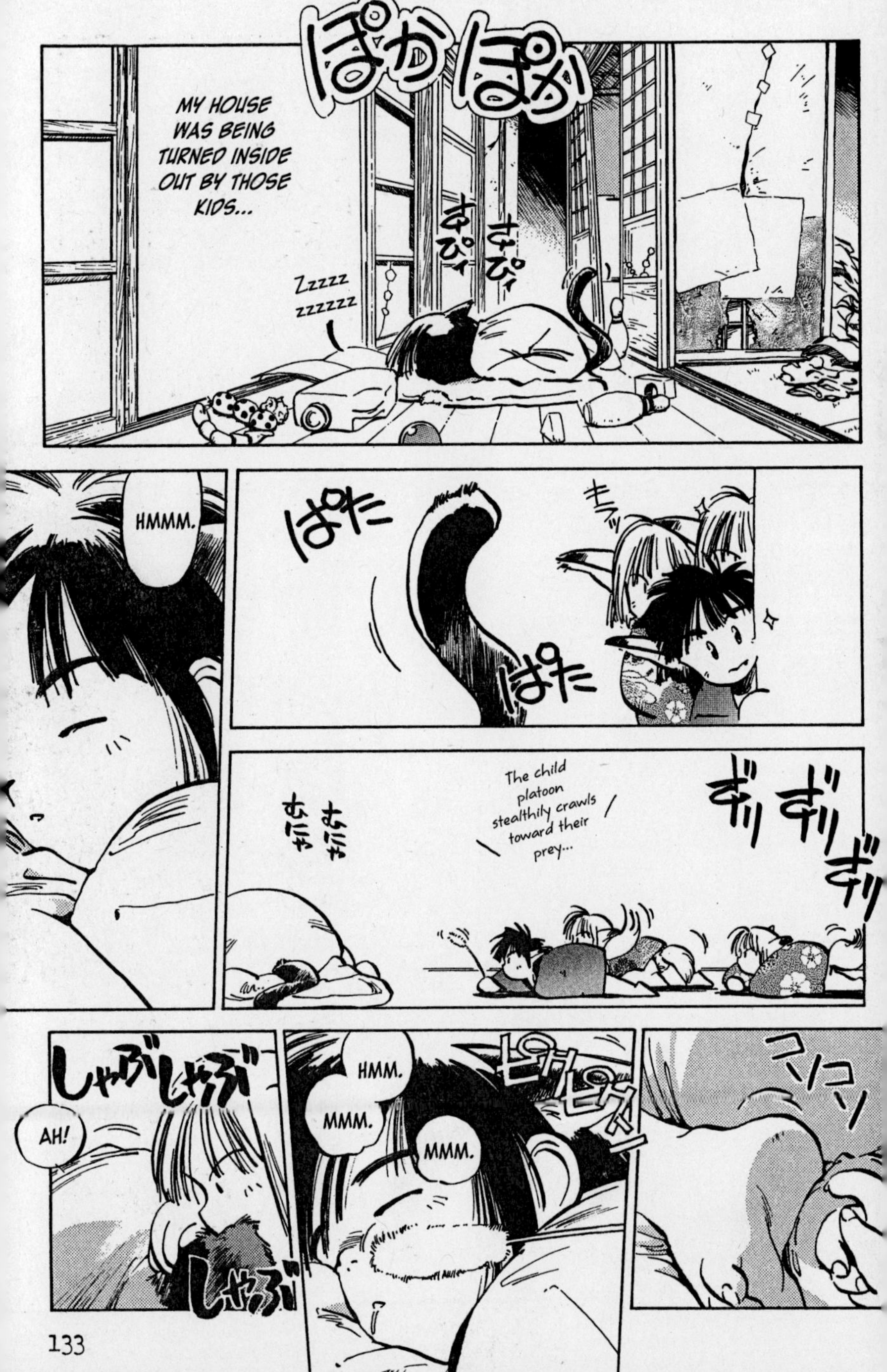
ぱかぱか
すぴ すぴ
すぴ すぴ
MY HOUSE WAS BEING TURNED INSIDE OUT BY THOSE KIDS...
Zzzzz zzzzzz
キラッ
ぱた
ぱた
ずり ずり ずり
The child platoon stealthily crawls toward their prey...
むにゃ むにゃ
HMMM.
コソコソ
HMM.
MMM.
MMM.
しゃぶしゃぶ
AH!
しゃぶ

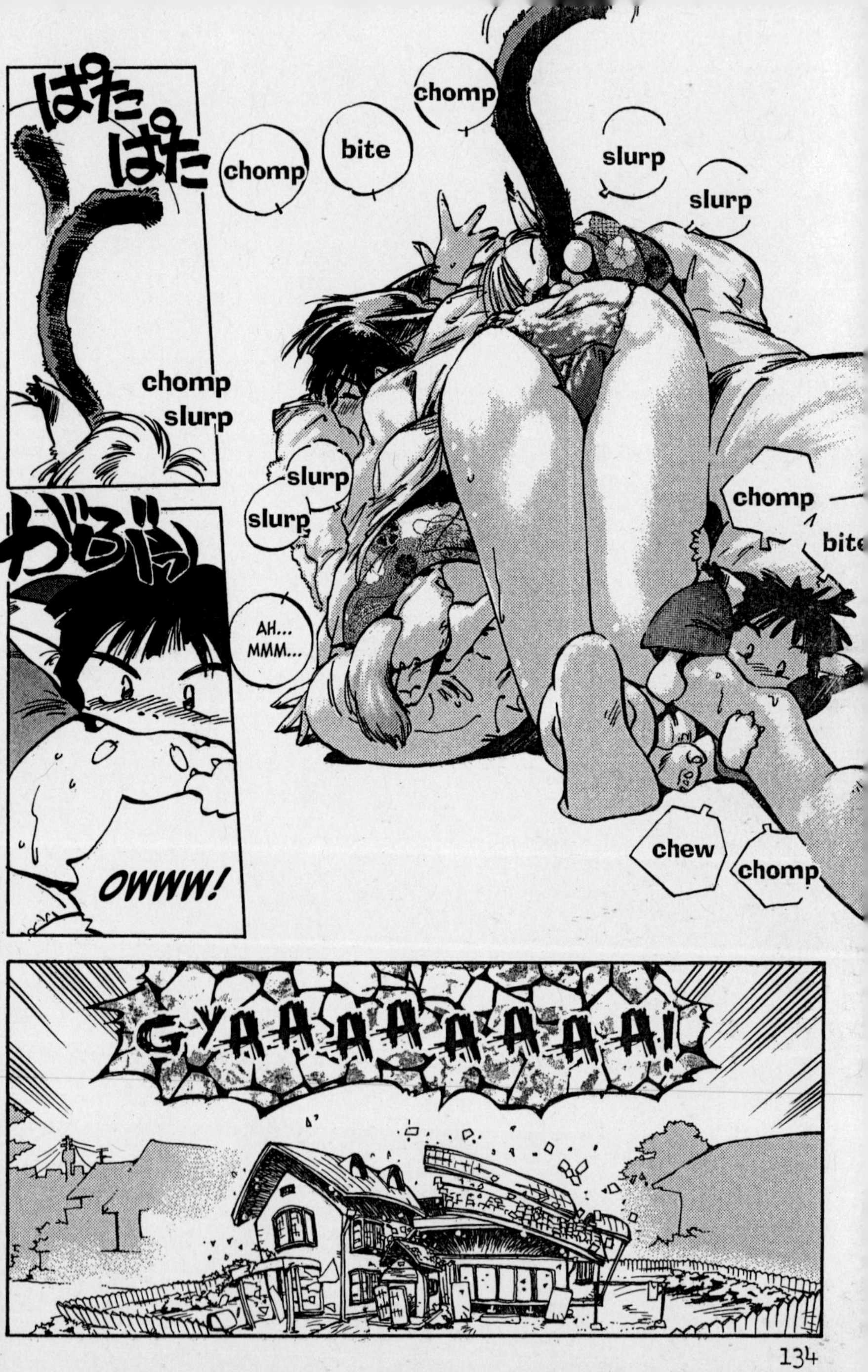
slurp
slurp
chomp
bite
chomp
chomp
bite
slurp
slurp
AH... MMM...
chomp
chew
ぱたぱた
chomp
slurp
OWWW!
GYAAAAAAAA!

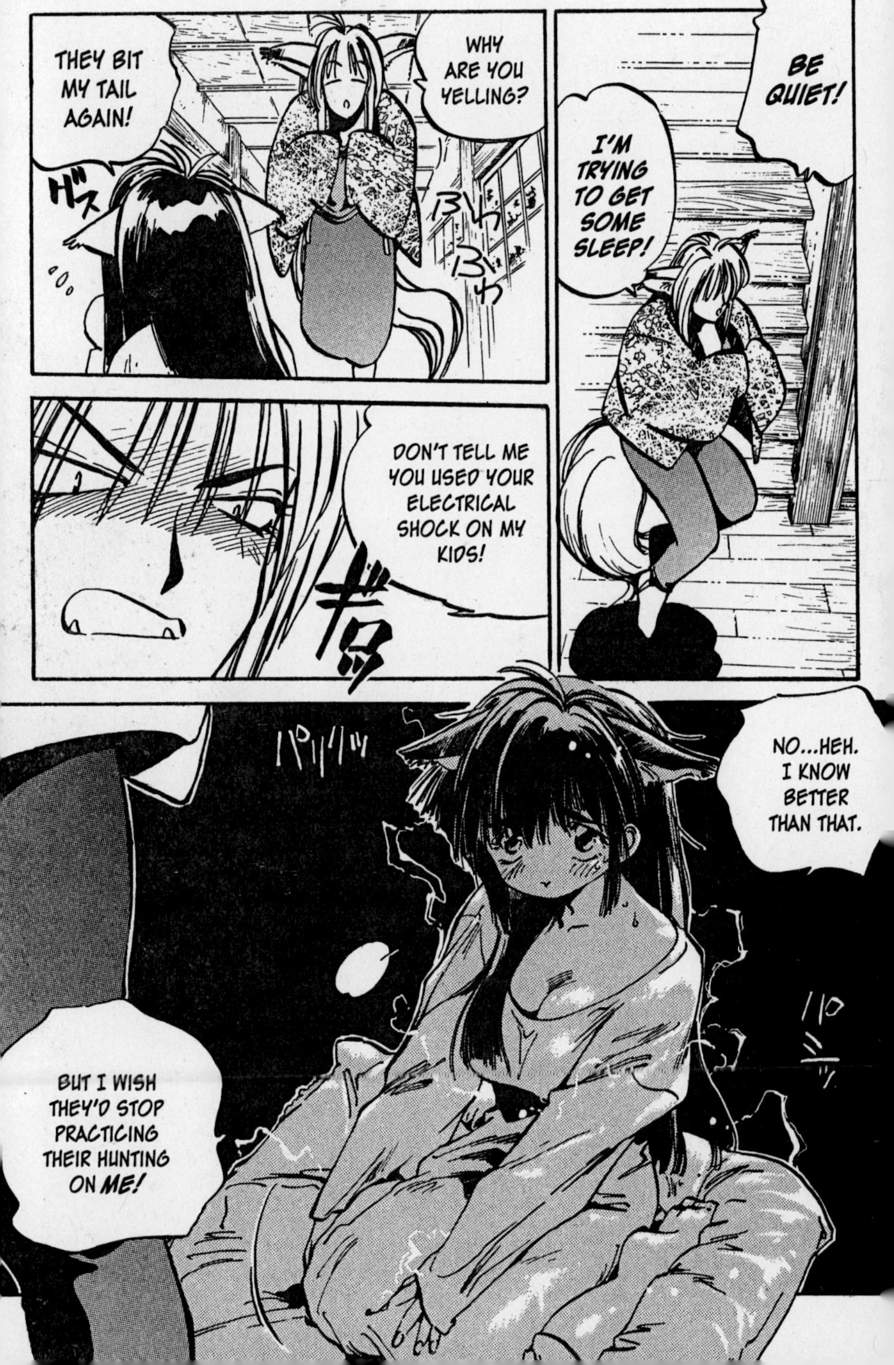
BE QUIET!
I'M TRYING TO GET SOME SLEEP!
WHY ARE YOU YELLING?
THEY BIT MY TAIL AGAIN!
DON'T TELL ME YOU USED YOUR ELECTRICAL SHOCK ON MY KIDS!
NO...HEH. I KNOW BETTER THAN THAT.
BUT I WISH THEY'D STOP PRACTICING THEIR HUNTING ON *ME*!

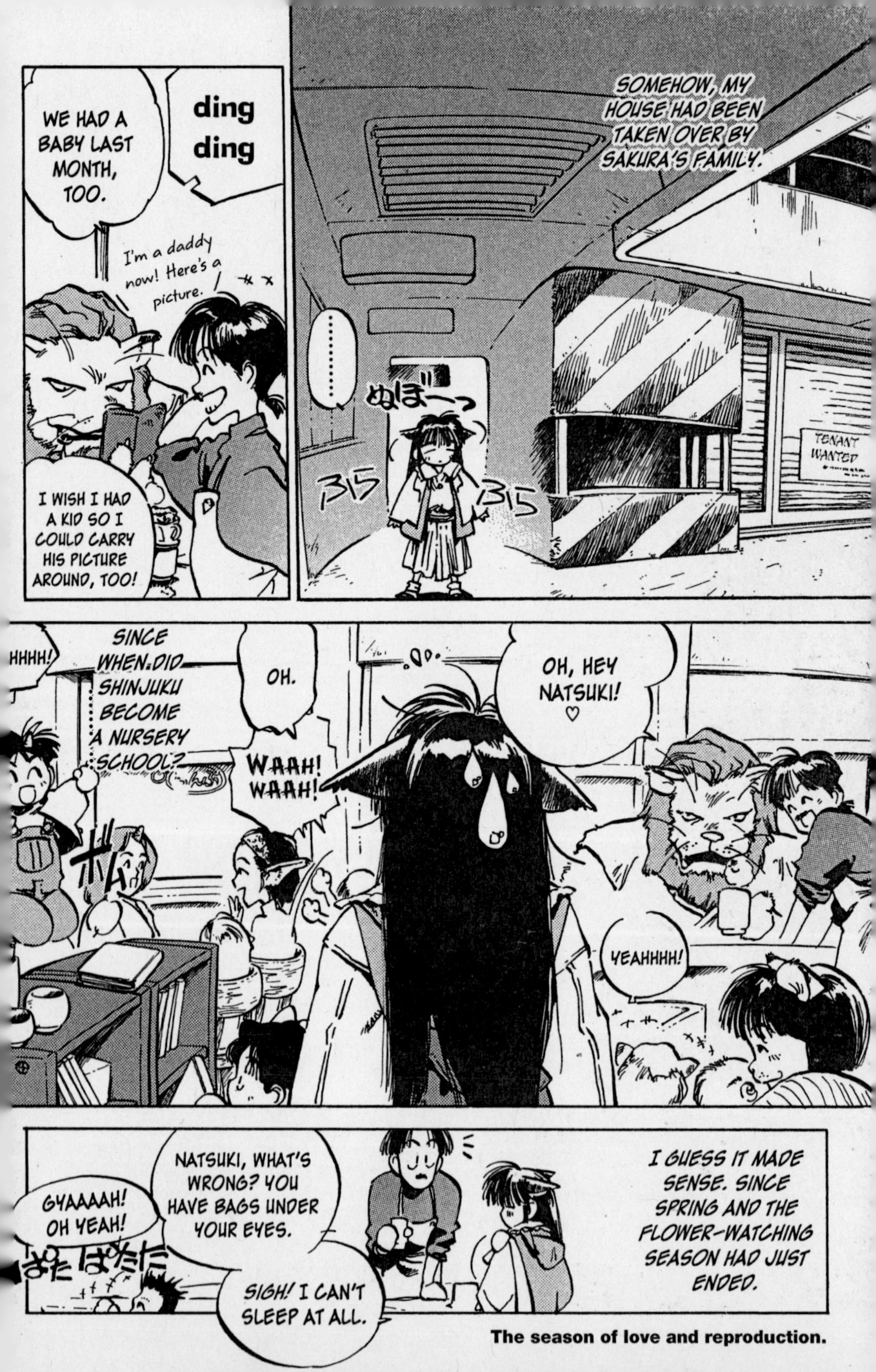
SOMEHOW, MY HOUSE HAD BEEN TAKEN OVER BY SAKURA'S FAMILY.
TENANT WANTED
ぬぼ〜っ
ふらふら
ふらふら
......
ding ding
WE HAD A BABY LAST MONTH, TOO.
I'm a daddy now! Here's a picture.
I WISH I HAD A KID SO I COULD CARRY HIS PICTURE AROUND, TOO!
OH, HEY NATSUKI! ♡
YEAHHHH!
OH.
WAAH! WAAH!
SINCE WHEN DID SHINJUKU BECOME A NURSERY SCHOOL?
HHHH!
I GUESS IT MADE SENSE. SINCE SPRING AND THE FLOWER-WATCHING SEASON HAD JUST ENDED.
NATSUKI, WHAT'S WRONG? YOU HAVE BAGS UNDER YOUR EYES.
SIGH! I CAN'T SLEEP AT ALL.
GYAAAAH! OH YEAH!

The season of love and reproduction.

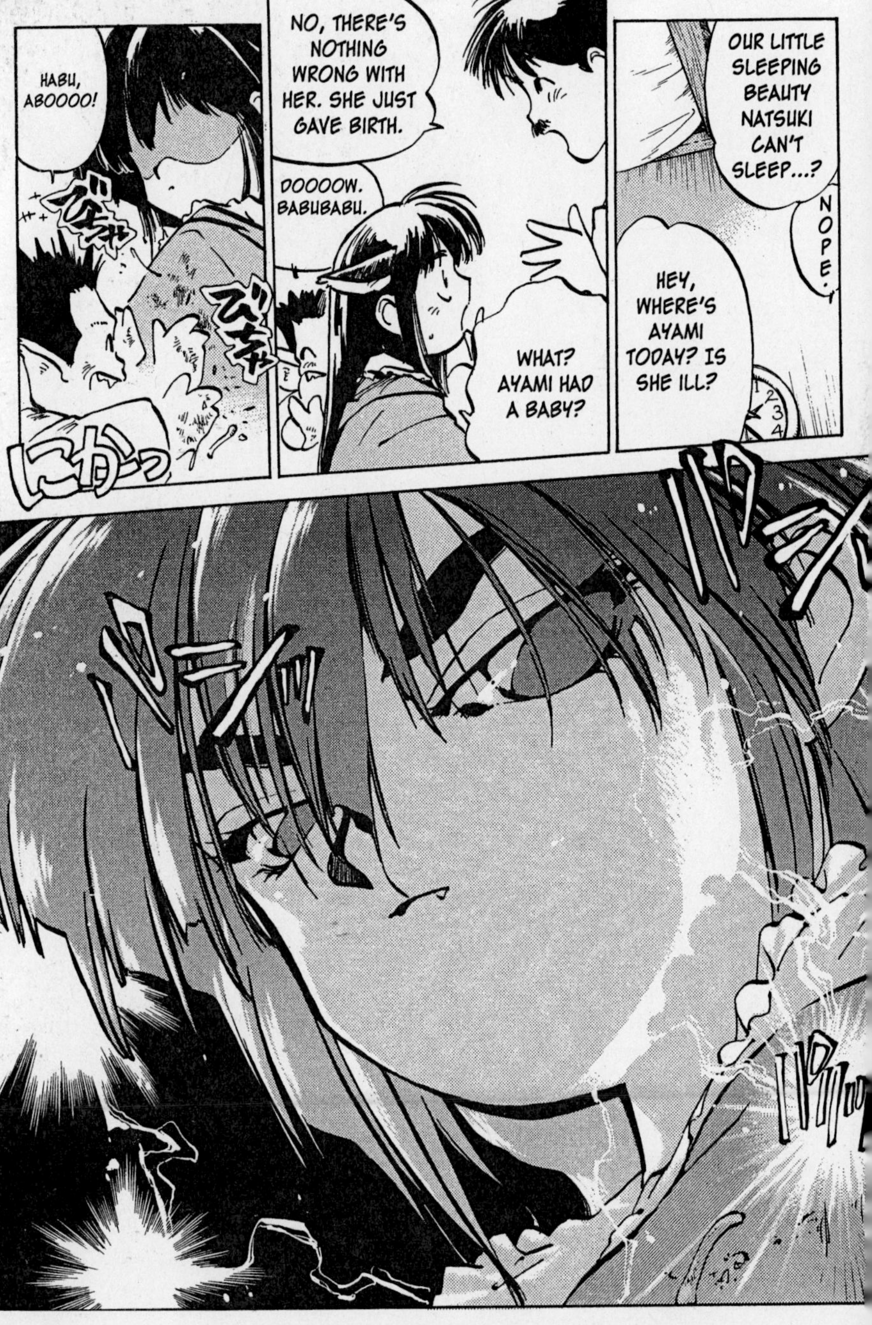
OUR LITTLE SLEEPING BEAUTY NATSUKI CAN'T SLEEP...?
NOPE.
HEY, WHERE'S AYAMI TODAY? IS SHE ILL?
NO, THERE'S NOTHING WRONG WITH HER. SHE JUST GAVE BIRTH.
DOOOOW. BABUBABU.
WHAT? AYAMI HAD A BABY?
HABU, ABOOOO!
にかっ

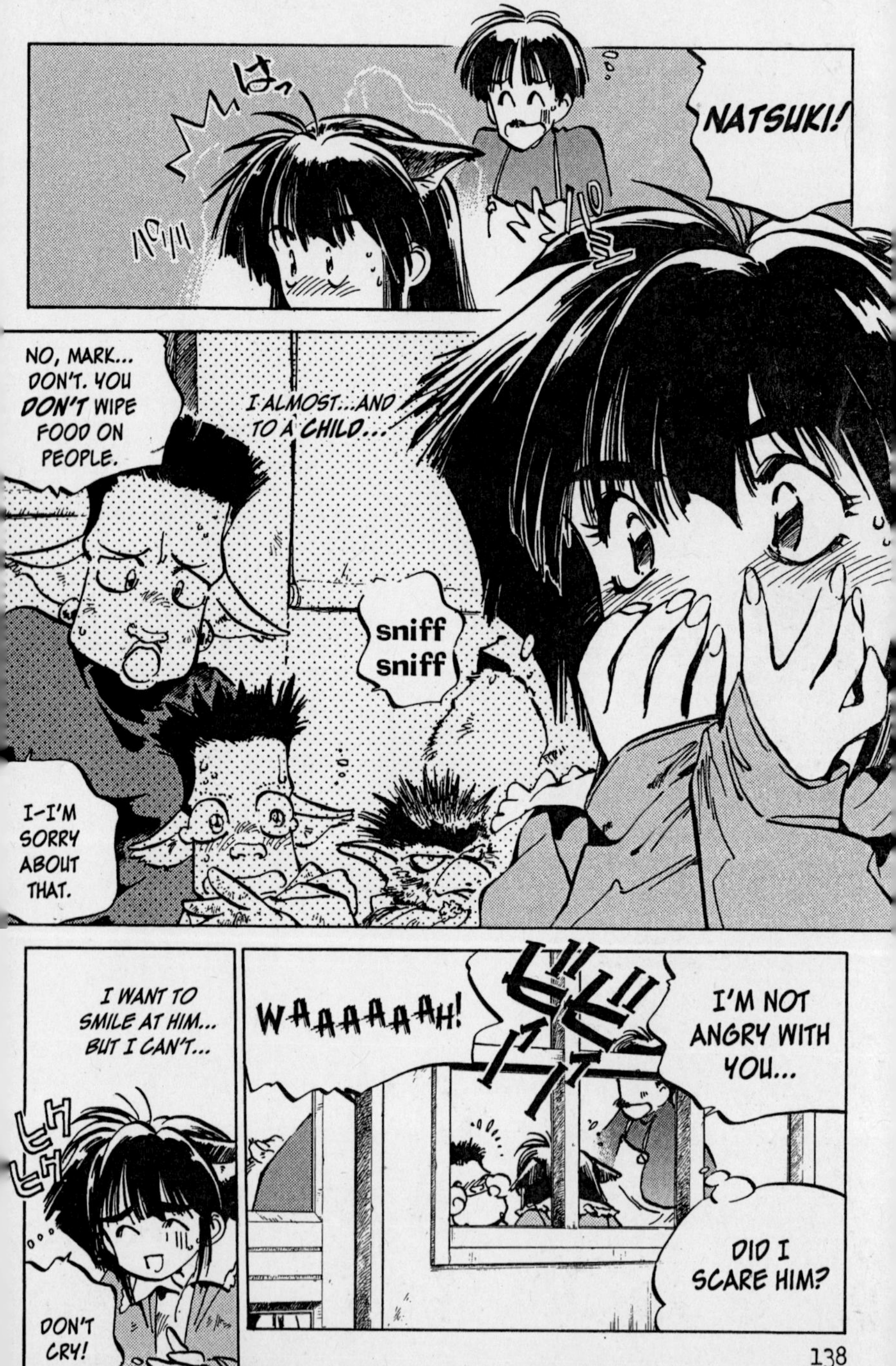
NATSUKI!
はっ
I ALMOST...AND TO A CHILD...
NO, MARK... DON'T. YOU DON'T WIPE FOOD ON PEOPLE.
sniff sniff
I-I'M SORRY ABOUT THAT.
I'M NOT ANGRY WITH YOU...
WAAAAAAAH!
DID I SCARE HIM?
I WANT TO SMILE AT HIM... BUT I CAN'T...
DON'T CRY!

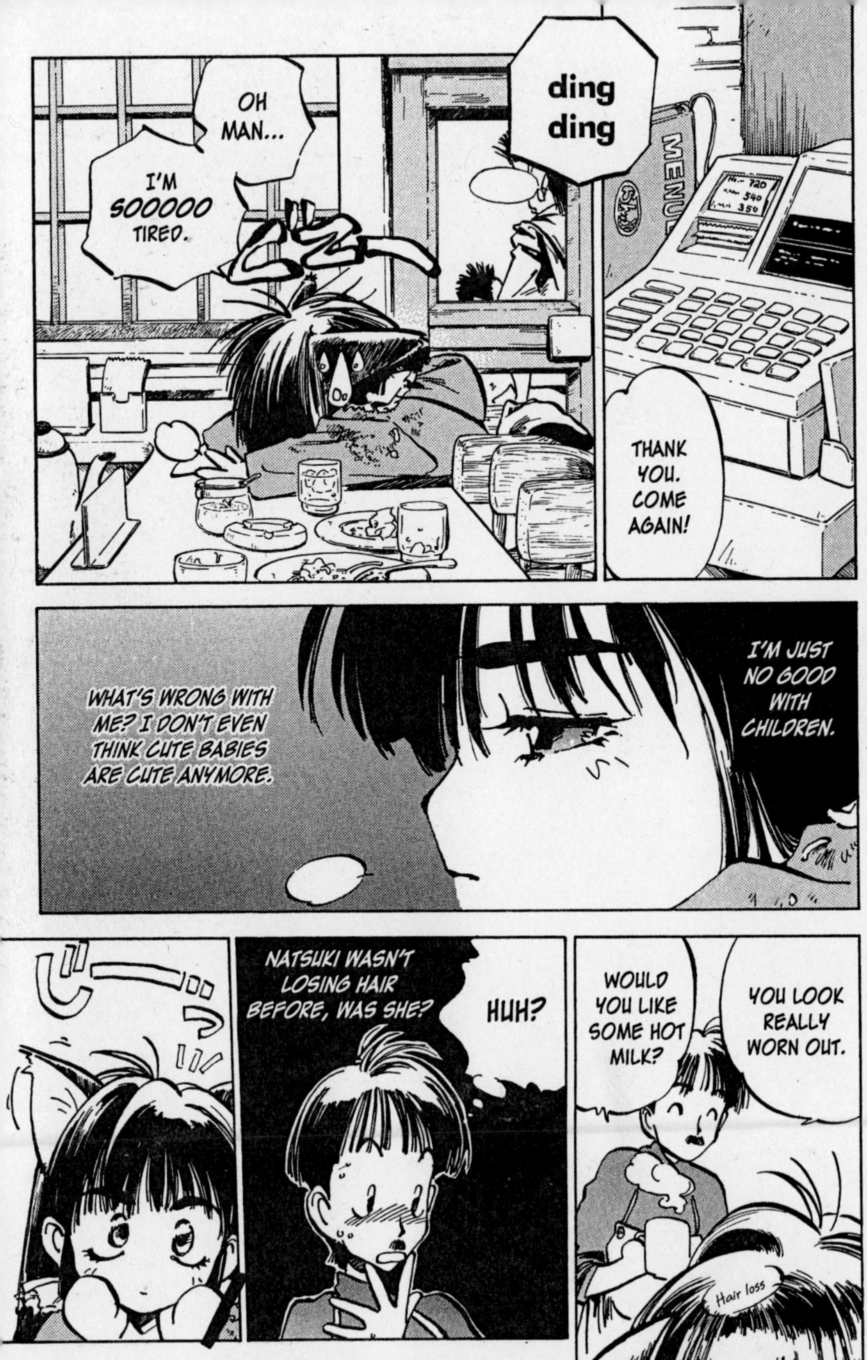
ding ding
THANK YOU. COME AGAIN!
OH MAN...
I'M SOOOOO TIRED.
I'M JUST NO GOOD WITH CHILDREN.
WHAT'S WRONG WITH ME? I DON'T EVEN THINK CUTE BABIES ARE CUTE ANYMORE.
YOU LOOK REALLY WORN OUT.
WOULD YOU LIKE SOME HOT MILK?
Hair loss
HUH?
NATSUKI WASN'T LOSING HAIR BEFORE, WAS SHE?

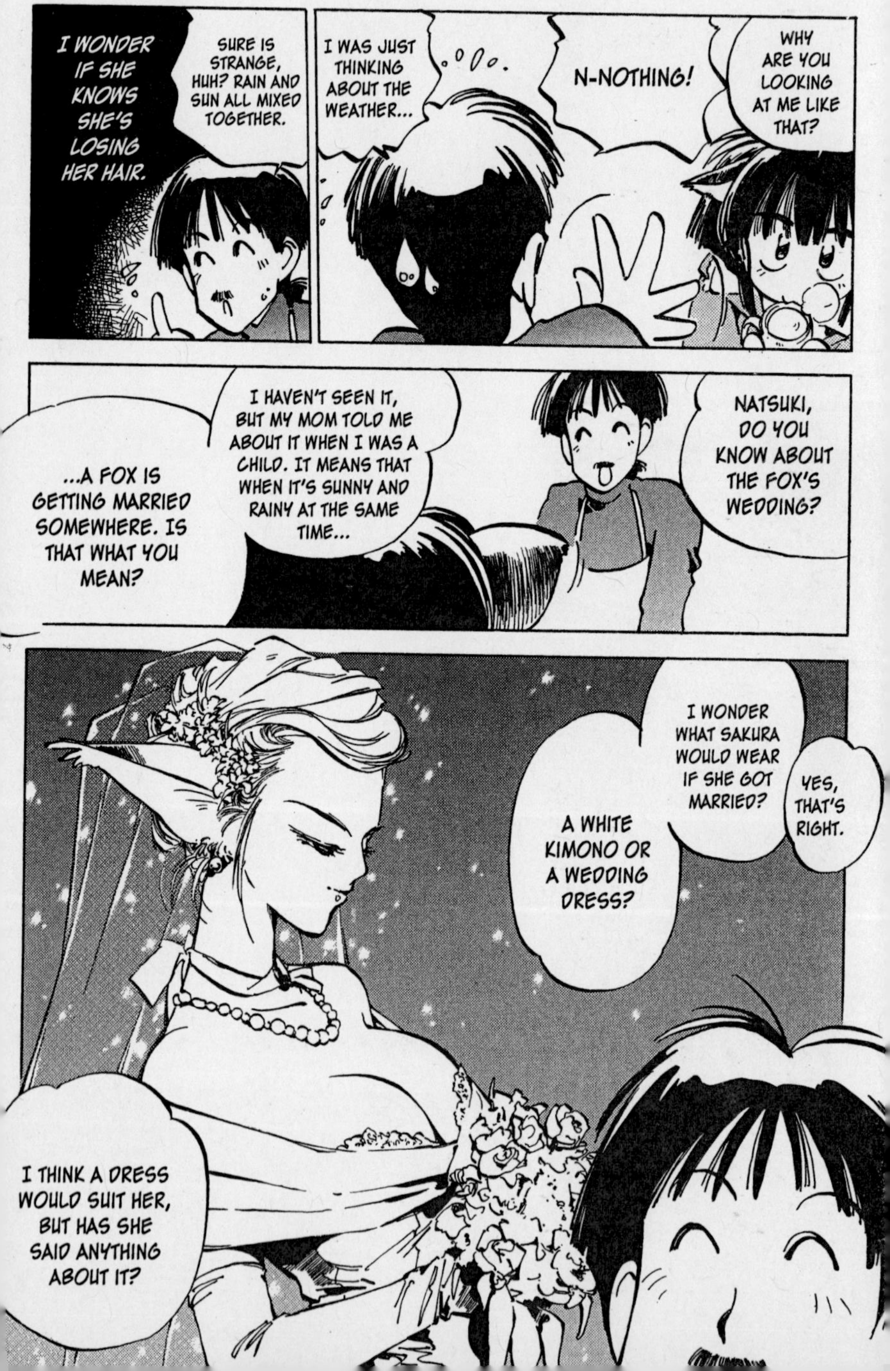
WHY ARE YOU LOOKING AT ME LIKE THAT?
N-NOTHING!
I WAS JUST THINKING ABOUT THE WEATHER...
SURE IS STRANGE, HUH? RAIN AND SUN ALL MIXED TOGETHER.
I WONDER IF SHE KNOWS SHE'S LOSING HER HAIR.
NATSUKI, DO YOU KNOW ABOUT THE FOX'S WEDDING?
I HAVEN'T SEEN IT, BUT MY MOM TOLD ME ABOUT IT WHEN I WAS A CHILD. IT MEANS THAT WHEN IT'S SUNNY AND RAINY AT THE SAME TIME...
...A FOX IS GETTING MARRIED SOMEWHERE. IS THAT WHAT YOU MEAN?
YES, THAT'S RIGHT.
I WONDER WHAT SAKURA WOULD WEAR IF SHE GOT MARRIED?
A WHITE KIMONO OR A WEDDING DRESS?
I THINK A DRESS WOULD SUIT HER, BUT HAS SHE SAID ANYTHING ABOUT IT?

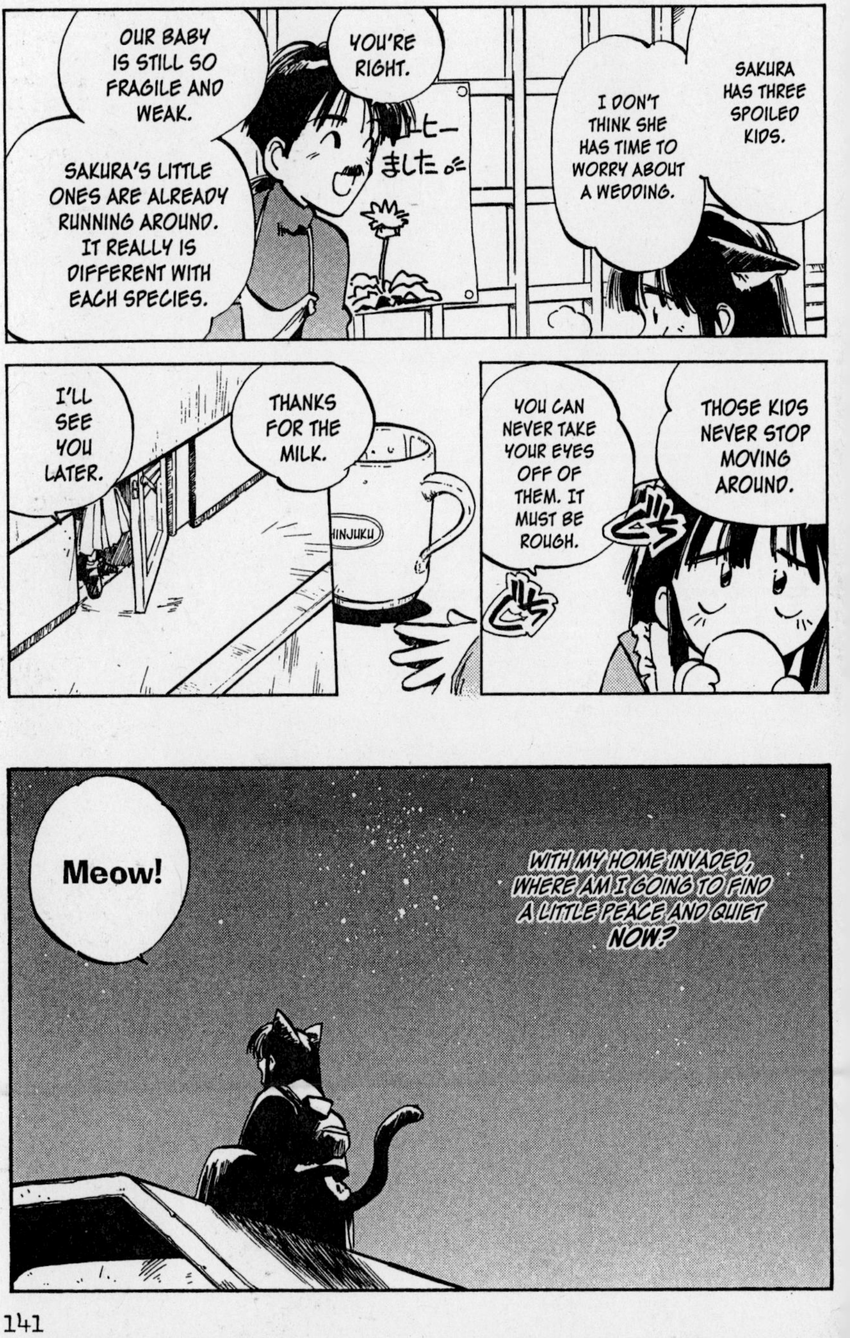

SAKURA HAS THREE SPOILED KIDS.
I DON'T THINK SHE HAS TIME TO WORRY ABOUT A WEDDING.
YOU'RE RIGHT.
OUR BABY IS STILL SO FRAGILE AND WEAK.
SAKURA'S LITTLE ONES ARE ALREADY RUNNING AROUND. IT REALLY IS DIFFERENT WITH EACH SPECIES.
THOSE KIDS NEVER STOP MOVING AROUND.
YOU CAN NEVER TAKE YOUR EYES OFF OF THEM. IT MUST BE ROUGH.
THANKS FOR THE MILK.
I'LL SEE YOU LATER.
WITH MY HOME INVADED, WHERE AM I GOING TO FIND A LITTLE PEACE AND QUIET NOW?
Meow!

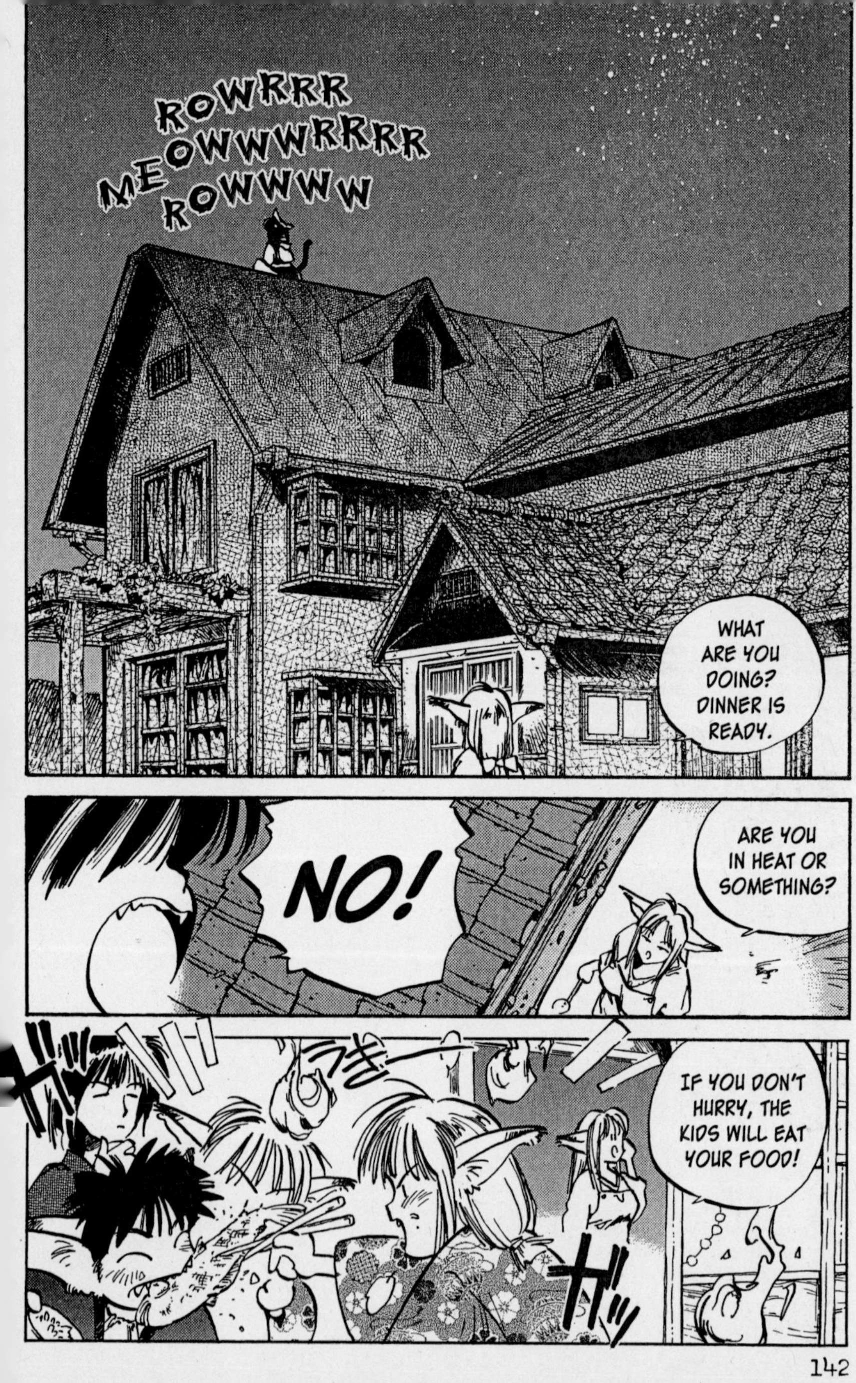
ROWRRR MEOWWWRRRR ROWWWW
WHAT ARE YOU DOING? DINNER IS READY.
ARE YOU IN HEAT OR SOMETHING?
NO!
IF YOU DON'T HURRY, THE KIDS WILL EAT YOUR FOOD!

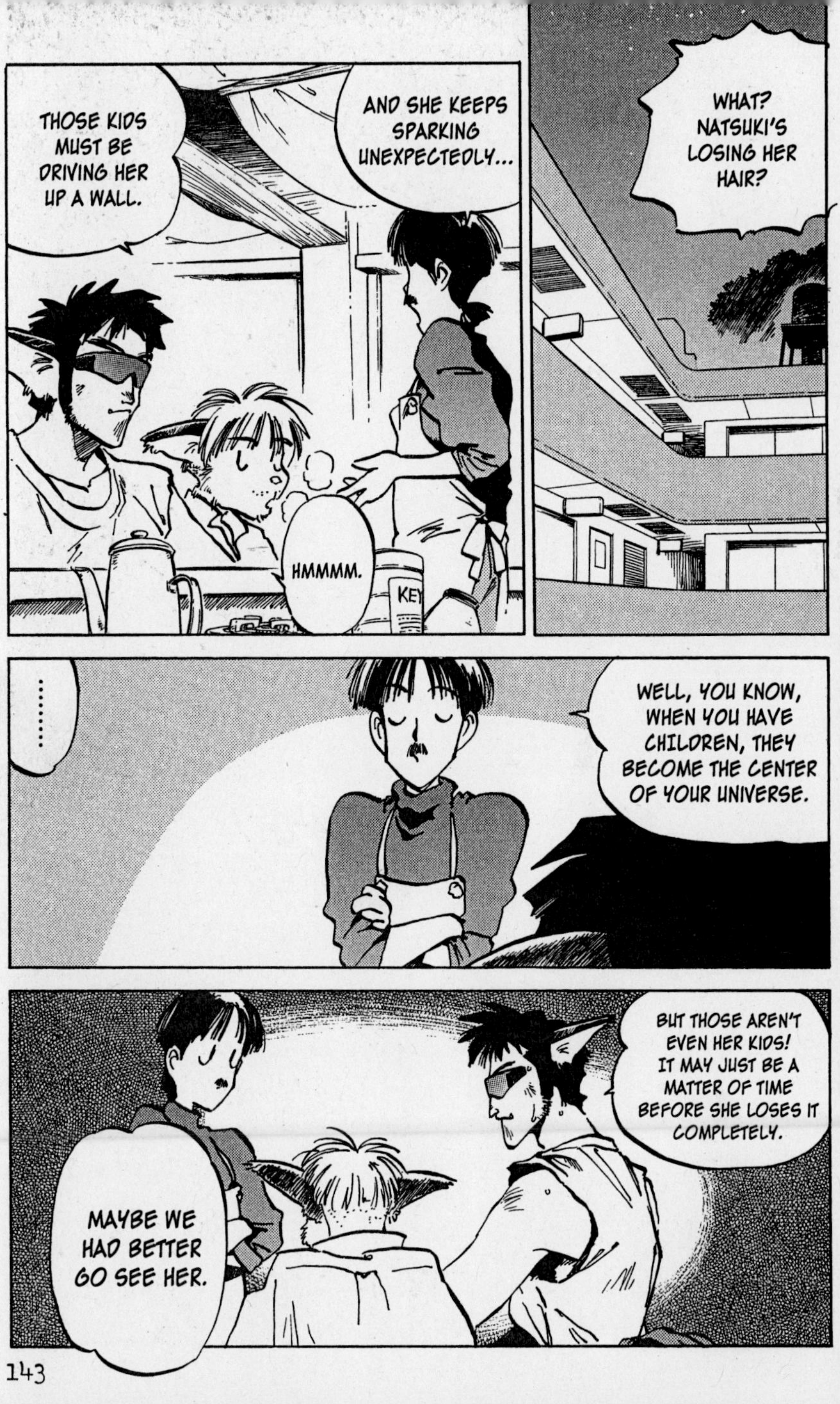
WHAT? NATSUKI'S LOSING HER HAIR?
AND SHE KEEPS SPARKING UNEXPECTEDLY...
THOSE KIDS MUST BE DRIVING HER UP A WALL.
HMMMM.
WELL, YOU KNOW, WHEN YOU HAVE CHILDREN, THEY BECOME THE CENTER OF YOUR UNIVERSE.
......
BUT THOSE AREN'T EVEN HER KIDS! IT MAY JUST BE A MATTER OF TIME BEFORE SHE LOSES IT COMPLETELY.
MAYBE WE HAD BETTER GO SEE HER.

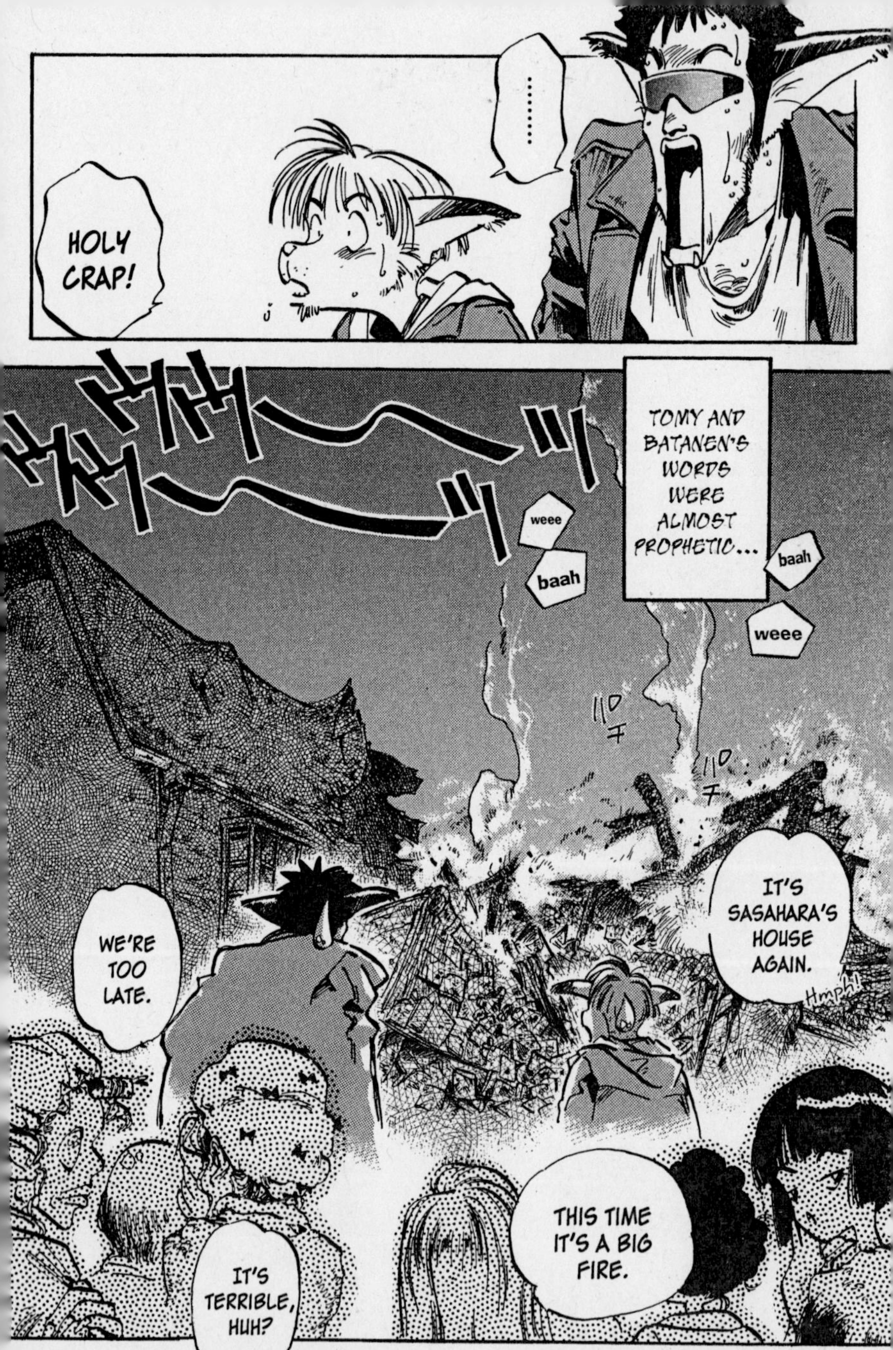
......
HOLY CRAP!
TOMY AND BATANEN'S WORDS WERE ALMOST PROPHETIC...
baah
weee
weee
baah
IT'S SASAHARA'S HOUSE AGAIN.
Hmph!
WE'RE TOO LATE.
THIS TIME IT'S A BIG FIRE.
IT'S TERRIBLE, HUH?

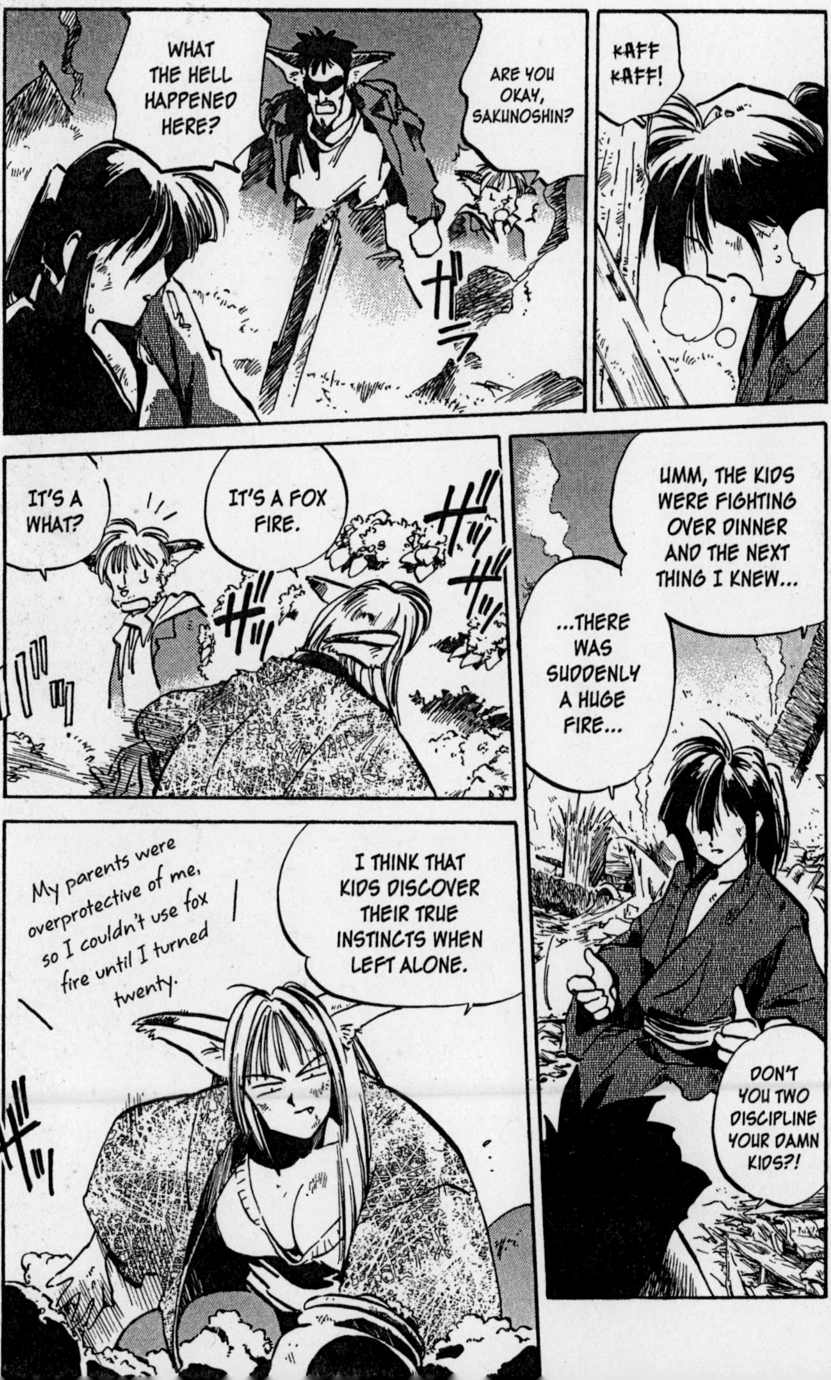
KAFF KAFF!
ARE YOU OKAY, SAKUNOSHIN?
WHAT THE HELL HAPPENED HERE?
ガラ
UMM, THE KIDS WERE FIGHTING OVER DINNER AND THE NEXT THING I KNEW...
...THERE WAS SUDDENLY A HUGE FIRE...
DON'T YOU TWO DISCIPLINE YOUR DAMN KIDS?!
IT'S A FOX FIRE.
IT'S A WHAT?
I THINK THAT KIDS DISCOVER THEIR TRUE INSTINCTS WHEN LEFT ALONE.
My parents were overprotective of me, so I couldn't use fox fire until I turned twenty.

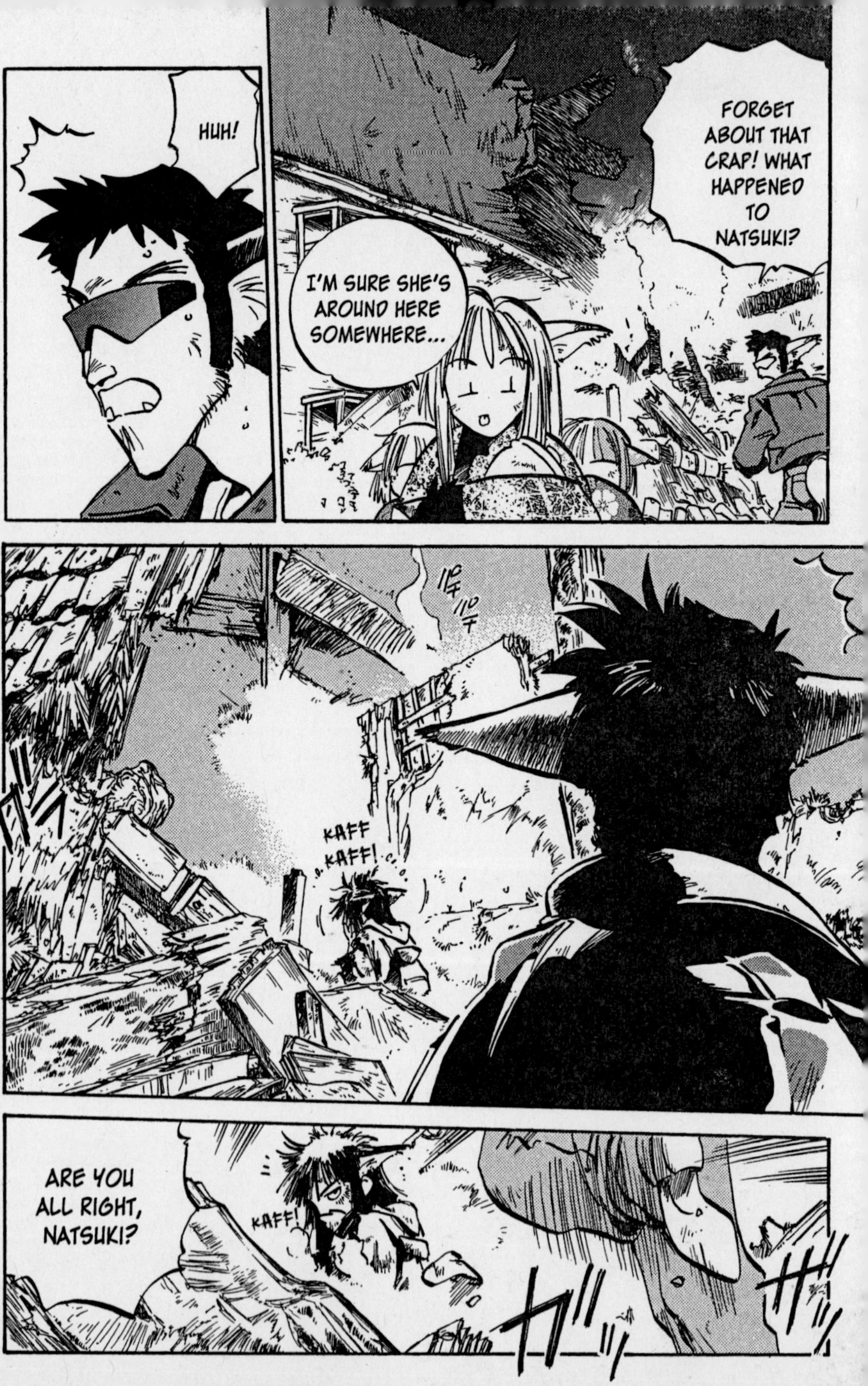
FORGET ABOUT THAT CRAP! WHAT HAPPENED TO NATSUKI?
I'M SURE SHE'S AROUND HERE SOMEWHERE...
HUH!
KAFF KAFF!
ARE YOU ALL RIGHT, NATSUKI?
KAFF!

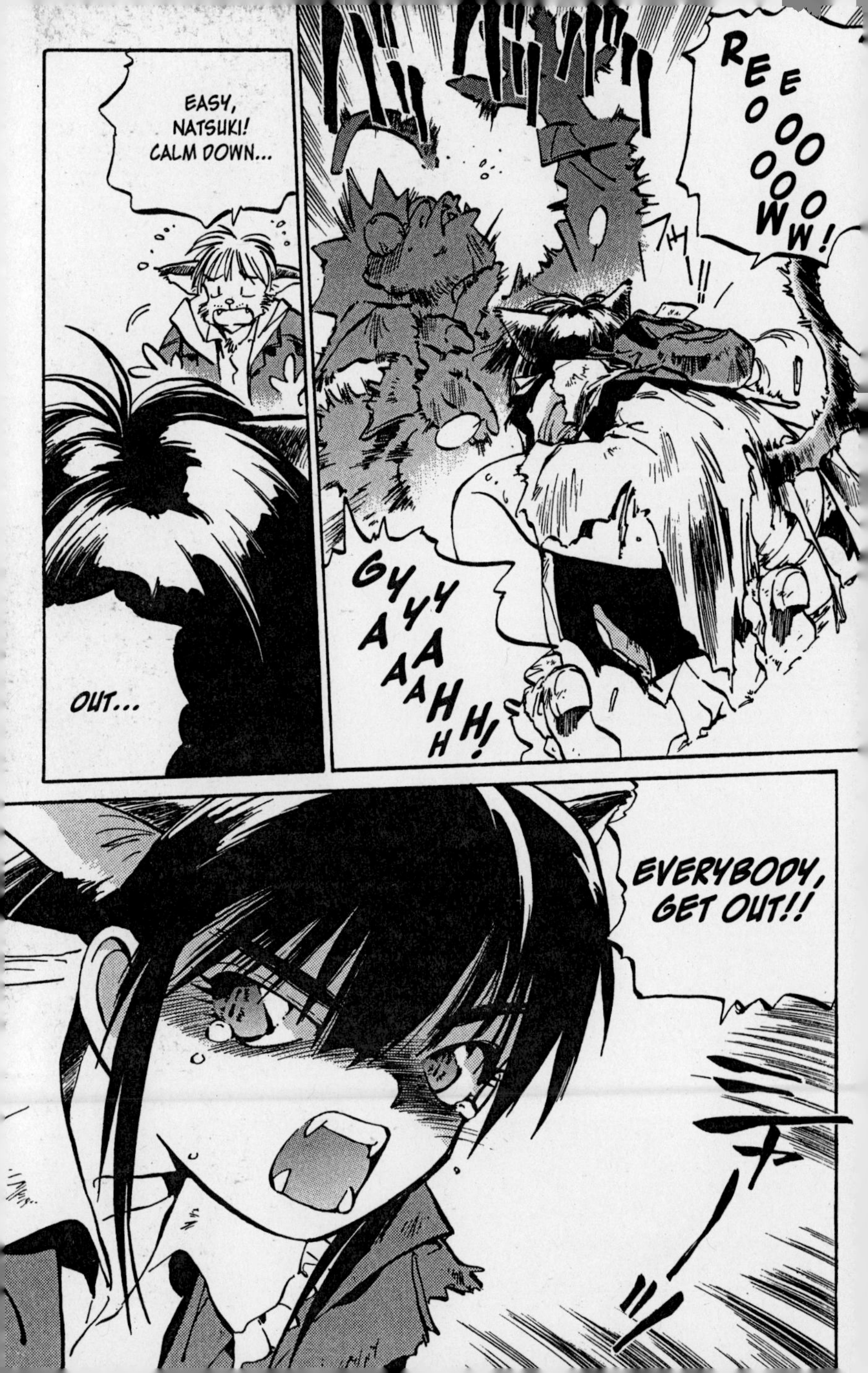
REEOOOOOOWW!
GYYYAAAAAHH!
EASY, NATSUKI! CALM DOWN...
OUT...
EVERYBODY, GET OUT!!

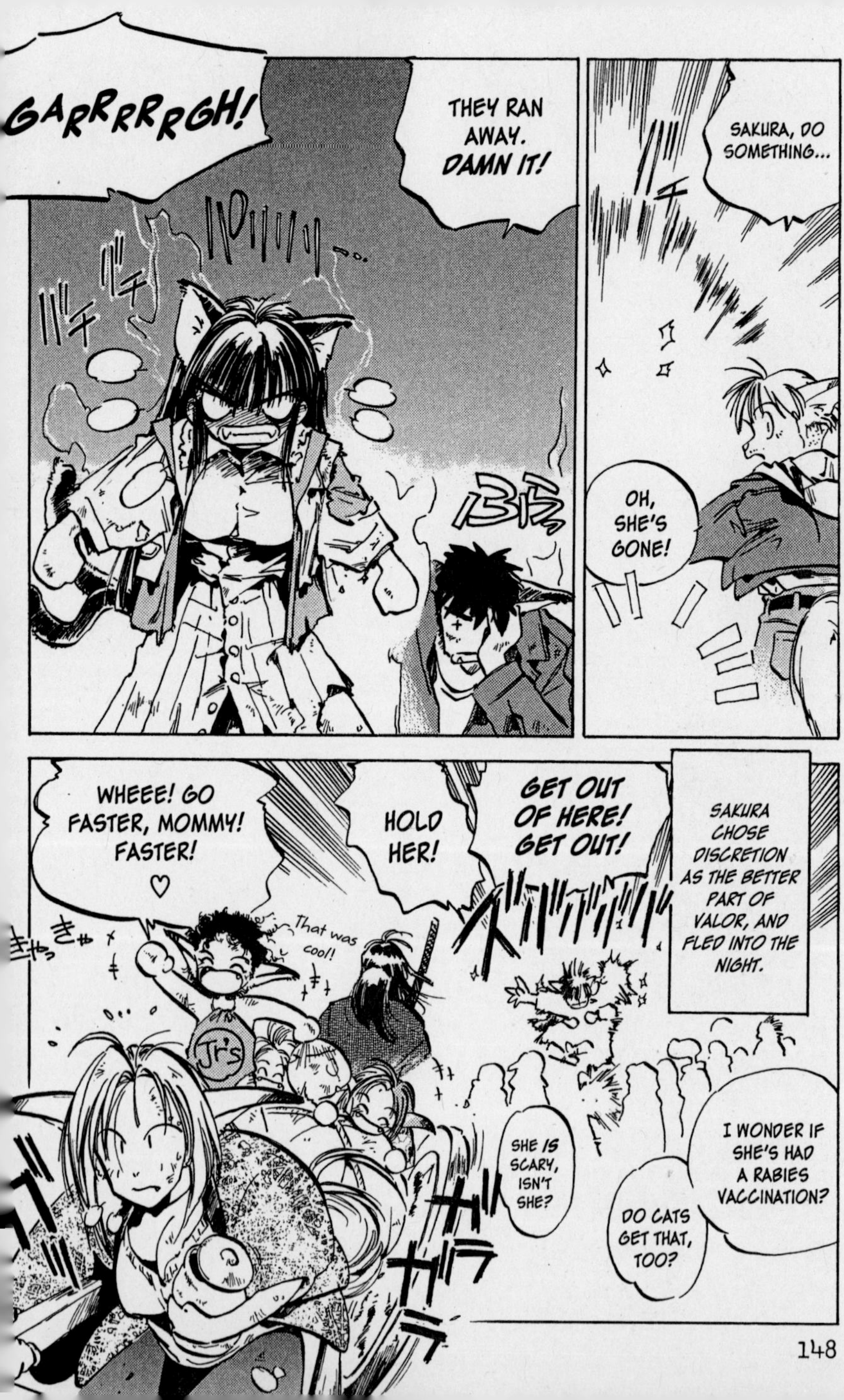
SAKURA, DO SOMETHING...
OH, SHE'S GONE!
THEY RAN AWAY. DAMN IT!
GARRRRRGH!
SAKURA CHOSE DISCRETION AS THE BETTER PART OF VALOR, AND FLED INTO THE NIGHT.
GET OUT OF HERE! GET OUT!
HOLD HER!
WHEEE! GO FASTER, MOMMY! FASTER! ♡
That was cool!
Jr's
I WONDER IF SHE'S HAD A RABIES VACCINATION?
SHE IS SCARY, ISN'T SHE?
DO CATS GET THAT, TOO?

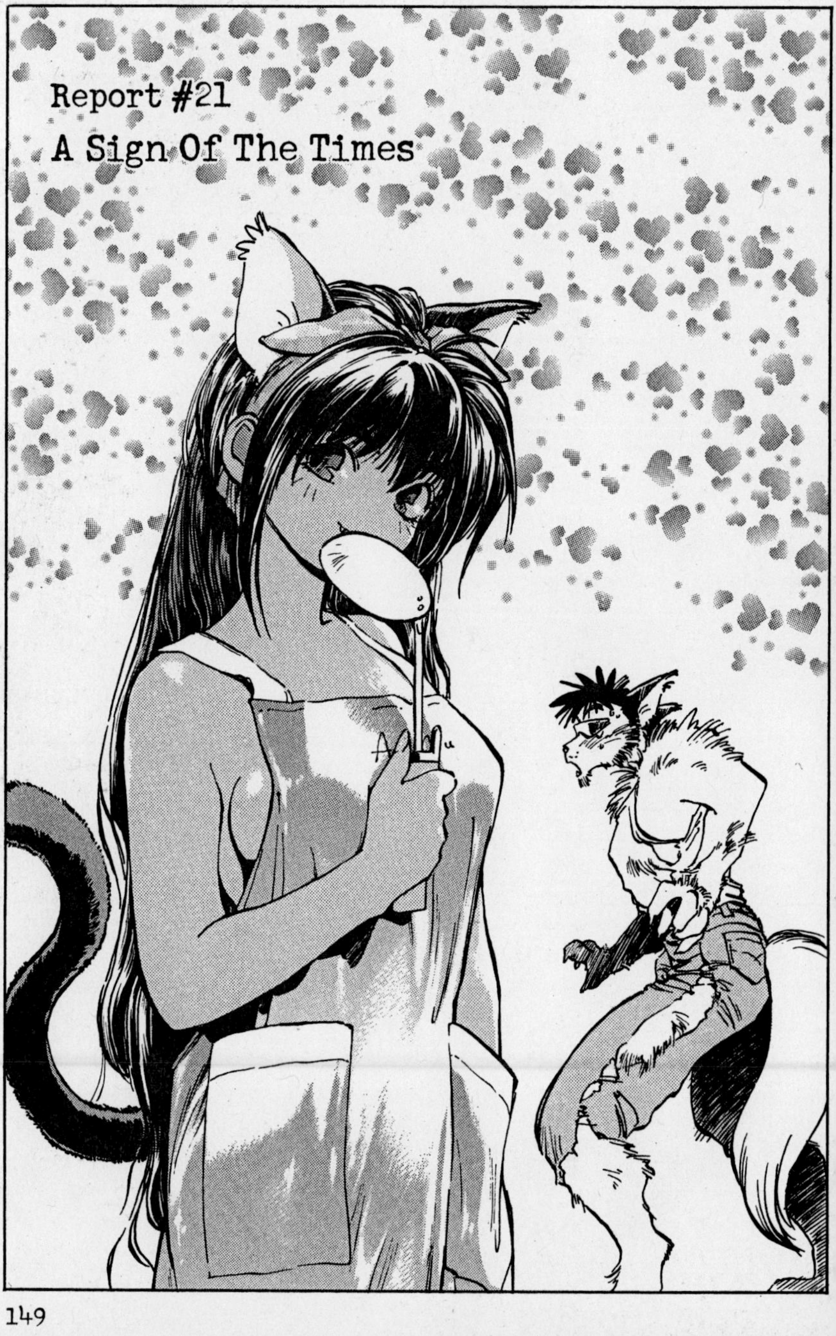
Report #21
A Sign Of The Times

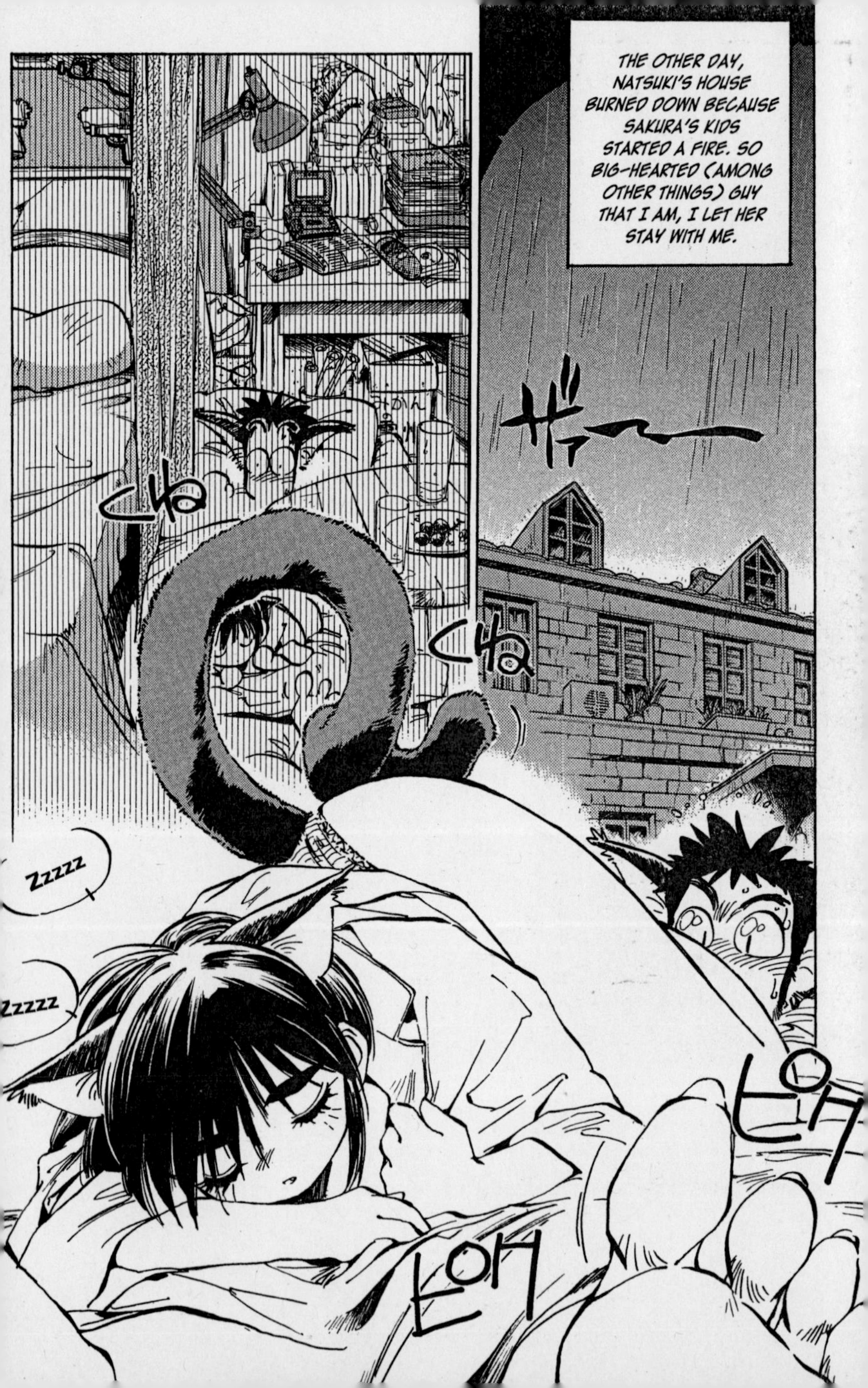
THE OTHER DAY, NATSUKI'S HOUSE BURNED DOWN BECAUSE SAKURA'S KIDS STARTED A FIRE. SO BIG-HEARTED (AMONG OTHER THINGS) GUY THAT I AM, I LET HER STAY WITH ME.
ザァーー
Zzzzz
Zzzzz

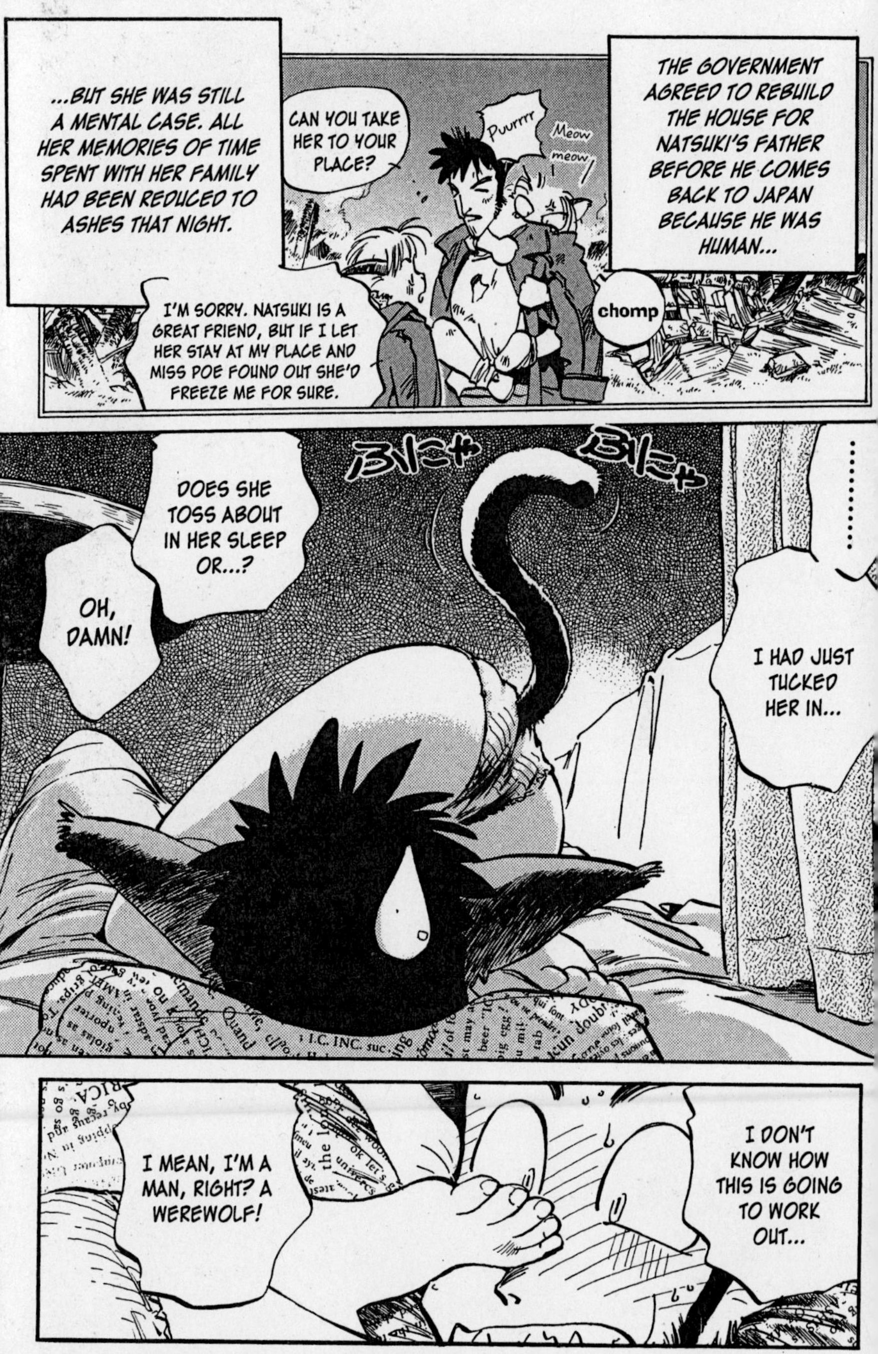
THE GOVERNMENT AGREED TO REBUILD THE HOUSE FOR NATSUKI'S FATHER BEFORE HE COMES BACK TO JAPAN BECAUSE HE WAS HUMAN...
Meow meow
Puurrrr
CAN YOU TAKE HER TO YOUR PLACE?
...BUT SHE WAS STILL A MENTAL CASE. ALL HER MEMORIES OF TIME SPENT WITH HER FAMILY HAD BEEN REDUCED TO ASHES THAT NIGHT.
chomp
I'M SORRY. NATSUKI IS A GREAT FRIEND, BUT IF I LET HER STAY AT MY PLACE AND MISS POE FOUND OUT SHE'D FREEZE ME FOR SURE.
......
I HAD JUST TUCKED HER IN...
ふにゃ
ふにゃ
DOES SHE TOSS ABOUT IN HER SLEEP OR...?
OH, DAMN!
I DON'T KNOW HOW THIS IS GOING TO WORK OUT...
I MEAN, I'M A MAN, RIGHT? A WEREWOLF!

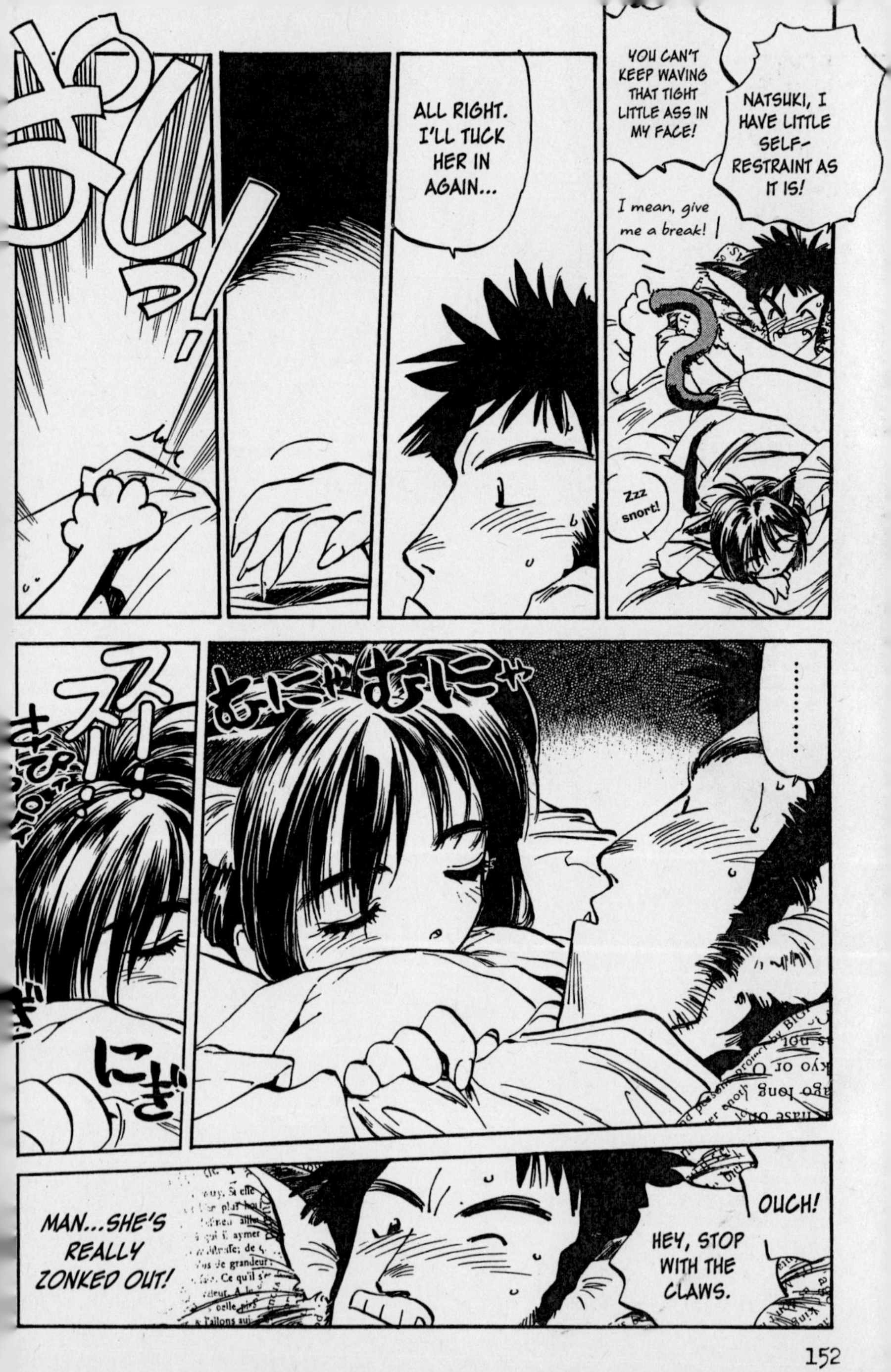
NATSUKI, I HAVE LITTLE SELF-RESTRAINT AS IT IS!
YOU CAN'T KEEP WAVING THAT TIGHT LITTLE ASS IN MY FACE!
I mean, give me a break!
Zzz snort!
ALL RIGHT. I'LL TUCK HER IN AGAIN...
......
むにゃむにゃ
スースー
にぎ
OUCH!
HEY, STOP WITH THE CLAWS.
MAN...SHE'S REALLY ZONKED OUT!

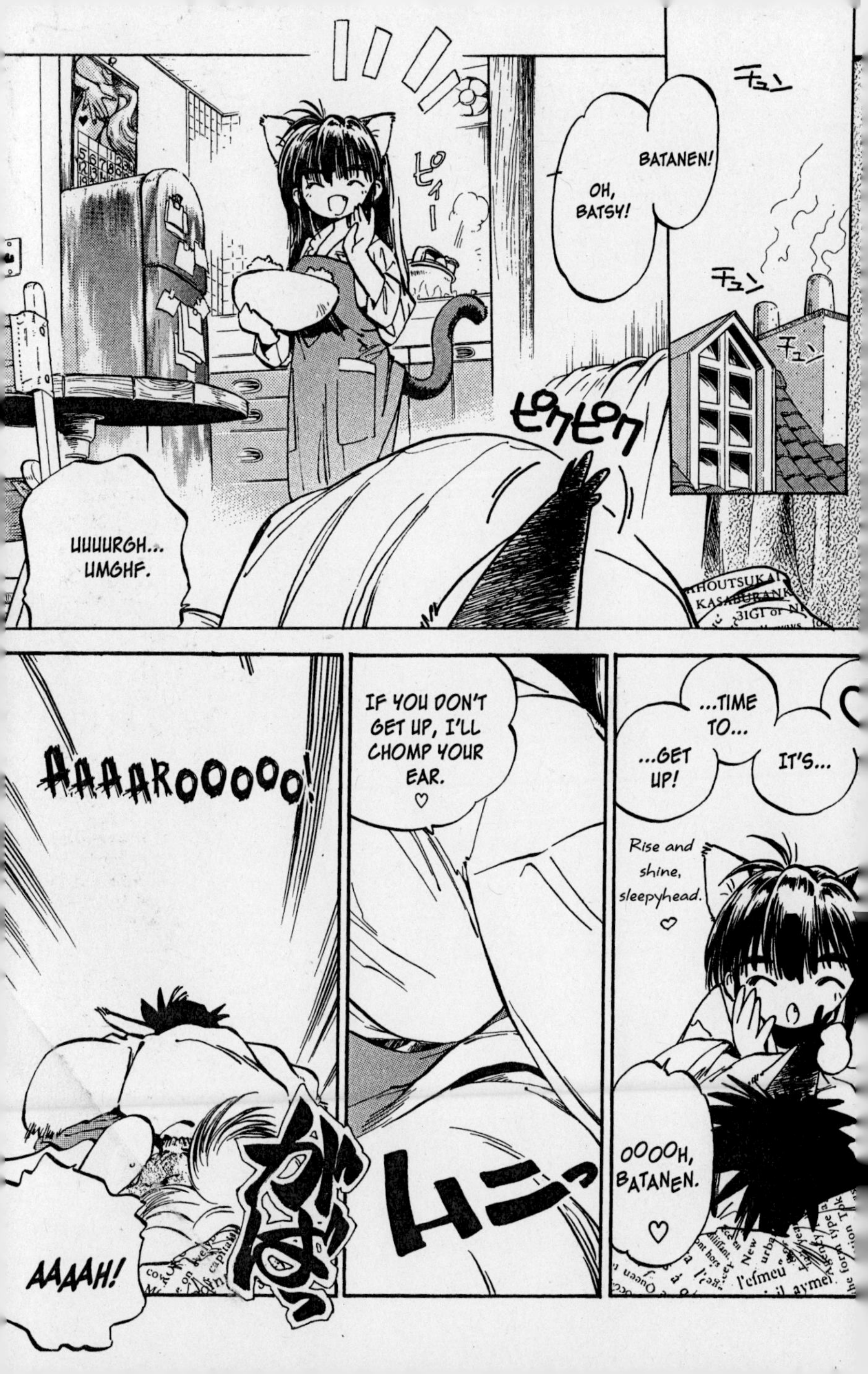
チュン
BATANEN!
OH, BATSY!
チュン
チュン
ピィー
ピクピク
UUUURGH... UMGHF.
IT'S...
...TIME TO...
...GET UP!
Rise and shine, sleepyhead. ♡
OOOOH, BATANEN. ♡
IF YOU DON'T GET UP, I'LL CHOMP YOUR EAR. ♡
ムニっ
AAAAROOOOO!
AAAAH!

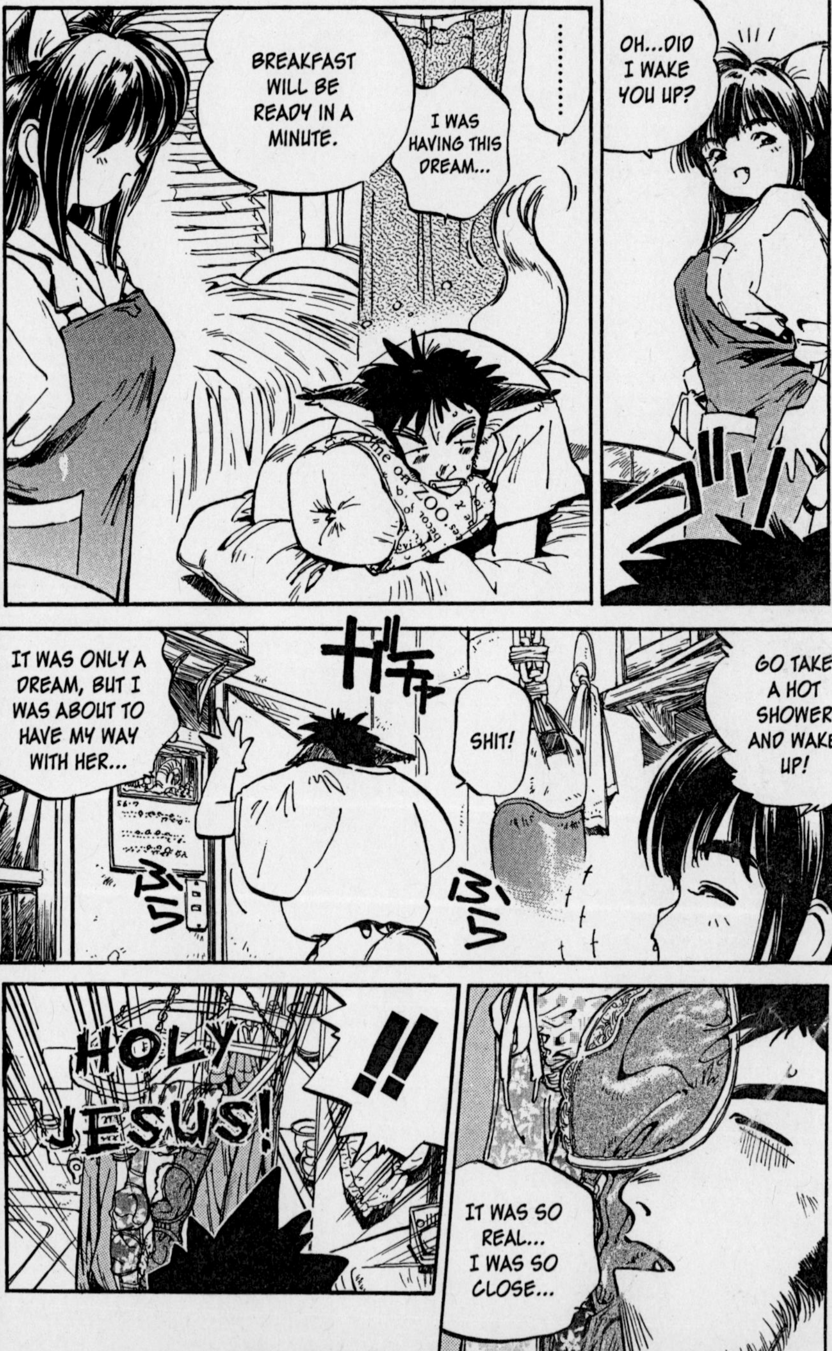
OH...DID I WAKE YOU UP?
......
I WAS HAVING THIS DREAM...
BREAKFAST WILL BE READY IN A MINUTE.
GO TAKE A HOT SHOWER AND WAKE UP!
SHIT!
ガチャ
IT WAS ONLY A DREAM, BUT I WAS ABOUT TO HAVE MY WAY WITH HER...
ぶら
ぶら
IT WAS SO REAL... I WAS SO CLOSE...
!!
HOLY JESUS!

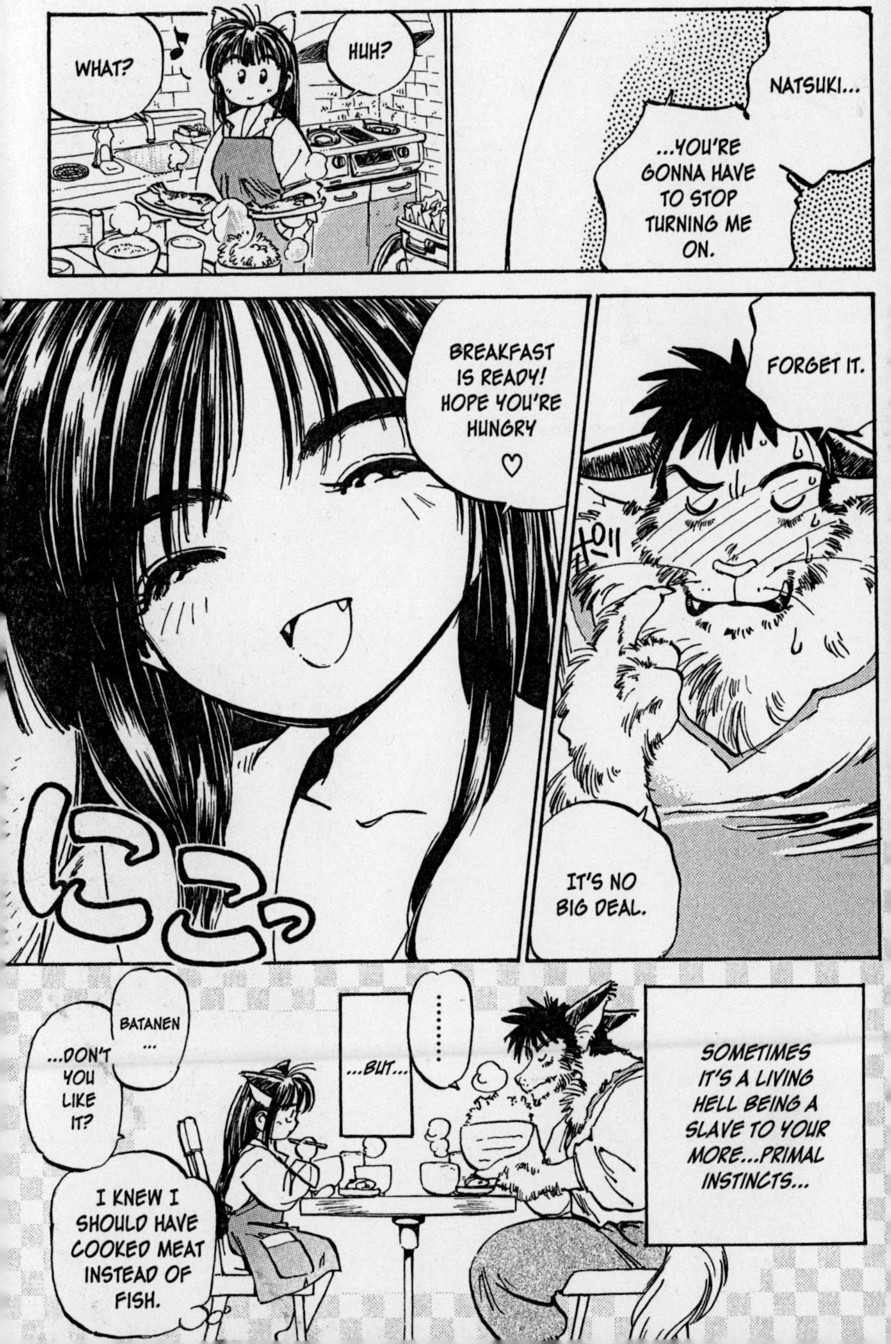
NATSUKI...
...YOU'RE GONNA HAVE TO STOP TURNING ME ON.
HUH?
WHAT?
FORGET IT.
IT'S NO BIG DEAL.
BREAKFAST IS READY! HOPE YOU'RE HUNGRY ♡
にこっ
SOMETIMES IT'S A LIVING HELL BEING A SLAVE TO YOUR MORE...PRIMAL INSTINCTS...
......
...BUT...
BATANEN ...
...DON'T YOU LIKE IT?
I KNEW I SHOULD HAVE COOKED MEAT INSTEAD OF FISH.

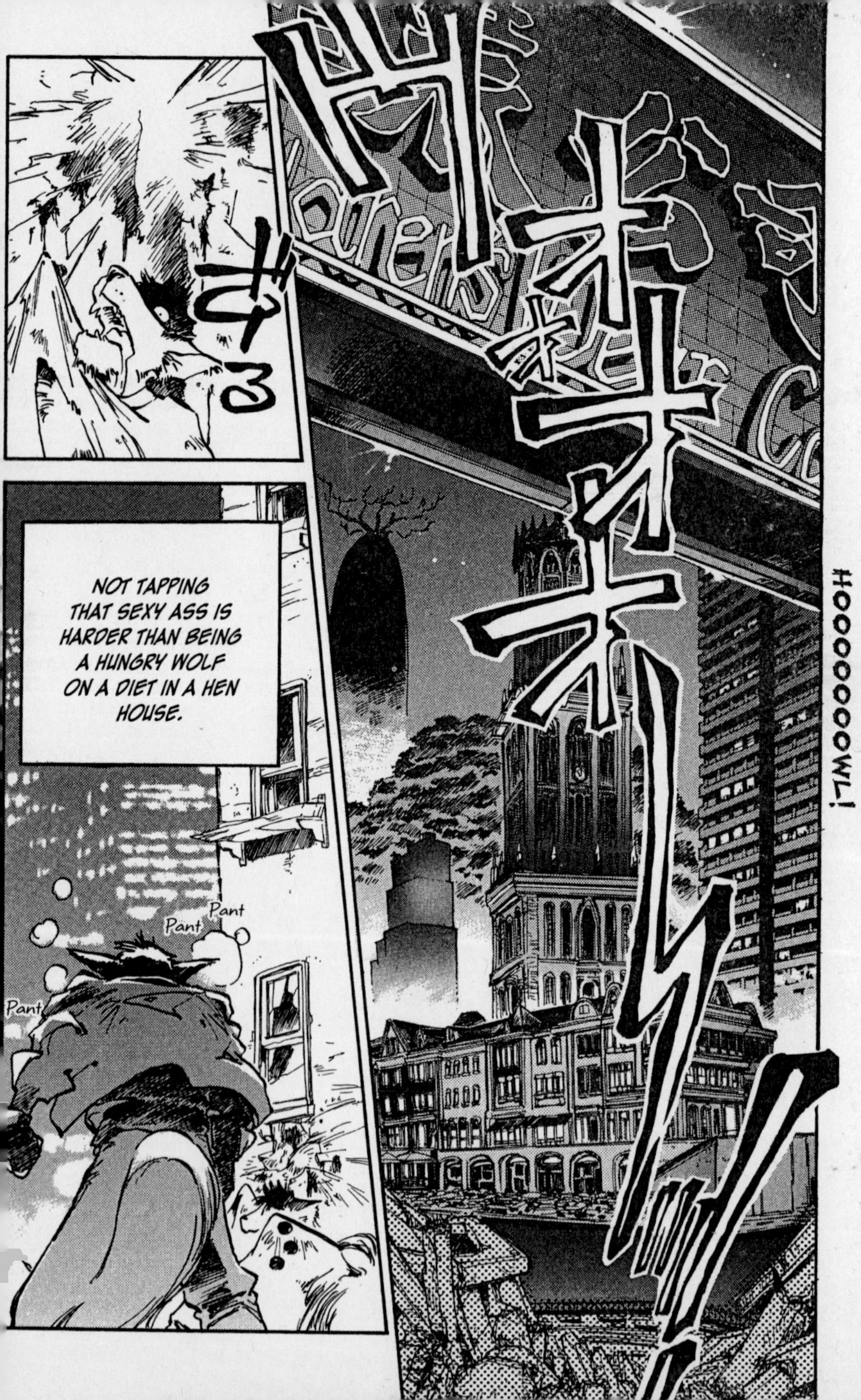
HOOOOOOOOWL!
NOT TAPPING THAT SEXY ASS IS HARDER THAN BEING A HUNGRY WOLF ON A DIET IN A HEN HOUSE.
Pant
Pant
Pant

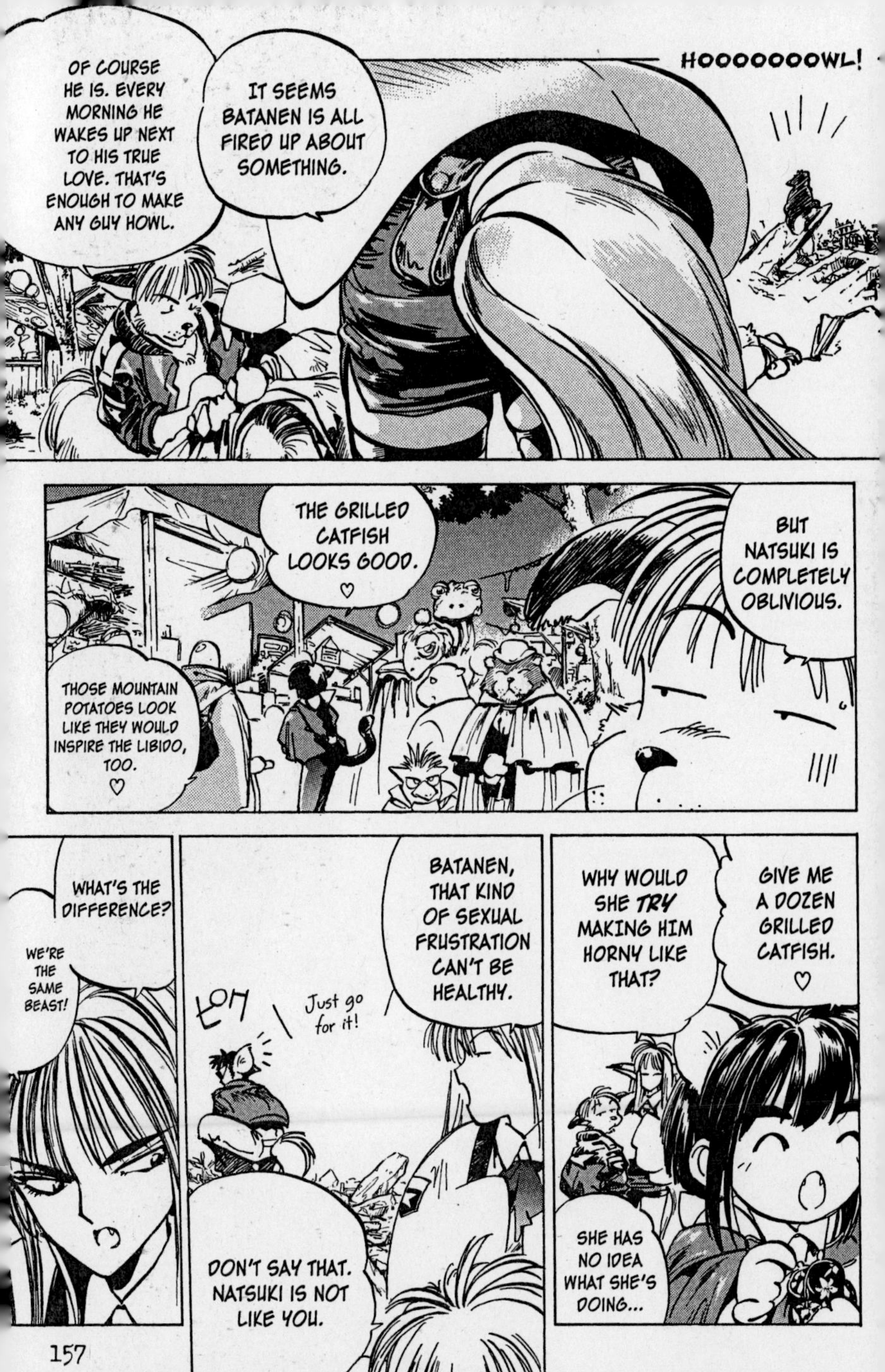
HOOOOOOOWL!
IT SEEMS BATANEN IS ALL FIRED UP ABOUT SOMETHING.
OF COURSE HE IS. EVERY MORNING HE WAKES UP NEXT TO HIS TRUE LOVE. THAT'S ENOUGH TO MAKE ANY GUY HOWL.
BUT NATSUKI IS COMPLETELY OBLIVIOUS.
THE GRILLED CATFISH LOOKS GOOD. ♡
THOSE MOUNTAIN POTATOES LOOK LIKE THEY WOULD INSPIRE THE LIBIDO, TOO. ♡
GIVE ME A DOZEN GRILLED CATFISH. ♡
WHY WOULD SHE *TRY* MAKING HIM HORNY LIKE THAT?
SHE HAS NO IDEA WHAT SHE'S DOING...
BATANEN, THAT KIND OF SEXUAL FRUSTRATION CAN'T BE HEALTHY.
Just go for it!
DON'T SAY THAT. NATSUKI IS NOT LIKE YOU.
WHAT'S THE DIFFERENCE?
WE'RE THE SAME BEAST!

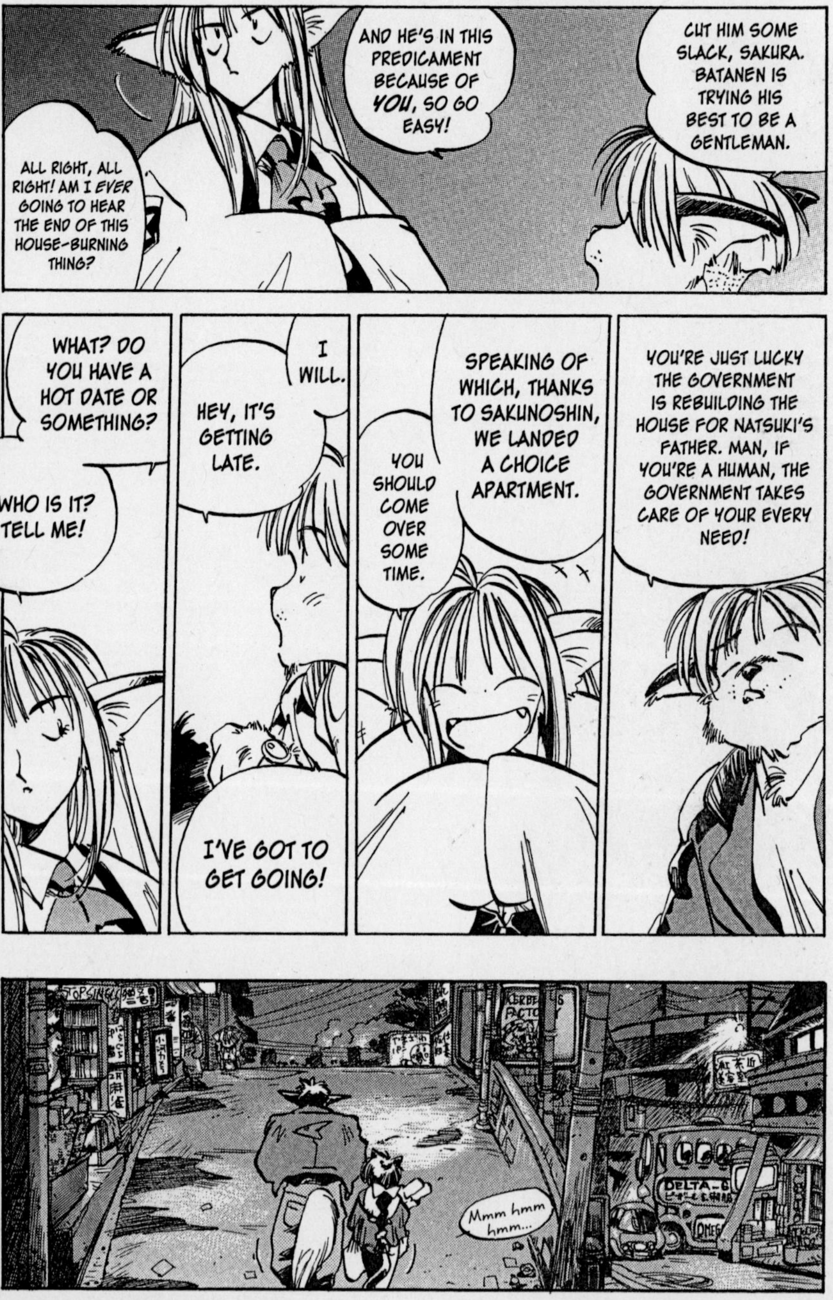
CUT HIM SOME SLACK, SAKURA. BATANEN IS TRYING HIS BEST TO BE A GENTLEMAN.
AND HE'S IN THIS PREDICAMENT BECAUSE OF *YOU*, SO GO EASY!
ALL RIGHT, ALL RIGHT! AM I *EVER* GOING TO HEAR THE END OF THIS HOUSE-BURNING THING?
YOU'RE JUST LUCKY THE GOVERNMENT IS REBUILDING THE HOUSE FOR NATSUKI'S FATHER. MAN, IF YOU'RE A HUMAN, THE GOVERNMENT TAKES CARE OF YOUR EVERY NEED!
SPEAKING OF WHICH, THANKS TO SAKUNOSHIN, WE LANDED A CHOICE APARTMENT.
YOU SHOULD COME OVER SOME TIME.
I WILL.
HEY, IT'S GETTING LATE.
I'VE GOT TO GET GOING!
WHAT? DO YOU HAVE A HOT DATE OR SOMETHING?
WHO IS IT? TELL ME!
Mmm hmm hmm...

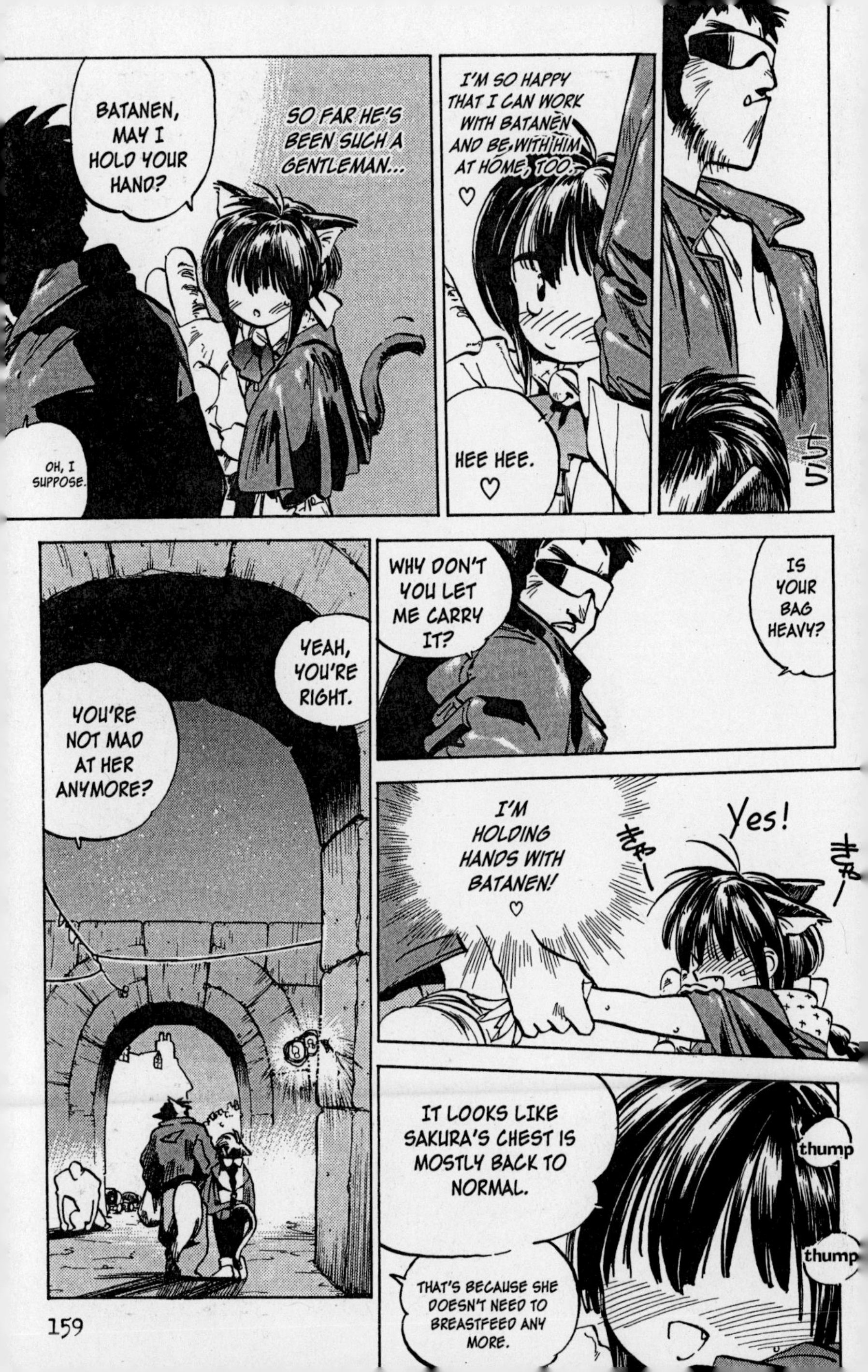
ちら
I'M SO HAPPY THAT I CAN WORK WITH BATANEN AND BE WITH HIM AT HOME, TOO. ♡
HEE HEE. ♡
SO FAR HE'S BEEN SUCH A GENTLEMAN...
BATANEN, MAY I HOLD YOUR HAND?
OH, I SUPPOSE.
IS YOUR BAG HEAVY?
WHY DON'T YOU LET ME CARRY IT?
Yes!
きゃー
I'M HOLDING HANDS WITH BATANEN! ♡
きゃー
thump
IT LOOKS LIKE SAKURA'S CHEST IS MOSTLY BACK TO NORMAL.
thump
THAT'S BECAUSE SHE DOESN'T NEED TO BREASTFEED ANY MORE.
YEAH, YOU'RE RIGHT.
YOU'RE NOT MAD AT HER ANYMORE?

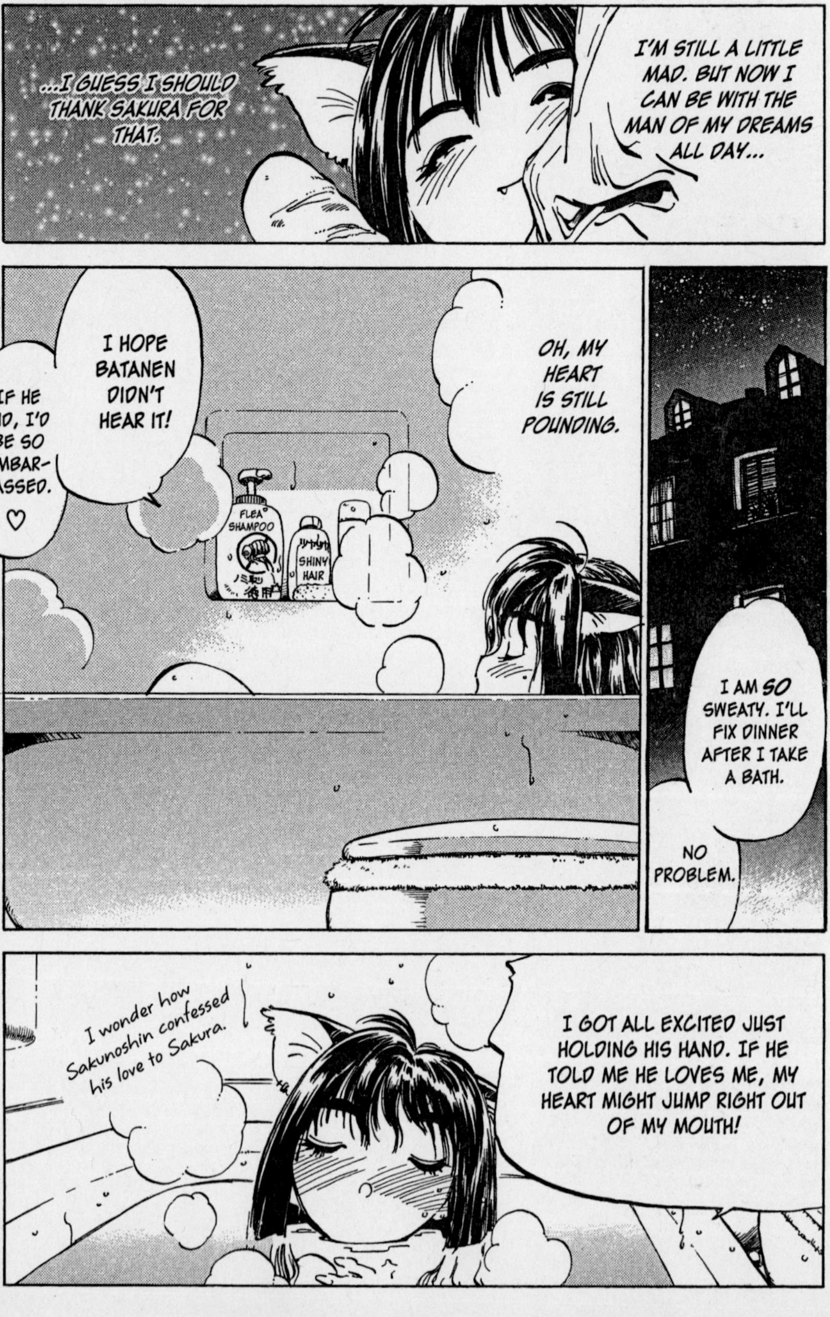
I'M STILL A LITTLE MAD. BUT NOW I CAN BE WITH THE MAN OF MY DREAMS ALL DAY...
...I GUESS I SHOULD THANK SAKURA FOR THAT.
I AM SO SWEATY. I'LL FIX DINNER AFTER I TAKE A BATH.
NO PROBLEM.
OH, MY HEART IS STILL POUNDING.
I HOPE BATANEN DIDN'T HEAR IT!
IF HE DID, I'D BE SO EMBARRASSED. ♡
FLEA SHAMPOO
SHINY HAIR
I GOT ALL EXCITED JUST HOLDING HIS HAND. IF HE TOLD ME HE LOVES ME, MY HEART MIGHT JUMP RIGHT OUT OF MY MOUTH!
I wonder how Sakunoshin confessed his love to Sakura.

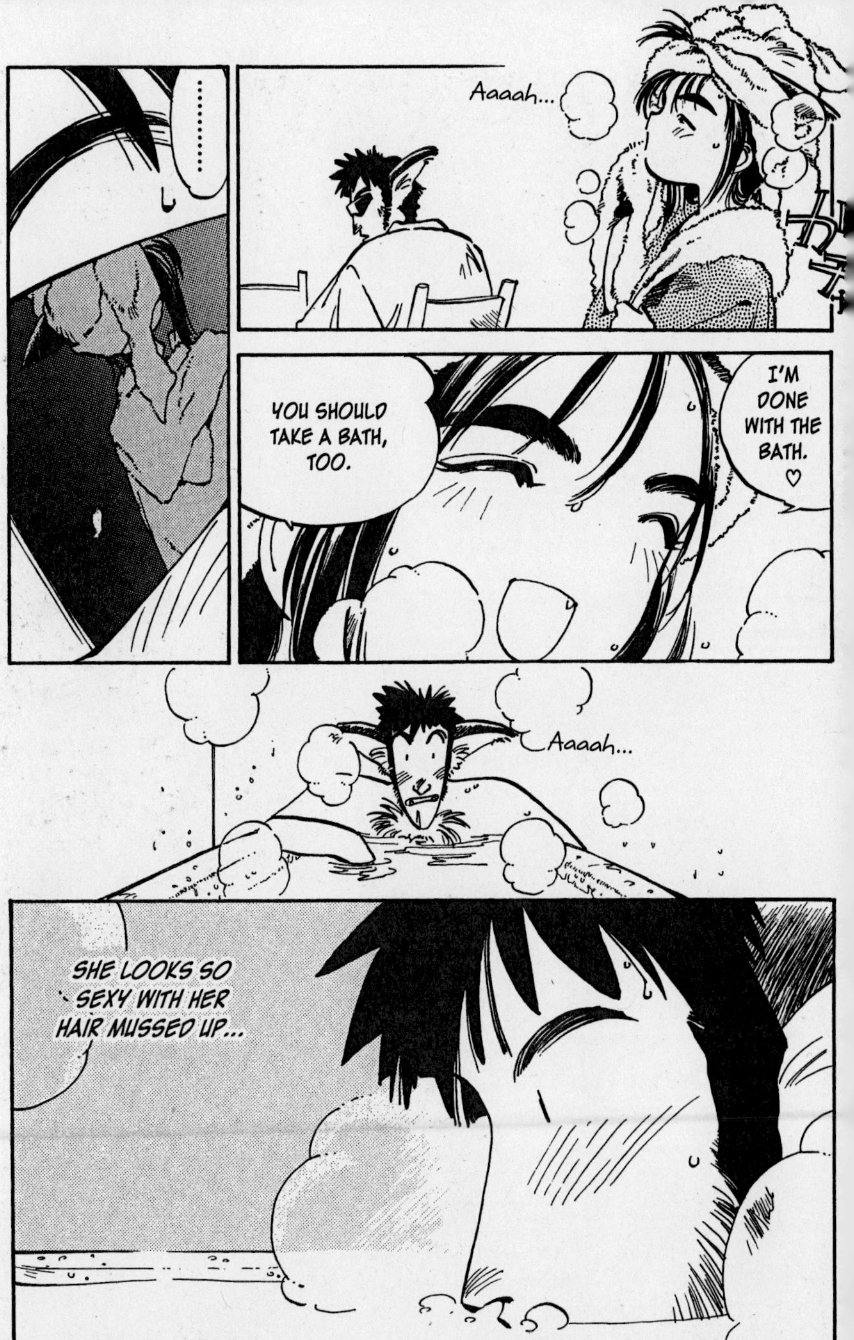
Aaaah...
I'M DONE WITH THE BATH. ♡
YOU SHOULD TAKE A BATH, TOO.
......
Aaaah...
SHE LOOKS SO SEXY WITH HER HAIR MUSSED UP...

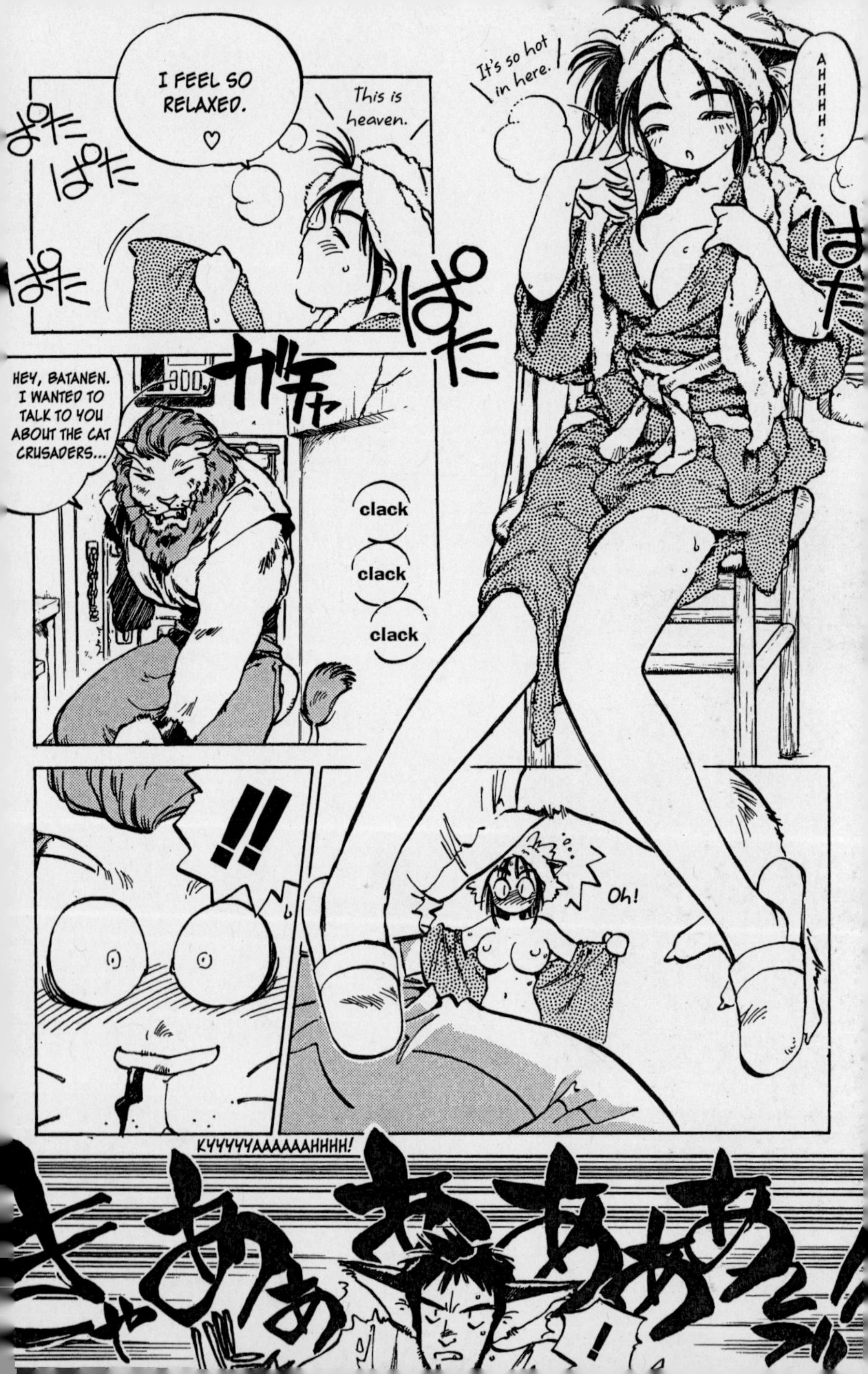
AHHHH...
It's so hot in here.
はた
ぱた
I FEEL SO RELAXED. ♡
This is heaven.
ぱたぱた
ぱた
ガチャ
HEY, BATANEN. I WANTED TO TALK TO YOU ABOUT THE CAT CRUSADERS...
clack
clack
clack
Oh!
!!
KYYYYYAAAAAAHHHH!

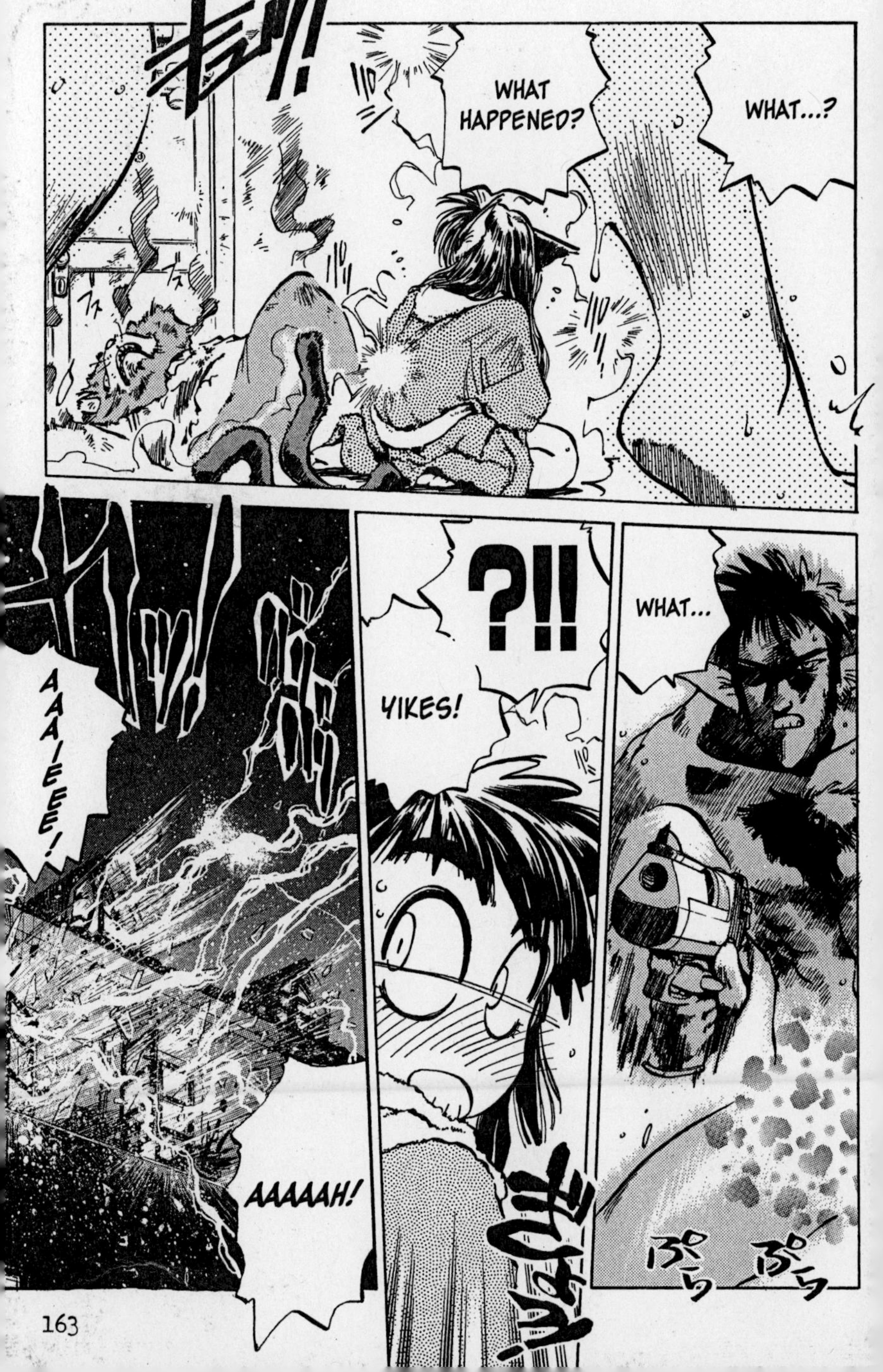
WHAT...?
WHAT HAPPENED?
WHAT...
ぷら ぷら
?!!
YIKES!
AAAIEEEE!
AAAAAH!

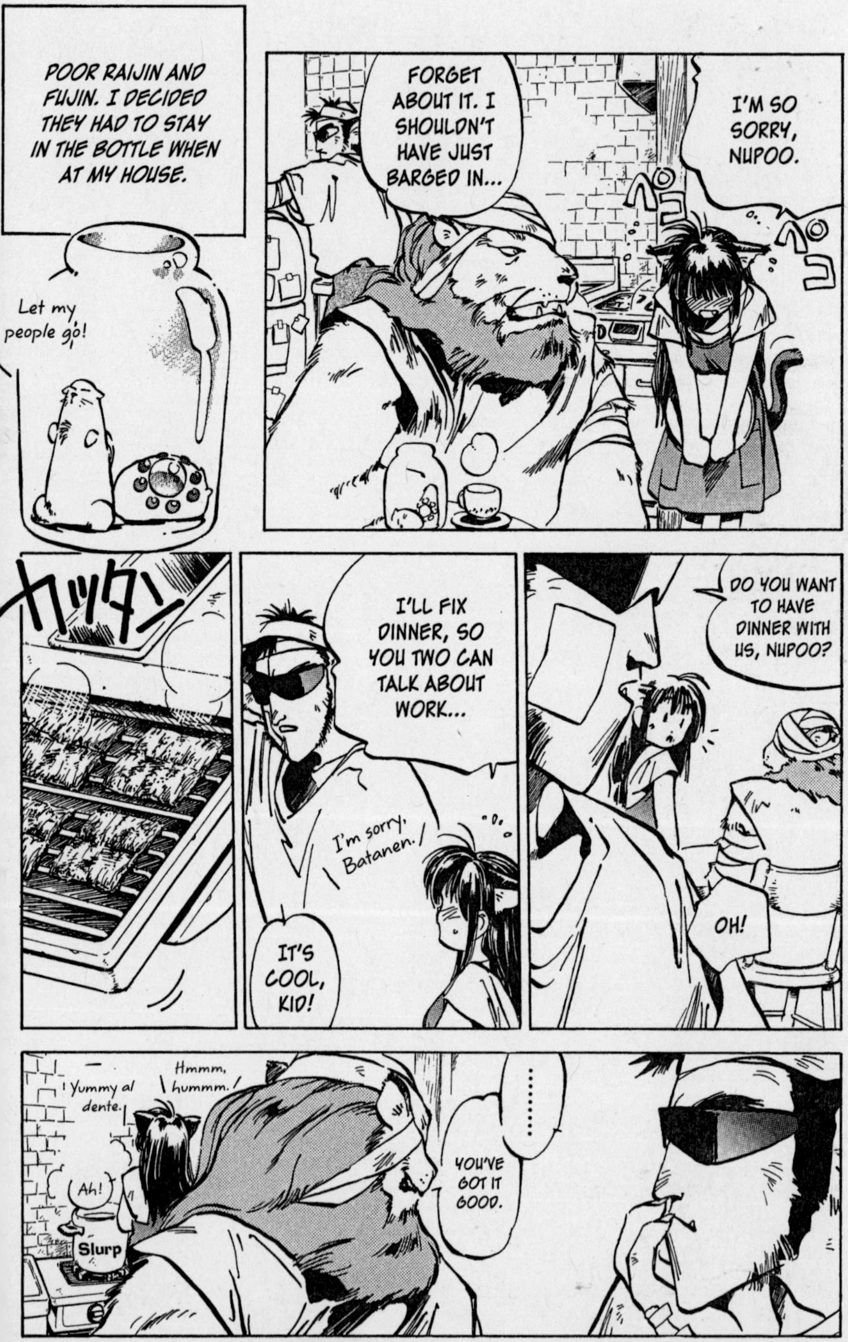
I'M SO SORRY, NUPOO.
ペコ
ペコ
FORGET ABOUT IT. I SHOULDN'T HAVE JUST BARGED IN...
POOR RAIJIN AND FUJIN. I DECIDED THEY HAD TO STAY IN THE BOTTLE WHEN AT MY HOUSE.
Let my people go!
DO YOU WANT TO HAVE DINNER WITH US, NUPOO?
OH!
I'LL FIX DINNER, SO YOU TWO CAN TALK ABOUT WORK...
I'm sorry, Batanen.
IT'S COOL, KID!
カッタン
......
YOU'VE GOT IT GOOD.
Hmmm, hummm.
Yummy al dente.
Ah!
Slurp

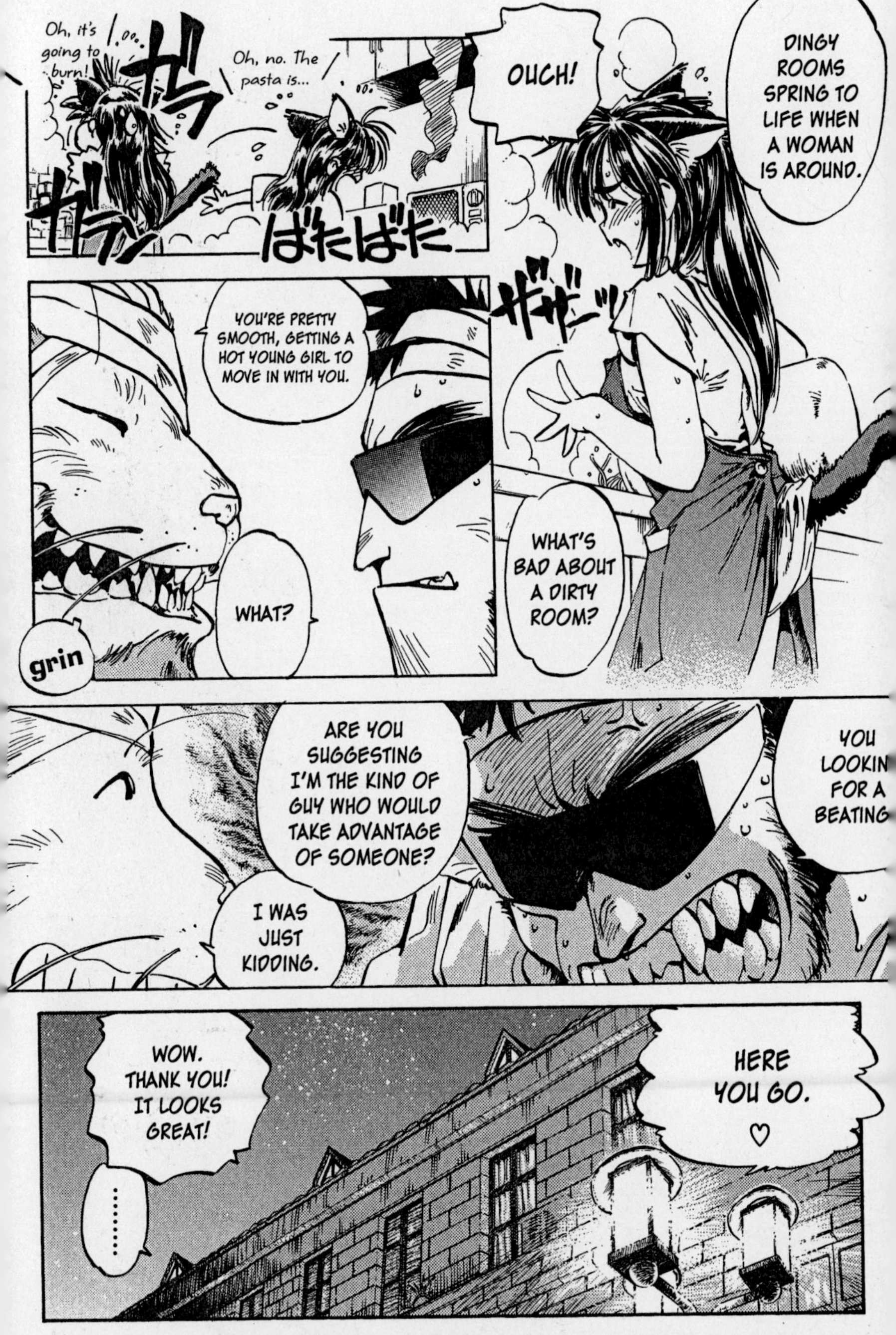
DINGY ROOMS SPRING TO LIFE WHEN A WOMAN IS AROUND.
OUCH!
WHAT'S BAD ABOUT A DIRTY ROOM?
Oh, no. The pasta is...
Oh, it's going to burn!
ばたばた
YOU'RE PRETTY SMOOTH, GETTING A HOT YOUNG GIRL TO MOVE IN WITH YOU.
WHAT?
grin
YOU LOOKIN FOR A BEATING
ARE YOU SUGGESTING I'M THE KIND OF GUY WHO WOULD TAKE ADVANTAGE OF SOMEONE?
I WAS JUST KIDDING.
HERE YOU GO. ♡
WOW. THANK YOU! IT LOOKS GREAT!
....

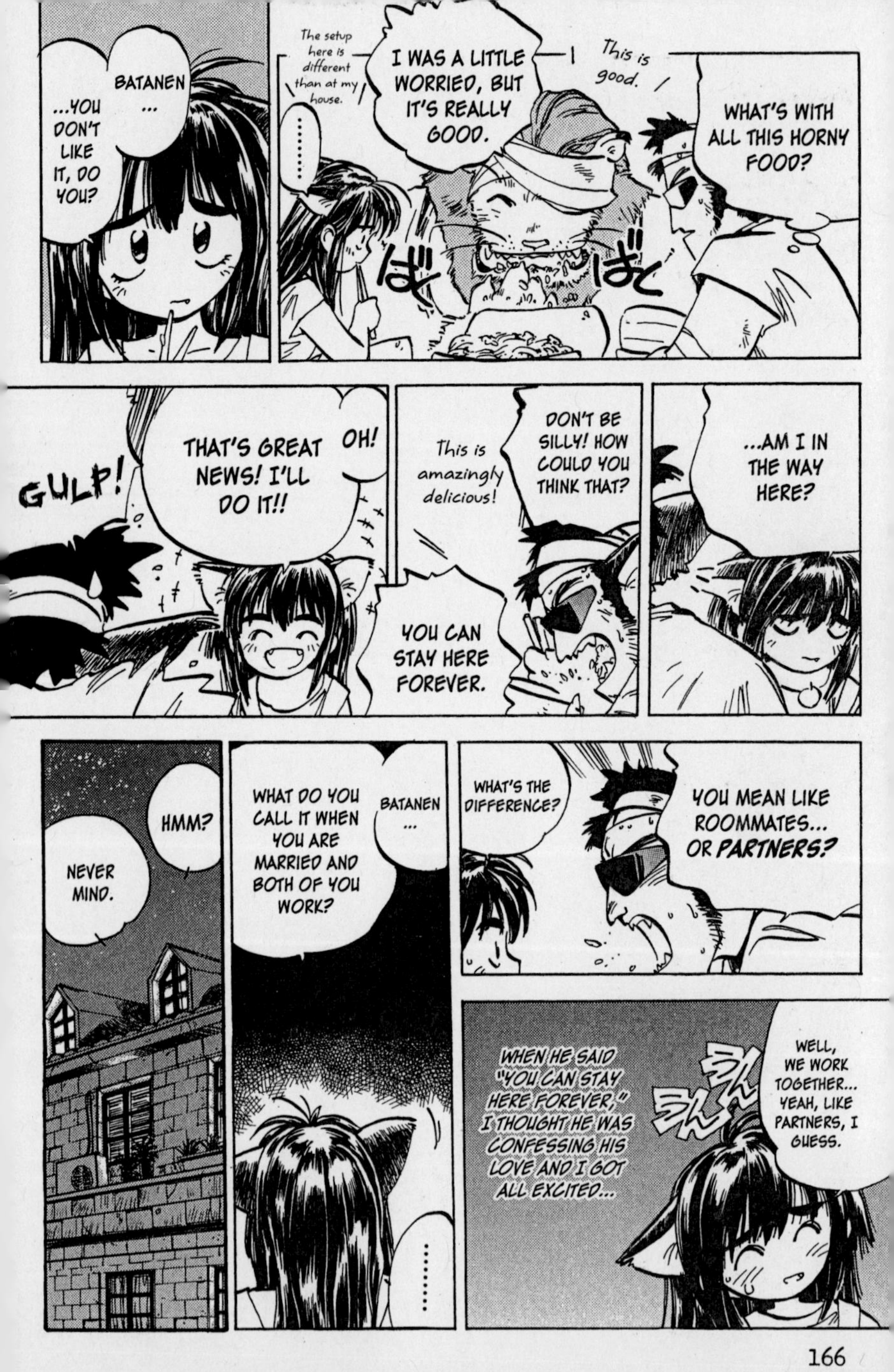
WHAT'S WITH ALL THIS HORNY FOOD?
This is good.
I WAS A LITTLE WORRIED, BUT IT'S REALLY GOOD.
The setup here is different than at my house.
......
ばく ばく
BATANEN ...
...YOU DON'T LIKE IT, DO YOU?
...AM I IN THE WAY HERE?
DON'T BE SILLY! HOW COULD YOU THINK THAT?
This is amazingly delicious!
YOU CAN STAY HERE FOREVER.
OH!
THAT'S GREAT NEWS! I'LL DO IT!!
GULP!
YOU MEAN LIKE ROOMMATES... OR PARTNERS?
WHAT'S THE DIFFERENCE?
WELL, WE WORK TOGETHER... YEAH, LIKE PARTNERS, I GUESS.
うん うん
WHEN HE SAID "YOU CAN STAY HERE FOREVER," I THOUGHT HE WAS CONFESSING HIS LOVE AND I GOT ALL EXCITED...
BATANEN ...
WHAT DO YOU CALL IT WHEN YOU ARE MARRIED AND BOTH OF YOU WORK?
......
HMM?
NEVER MIND.

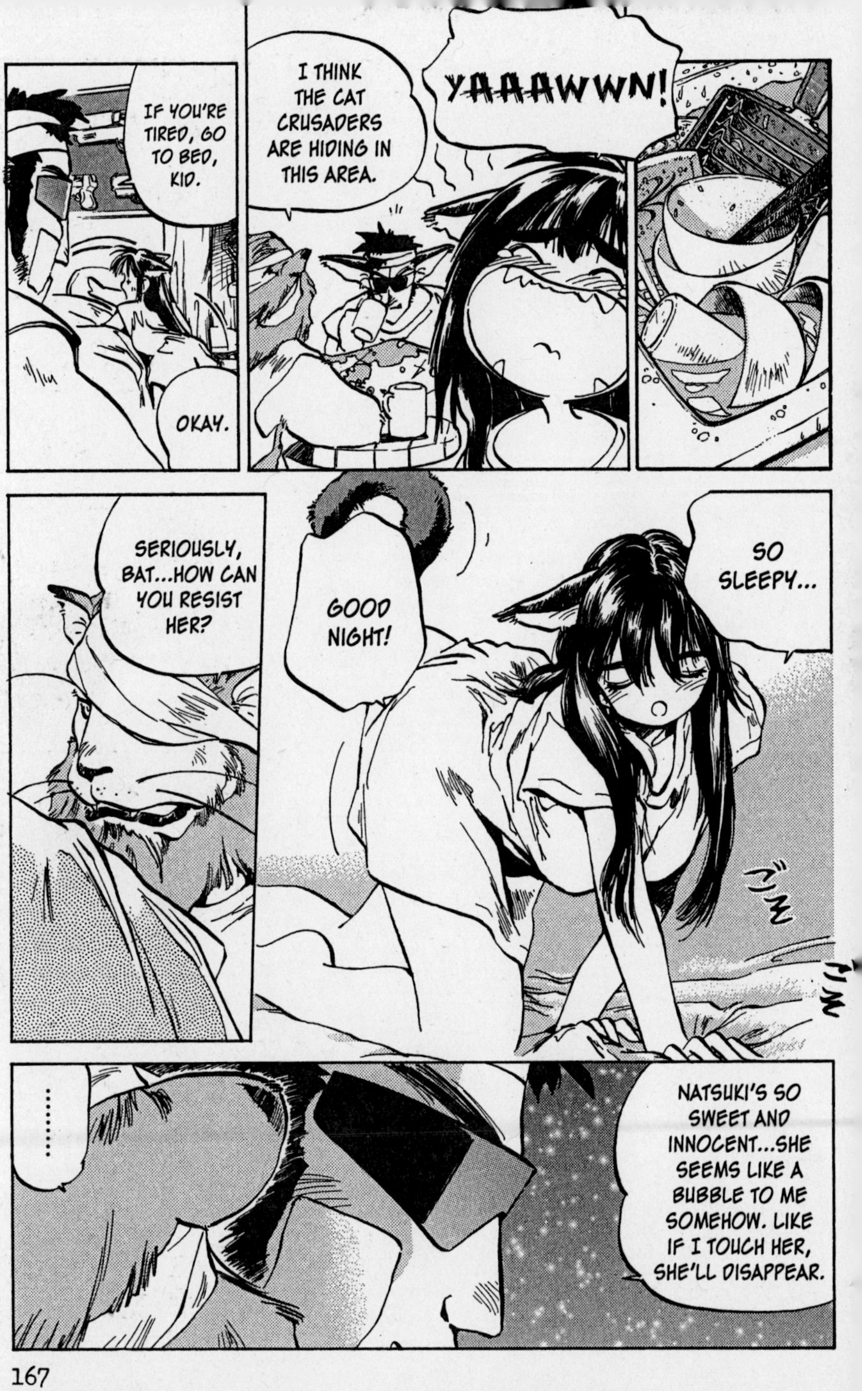
YAAAWWN!
I THINK THE CAT CRUSADERS ARE HIDING IN THIS AREA.
IF YOU'RE TIRED, GO TO BED, KID.
OKAY.
SO SLEEPY...
GOOD NIGHT!
SERIOUSLY, BAT...HOW CAN YOU RESIST HER?
NATSUKI'S SO SWEET AND INNOCENT...SHE SEEMS LIKE A BUBBLE TO ME SOMEHOW. LIKE IF I TOUCH HER, SHE'LL DISAPPEAR.
......

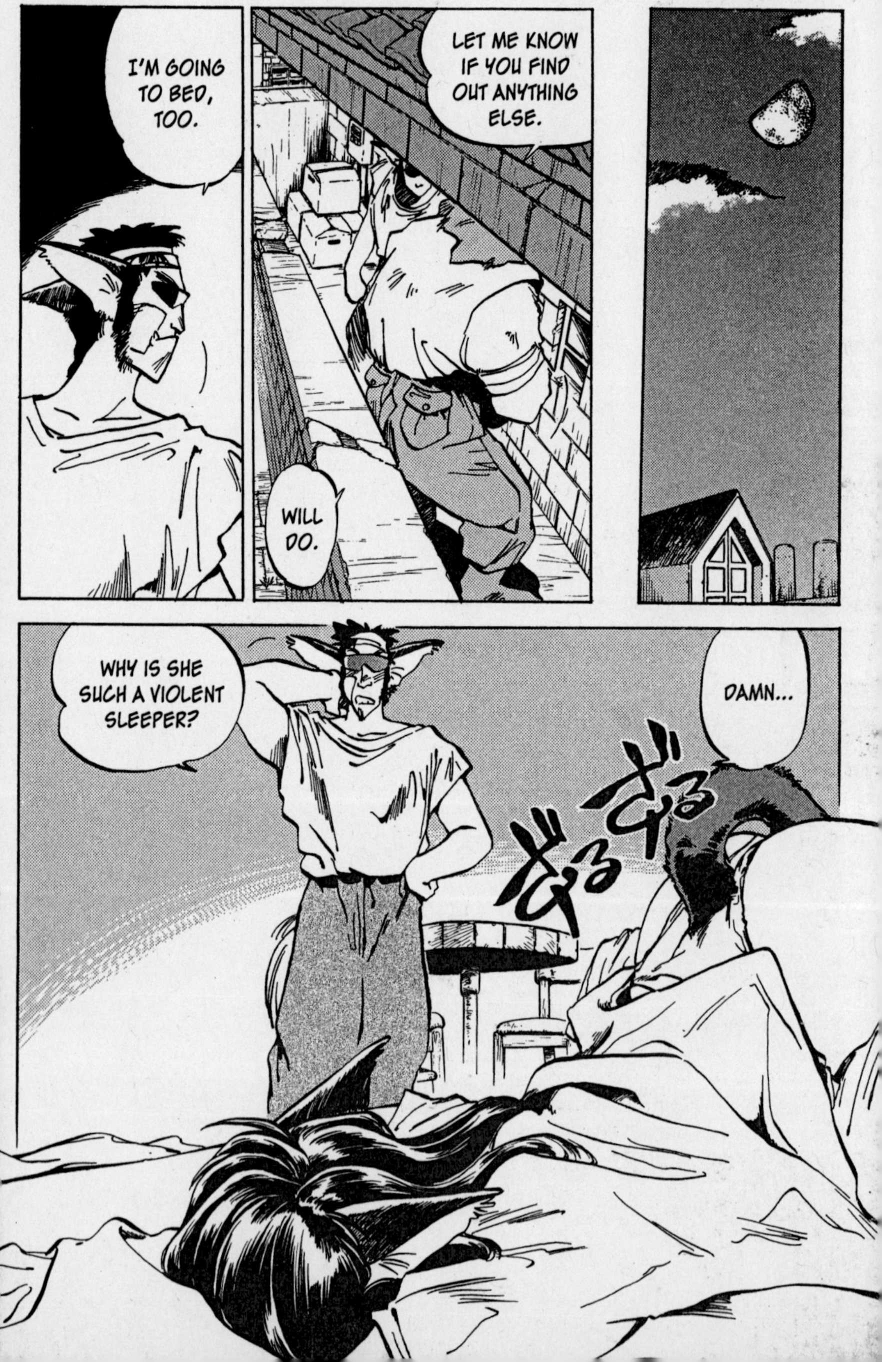
LET ME KNOW IF YOU FIND OUT ANYTHING ELSE.
WILL DO.
I'M GOING TO BED, TOO.
DAMN...
WHY IS SHE SUCH A VIOLENT SLEEPER?

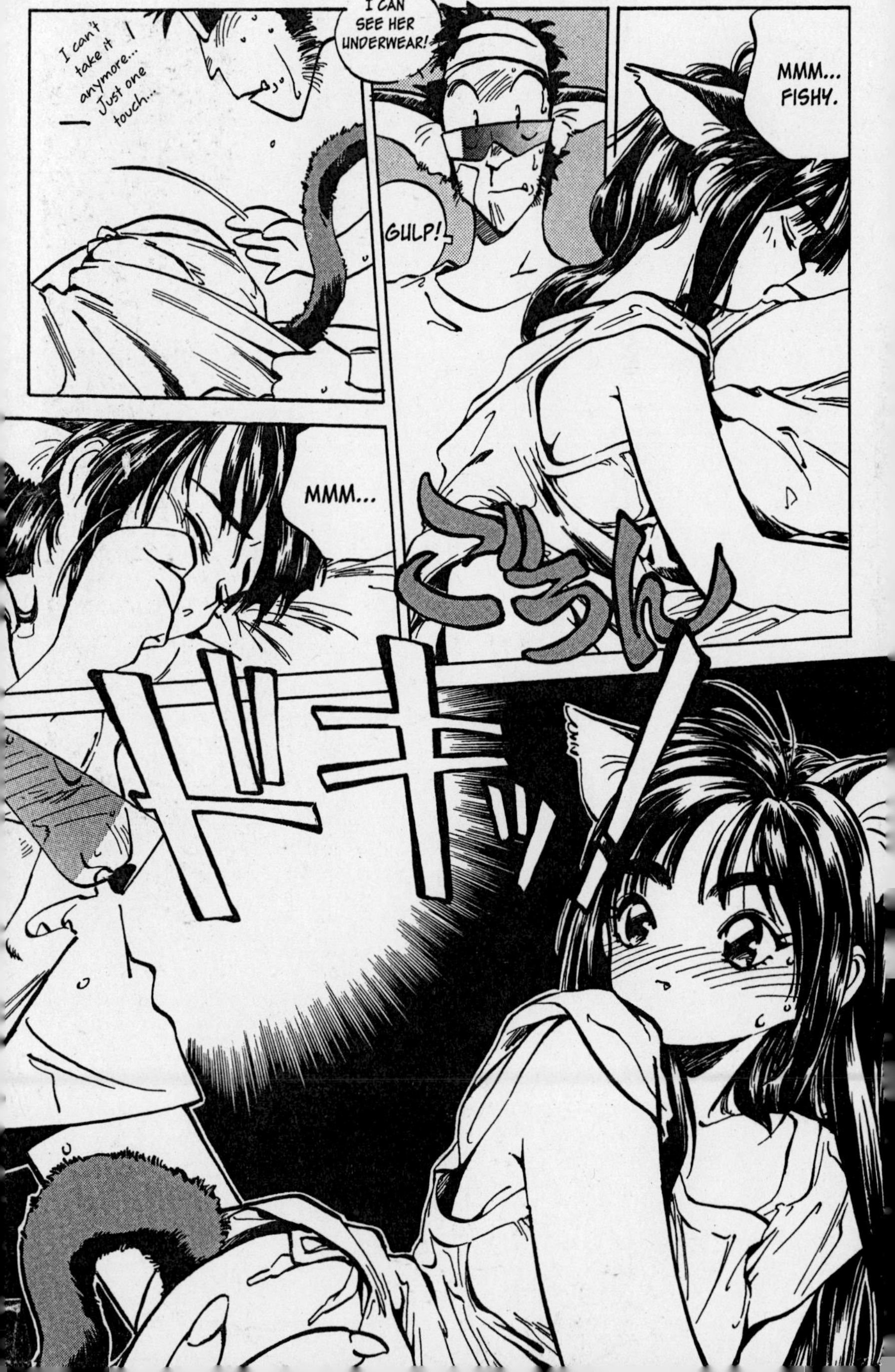
MMM... FISHY.
I CAN SEE HER UNDERWEAR!
GULP!
I can't take it anymore... Just one touch...
ごろん
MMM...
ドキッ

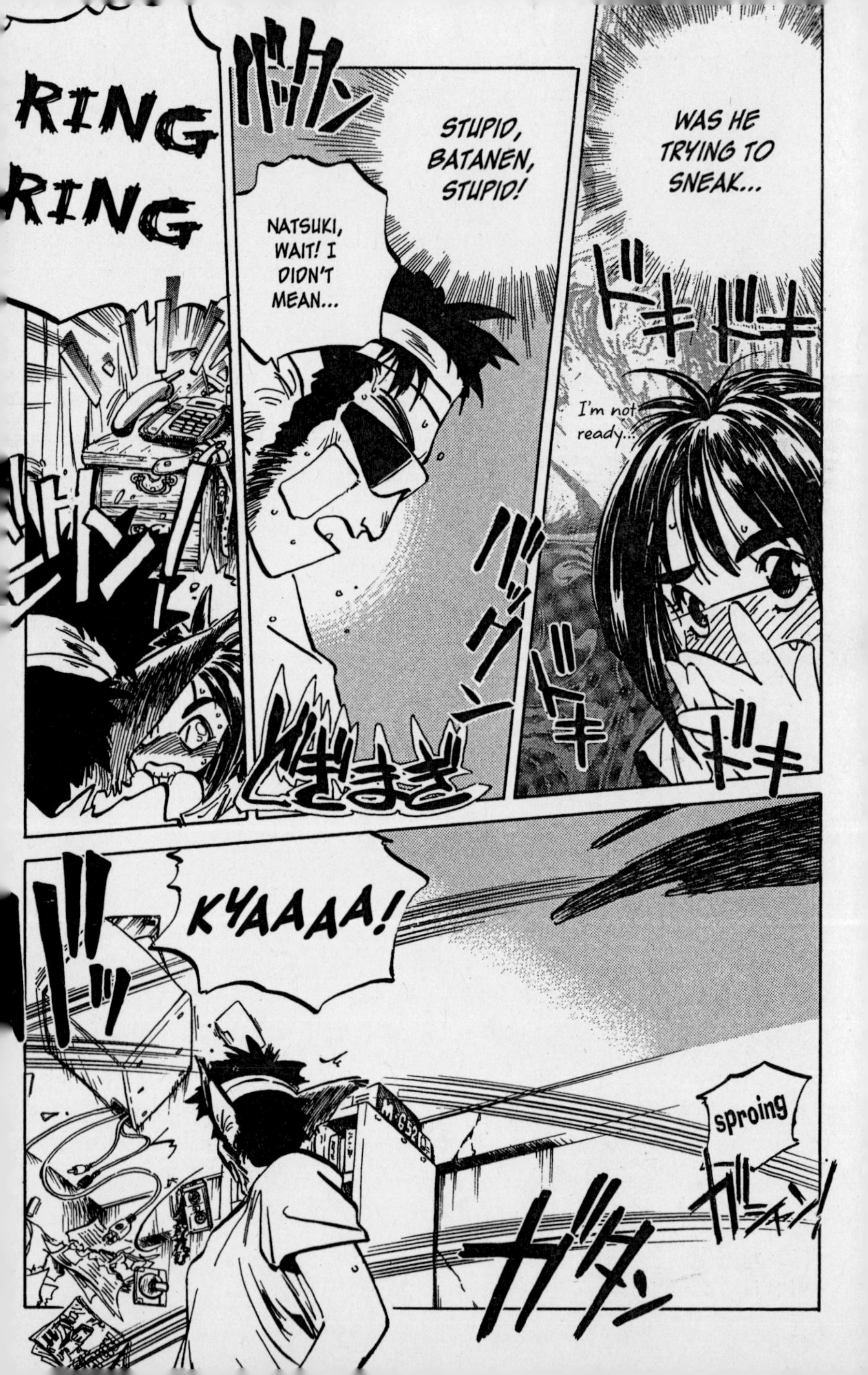
WAS HE TRYING TO SNEAK...
I'm not ready...
STUPID, BATANEN, STUPID!
NATSUKI, WAIT! I DIDN'T MEAN...
RING RING
KYAAAA!
sproing

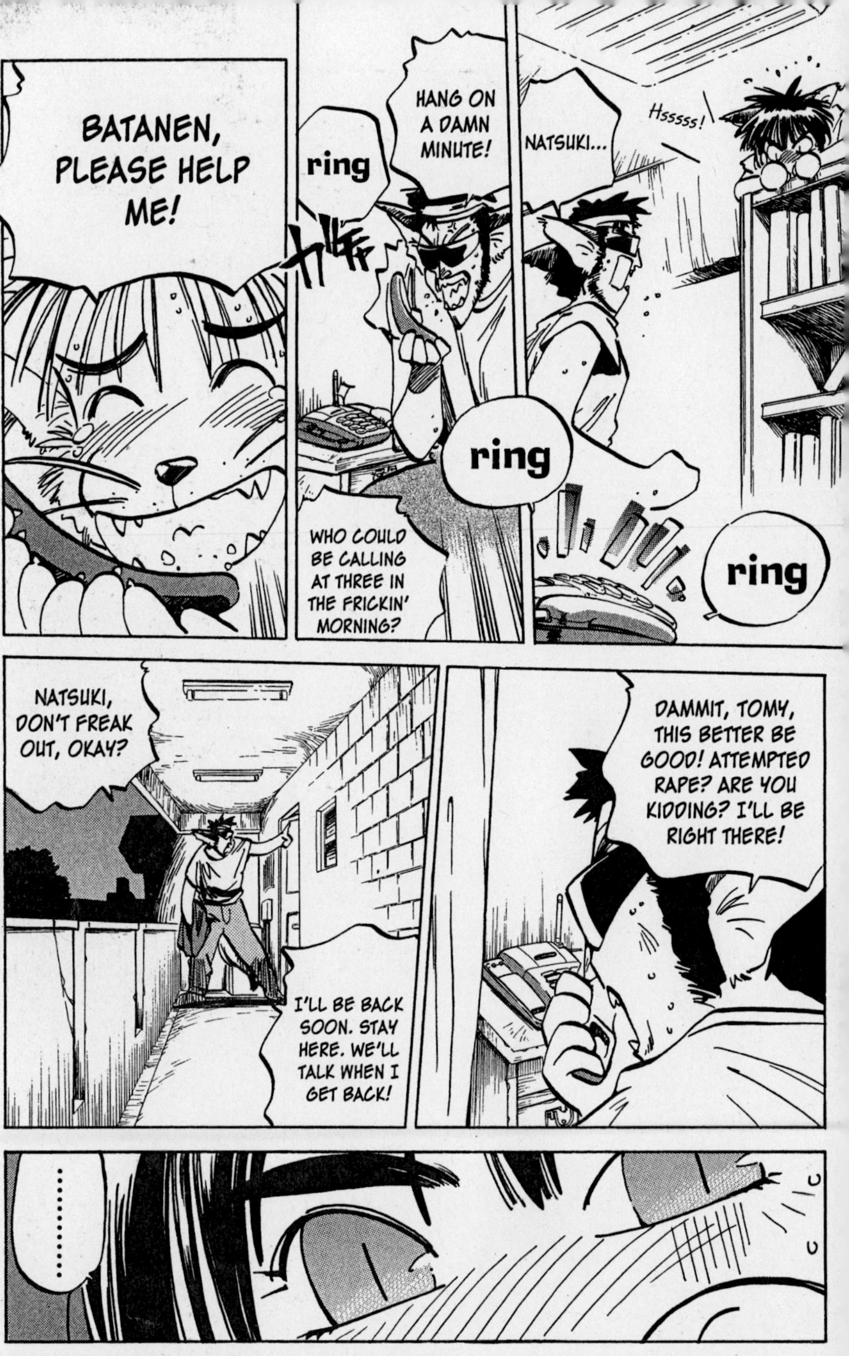
Hsssss!
NATSUKI...
ring
ring
HANG ON A DAMN MINUTE!
ring
WHO COULD BE CALLING AT THREE IN THE FRICKIN' MORNING?
BATANEN, PLEASE HELP ME!
DAMMIT, TOMY, THIS BETTER BE GOOD! ATTEMPTED RAPE? ARE YOU KIDDING? I'LL BE RIGHT THERE!
NATSUKI, DON'T FREAK OUT, OKAY?
I'LL BE BACK SOON. STAY HERE. WE'LL TALK WHEN I GET BACK!
....

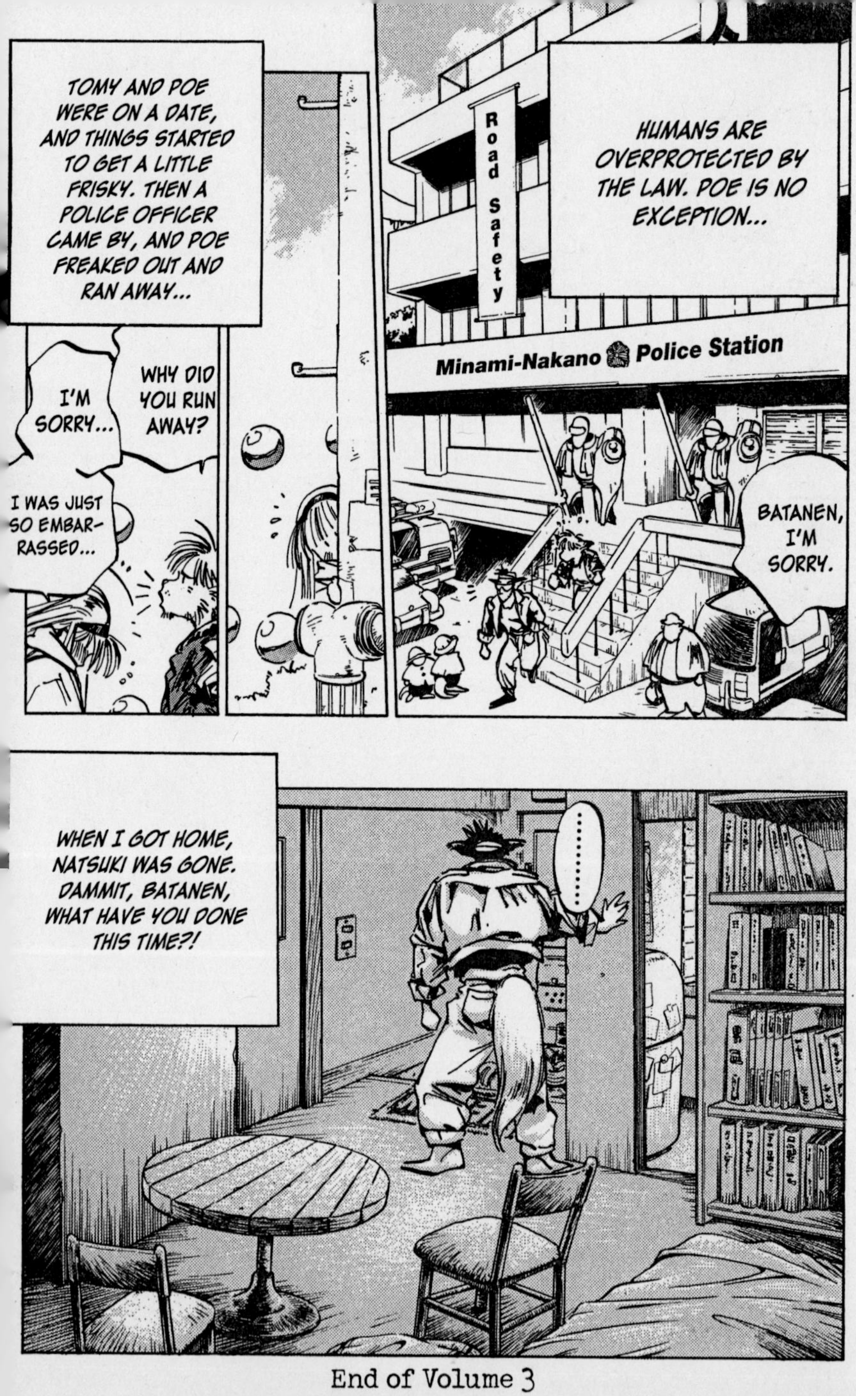
HUMANS ARE OVERPROTECTED BY THE LAW. POE IS NO EXCEPTION...
Road Safety
Minami-Nakano Police Station
BATANEN, I'M SORRY.
TOMY AND POE WERE ON A DATE, AND THINGS STARTED TO GET A LITTLE FRISKY. THEN A POLICE OFFICER CAME BY, AND POE FREAKED OUT AND RAN AWAY...
WHY DID YOU RUN AWAY?
I'M SORRY...
I WAS JUST SO EMBAR-RASSED...
WHEN I GOT HOME, NATSUKI WAS GONE. DAMMIT, BATANEN, WHAT HAVE YOU DONE THIS TIME?!
....

End of Volume 3

BONUS REPORT

This time the topic is bathing.

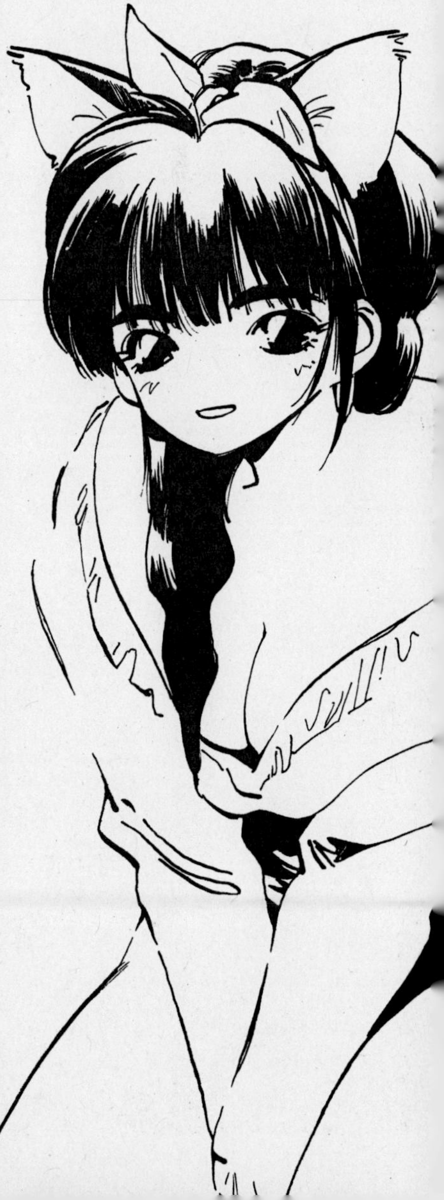

Bathing 1 ♡

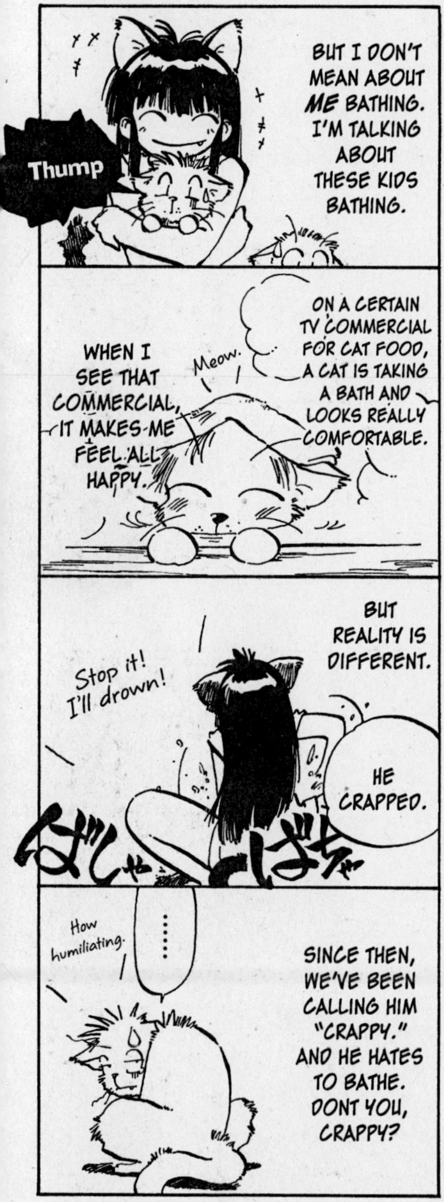
BUT I DON'T MEAN ABOUT *ME* BATHING. I'M TALKING ABOUT THESE KIDS BATHING.
Thump
ON A CERTAIN TV COMMERCIAL FOR CAT FOOD, A CAT IS TAKING A BATH AND LOOKS REALLY COMFORTABLE.
Meow.
WHEN I SEE THAT COMMERCIAL, IT MAKES ME FEEL ALL HAPPY.
BUT REALITY IS DIFFERENT.
HE CRAPPED.
Stop it! I'll drown!
SINCE THEN, WE'VE BEEN CALLING HIM "CRAPPY." AND HE HATES TO BATHE. DONT YOU, CRAPPY?
......
How humiliating.

Bathing 2 ♡

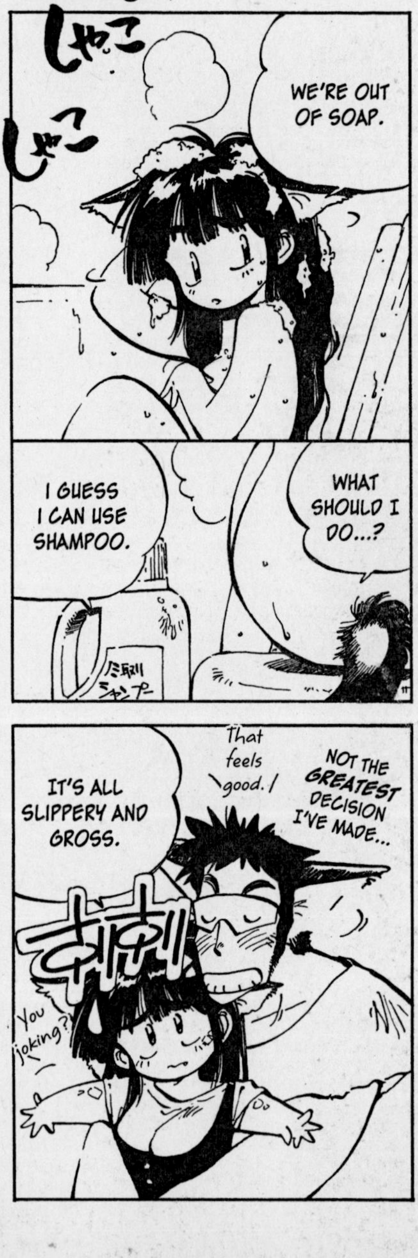
しゃこ
しゃこ
WE'RE OUT OF SOAP.
WHAT SHOULD I DO...?
I GUESS I CAN USE SHAMPOO.
NOT THE GREATEST DECISION I'VE MADE...
That feels good.
IT'S ALL SLIPPERY AND GROSS.
You joking?

Bathing 3 ♡

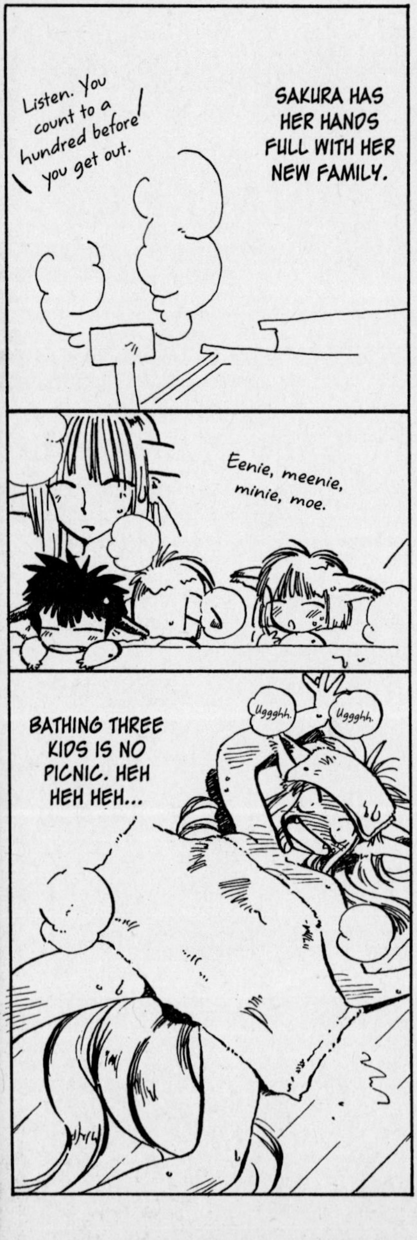
SAKURA HAS HER HANDS FULL WITH HER NEW FAMILY.
Listen. You count to a hundred before you get out.
Eenie, meenie, minie, moe.
Uggghh.
Uggghh.
BATHING THREE KIDS IS NO PICNIC. HEH HEH HEH...

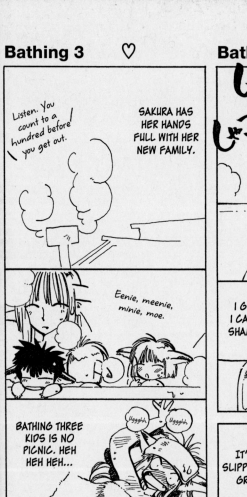

WANTED

MEE

FOR THE PERPETRATION AND SALE OF TRULY TWISTED MANGA FEATURING FURRY FEMME FATALES.

A PRODUCT OF YANAGAWA IN THE FUKUOKA PREFECTURE, MEE WAS BORN ON JUNE 24 IN 1963. PAST ACTIVITY HAS INCLUDED WRITING AND ILLUSTRATING KOTETSU NO DAIBOKEN (KOTETETSU'S GREAT ADVENTURES) FOR WANI MAGAZINE COMICS. CURRENTLY BELIEVED TO BE WORKING ON THE HYPER POLICE MANGA (THOUGH THIS INFORMATION MAY BE OUT OF DATE).

SUSPECT HAS ISSUED THE FOLLOWING STATEMENT TO POLICE COMPANY: "I WOULD LIKE TO HOOK SAKURA UP WITH A BOYFRIEND AND NATSUKI WITH A FIANCE, BUT IT LOOKS LIKE THIS MAY TAKE A WHILE. NEVERTHELESS, I THANK YOU FOR YOUR SUPPORT."

POLICE COMPANY

UNSOLVED CASE REPORT

GENERAL INFORMATION	
Case file number: JJL-5211314-JY	

Investigation status:

Attention All Units: A band of thieves who call themselves the Cat Crusaders are on the loose. These felonious felines are believed to be holed up in an abandoned church in one of the downtown slums. Subjects are to be considered extremely dangerous. Bounty Hunter Batanen Fujioka has reportedly got an inside agent working to crack this case, one Natsuki Sasahara—try not to shoot her if at all possible, but don't hold back too much...after all, she's just a freelancer.

Okay, boys, you're going to love this one... Reports coming in of a dinosaur rampaging through the downtown area. Officer Poe and flea-bitten freelancer Tomy are reportedly en route to apprehend. Be careful downtown...we're getting reports of unexplained phenomenon which may be mystical or even extraterrestrial in nature. Officers are advised to pack a tinfoil hat along with their flack jackets before dispatching.

All Points Bulletin: All available units converge on the Chiba Prefecture Power Plant. Seems the power plant has a rodent problem, but these rats are packing roscoes and have taken hostages. If none of you trigger-happy goons gunned down that undercover cat-girl, see if we can't get her to put those feline instincts to the test...

PD 292 (Rev. 2-99) *This information is available in alternative formats upon request.* Printed on Recycled Paper

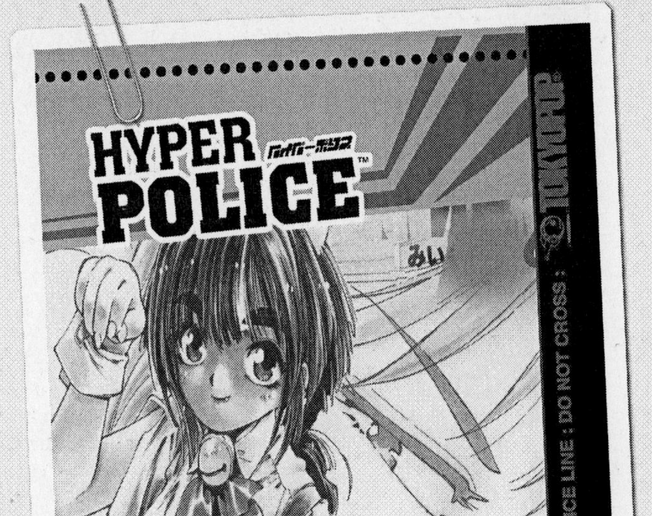
HYPER POLICE™
VOLUME 04 • STORY & ART BY MEE
TOKYOPOP
: POLICE LINE : DO NOT CROSS : POLICE LINE : DO NOT CROSS :

TOKYOPOP SHOP

WWW.TOKYOPOP.COM/SHOP

HOT NEWS!

Check out the TOKYOPOP SHOP! The world's best collection of manga in English is now available online in one place!

ARCANA

TOKYO MEW MEW A LA MODE

MBQ and other hot titles are available at the store that never closes!

MBQ

- LOOK FOR SPECIAL OFFERS
- PRE-ORDER UPCOMING RELEASES!
- COMPLETE YOUR COLLECTIONS

SPOTLIGHT TOKYOPOP MANGA SUPPLEMENT

BECK: MONGOLIAN CHOP SQUAD

OT
OLDER TEEN
AGE 16+

ROCK IN MANGA!

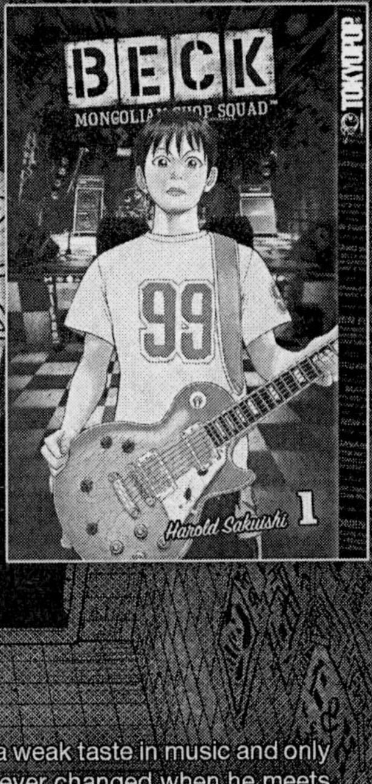

BECK
MONGOLIAN CHOP SQUAD™
TOKYOPOP
Harold Sakuishi
1

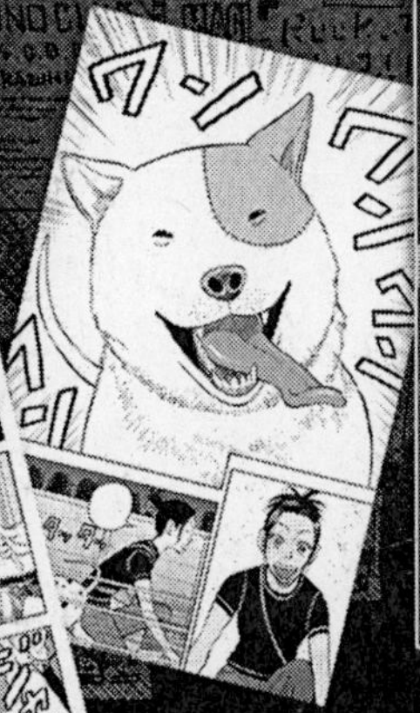

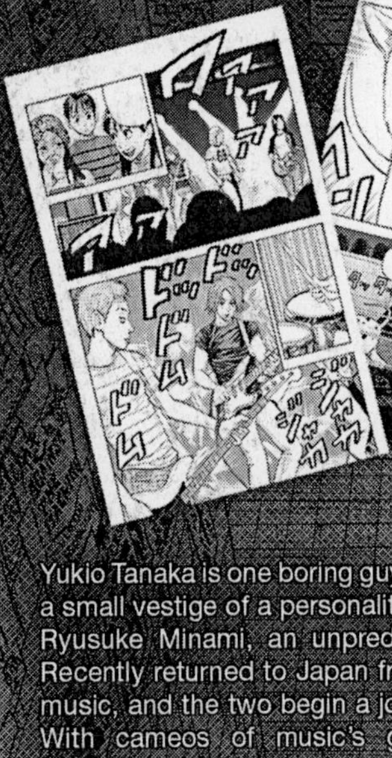

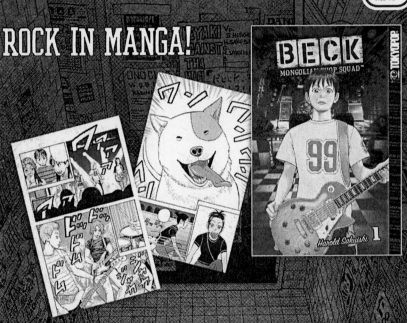

Yukio Tanaka is one boring guy with no hobbies, a weak taste in music and only a small vestige of a personality. But his life is forever changed when he meets Ryusuke Minami, an unpredictable rocker with a cool dog named Beck. Recently returned to Japan from America, Ryusuke inspires Yukio to get into music, and the two begin a journey through the world of rock 'n' roll dreams! With cameos of music's greatest stars—from John Lennon to David Bowie—and homages to supergroups such as Led Zeppelin and Nirvana, anyone who's anyone can make an appearance in *Beck*...even Beck himself! With action, music and gobs of comedy, *Beck* puts the rock in manga!

HAROLD SAKUISHI'S HIGHLY ADDICTIVE MANGA SERIES THAT SPAWNED A HIT ANIME HAS FINALLY REACHED THE STATES!

FOR MORE INFORMATION VISIT: WWW.TOKYOPOP.COM

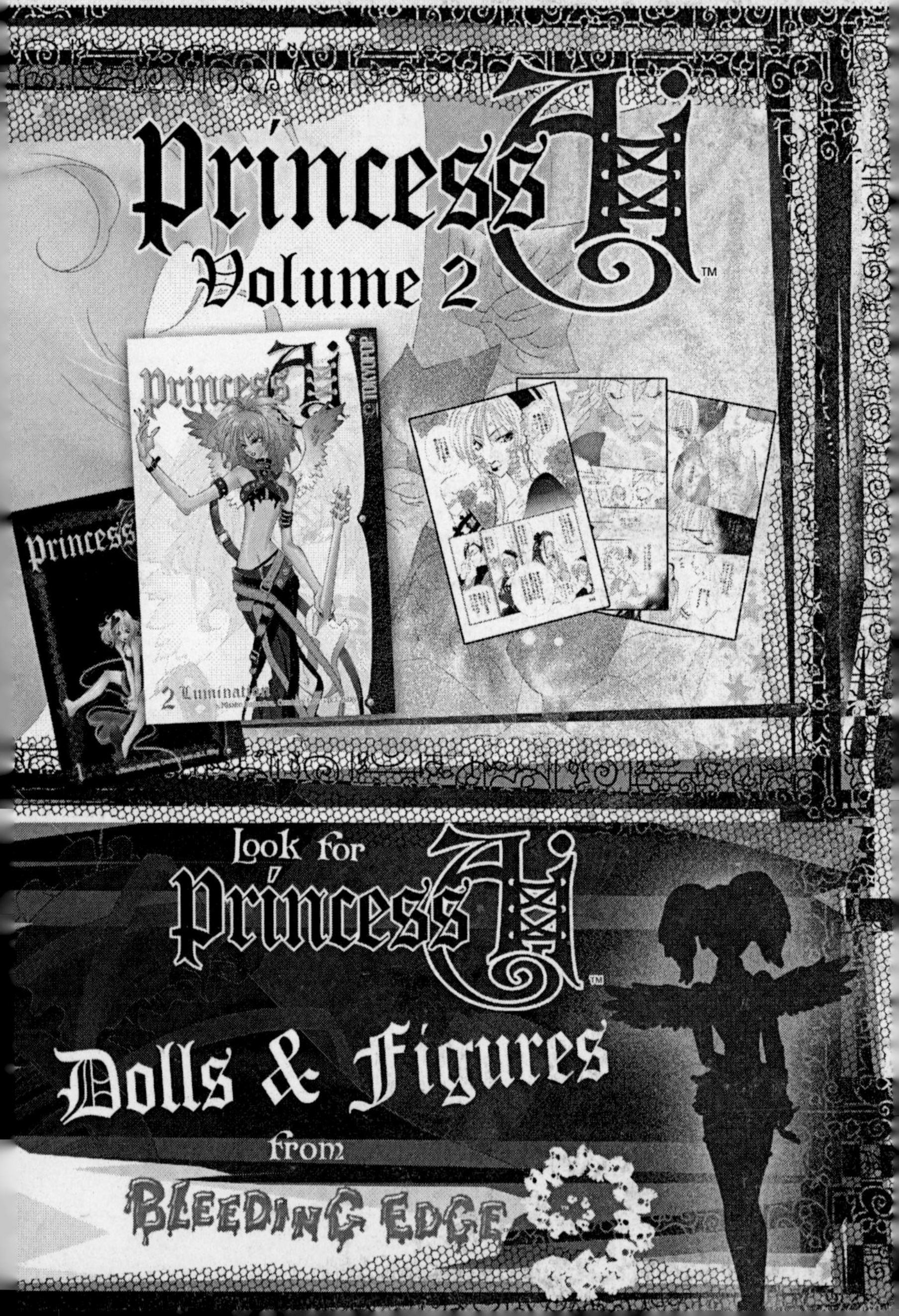
Princess Ai™
Volume 2
Look for
Princess Ai™
Dolls & Figures
from
BLEEDING EDGE

PRINCESS AI

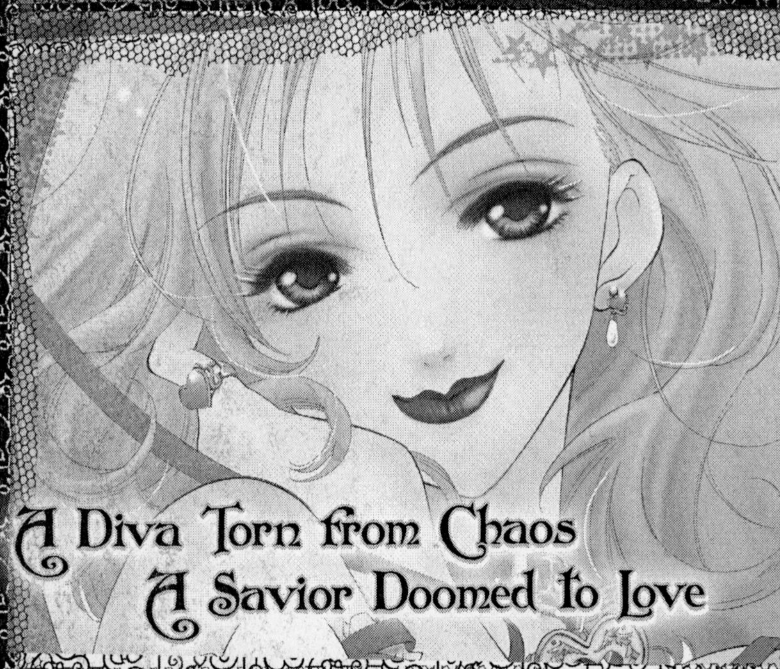
A Diva Torn from Chaos
A Savior Doomed to Love

Volume 2 Lumination

Ai continues to search for her place in our world on the streets of Tokyo. Using her talent to support herself, Ai signs a contract with a top record label and begins her rise to stardom. But fame is unpredictable—as her talent blooms, all eyes are on Ai. When scandal surfaces, will she burn out in the spotlight of celebrity?

T
TEEN
AGE 13+

Preview the manga at:

www.TOKYOPOP.com/princessai

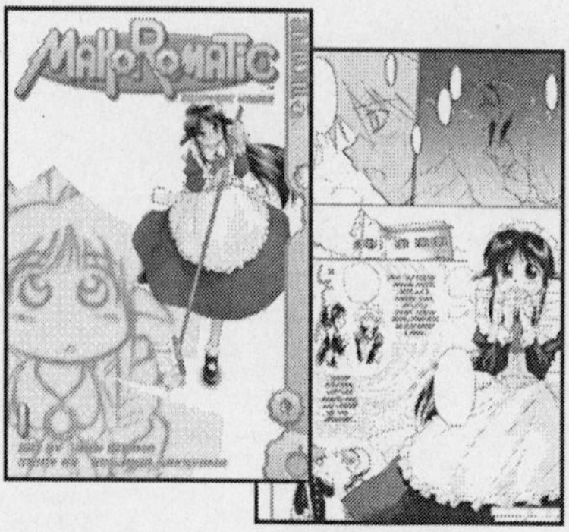
MAHOROMATIC

BY BUNJURO NAKAYAMA AND BOW DITAMA

MAHOROMATIC: AUTOMATIC MAIDEN

Mahoro is a sweet, cute, female battle android who decides to go from mopping up alien invaders to mopping up after Suguru Misato, a teenaged orphan boy... and hilarity most definitely ensues. This series has great art and a slick story that easily switches from truly funny to downright heartwarming...but always with a large shadow looming over it. You see, only Mahoro knows that her days are quite literally numbered, and the end of each chapter lets you know exactly how much—or how little—time she has left!

~Rob Tokar, Sr. Editor

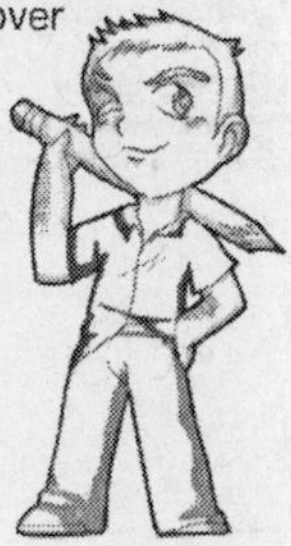

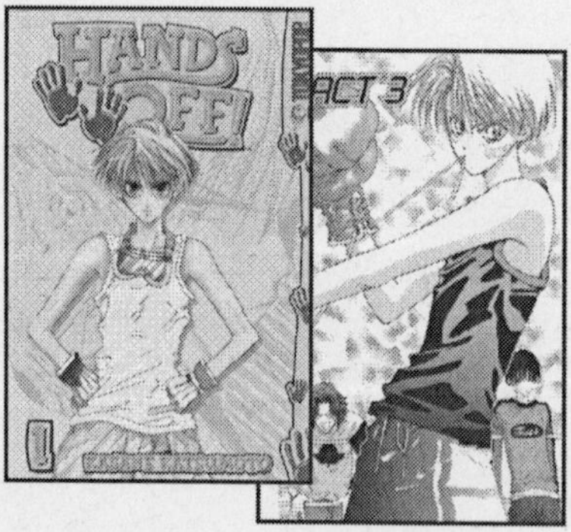
HANDS OFF!
ACT 3

BY KASANE KATSUMOTO

HANDS OFF!

Cute boys with ESP who share a special bond... If you think this is familiar (e.g. *Legal Drug*), well, you're wrong. *Hands Off!* totally stands alone as a unique and thoroughly enjoyable series. Kotarou and Tatsuki's (platonic!) relationship is complex, fascinating and heart-wrenching. Throw in Yuuto, the playboy who can read auras, and you've got a fantastic setup for drama and comedy, with incredible themes of friendship running throughout. Don't be put off by Kotarou's danger-magnet status, either. The episodic stuff gradually changes, and the full arc of the characters' development is well worth waiting for.

~Lillian Diaz-Przybyl, Jr. Editor

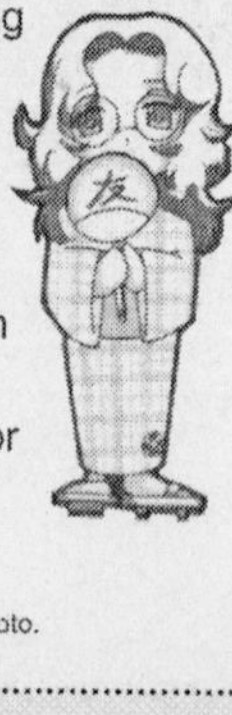

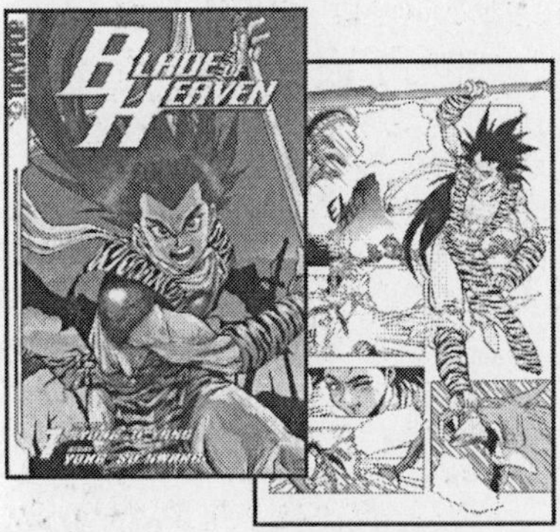
Blade of Heaven

BY YONG-SU HWANG
AND KYUNG-IL YANG

BLADE OF HEAVEN

Wildly popular in its homeland of Korea, *Blade of Heaven* enjoys the rare distinction of not only being a hit in its own country, but in Japan and several other countries, as well. On the surface, Yong-Su Hwang and Kyung-Il Yang's fantasy-adventure may look like yet another "Heaven vs. Demons" sword opera, but the story of the mischievous Soma, a pawn caught in a struggle of mythic proportions, is filled with so much humor, pathos, imagination—and yes, action, that it's easy to see why *Blade of Heaven* has been so popular worldwide.

~Bryce P. Coleman, Editor

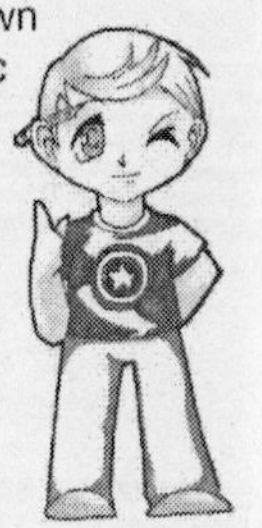

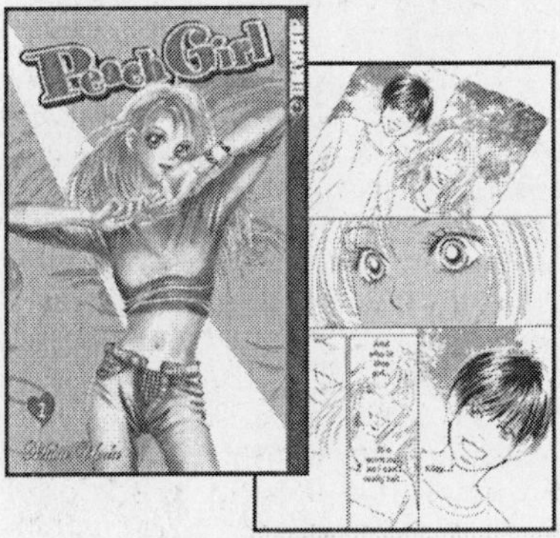
Peach Girl

BY MIWA UEDA

PEACH GIRL

Am I the only person who thinks that *Peach Girl* is just like *The O.C.*? Just imagine Ryan as Toji, Seth as Kiley, Marissa as Momo and Summer as Sae. (The similarities are almost spooky!) Plus, Seth is way into comics and manga—and I'm sure he'd love *Peach Girl*. It has everything that my favorite TV show has and then some—drama, intrigue, romance and lots of will-they-or-won't-they suspense. I love it! *Peach Girl* rules, seriously. If you haven't read it, do so. Now.

~Julie Taylor, Sr. Editor

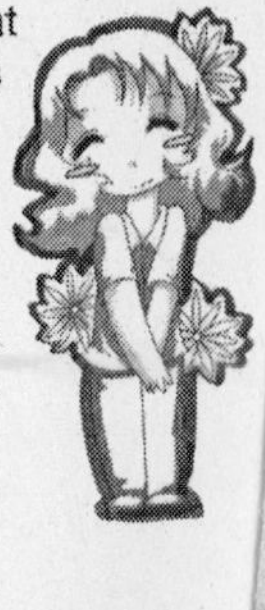

STOP!

This is the back of the book.
You wouldn't want to spoil a great ending!

This book is printed "manga-style," in the authentic Japanese right-to-left format. Since none of the artwork has been flipped or altered, readers get to experience the story just as the creator intended. You've been asking for it, so TOKYOPOP® delivered: authentic, hot-off-the-press, and far more fun!

DIRECTIONS

If this is your first time reading manga-style, here's a quick guide to help you understand how it works.

It's easy... just start in the top right panel and follow the numbers. Have fun, and look for more 100% authentic manga from TOKYOPOP®!